American Civilization in the First Machine Age: 1890-1940

Gilman M. Ostrander

HARPER TORCHBOOKS ▼
Harper & Row, Publishers
New York, Evanston, San Francisco, London

The author makes grateful acknowledgment to Funk & Wagnalls, New York, for excerpts on pages 246–249, 264 reprinted from *Dorothy Dix, Her Book: Every-Day Help For Every-Day People* (1926). Reprinted by permission of the publishers, Funk & Wagnalls, New York.

First HARPER TORCHBOOK edition published 1972

STANDARD BOOK NUMBER: 06–131652–0

Contents

Acknowledgments

The first draft of *American Civilization in the First Machine Age: 1890–1940* benefited from readings by Douglas T. Miller, Russel B. Nye, Joan Rich, and Allan Shaffer in the spring of 1966. John Higham read an altered version in the fall of 1967, and his critique was the basis for a thorough redrafting. Arthur Shaffer criticized the "Melting Pot" section for me and, finally, in the spring of 1969, Carl Degler read the manuscript and made numerous suggestions that were incorporated into the final draft. Jean Withers Ostrander was called upon for critical remarks at all stages of the manuscript. Jere Grant gave the manuscript perceptive editorial attention, and David M. Ostrander assisted with the index.

Where I have been aware of having placed myself under major obligation to another scholar, I have cited the scholar and his work in passing, together with some indication of the nature of my indebtedness to his scholarship. Additionally, the sources of the quotations used in this work are cited in the chapter-by-chapter bibliographical acknowledgments at the end of the book, as, indeed, are all sources from which I am conscious of having derived specific information or insights, relevant to this study.

GILMAN M. OSTRANDER

ONE

●

An Overview: Technology, Immigration, and the American Character

....

Note to
the Reader

Two words that are not to be found in most dictionaries are used in this book and are basic to the main lines of argument presented here. The following definitions of these two words ought therefore to be kept in mind:

Filiarchy. 1. Rule by the young; the young as a ruling class. **2.** In a continually developing technological environment, a society which relies on the young to acquire the new skills necessary to maintain and further re-create the environment; a society, furthermore, where social values are in a continual process of reinterpretation in relation to the changing environment, and where the young, as the social product of the new environment, are superior to their elders in adaptability to the environment and in their understanding of it, and on that basis are qualified to act as authoritative exemplars of social change.

Ethnocracy. 1. A society composed of racial, ethnic, and religious minority groups. **2.** An ethnically pluralistic society that conceives of its national character as the sum of its interacting subcultures, under laws that protect the liberties of the individual as well as those of the group. **3.** A democratic and legally integrated polyethnic society, pursuing the goal of ethnic assimilation into the national culture through indoctrination of successive younger generations amid a continually developing technological environment, that tends to divide society horizontally, along generational lines, rather than vertically, along racial, ethnic, and religious lines.

An Overview: Technology, Immigration, and the American Character

....

FREDERICK JACKSON TURNER concluded his paper "The Significance of the Frontier in American History" with the observation that "now, four centuries from the discovery of America, at the end of a hundred years of life under the Constitution, the frontier has gone, and with its going has closed the first period of American history." There was a quality of pathos in that conclusion which was enhanced by the circumstances of its presentation. Turner was addressing a historical meeting held in conjunction with Chicago's Columbian Exposition of 1893, where applied science and industry were on display in the Machinery Hall and where the hootchy-kootchy dancer Little Egypt was the stellar attraction on the Midway. The Columbian Exposition was a triumphant celebration of the emergent second period of American history, the age of the machine.

In fact the whole city of Chicago, which had been organized as a town just sixty years earlier, was an outstanding American exhibit of this new age of the machine.

America is still in the perpetually new age of the machine, but the present electronically automated era is evidently of a different order from the railroad era of the Chicago Exposition. Indeed Norbert Wiener, in *The Human Use of Human Beings* (1954), argued that World War II had launched a second industrial revolution, when the machine began to supplant the human brain, just as it had supplanted manpower in the first industrial revolution. Wiener was concerned with the question of how society could adjust, without sacrificing human values, to this second industrial revolution, where "the machine plays no favorites as between overall labor and white collar labor."

The century of America's first machine age was also the century of the great European exodus, and the European migration to America during the century after 1820 equaled three times the total population of the United States in 1820. German and Irish immigrants arrived in northeastern United States by the hundreds of thousands annually from the 1840's on; beginning in the 1880's they were joined by the "New Immigration" from southeastern and central Europe; and beginning early in the twentieth century American cities absorbed the mass migration of Negroes from the southern countryside as well. This ethnic accumulation, compounded by technological revolution, had comprehensively transformed the American national character by the eve of World War II.

The new American national character of the twentieth century was hardly a completed product by the eve of World War II, any more than Crèvecoeur's "new American" of the Revolutionary era remained entirely true to form two generations later in the democratic America which Tocqueville analyzed. Nevertheless the decade of the 1920's witnessed a momentous technological reorientation of American social values, and the decade of the 1930's witnessed a momentous ethnic reorientation. American civilization in the late twentieth century is in large measure the continuing development of these essentially post-Christian reformations of the interwar generation that experienced the great prosperity and then the Great Depression.

That such a thing as an American national character exists to begin with is a proposition that has been generally accepted throughout America's national history. To European observers, whether favorably disposed or otherwise, the United States has appeared to be an exceptionally easy nation to generalize upon, by comparison to European nations such as England or France or Italy. James Bryce wrote that it is "rather more difficult to take any assemblage of attributes in any of these European countries and call it the national type than it is to do the like in the United States." European observers have also tended to believe that the America of their own day was to some extent prophetic of conditions they might be obliged to face in the Europe of their own tomorrow.

Americans have agreed with foreigners that an American character exists; and American historians, after several generations of argument, arrived, following World War II, at a rough consensus of what the American character was and is. The argument had been waged mainly between those who had interpreted American civilization in terms of New England Puritan origins and those who had supported the Turner thesis, that American civilization was the product of the American frontier experience. During the past generation the consensus of the historical profession has been that the American character is essentially the ethnically mixed but predominantly English culture of the Protestant Reformation as that culture was reformed once more by the American wilderness environment. The absence of an American feudal past is stressed in this consensus.

According to this consensus the American character took final form during and after the American Revolution, and its essential nature has not changed from that time to the present. Despite momentous alterations in modes of existence, so it is argued, American social values remain essentially those of its early Puritan-frontier-Revolution-originated ethos.

But even while American historians have agreed with what European observers have said about America, they have seen the American character differently by not seeing it from the European vantage point. To European observers in the times of Crèvecoeur and Tocqueville, and to some extent of Bryce, the American character was a largely negative concept. To them American society was essentially European society after it had been stripped of the centuries of accumulations of cultural heritage by transplantation to the New World.

To be sure, American society could not be viewed as simply European society in a new setting, if only because of the presence of Indian tribes and of Negro slavery; but from a European point of view, what was more revealing to Europe about the American character was the riddance of the European heritage which the transplantation had accomplished upon what was essentially still a European society. By European standards, Anglo-America possessed no history of its own and no traditions. Here was to be seen European society with the integuments of ancient and medieval civilization removed, resulting in a relatively undifferentiated mass society called American democracy.

The "general equality of conditions," which so forcibly struck Tocqueville during his stay in America, expressed this absence of ingrained regional and hierarchal distinctions which everywhere characterized European society. Crèvecoeur's American was "a new man, who acts upon new principles; he must therefore entertain new ideas, and form new opinions." It is true that the Old Dominion of Virginia and the Commonwealth of Massachusetts had to some extent formed their own characters by the time of the Revolution, but not by comparison to Pomerania or Normandy or Andalusia.

To the extent that the newness or youthfulness of American society was fundamental to the character of the young Republic, one might expect the national character to change as the nation aged. And if, initially, the national character had, to some extent, been shaped by its forest environment, one might expect that it would later have been altered by the increasingly urban and industrial setting. Finally, if the culture of the young Republic was, to begin with, essentially the rudimentary culture of Britain and West Europe, one might expect it to be altered in time by a century of mass immigration from southern and eastern Europe, together with the emancipation of its millions of Negro slaves.

Social scientists have argued for the idea of a changing national character, but historians have not been convinced by the social scientists in this matter. In a critique of David Riesman's *The Lonely Crowd,* Seymour Martin Lipset has presented, in social scientists' terms, the position against a changing American character which represents the historians' consensus. Lipset cited Tocqueville and other nineteenth-century witnesses to indicate that social tendencies which Riesman associated with the late stages of the industrial revolution were already observable a century and more earlier.

And then Lipset went on to assert that

basic alterations of social character or values are rarely produced by change in population or in the means of production, distribution, and exchange *alone*. Rather, as a society becomes more complex, its institutional arrangements adjust to new conditions within the framework of a dominant value-system. . . . Only a profound social revolution . . . can produce sudden major changes in values and social character . . . American nationhood emerged from such a revolutionary break with the ways of the Old World.

This argument is particularly vulnerable in two respects where the United States is concerned. In the first place, the American character differs from the English or French or Italian character in that it is not rooted in an ancient and medieval past of its own. Secondly, the United States cannot be held to any previous rule concerning the extent to which changes in population and the means of production and distribution can affect national values and social character. The United States represents the extreme example of both demographic and technological change in modern times; the United States is therefore, itself, the test of whether such changes can, in turn, "produce sudden major changes in values and social character."

The American character in the times of Crèvecoeur and Tocqueville had great negative significance for European observers, as indicating how European society appeared when it was divested of old cultural accretions and reconstructed in a distant primitive environment. This view of the American as an unfinished European is most thoroughgoing in the writings of unsympathetic British visitors, such as Hall and Marryat and Dickens and the Trollopes. Later, as the industrial revolution reshaped American society, foreign observers could still find grounds to condescend to America, if they wished to, but they could no longer do so convincingly on the old grounds that America lacked a culture of its own. Whether they liked it or not, they were obliged to concede that an American civilization existed which was distinct from European civilization.

This American civilization, which manifested itself full-bloom to the world in the Roaring Twenties, was the modern technological civilization toward which the world had been tending since the beginning of the industrial revolution. Far more fundamentally than was the case with Revolutionary America or Revolutionary France or Revolutionary Russia, the American twenties was the revolutionary foundation of the modern era for the world at large.

••

However variously history may be subdivided into epochs and eras and reigns and administrations, all of recorded history falls meaningfully into two main periods: ancient history, extending from earliest recorded times to the onset of the industrial revolution, and modern history, beginning with the age of steam power and continuing through ever-accelerating stages of technological change to the onrushing present. Henry Adams' description of the United States in 1800 as an ancient society is classic:

The man who in the year 1800 ventured to hope for a new era in the coming century, could lay his hand on no statistics that silenced doubt. The machinery of production showed no radical difference from that familiar to ages long past. The Saxon farmer of the eighth century enjoyed most of the comforts known to Saxon farmers of the eighteenth. . . . The plough was rude and clumsy; the sickle as old as Tubal Cain, and even the cradle not in general use; the flail was unchanged since the Aryan exodus.

Human society as the signers of the Declaration of Independence knew it was one which was ordered by sunrise and sunset and from season to season, and it was a society which was at the mercy of wind and weather. Both the predictable order and the accidental variations were part of the natural laws which governed the universe as they governed the daily rounds of society and the individual. With the rise of urban, industrial America, however, nature ceased to hold the individual or society so immediately to account. Man increasingly lived by an artificial rather than a natural order. For him the yield of the land was what was on the shelves at the store, processed and packaged and refrigerated. The factory worker's life was ordered by the schedule of the machine, and so, in varying degrees, were the lives of all who were affected by the machine, which was to say society as a whole.

Jefferson had held to the principle that "the earth belongs to the living," but he had thought of it as an earth that would be farmed for a living by the majority of each successive generation. In the technological age of the twentieth century it had become the machinery of civilization, rather than simply the earth, which belonged to the living, and this machinery was continually re-creating itself with the devoted and skillful but not, on the whole, philosophically purposeful assistance of the oncoming generations.

The artificial environment had taken on a life of its own; and while it suited man's needs much better than John Locke's state of nature had, it was much trickier to work with than Locke's state of nature had been. And progress had come to refer primarily to this tricky, changing, unpredictable technological environment and not separately to the society which continued to service and improve it and to be, itself, in a continual state of adjustment to the improvements.

The moral order which had been decreed by the Declaration and the Constitution had been based upon an economic order in which the natural right to property was fundamentally conceived of as the right of the farmer to his land and to the yield of his land. By the American twenties, however, machine-made possessions had replaced land as the most conspicuous evidence of man's stake in society. This was an American development which later deeply impressed British industrial missions sent to study American production methods after World War II. Products, especially automobiles, were more important than landed property in fixing a man's position in society, and they were also more important than were the means by which the owner had managed to acquire the products. That marked, the British investigators believed, a crucial difference between the British and the American cultures.

When manufactured goods instead of land and improvements on land came to determine social status, the newness of one's property came to be prized, whereas formerly its age had commanded respect. In fact, when the natural environment was replaced by the technological environment, there occurred a comprehensive reorientation—from a patriarchal faith in the wisdom of age and experience to a filiarchal faith in the promise of youth and innovation and in technologically oriented and therefore continually changing values (see p. 2).

How this filiarchal reorientation of social values operates upon the individual living in this technological society is illustrated by the domestic problems of a man I met in a bar a number of years ago, who got around to telling me some of his problems. This man was married and had several children, the oldest of whom had just reached school age. They lived in a trailer and valued the mobility and sense of freedom of life in trailer courts. Now, however, with a school-age child in the mobile home, the man's wife was arguing that they ought to buy a house in a conventional neighborhood with its own school, for the sake of the children. And, having gotten onto the subject, his wife had decided that if they were not going to move into a house in a conventional neighborhood, they would have to get a new trailer because theirs was an older model which reflected badly upon them in the trailer court.

And then this man went on to observe that his life was in this respect going in the opposite direction from other people's. In most towns, he said, there will be a family living in a house that is maybe fifty or a hundred years old or more, and people will look up to the family because of it; but with him, when his trailer gets to be a few years old, people begin to look down on him. The manager of the trailer court had even hinted that he might move his trailer to a less conspicuous location.

This is an illustration of how what may be called a technological filiarchy operates, including the compulsion felt by parents to reorder their own lives to suit the needs of their children. This man did not question the fact that his children had to go to school and that the quality of the school was a matter of sufficient importance to unsettle the accustomed way of life of the parents. It was not simply that the law required him to send his children to school, because that could have been managed from the trailer court. It was that youth in the technological society is instinctively deferred to, much as age was instinctively deferred to in the patriarchal order which was characteristic of Western society before the industrial revolution.

Nothing was said about what practical benefits the children would derive from this education, and the man probably had no idea, just as most modern parents do not know what education is going to do for their children. In a technological society things will be so different for

each successive generation that parents can do little more than give
their children the chance to take advantage of new opportunities as
they arise. It is likely that the boy who is forced to follow in his
father's footsteps will be unable to keep abreast of his own generation.

This man did not mention anything about his own parents or those
of his wife, but it is unlikely that any of the four parents were living
with them in the trailer. In the mechanical filiarchy the commandment to honor one's father and mother loses its force. There is no
longer the basis for the dignity of age, which characterized patriarchal
agrarian societies. Once the children are grown and are raising families of their own, their parents normally no longer have any clearly
recognized role to play in the home. And at the age of 65 they
arbitrarily cease to play a useful role in society; they become like old
trailers instead of old mansions and old cottages.

Filiarchy visibly became the new order in American society following World War I, and it was this new filiarchal order that gave the
1920's its distinctive character. A spectacularly protean decade, the
Roaring Twenties or Jazz Age or Dollar Decade or Prosperity
Decade was also the Era of the Flapper, of the Lost Generation, of
Coolidge Republicanism, of Postwar Reaction. Frederick Lewis Allen
in *Only Yesterday* (1931) discovered a central theme for the decade
in the "manners and customs, fads and follies, and everyday circumstances of life," and he emphasized the youthful as well as the technological characteristics of the age. He was right about this, and he
might have given these attributes even greater emphasis and wider
application and profounder significance than he did.

The flapper was the authentic personification of the twenties: a
happily motherless child, smoking, boozing, petting, necking, joyriding, doing the Charleston and Black Bottom; living for the moment; trying out every new thing and discarding every old thing.
Against this fast-stepping flapper, the moral forces of the day—
sobersided Progressives and concerned parents, as well as fundamentalists and prohibitionists—strove fruitlessly to save old values. It
was to no apparent avail. In the Era of the Flapper the wisdom,
experience, and authority of age tended to turn into the caricature of
the bluenosed dry. The moral forces became ridiculous, frequently
rabid, as with the Ku Klux Klan, and sadly out of date.

The Lost Generation was defiantly youthful, and even the Business

Civilization prided itself on its young ideas. Chronologically, Herbert Hoover was a middle-aged man when he became Secretary of Commerce; but he was the heroic spokesman for the youthful spirit of innovative business enterprise, and, in the words of Calvin Coolidge, he remained "that wonderful boy" throughout the twenties.

Idealism was not the forte of the twenties, but insofar as it was an idealistic age, Charles A. Lindbergh was the heroic embodiment of its ideals. Lindbergh appealed to the American people as the youth who would lead the nation upward into the unprophesied future. There had never been a hero in American history to match Lindbergh; there had never been one who had dramatized the idea of youthful leadership as Lindbergh did. Young heroes and leaders had made their names in American history, but their youth had not been in their favor—had not been ecstatically emphasized. Until Lindbergh's day, the men were separated from the boys, in the doing of deeds, to the dishonor of the boys; in the age of the technological filiarchy, this was no longer so clearly true.

The leaders of the American Revolution had been fairly young men by political standards, being mainly in their thirties and forties. When the Declaration of Independence was signed, Alexander Hamilton was 19 and James Madison was 25, and both had already been active in the cause of liberty for several years. As founding fathers of the Constitution in the next decade, they were still rather young men, and so were most of their fellow delegates at the Constitutional Convention.

It is therefore significant that these men were not remembered as young revolutionists and state-makers, except, perhaps, in the case of the teenager Hamilton. Their portraits depict them as men who were advanced in years, and that is how their nation wished them to be remembered: as Founding Fathers, and not subordinately as Sons of Liberty. Washington was singled out from the rest as the Father of His Country, and in the patriotic public mind, he was not permitted ever to have experienced the frailties of childhood and youth. Instead he was required always to have behaved as a responsible adult, from the day when, according to Parson Weems, he took manly responsibility for chopping down the cherry tree.

The patriotic mind of the early Republic preferred to envision America as a new nation rather than a young one. The cartoon image of the young Brother Jonathon rebuking old John Bull may have been a faithful reflection of Anglo-American relations, but Uncle Sam satisfied the American ego better, and consequently he replaced Jonathan after the War of 1812.

Two generations later, on the other hand, the industrial revolution was well advanced in the United States, and the expansionists in the Democratic party were now glorying in the phrase "Young America." Their America was now young in the new context of the machine age, when the anticipated transcontinental railroad was envisioned as the nation's most brilliant and exciting symbol of progress. There were many new things under the sun in the early railroad era, and Young America was ambitious to take the lead in them against the seemingly outmoded Old World.

The history of the rise of filiarchy parallels the history of the American industrial revolution, when the old ways tended in increasing degree to be outmoded by the progressively changing circumstances of modern existence. It is no doubt true that by comparison to Europe, America was relatively unpatriarchal, and even youth-oriented, before American society had been much affected by the industrial revolution. Nevertheless, it was not filiarchal, as I have defined the term *filiarchy* (p. 2).

Filiarchy, by my definition, is characteristic of twentieth- rather than nineteenth-century American society; and in the twentieth century, filiarchy has conspicuously advanced its claims only during comparatively peaceful and affluent times. During the prosperous Progressive era a younger generation of Ivy League Bohemian intellectuals gathered in Greenwich Village in the 1910's and acted on the assumption that they were superior in wisdom to their parents because their parents were out of step with the changing times. They were harshly dealt with for their presumption during World War I, but during the 1920's filiarchy triumphed in America in the thoroughly apolitical Jazz Age.

Then came the Great Depression, which proved unfavorable to filiarchy, and then World War II, which imposed the absolute patriarchy of the military system on the youth of the nation. Little was heard on the subject of rebellious youth for more than a decade after the close of World War II, and talk in the mid-fifties was about the "Silent Generation"; then out burst bop and rock and beat and hip and twist and frug and grass and pot and pop and op and LSD and SDS and the whole new revolt of youth. American youth never before behaved quite as it did in the 1960's; but it had never before behaved as it did in the 1920's, and it had never before behaved as it did in the 1910's. Together, these two earlier decades have much to say concerning the meaning of filiarchy in the present day.

••

Moralists have assumed that the family, since Adam and Eve, has always been the essential building block for sound social order and that, unhappily, since the rise of industry, the family in Western civilization has been weakening, if not approaching actual disintegration. Today, after two centuries of industrialization, the disintegrative influences of technology on family life are everywhere apparent; yet young people enthusiastically marry and dutifully raise children, and the sentiment of society as a whole remains overwhelmingly in their favor.

This evidence of the continued vitality of the marriage institution, despite apparently adverse influences, persuaded the French demographic historian Philip Aries to doubt that the family was, despite some appearances, on its way out. "It seemed to me," he wrote, "that the family occupied a tremendous place in our industrial societies, and that it perhaps never before exercised so much influence over the human condition."

Examining Western civilization from this point of view, Aries discovered that the family circle had been nowhere in evidence in medieval times and that it had only gradually made its modern appearance in the course of the fifteenth, sixteenth, and seventeenth centuries. Before that, "people had lived on top of one another, masters and servants, children and adults, in houses open at all hours" to all comers and goers. Medieval society had "concentrated the maximum number of ways of life into the minimum of space" in a "rigid, polymorphous social body." Privacy had scarcely existed on any level. "Not that the family did not exist as a reality; it would be paradoxical to deny that it did. But it did not exist as a concept."

Neither had the idea of childhood existed in this polymorphous society. Instead, "as soon as the child could live without the constant solicitude of his mother, his nanny or his cradle-rocker, he belonged to adult society." The idea of a transitional stage between the world of infancy and the adult world, an idea that had been accepted in some ancient and prehistoric European societies, was absent from medieval thought.

Aries discovered the modern beginnings of the idea of childhood —and with it, the idea of the family—in the revival of interest in education, a revival sponsored by certain churchmen, lawyers, and scholars in the fifteenth century, joined by advocates of religious reform in the sixteenth and seventeenth centuries. These reformers were "primarily moralists rather than humanists: the humanists remained attached to the idea of a general culture spread over the whole of life and showed scant interest in education confined to children." But as "the moral aspect of religion was gradually triumphing in practice over the sacred or eschatological aspect," so it came increasingly to be "recognized that the child was not ready for life, and that he had to be subjected to a special treatment, a sort of quarantine, before he was allowed to join the adults."

This new concern about education would gradually install itself in the heart of society and transform it from top to bottom. The family ceased to be simply an institution for the transmission of a name and an estate— it assumed a moral and spiritual function, it moulded bodies and souls. The care expended on children inspired new feelings, a new emotional attitude, to which the iconography of the seventeenth century gave brilliant and insistent expression: the modern concept of the family.

As Philip Aries noted, this concept of the family emerged together with the emergence of the middle class in Western society and was part of the same general tendency.

It was as if a rigid, polymorphous social body had broken up and had been replaced by a host of little societies, the families, and by a few massive groups, the classes . . . there came a time when the middle class could no longer bear the pressure of the multitude or the contact of the lower class. It seceded: it withdrew from the vast polymorphous society. . . . The concept of the family, the concept of class, and perhaps elsewhere the concept of race, appear as manifestations of the same intolerance toward variety, the same insistence on uniformity.

Among the European middle classes, the seventeenth, eighteenth, and nineteenth centuries were a time of transition from the hierarchal, extended family to the conjugal family and to an expanding role of schools in the subduing as well as the educating of boys; in the seventeenth-century New England wilderness a similar transition occurred more abruptly and radically, amid the fearful warnings of ministers and magistrates. Of the numerous laws passed in the various colonies relating to the training and discipline of children, the school laws of Massachusetts are the most famous and the most important, attempting to repair "the great neglect of many parents and masters in training up their children in learning and labor."

Aside from coping with the extraordinary circumstances of frontier life, a school system was found necessary in New England to guard against the tendency of parents to coddle their children, a tendency which was evident to middle-class parents themselves on both sides of the Atlantic. This characteristic parental weakness was morally disastrous, as it led children to behave "as if hail-fellow well met (as they say) and no difference twixt parent and child." In both England and New England, children were frequently sent to live in other families, where discipline would be more stringent than at home. Apprenticeship carried with it the same moral advantage.

To a greater extent than elsewhere in the colonies, New England was settled by families rather than by individuals. Puritan church membership was by family rather than by individual; the Puritans justified this practice by God's covenant with Abraham, which, they said, had included Abraham's family. The argument arose as to whether "family" in this context meant all members of the household, including servants, or only the children of parents who were church members. The narrower interpretation of family became the commonly accepted one, and in 1662, in the Half-Way Covenant, this interpretation was in turn modified to permit the children to continue as church members, to a limited extent, and to bring their own children into the church, even though they themselves were still unable, as adults, to give evidence of sanctification. "The Puritans had, in fact," wrote Edmund Morgan, "committed the very sin that they so often admonished themselves to avoid; they had allowed their children to usurp a higher place than God in their affections."

Throughout the more worldly eighteenth century, while zeal for God flagged in middle-class society, zeal for family—the conjugal family of parents and children—increased, and its sanctification became liberal dogma. What Aries remarked about European liberalism was at least equally true of Revolutionary liberalism in America—that it sought the liberty, not so much of the individual, as of the family.

The signers of the Declaration of Independence were not demonstrably concerned about the unalienable rights of women—although some of their wives, Abigail Adams, for instance, were—and nobody supposed that children should think and act for themselves. Bachelors were eligible for the rights of man but only grudgingly so; colonial legislation had in some instances treated them virtually as outlaws. The true basis for a libertarian republican government was an electorate composed of property-owning husbands and fathers representing their households at the polling booths.

As a preeminently middle-class phenomenon, the conjugal family morally dedicated to child-rearing prevailed in eighteenth-century America more or less in proportion to the extent that middle-class circumstances prevailed. It was more thoroughly characteristic of the farmers and townspeople of New England and the Middle States than it was of the slave-plantation owners of the Chesapeake region and the South Carolina low country. The diaries of William Byrd II, the model aristocrat of mid-eighteenth-century Virginia, describe a life at Westover which is faintly reminiscent of Aries' description of the medieval great house where "people had lived on top of one another, masters and servants, children and adults, in houses open at all hours." In a later age, the phrase "southern hospitality" described a phenomenon similar to the medieval quality which Aries identifies as "sociability," in contrast to the privacy of "domesticity." Byrd's sarcastic description of North Carolina country people presents a picture of the squalid "sociability" of the lower classes in "lubber-land."

There were Squire Allworthys as well as Squire Westerns among the Virginia gentry, however, as is attested to by the high moral quality of the Virginian leadership in the Revolutionary and early national period. During the Revolutionary era, the laws of primogeniture were repealed in Virginia, as in other of the newly independent states, and this reform simply brought the state law into harmony with what was already widespread practice. Thomas Jefferson, who led in abolishing primogeniture in Virginia, assumed without question—as appears perhaps most clearly in his correspondence with his daughters

—that the basic purpose of government was to preserve the tranquility and sacred privacy of family life in the nation.

The era of Jeffersonian republicanism opened at a time when, as Henry Adams said, there was no persuasive evidence at hand to indicate that great changes were in the offing. What Bernard Bailyn wrote of English Puritans on the eve of colonization was equally true two centuries later of Americans on the eve of the industrial revolution: "Nothing disturbed the confident expectation that the world of the child's maturity would be the same as that of the parents' youth, and that the past would continue to be an effective guide to the future."

The child was the central concern of the American family in the anciently agrarian world of 1800, just as he was in the technological society a century and more later. The family was not child-centered, however, in the sense that that term later came to be used by progressive educationalists, but rather father-centered, or parent-centered. Whether parental training was strict or indulgent, the patriarchal principle went unquestioned: that father knew best what the child's future would be like. The filiarchal outlook of the technological society was as yet inconceivable.

....

Those enlightened Americans who in 1800 did venture to hope for a new era in the coming century shared a severely limited conception of human progress by comparison to the ideas of progress which became current in Jacksonian America. American gentlemen in 1800 still tended to accept the cyclical theory of history—that nations and societies had been experiencing ups and downs since the beginning of human history and that this would continue to be so in future ages, without resulting in significant cumulative benefits to the human race. Enlightened American hopes for a new era rested upon the fact that America was, itself, a new nation, founded upon new principles, and that it was moving upward in its historical cycle. Few believed that America could, in the long run, escape from the laws of history, which appeared to have been in force since before Noah and the flood.

The classical training that educated Americans shared in 1800 did not teach them to suppose that the bygone civilizations of Greece and Rome were inferior to their own, while Protestant Christianity taught them to reverence the age of the primitive Church. They might look down upon the Middle Ages, before the Reformation had restored primitive Christianity; but, in another context, the Middle Ages were seen as the battleground on which Englishmen, and ultimately Americans, had secured their liberties in the Magna Carta. Interpreting the Magna Carta according to seventeenth- and eighteenth-century concepts of law and liberty, eighteenth-century Anglo-Saxons remained correspondingly unaware of how absolutely alien the medieval world of King John and his barons really was to their own.

The cyclical theory of history gained authority from the observable fact that the workaday world had remained recognizably similar from biblical times to the age of the American and French revolutions. Jefferson's *Notes on Virginia* expresses this point of view; yet Jefferson, as an old man, in the early nineteenth century arrived at the new opinion that "science has liberated the ideas of those who can read and reflect" and that belief in the "improvability of the condition of man" had become an article of republican faith. Statements such as these, together with Jefferson's optimistic faith in the possibilities of mechanical inventions, exhibit, as Stow Persons has observed, those authentic features of the new faith in human progress: "the cumulative character of technology, the liberating power in science, the kindling of feelings of right, and the improvement of the condition of mankind."

There followed the romantic age of Jacksonian democracy—an age of perfectionism, postmillennialism, utopianism, and transcendentalism; human progress had become a fundamental article of American faith. As the Jacksonian editor John O'Sullivan put it, "On all is written the great Law of Progress. That is the distinguishing mark of our species. . . . Every age takes one step in advance of its predecessors." Some, like Emerson, felt that progress was a spiritual rather than a mechanical process, but the moral philosopher Francis Wayland more truly represented the thinking of educated men and women when he wrote, "The progress of a nation in wealth, happiness and refinement, is measured by the university of its knowledge of the laws and nature and its skill in adapting these laws to the purposes of man." Or, as James K. Paulding put it even more baldly,

"Machinery and steam engines have had more influence on the Christian world than Locke's metaphysics, Napoleon's code or Jeremy Bentham's codifications."

Relatively well-educated men and women have tended to nourish traditional social values and to guard against technologically oriented social values, but they have also been the ones who have been obliged to reconcile their social values with the changing conditions of life. Accordingly, during the first machine age Darwinian biology replaced Newtonian physics as the scientific basis for social thought. Society was understood to be conforming to the newly accepted universal law of evolution; and progress came to mean, not simply the perfecting of existing arrangements, but the creation of a materially superior civilization.

Victorian America assumed a very condescending attitude toward the more primitive previous periods of the nation's development. But although it became natural to think in terms of past evolution to the present, it did not become natural to think in terms of contemporary evolution toward an unrecognizable future. Philosophical relativism emerged in the form of pragmatism, but the typical American had always been pragmatic in the sense of putting more stock in how things worked out in practice than in the theory of it. The social evolutionist remained a moral man, and the relativistic humanism of William James and of John Dewey remained invisibly framed in the eternally fixed moral order.

What proved truly subversive was not pragmatism as it was seen from the point of view of those philosophers, but pragmatism as seen from the point of view of their students. The conclusions that Max Eastman drew from John Dewey, and Hutchins Hapgood from William James, were the radical conclusions of members of the younger generation who were entering a world which their generation was about to change. Their point of view toward progressive education was not the paternal one of the teacher—ambitious to train a community of pupils to be better than their parents. Their point of view was the filiarchal one of the pupil—ambitious to be better than his teacher in a better community of his own making.

It was during the Progressive era that the younger generation emerged in America as a recognized class in society, proclaiming its radical doctrines from its national capital in Greenwich Village. The younger generation has traditionally been a trial to its elders since Plato complained about it and before; but beginning with the twentieth century, the younger generation spoke with the legitimate authority of youthful experience. Their generation had grown up in a changing technological society, which was materially unlike the society the older generation had known in its youth. The new generation was, in that sense, a truly new generation; and the new world to come would be uniquely a world of its own making.

The confidence of this first new generation of youth who grew up in a changing technological society proved woefully ill-founded, and following World War I, the Greenwich Villagers of the 1910's joined the Lost Generation of the 1920's. The phenomenon of the younger generation as the exclusive custodians of the new wisdom continued to characterize American life, however, after the Lost Generation had grown old and largely failed, in its turn, to bring up another younger generation according to its own once-new lights.

The American experience suggests that filiarchy is incompatible with philosophy. Pragmatism enjoyed its greatest influence in the Progressive era and when its influence declined, no subsequent philosophical school emerged to take its place. During the fifties and sixties existentialism enjoyed a vogue in America; but it failed to achieve a recognized status, either as an academic subject or as a popular line of argument, comparable to the earlier status of philosophical idealism in the late nineteenth century and pragmatism in the early twentieth. Filiarchy is concerned with technique rather than philosophy, for nobody can imagine with any assurance what the long-range results of the new techniques will be or what further new techniques they will lead to.

It is not so evident that filiarchy is incompatible with the idea of progress; certainly not from the youthful point of view, which is continually discovering the answers that were evidently not known to earlier generations of men and women. Technology continues to manufacture the wherewithal for material progress and to provide the means by which a rational world can live by standards such as were formerly inconceivable. There remains the problem of man, himself, who is evidently not rational by nature. Technology offers promises of progress in this area also through such means as computerized controls and chemical psychology, but this inhuman use of human beings alters out of recognition the traditional humanistic and libertarian idea of progress.

The technological filiarchy tends to live day by day and year by year because it does not have the foreknowledge or the usable retrospect to do otherwise; and faith in human progress, which remains strong in America, must to this extent necessarily be blind faith, strengthened by faith in education and faith in the younger generation. Belief in continuing progress depends, to a greater extent than was true a century ago, on the conviction that the oncoming generation is the best-trained and generally finest generation the nation has produced; at the same time, the younger generations are just children growing up. Questions arise such as who represents the younger generation at what age, and how the new wisdom is to be distinguished from the old immaturity.

....

Following the progress of the younger generation through twentieth-century America is akin to playing croquet in Wonderland with flamingoes as mallets, hedgehogs as croquet balls, and pages as wickets. The younger generation is at all times simultaneously appearing on the field and moving off the field and trying to stay on the field while turning into something else. No sooner have the rules of the game been officially explained by the younger generation, than another game is discovered to be in progress on the same field under different rules by a somewhat different younger generation.

In defining what the younger generation is, one qualification may perhaps be insisted upon: that all members be under thirty. Radical spokesmen for youth from Randolph Bourne to Mario Savio have set this upward limit; so they, themselves, may be held to it. It would further clarify the subject if a similar line could be drawn marking the age at which the growing child becomes a part of the younger generation, but it cannot be. The younger generation begins in the womb; before it is three years old, major industries, such as the breakfast food manufacturers, are vying for its favor. By the time it is in its teens, its purchasing power is immense; and it has by then developed a social style of its own, which the older generations react to, chiefly with aversion but to some extent with emulation.

Except for prodigies, child laborers, and juvenile delinquents, however, adolescents do not characteristically think of themselves as a part of the adult world until they arrive at college age. In the pre-World War I Greenwich Village era of Randolph Bourne, this intellectual awareness of incipient adulthood typically awaited graduation from college. A minimum age limit therefore can be imposed upon the younger generation in dealing with it as a deliberately formative influence upon society as a whole. In this sense, the younger generation ideologically enters the adult world four or five years earlier than tended to be the case a half century or more ago.

But there are generations within younger generations. Testifying before the President's National Commission on the Causes and Prevention of Violence in October 1968, Tom Hayden, founder of the Students for a Democratic Society (SDS), declared that the presidential primary campaigns of Senators Kennedy and McCarthy that year had "rekindled a last hope in some young people of working within the channels of society." In that respect, Hayden concluded, they resembled "the original Peace Corps volunteers of my generation." By this implied reckoning, younger generations may occur at intervals of four or five or six years; and indeed that seems to have been roughly the recognized interval between younger generations early in the century.

Floyd Dell, editor of *Masses* and later of *Liberator,* who had arrived in Greenwich Village in 1913, later violated the feelings of the community by the manner in which he changed sweethearts. He was therefore driven to finding new company among the newer Villagers, who had arrived around 1916 or after. When that happened, he wrote

I found that I was regarded by these younger people as one of the pillars of hated Village orthodoxy. The *Liberator,* though regarded by the rest of America (wherever it was known at all) as daringly modern in its pictures and poetry, was thought of by the younger Villagers as tame, old-fogy, stupidly conservative.

Presently in the early post-World War I period, another younger generation entered Greenwich Village, the one for whom Malcolm Cowley spoke in *Exile's Return* (1934). Cowley wrote,

There were two sorts of people here: those who had lived in the Village before 1917 and those who had just arrived from France or college. . . .

'They' wore funny clothes: it was the first thing that struck you about them. . . . 'They' were older, and this simple fact continued to impress me long after I ceased to notice their clothes. Their ages ran from sixty down to twenty-three, some of the older ones sporting the authentic Windsor ties that marked the bohemians of the 1890's. 'They' had been rebels. . . . 'We' were convinced at the time that society could never be changed by an effort of the will.

During the 1920's all of the younger generations, from Floyd Dell's to Malcolm Cowley's and on down, could unite in the common sense of being the Lost Generation, because they shared a common sense of alienation from what they conceived to be the dominant older generation. During the 1960's the younger generation, from Ginsberg and Kerouac to Savio and Hayden and on down, shared this same common sense of alienation from "The Establishment," rather than any commonly shared outlook on life or program for America. Nor did Floyd Dell nor Malcolm Cowley nor Allen Ginsberg nor Tom Hayden speak for more than a small segment of what each considered to be his own generation chronologically.

Endemic revolts of youth in the twentieth century have left an exaggerated impression of the radical and nonconformist tendencies inherent in the state of postadolescence or incipient adulthood in the technological society. College age is a revolutionary age of new ideas and new opportunities; but it is, for that very reason, an age of uncertainty and insecurity, when the felt need for fraternity or sorority with one's contemporaries is unusually strong. This need for belongingness can be satisfied equally well in the Greek fraternity or in the beat fraternity. Later on, in the state of what is called maturity, a sense of belongingness is provided by the line of work one enters and by the family that one mothers or fathers, with its accumulating possessions and obligations.

Dell wrote of the pre-World War I Greenwich Villagers that they "were almost invariably the children of people of some importance in the home town." They were from the top 5 percent or so of their generation, economically and socially—those who had been given "opportunities," probably including a college education—and they represented that small minority of their privileged class which had not returned to the hometown or at least entered a hometown-approved marriage and career. Among the college generations of the twentieth century, social revolt against parental admonitions has been usual; on the other hand, ideological revolt against the politics of the parents has always been a minority movement.

Campus radicalism was more in evidence during the 1930's than at any time until the sixties, but a survey of predominant college attitudes by *Fortune* in 1936 drew a picture of "a generation that will not stick its neck out . . . a cautious, subdued, unadventurous generation. . . . Security is the summum bonum of the present college generation." Security is no doubt the summum bonum of any generation that finds its security in jeopardy. Revolts of youth in America have been chiefly carried out by those who have had no reason to worry about economic insecurity.

The quality in American democratic life which, more than any other, inspires rebelliousness among young people is the hypocrisy of overextended moralism—the hypocrisy of American ideals as these ideals are put into practice and, closer to home, the hypocrisy which parents and teachers have customarily employed in dealing with children. "The world created in nineteenth-century schoolbooks," according to Ruth Miller Elson, "is essentially a world of fantasy—a fantasy made up by adults as a guide for their children, but inhabited by no one outside the pages of schoolbooks." Efforts have been made continuously in the twentieth century to correct this situation, but children continue to be taught about a world other than the real one as they come to recognize it upon growing up.

This is the cycle of innocence and experience which traditionally has gone on from one generation to the next, except that in the technological filiarchy the younger generation brings something beyond innocence to the contest. In a rapidly evolving technological society much new knowledge will come naturally to the child, which his elders must learn laboriously or superficially. The child has a grasp of contemporary reality which is in some ways superior to that of his elders, and he knows this. It is in the world of ideas, rather than in the world of reality, that the child will be more likely to be kept innocent, deferring to the wisdom of his elders until he goes to college and learns about the larger world for himself.

Intellectually, the most important thing about modern college life is the fact that in practice as well as theory it confers upon the student the adult right to enter the world of ideas, as had not been the case in high school. The awareness of this new right can change a student's outlook on life almost overnight. A rich variety of subversive ideas are available to the entering freshman, including those upholding free love, atheism, communism, and pot; but in politics, collegiate and postcollegiate radicalism in twentieth-century America has not tended to reject schoolbook ideals for alien ideologies. Rather it has tended to subject adult American political and cultural behavior to schoolbook standards and to give adult America a failing grade. The Declaration of Independence has been the main ideological basis for student radicalism throughout this century, despite an intellectual vogue for Marxism in the thirties and a more enduring vogue for the quasi-Marxism of the Charles Beard school.

Greenwich Villagers in the pre-World War I era applied the doctrine of the Declaration to the Progressive movement and found that Progressivism represented the ethnocentric attitudes of the privileged Protestant Anglo-Saxon middle classes against the great American masses. Then Wilson spoke for a war to make the world safe for democracy and followed it with support for the Treaty of Versailles and, as Cowley said, young intellectuals simply gave up hope for the system. Franklin D. Roosevelt and the New Deal and the radical movements revived the idealistic hope of youthful intellectuals in the struggle for the rights of labor and for the improvement of the underprivileged one-third of the nation. Then came the war against fascism and then the Cold War.

Cold War America has been a hothouse for both libertarianism and militarism, as well as for economic expansion and technological-filiarchal development; the younger generations of the past decade and a half are the products of this hothouse, including new conservatives, beats, hippies, professional soldiers, draft-card burners, black nationalists, teenie boppers, and New Leftists. What Eisenhower called the military-industrial complex has continued to expand prodigiously in the era of the Vietnam War; while the civil rights movement has made giant advances in line with the Cold War requirement that America make a good impression on the nonwhite world majority. And in this same Cold War context, individual liberty for youthful agitators has received a degree of support in the mass media and protection in the courts unprecedented in the nation's history.

The younger generation in the sixties has been freer to behave as it pleases than ever before, except that it has been confronted with military duty and perhaps combat duty in a war which has inspired American idealism and hypocrisy in a nationally volatile combination. This generation has been continuously stimulated by technological-social change; it has been encouraged by its elders to help forward a revolution in Negro rights which is far more sweeping than the older generation, itself, had been brought up to be able to tolerate.

Writing during the fall of 1968, Walter Lippmann observed that "never before or in any place have 200 million people confronted the consequences of the technological revolution with a heterogeneous population no longer bound by ancestral habits and customs. Nothing on this scale or diversity has ever before been attempted. . . ." Lippmann was concerned to dispel illusions that the consequent problems confronting the nation could be solved in the next four or eight years, providing only that the right man were elected to the Presidency.

Indeed, the history of the problem as Lippmann formulated it, first received articulate recognition from Lippmann's own younger generation—which emerged nearly sixty years ago in Greenwich Village—of which he was the leading political philosopher. In that sense, Lippmann is an intellectual patriarch of the technological filiarchy. This is a position which is not recognized and which holds no authority; and Lippmann is wise in not appealing to the filiarchy, as some old men and women are inclined to do, on the basis of his prior youth.

....

The younger generation to which Lippmann belonged was conscious of possessing a new wisdom that had been acquired in part by the experience of growing up during the period of the New Immigration from southeastern and central Europe and witnessing in its youth the decline of the old Anglo-Saxon elements to a minority position in the nation. To the Greenwich Villagers, this presaged the end of puritanical Anglo-Saxon provincialism. To a great many more Americans, however, it threatened the destruction of the Protestant Republic, and the nation reacted with immigration restriction legislation culminating in the National Origins Act of 1924.

It is customary for historians to make sentimental reference to the

Statue of Liberty when discussing the National Origins Act, which closed the gates to the huddled masses of the world except for selected quotas of them. Its passage is attributed to nativism and racial bigotry, although at the time, the major organized opposition to it came, not from Progressives, but from the National Association of Manufacturers. Many reasonable men believed that the nation would be better off if immigration were sharply curtailed, and they proved right.

The National Origins Act represented the climax of two generations of rising racism in America; it also marked the end of racism as a significant organized force in American political life. The collapse of the Ku Klux Klan as a national force was related to the nativist victory of immigration restriction because no major legislative goal remained around which to rally the Klan. Other racist organizations dwindled and died for sudden lack of support following passage of the 1924 act, while racist books, of the sort that had been well received by educated people early in the twenties, began to get adverse, even contemptuous, reviews by the close of the decade. A flurry of nativism was occasioned in 1928 by the candidacy of the Irish-American Catholic Al Smith, it is true, and anti-Semitic Bundist rallies were carried on during the thirties; but the National Origins Act nevertheless stands as the beginning of that age when self-conscious American race tolerance began to become a cardinal tenet of American liberalism.

Arnold Toynbee, in a long and lordly denunciation of the United States entitled *America and the World Revolution,* has asserted that the immigration restriction laws of the twenties, in their "political and psychological consequences . . . have been unfortunate for America." But the truth is precisely the opposite of this. Politically and psychologically, the National Origins Act manifested its influence directly in the New Deal, which was the first truly cosmopolitan reform movement in American history. This cosmopolitan character of the New Deal was directly facilitated politically and psychologically by the national sense of comparative ethnic security which resulted from the immigration restriction legislation of the twenties. One of the most fundamental achievements of the New Deal was the incorporation of the New Immigration, not merely into American political life, which already had been accomplished to some extent, but into a tradition of reform associated with the ideals of the nation's Revolutionary origins—a tradition which, in the Progressive era, had been distinctively Protestant and Anglo-Saxon. It is hardly conceivable that this development could have taken place while unlimited immigration continued to play on the fears and prejudices of old-stock Americans, as it increasingly had done from the late nineteenth century to the law of 1924.

American society had ceased to be predominantly white old-stock American by the 1920's, but it was far from clear what it was becoming instead. The National Origins Act was the beginning of a new answer to the question of what American nationality was. By sealing off the nation from any further mass migrations, it fixed the national character, psychologically much more than actually, and defined it in terms of its existing ethnic components. Thereafter the ideal American ceased to be thought of as quite so Anglo-Saxon as he had formerly been and tended to be thought of as a composite of that cosmopolitan mixture that had existed at the time the National Origins Act went into effect.

The New Deal, unlike the Progressive movement, drew strength from the entire American ethnic spectrum. White Anglo-Saxon Protestants continued to predominate in high New Deal councils; and FDR was himself the great WASP under whom the new Americanism was taking form. But New Deal ideals were explicitly not formed out of that WASP America, which, according to the formerly authorized version, had developed from the Pilgrim landing into the national character.

The faith of the founding fathers had been Protestantism, and during World War I the main spiritual agency of the nation had been the YMCA. During the New Deal the American character ceased to be thought of as distinctly Protestant, either ideally or actually. The American faith became the American faiths, and spread out from "the God of our fathers" into "our Judeo-Christian heritage." During World War II the three-faith character of American religion was heavily stressed.

In World War I the American soldier was called a Yank, in reference to the archetypally New England characteristics he was supposed to represent. In World War II the American soldier was called a G.I., the initials standing for Government Issue and the concept being that of the end product of the American assembly line, or the modern equivalent of the melting pot. A lot of things had happened between the two wars to alter the American self-image, but the most decisive thing was the Immigration Act of 1924.

The New Deal renationalized American ideals, and in so doing it necessarily reshaped them in harmony with the neoequalitarianism of the machine age. This new Americanism did not take the form of the cultural pluralism that had been advocated by Jane Addams and others. It consisted instead of loyalty to an American Way of Life which, though it celebrated a heritage on Thanksgiving and Fourth of July, was not so much a loyalty to a historical development as to a highly prized contemporary, social, political, economic, and technological condition. Second- and third-generation Americans were drawn into it away from the vestiges of Old World culture which were preserved in their homes and neighborhoods.

Gunnar Myrdal wrote of the American foreign-born in *An American Dilemma*:

The first stages of their assimilation often took them through the worst slums of the nation . . . [their] first course in Americanism [was] in the midst of utter poverty, crime, prostitution, lawlessness . . . uncontrolled labor conditions and often through personal misery and social pressures of all kinds.

Myrdal supposed that the resulting failures might be such as to occupy the curiosity of American social scientists.

To the outside observer, on the other hand, the relative success will forever remain the first and greatest riddle to solve, when he sees that the children and grandchildren of these unassimilated foreigners are well-adjusted Americans. He will have to account for the basic human power of resistance and the flexibility of peoples' minds and cultures. He will have to appreciate the tremendous force in the American educational system, but it will not suffice as an explanation. He will be tempted to infer the influence upon the immigrant of a great national *ethos,* in which optimism and carelessness, generosity and callousness, were so blended as to provide him with hope and endurance.

Myrdal was writing at the close of the New Deal period, when the application of that national ethos to non-Anglo-Saxon ethnic groups was better realized than it had been in the twenties or at any time before the passage of the National Origins Act of 1924. The National Origins Act marks the end of an era more concretely than did that announcement of the end of the frontier in the census report of 1890, which had provided Frederick Jackson Turner with the text for his paper on the significance of the frontier in American history.

World War II was followed by a postwar period that was in many ways reminiscent of those ill-remembered postwar years of a generation earlier. Business was back in the saddle; and Senator Robert A. Taft was the dominating figure in what President Truman immortalized as the "do-nothing" Eightieth Congress. What had been termed demobilization after World War I was now called reconversion, and it seemed to be the evident intention of the old-stock American congressional coalition of Republicans and southern Democrats to reconvert the nation, so far as possible, to the old order of the ante-New Deal twenties.

Another great Red Scare swept the nation, which far outlasted its predecessor and culminated in Senator Joseph McCarthy's personal reign of terror. Together with this new postwar Red Scare, postwar nativism expressed itself in new immigration restriction legislation, the McCarran Act of 1952. Adlai Stevenson emerged in that year as an extraordinarily eloquent spokesman for the cosmopolitan humanism of the New Deal, and he was decisively defeated at the polls.

Eisenhower Republicanism, however, did not turn out to be a recapitulation of Coolidge Republicanism. The national circumstances were unalterably changed, and the Eisenhower administration, on taking office, adjusted to the changed circumstances. It substantially accepted, and in some respects even extended, the social reforms of the New Deal; and it was in turn substantially accepted by those descendants of the New Immigration who had achieved their sense of national identity during the New Deal period. In 1956 Eisenhower's margin of victory over Stevenson was half again as large as it had been four years earlier; this added support apparently came in large measure from the children and grandchildren of the New Immigration.

Amid the Cold War contest with atheistic communism, Catholic and Jewish descendants of the New Immigration found themselves securely within the wagon circle, inside the camp of the new Americanism, where a generation before they had been the enemy at the edge of the forest. The Protestant crusade was over as a national movement; American Catholicism and American Judaism had become nationally recognized variations of the established American Way of Life. For a century and a half the American Catholic Church had remained mobilized against the Protestant crusade. In the age of the new Americanism, the Church faced new problems of maintaining its authority—in an age when it was unsustained by the old anti-Catholic pressures from without. In the new age of the technological filiarchy, it faced unprecedented challenges on the campuses of the nation's Catholic colleges and universities.

In 1960, in the Democratic primary campaign in Anglo-Saxon West Virginia, John F. Kennedy put the new Americanism to the test. He appealed for support for his American right to his Catholic faith, and West Virginians responded with a mandate for him against his awkwardly Protestant opponent Hubert Humphrey. The Kennedy-Nixon presidential contest that followed was a close one; and it stirred up some old nativist sentiments. However, Kennedy, as President, won broad support throughout the nation, and American democracy took a giant step toward becoming the American ethnocracy (see p. 2).

How great a change this was may be seen in the contrast between Kennedy in 1960 and Alfred E. Smith in 1928, when Smith's landslide defeat convinced many that no Catholic could ever become President. Smith was a product of the old political system, who had worked his way up through the ranks of Tammany Hall. In the election of 1928, he represented urban America of the immigrant, the saloon, and the Catholic Church, and he was savagely rejected by the embattled forces of the old Protestant Republic. In the election of 1960, the young, wealthy, Harvard-educated Kennedy represented urban America of both the new ethnocracy and the new technological filiarchy, which tended to reject old ways, including the ways of the old Americanism. The televised and computerized political campaign of 1960 may perhaps be considered the first truly modern presidential campaign of the second industrial revolution. Al Smith's old-style political image had been his worst liability; Kennedy's new-style image was his greatest asset and won him his victory through the medium of television.

Kennedy's Presidency constituted the fulfillment of ethnocracy, where white America was concerned, in the political world. Culturally, America retained its Anglo-Saxon Protestant heritage; and it was only by becoming a surrogate descendant of the founding fathers that Kennedy qualified himself for the Presidency in the public mind. In the meanwhile, however, the Anglo-Saxon Protestant heritage itself was increasingly challenged by successive younger generations of writers and scholars.

During the depression, proletarian literature had been published in quantity and had been well received critically, and intellectual publications had subjected the American heritage to critical devaluation as a matter of course. Indeed, "serious" literature came to be, almost by definition, adversely critical literature, where American society was concerned.

With the G.I. Bill of Rights, at the close of World War II, higher education in America ceased to be the preserve of the old-stock children of well-to-do, who had formerly made up 90 percent of college enrollments. Children of the New Immigration in their turn immigrated to the campuses of the nation in the postwar period. The prodigious expansion in higher education of recent years has provided a massive new program of higher Americanization, which is increasingly extending itself into postgraduate study. This has been the trend in the private colleges and universities as well as in the state institutions.

One striking intellectual development that is related to this trend is the emergence of what is somewhat misleadingly called the New Left in historical writing. Young historians, whose own personal histories go back to the New Immigration, are reexamining the American past with an alien, as well as a critical, eye. To the extent that there has been a Nestor to these young historians, he was Charles Beard; but Beard thought of the founding fathers as his own people, and he thought of American history as "The Rise of American Civilization." The New Left historians count a good many old-stock Americans among their number: some are historically in the tradition of the idealistic abolitionists or of the despairing Lost Generation; others may simply be sharing in the expression by their generation of the filiarchal wisdom of the age.

What appears likely to result from this new trend is a revised version or revised versions of American history which will better suit the inner needs of the new ethnocracy than is the case with the present American historiography, representing, as it does, the devoted labors of generation after generation of Anglo-Saxon scholars. And in this new history, which the new ethnocracy is writing, the American Negro is finding a place for himself much more readily than he is finding a place for himself in the society of the new ethnocracy itself. In society at large, he remains the "American dilemma," in Gunnar Myrdal's phrase, which confronts the nation today with unprecedented urgency.

• •

Concerning this American dilemma, Thomas Jefferson long ago wrote that

deep rooted prejudices entertained by the whites; ten thousand recollections, by the blacks, of the injuries they have sustained; new provocations; the real distinctions which nature has made; and many other circumstances, will divide us into parties, and produce convulsions which will probably never end but in the extermination of one or the other race.

American society has altered out of recognition during the nearly two centuries which have passed since Jefferson's prophecy, but the race problem has not altered out of recognition. Indeed, it has only been within the past two decades that white America has seriously undertaken the task of understanding the meaning of those "ten thousand recollections, by the blacks, of the injuries they have sustained." A new era in race relations is at hand; but it is an era of unparalleled racial convulsions, leading to no clearly discernible permanent resolutions.

Abolition of slavery by northern force more than a century ago was not accompanied by substantive progress toward Negro equality even in the North, itself; and at the end of the nineteenth century, Jim Crow segregation became the nationally agreed upon white solution to the problem. Jim Crow continued to extend itself nationally, together with the continuing surge of racist sentiment which reached its climax with the Ku Klux Klan in the early 1920's. By that time, however, racist theories were beginning to cease to be respectable in educated circles; while the cause of Negro rights was attracting the support of some white liberals through the National Association for the Advancement of Colored People. The New Deal extended major federal assistance to Negroes for the first time since Reconstruction, chiefly through relief programs; but in deference to southern Democrats, it would not support civil rights for Negroes even to the point of a federal antilynch law. Amid the war against the racist Nazis, fair employment practices toward Negro workers became a federal concern and a national liberal cause, but comprehensively equal civil rights for Negroes became a major national issue only after the onset of the Cold War.

Confronted by the Cold War, America, for the first time since the Revolutionary War, became vitally concerned about the impression it was making upon the world at large. The United Nations, a distinctively American conception, brought the representatives of the world together in a General Assembly—and the majority of them were not white. It was most fundamentally within this international context that the Democratic party sacrificed the Solid South in 1948 and committed itself to a second Reconstruction. In 1954 the Supreme Court reversed the Jim Crow decisions of the 1890's. A year later the black nonviolence movement began with the year-long bus boycott in Montgomery, Alabama. National civil rights legislation followed, amid sit-ins, civil rights marches, and from 1963 on, increasing violence, the centers of its ferocity tending to shift from the South to the northern cities.

As long as Martin Luther King could still be said to represent the Negro rights movement, its character was southern and agrarian-oriented and deeply religious and compellingly comprehensible to millions of whites. With the shift in major emphasis to northern cities, however, the movement took on the character of a new social force, the black ghetto, which was mainly the product of the two great wartime Negro migrations out of the South. Originally uprooted from Africa and then uprooted from the southern countryside, the Negro migrants did not bring to the ghetto those ingrained village traditions of the Old World which the New Immigrants had brought with them and had stubbornly adapted to American urban circumstances. The black ghetto is a society that is culturally an indigenous product; yet one that, despite decades of intensive study, is still a fearfully new and unknown quantity. The tragic American dilemma has become the dangerous American enigma.

However little white America may have been aware of the Negro as a human problem in the past, American culture has always been influenced by Negro culture, and perhaps never more so than during the Jim Crow era of the early twentieth century. During the nineteenth century Negro cultural influence had made itself felt most strongly in white America through the minstrel show, which was a natively American, yet joyfully antipuritanical, form of extremely popular entertainment. During the first quarter of the twentieth century this influence of Negro music and Negro rhythm was more insistently exerted through spirituals, blues, ragtime and jazz, which, in whitened forms, accompanied the filiarchal "dance craze" into the Jazz Age.

Together with other manifestations of filiarchy, Negro musical culture, chiefly in its white modifications, persisted through the Great Depression in the big band and Big Apple era. In the 1960's the Negro hot style in music again became a dominant undercurrent of a new filiarchal culture, to the new sound of the electric guitar. The phrase "white Negro" described a clearly observable phenomenon of Negro cultural influence upon the younger generations through rhythm and music.

Deep-rooted prejudices of whites and the volatile and enigmatic nature of black nationalism will perhaps prevail against any stable solution to the American race problem in the foreseeable future; but in the age of the technological filiarchy, the fatalism of Jefferson's prophecy may finally have become dated. The "heterogeneous population no longer bound by ancestral habits and customs" threatens social stability, as Lippmann pointed out, but it also offers hope for a workable national solution to the American dilemma. The achievement of full citizenship for Negroes, if it comes to be achieved, will be worked out according to the anciently formulated principles of the Declaration of Independence. But the process by which the achievement will be accomplished must be the process of the technological filiarchy, both black and white, in which successive generations at rapid four- or five-year intervals will tend to reject the wisdom—including the race wisdom—of the fathers, in favor of their own new experience and filiarchal wisdom.

••

According to the Turner thesis, in its most unmitigated form American democracy was declared to be wholly the product of environment. It had not been brought to America aboard the *Susan Constant* or the *Mayflower*; it had been born in the American wilderness, and it had gained new strength on each new frontier. Few if any modern historians would deny that such an interpretation represents an excessively deterministic view of the origins of late nineteenth-century American democracy. Similarly, it would be excessively deterministic to assert that late twentieth-century American democracy was born in the cities and on the assembly line and that it gained new strength with each new urban development and factory.

The central tenets of American democracy—liberty and equality—are not indigenous concepts, but are, rather, tenets inherited from European humanism. They were not the special handiwork of the founding fathers or of the provincial American nation for which the founding fathers spoke. They were tenets of western European and American liberalism which varied in meaning according to historical and material circumstances. They became distinctively American, however, when they became the basic principles underlying the American system of government; and since then, they have remained distinctively American. But though the principles have remained the same, their American meaning has continued to change with the changing historical and material circumstances.

The founding fathers held assumptions concerning liberty and equality which were conservatively related to property ownership. The Jacksonians broadened the conception to include equal political rights for all adult white males, and northern evangelists demanded the abolition of slavery in the name of spiritual equality. Catholic and Jewish humanism emerged with the New Immigration and served to broaden the existing concept of Anglo-American liberty and equality into the more cosmopolitan liberalism of the New Deal. These were historical developments in American democracy which were more basically cultural than environmental in origin.

These are also historical developments in American democracy which are comparatively rational and articulate in character. The highest excellence and originality of the Turner thesis is its depiction of the irrational and inarticulate qualities that the frontier contributed to American democracy. "The wilderness masters the colonist," Turner wrote. ". . . It strips off the garments of civilization and arrays him in the hunting shirt and the moccasin. . . . The fact is that here is a new product that is American." Unlike this new American of Turner's, Crèvecoeur's new American had been the farmer who had arrived on the heels of that frontiersman, for whose wild ways Crèvecoeur had no word of praise. Crèvecoeur's new American was domesticated and rational; Turner's retained the marks of the wilderness:

The result is that to the frontier the American intellect owes its striking characteristics. That coarseness and strength combined with acuteness and inquisitiveness; that practical, inventive turn of mind, quick to find expedients; that masterful grasp of material things, lacking in the artistic but powerful to effect great ends; that restless, nervous energy; that dominant individualism, working for good and for evil; and withal that buoyancy and exuberance which comes with freedom.

The eighteenth-century republicanism of John Adams and Thomas Jefferson was a rational and fully articulated conception, but the democracy of Andrew Jackson and Zachary Taylor was not. From the age of Jackson to the present, American democracy has represented the will of the majority, and it has necessarily taken on the inarticulate character of the whole people. And what the frontiersman personified for mid-nineteenth-century democracy, the factory worker may be said to have personified for democracy at the climax of the first machine age, sustaining the full force of an environment that was reshaping the national character as a whole.

J. Franklin Jameson wrote in *The American Revolution Considered as a Social Movement* of his agreement with historians who "have been much impressed with the thought that the average man, in all ages, has been more occupied with making a living than with any other one thing." This had "led them to doubt whether economic phenomena are not more often the cause than the effect of political institutions and arrangements." Political democracy came to the United States, Jameson explained, as the result of economic democracy. Furthermore, it was an economic democracy based upon an agrarian order which has vanished and is now, Jameson noted two generations ago, difficult even to imagine.

Liberty and equality continue to be the watchwords of American democracy in the second machine age as in the first machine age and before that in the age of Jefferson and Jackson, and they continue to assume new meanings as material conditions change and as "the people" reveals itself in new aspects. As black America asserts its birthright, it inevitably must do so in the name of liberty and equality. But the achievement of its goal will require new dimensions of meaning for American democracy beyond those evangelically middle-class and legalistically Anglo-Saxon dimensions originally contemplated by the predominantly white founders of the National Association for the Advancement of Colored People. Any resolution of this American dilemma which can be counted successful must involve at the same time a fulfillment of the doctrine of the Declaration of Independence and a basic alteration in American social values.

Perhaps the most significant modern social change that is outmoding the social values of earlier times is the fact that for the first time in all ages the average man is no longer indisputably more occupied with making a living than with any other one thing. The average man today is occupied more by his leisure and less completely by his livelihood than ever before in history; and in the democratic world of leisure, as in the aristocratic, the fashions tend to be set by youth.

Teenie boppers and their older sisters in miniskirts have enlivened the scene in the 1960's, much as the flappers did more than a generation ago. The dance craze, which began in the pre-World I era, continued on in the sixties to the electronic rhythm of rock 'n' roll. Among the hippies, boys grew their hair in flowing locks, and girls went around in trousers, to the point where one did not always know which were boys and which girls. Jonathan Miller has suggested, probably rightly, that this sexual nondifferentiation was an attempt at expression of prepubertal love. Similarly, the English fashion model Twiggy was arguably the expression of prepubertal glamor.

Traditional religion, ancient and patriarchal in orientation, is out of place in filiarchal America—no matter how effectively the dynamically youthful Billy Graham may have mastered the new media and no matter how compelling his influence has been on many of the younger generation. The conviction is widespread among clergymen that religious faith must assume new forms to remain vital. In the sixties much attention was attracted to the God-Is-Dead argument that modern society has lost the power of belief in the concept of God-the-Father while retaining the power of belief in the concept of God-the-Son. The filiarchal religious tendency that this argument illustrates will surely persist in the youth-oriented society of the second machine age.

As recently as a decade ago the colleges and universities of the nation accepted without thought of serious challenge the principle that they were *in loco parentis* to their students; they are now in the revolutionary process of accepting the principle that the students are *in loco parentis* to themselves. Vietnam, the draft, university defense contracts, censorship, civil rights, and black studies have inspired violent student demonstrations to an unprecedented extent; but freedom from supervision by deans and housemothers has attracted the broadest grass-roots support from the students as a whole.

The present generation of college youth, raised, as it has been, on television, may or may not be the most intelligent in the nation's history. But it is unquestionably the most sophisticated, just as the youth of the 1920's, in another era of revolutionary technological change, was the most sophisticated in the nation's history until that time. Tom Hayden, who is now approaching his thirtieth year, has warned the nation that the generations growing up after him are more radical than his own generation; and he may be right. Where he may well be in error is in assuming that the form their radicalism will take will be recognizably similar to his own and will meet with his paternalistic approval.

The startlingly filiarchal phenomena of the 1960's are in some respects new phenomena, as is characteristic of filiarchy; but they also are continuations of those filiarchal tendencies that have paralleled the development of the machine process in American society from the early age of the steam engine and the calliope to the latest age of the electronic computer and the electric guitar.

TWO

The Moral Order in the Railroad Era

1.

The
Protestant
Republic

....

IN 1900 THE AMERICAN POPULATION was 76 million, of
which 9 million were Negroes, 26 million were immigrants or children of immigrants, and 41 million were white Americans of primarily British ancestry, whose parents had been born in the United
States.

The Negroes, who were in the violent process of losing the civil
rights they had held after the Civil War, were only just beginning to
move out of the South in large numbers and were quite separate from
the national community. The immigrants and their children were concentrated in factory towns and in the tenement districts of the cities.
Only the Germans and Scandinavians among them had settled rural
and small-town America on a large scale. The population of the

major cities was from 60 to 80 percent immigrant or first-generation American.

Political control of the cities was based upon these immigrant groups; but the business life of the cities was predominantly in the hands of Americans of native stock, who, from the middle classes upward, lived separate, privileged lives. Except at election time they tended to be unconscious of being a minority group, for they habitually divided the urban majority in their minds into "the foreign elements" and reduced them to the slum problem, the servant problem, and other problems.

Three out of five Americans still lived on the farm or in communities of 2,500 or less; but for a generation the rural population had been on the decline—not just in relation to the total population, but absolutely—in most of the nation's counties east of the Mississippi. The United States was the leading industrial nation in the world, and the countryside had largely ceased to be associated with the idea of expanding opportunity.

Except for the new immigrants and their children, the nation was overwhelmingly Protestant. The New Immigration then under way was overwhelmingly non-Protestant, and it was continuing to increase in volume; but old-stock Americans did not think of these immigrants as influencing the national character in any positive way, though some thought they were threatening to destroy it.

The American nation presented itself to the twentieth century as The Great Protestant Republic, a "heav'n rescued land," in the words of its national anthem, standing forth indivisible, with liberty and justice for all. Critics were saying little in the year of McKinley's reelection, or they were not being much listened to. The arrival of the year 1900 was inevitably the occasion for comments in national publications on the changes of the preceding century and speculations concerning the century to come. Mark Sullivan, who made a survey of these comments for his uniquely informative *Our Times,* found that "the writers who pointed out these contrasts for the delectation of the reader of 1900 had the air of regarding the country as having done marvelously; and not a little the manner of one who thinks not much else needs to be done."

However bitterly the native Americans might quarrel among themselves, as during the Bryan-McKinley campaign of 1896, they shared broad common assumptions concerning the national character and how and why it had been achieved. The fertile lands of America had been providentially withheld from settlement until the Reformation had purified Christianity; and then they had been settled by Protestants of Anglo-Saxon stock, whose mission it had been to preserve and extend liberty for the benefit of the human race. To this end, the nation had been carried triumphantly through the Revolution and the establishment of the Constitution and then tragically through the Civil War.

The Civil War, viewed through the mists of thirty-five years, had been a terrible trial, willed by God and gloriously fought by the victors and the vanquished. Victory had sealed God's approval of the northern cause and launched the Republic upon an age of material progress such as no other nation had known. In the South the Lost Cause was a memory; southern patriotism called for a New South, which would be converted to the enterprising spirit and accomplishments of the North. To the extent that the South did not respond, it remained a backwater—apart from the national mainstream.

Amid the welter of immigration, urbanization, and industrialization, the old-stock American majority held fast to ideals associated with the nation's Anglo-Saxon, Protestant, provincial and predominantly agrarian past.

....

Moral philosophy was a required course for students at the University of Missouri in the late nineteenth century, together with a twelve-lecture series, Evidences of Christianity. Agriculture students were exempted from these requirements, however, and the university catalog explained why. Moral philosophy "may not be so necessary for a farmer," it noted. "He communes with nature so much that his moral powers are better developed."

The idealization of agrarian virtues, of which this is an example, is associated in America particularly with Thomas Jefferson, whom the University of Missouri acknowledged as its spiritual founder. At a time when nine out of ten Americans were farmers, however, even Jefferson's citified opponent Alexander Hamilton had found it advisable to pay his respects to the idea. "It ought readily to be conceded," Hamilton had conceded in his Report on Manufacturers, "that the cultivation of the earth, as the primary and most certain source of national supply . . . as including a state most favorable to the freedom and independence of the human mind . . . has intrinsically a strong claim to pre-eminence over every other kind of industry."

Emerson, the foremost mid-nineteenth-century spokesman for American idealism, had not been gifted with a green thumb, and his ten-acre farm was worked for him by a hired man. He had enjoyed gardening, however, and on the national theme of agrarian virtue he waxed eloquent.

The glory of the farmer is ɪnat, in the division of labors, it is his part to create. All trade rests at last on his primitive activity. He stands close to Nature. . . . And the profession has in all eyes its ancient charm, as standing nearest to God, the first cause. . . . [The] uncorrupted behavior which we admire in animals and in young children belongs to him . . . the man who lives in the presence of nature.

By the close of the nineteenth century, America was ceasing to be predominantly agricultural; but William Jennings Bryan, in his "cross of gold" speech at the 1896 Democratic Convention, could still convincingly depict the American majority as being represented by the attorney in the country town, the merchant at the cross-roads store, "the farmer who goes forth in the morning and toils all day," and "the pioneers away out there who rear their children near to Nature's heart."

In alluding to "Nature's heart," Bryan was departing from strict Jeffersonian agrarianism into Emersonian romanticism and into the then currently popular sentimentalization of rural life (which may also have influenced the curriculum committee of the University of Missouri). Jefferson's attitude toward farmers and farming had been enlightened rather than romantic. He had believed it to be a fact that "corruption of morals in the mass of cultivators is a phenomenon of which no age nor nation has furnished an example." He had believed that this was true because the yeoman farmer lived a healthy and productive life and also because the small farmer was not in a position to engage in corruption except in small and relatively harmless ways.

Jefferson distrusted the "swinish multitude," and he did not exempt farmers from this distrust; but "farmers, whose interests are entirely agricultural . . . are the true representatives of the great American interest, and are alone to be relied on for expressing the proper American sentiments." And, most basically of all, farmers produced food so that people might live, which put them, without comparison, in the one major class of the world's fundamentally worthwhile people.

Food had not lost its moral priority during the century that separated Jefferson's first presidential campaign from Bryan's first, but great changes had taken place in the way food was produced. The yeoman farmer of Jefferson's day had, in the course of the century, either degenerated into the economically marginal subsistence farmer —who was the mudsill rather than the bedrock of society—or had modernized his operation and come to specialize in some phase of commercial farming.

Food production on a scale that was socially worthwhile in 1900 was an operation that required the cooperative activities of manufacturers of farm tools, farm machinery and fertilizers, of grain elevator and railroad operators, of food processors, and distributors and bankers. The chief campaign slogan of McKinley's in his 1896 contest with Bryan, "The Full Dinner Pail," was a good enough up-to-date metaphor for the staff of life to help McKinley to his substantial victory.

Actually the yeoman farmer of the type that figured in Jefferson's philosophy had been looked upon as something of a bumpkin by his more ambitious contemporaries, just as, for that matter, Jefferson had looked upon him as something of a bumpkin. A farmer who was content to plow his own field and sit under his own fig tree might have virtue, but he did not have much get-up-and-go. He might have the makings of a good enough voter, but he was not going to be the one who would represent his community in any matter of importance. Where they had the choice, the people would always choose a man of affairs, a businessman, as their representative.

Judging from the class of men who became President from Jackson to McKinley, and the styles of the campaigns which elected them, American democracy wished to be represented as being in touch with Nature or rural values or farm life without being stuck in it. These Presidents came from rural or small-town America, and it was thought important that they should. Thus McKinley was ordered by his manager, Mark Hanna, to do all his personal campaigning from his front porch in Canton, Ohio. Lincoln was associated with rail-splitting for campaign purposes, and William Henry Harrison with log cabins. Lincoln and Jackson, who chose the path of law and business to rise above their log cabin origins, epitomized the successful operation of the American System, which was a business system, even when agriculture was still the main business of the nation.

The choice of Uncle Sam to personify the American Republic in the nineteenth century demonstrated this American preference for appearing down-to-earth and practical, but not still down on the farm. Uncle Sam began his life in political cartoons during the War of 1812; but until Lincoln's Presidency, cartoonists were not in agreement as to his appearance, except that he was frequently a tall man in striped pants. Then Lincoln became Uncle Sam, with the chin whiskers whitened to make him older and wiser and more authoritative. As drawn by Thomas Nast, the great cartoonist for the staunchly Republican *Harper's Weekly,* the modern Uncle Sam took form. He appeared then as, one might suppose, Lincoln's own Uncle Sam, who might have split rails himself once but who had moved up in the world and now was a wise old gentleman, strong in experience and common sense.

Farming was preeminently the virtuous profession; but a man was supposed to be something more in this world than a paragon of virtue, and American farmers struggled to rise above the simple farming life as a matter of manly ambition. "Almost all the farmers of the United States," wrote Tocqueville,

combine some trade with agriculture; most of them make agriculture itself a trade. It seldom happens that an American farmer settles for good upon the land which he occupies: especially in the districts of the Far West he brings land into tillage in order to sell it again, and not to farm it. . . . Thus the Americans carry their business-like qualities into agriculture; and their trading passions are displayed in that as in their other pursuits.

Business was bad for much of the American farming community throughout the last third of the nineteenth century. Competing in a world market against other expanding agricultural regions, American farmers were caught in the continuing worldwide deflation of farm prices. Deflation affected the national economy generally, but the farmers suffered worse from it than did any other major segment of the nation; and as the traditional custodians of the national virtue, they were bound to see declining profits from farming in the light of a threat to the national moral health.

During the late sixties and early seventies farmers organized in the Granger movement, which captured the state governments of the Midwest and passed laws unsuccessfully attempting to control the railroads, especially in the rate-making area. They organized farm cooperatives to free themselves from the business community. Failing in this also, they increasingly thereafter put their faith in monetary reform. In the congressional elections of 1878 the Greenback party won more than a million votes and elected fourteen congressmen. Then, in the presidential election of 1880, farm conditions having temporarily improved, the party won only 308,000 votes with the highly respected James B. Weaver of Iowa.

A new wave of farm discontent, the Populist movement, arose in the late eighties, this time not so much in the Middle West, but in the cotton country of the South and in the wheat region of the Great Plains. The Middle West, with a more stabilized railroad system, increasingly diversified agriculture, and growing urban markets close at hand, tended to stay Republican through the whole period of agitation. In the South and in the plains region, however, farmers' alliances were formed which entered politics in 1890 and two years later at Omaha founded the Populist party. This time James B. Weaver, the Populist candidate, got more than 1 million popular and 22 electoral votes.

Agrarian radicalism gained strength during the Panic of 1893, and in the Democratic convention of 1896, William Jennings Bryan won the nomination and thereafter received the endorsement of the Populist convention. Against McKinley, Bryan carried the Solid South, the plains states, and the silver states but lost the Midwest and Northeast, as well as California and Oregon. His defeat by a margin of 600,000 votes was the worst since 1872. The Populist party was destroyed by its support of the Democratic Bryan and by the return of prosperity to the farm. Hard times did not come again to the American commercial farmer until after World War I, well past the time when the farmer could any longer think of himself as the representative American.

Rural America, the seedbed of national virtue, was visibly on the downgrade in Populist America. During the eighties, while the national population increased by more than 12 million, an absolute decline in population was registered in 10,063 of 25,746 townships in the United States. The trend was strongest in New England and New York, where two-thirds of the townships experienced a decline; but it was true of more than half of the townships in Ohio and Illinois as well. By the close of the century the deserted farm and the depleted village were mournful themes that were widely discussed.

Some viewed the situation positively, by pointing to areas of rural growth on the one hand and on the other, to increased productivity per man-hour in the areas of depleted population. It was further pointed out that the population of communities of from 4,000 and 8,000 had increased by more than 2 million during the nineties, indicating that the movement was not all from the farm to the big city. Some supposed that the process was a purifying one, the fittest of the sons remaining with the land. At the same time, much evidence was produced to indicate that nearly the opposite was true.

Journalistic exposures of rural degeneracy appeared increasingly, such as one in the New York *Evening Post* headlined "Decay of Religion in Rural Communities—A Mournful Review." The *Post* declared,

Rural life is monotonous and hard, with nothing in it to stimulate the imagination or refine the taste. The closest observers will soonest admit that by consequence the grosser forms of vice and crime in rural communities abound more than in great cities with all the slums counted in.

Much evidence appeared to indicate a tendency toward moral degeneration in towns where decline in population was taking place. Josiah Strong, the Social Gospel minister, outlined the process that took place: deterioration of roads, property depreciation, impairment of churches and schools, decline of native stock in proportion to immigrants, isolation, degeneration and demoralization, tending toward "a rural American peasantry, illiterate and immoral, possessing the rights of citizenship, but utterly incapable of performing or comprehending its duties." Wrote one disturbed rural sociologist, "What

we are here to recognize is the inevitable movement towards decadence,—a movement everywhere felt, and where not resisted, producing that visible degeneracy described by so many witnesses."

There were two sides to the track in small-town America in 1900
in spite of the exertions of the WCTU. Saloons were beginning to be
voted out, but not much had as yet been done about them. They were
still frequented during the day by respected men in the community
and at night, especially Saturday night, by a rowdier element. Farm
laborers, who did not stay long in any one community, got drunk
regularly on Saturday night and brawled in the streets, along with
disreputable native sons. The town harlot was usually around somewhere, and the boys at the saloon or the store generally knew where
she could be found at any given time. The large towns supported
sizable red-light districts.

There were the immigrant families of which the Germans were the
most numerous and the best respected. The Germans, however, in
common with other immigrant farmers and townspeople, saw no
harm in drinking on Sunday, and as often as not they were Catholics.
The Sunday Closing Law issue, even more than the general saloon
closing issue, was the one that most particularly expressed the hostility of the native American farmers and townspeople for the foreigners in their midst.

There was a further element disturbing to small-town and rural
orthodoxy. The well-to-do in the area tended to remove themselves
from the community in some ways and live according to a somewhat
different set of moral precepts. They might leave the Methodist
Church or the Baptist Church for the Episcopalian, where the doctrine of original sin was not rightly understood and where a lati-
tudinarian view was taken of moral conduct. They took trips to Chicago and to New York, and perhaps even to London and to Paris,
and they were likely to play cards and scoff at the temperance movement and go out socially on Sunday. Nevertheless they were still
looked up to because of their wealth and position, and that, in spite
of what boys and girls learned in McGuffey's Readers about the
sinfulness of pursuing wealth.

Anglo-Saxon Protestant rural Americans considered themselves to
be the heart and conscience of America; yet many were aware of a
decline in quality in rural life as well as a declining importance of the

farm in an increasingly urban nation. Population decline was accompanied by an increasing number of single women. The sour idealism which flourished in this situation was given its chief public expression in the prohibition movement, the panacea by which the home would be brightened, the town spirit revived, the sinful city scoured, and the Republic saved.

* *

Virtue, which was associated with rural rather than urban life in America, was even more pronouncedly associated with American womanhood rather than American manhood. The duty of the man to make his way in the world required qualities which were other than virtuous, and it was the duty of woman, according to *The Young Ladies' Class Book,* to maintain "the domestic fireside" as "the great guardian of society against the excesses of human passions." According to *The Lady at Home,* "even if we cannot reform the world in a moment, we can begin the work by reforming ourselves and our households—it is a woman's mission."

Women derived moral authority in society by their meekness and defenselessness and also by the superior virtues of their sex. Women were "the *better half* of *humanity*—with a more *delicate* and *sensitive* nature than man—with a more refined and spiritual organization." God had created man to wrest a living from a hard world for the support of himself and his family. Woman was created to make a home for husband and children which would reflect her finer nature.

The attitudes fostered by the churches regarding sexual matters did much to strengthen the women's sense of moral superiority to men. Sexual intercourse, except for the exclusive purpose of procreation, was considered to be a vice, and one to which, normally, only men were addicted. Woman was "more mental than physical" and "more virtuous and less passionate than man," but she was obliged to submit to the lust of her husband, when he demanded "that forbidden fruit, that original sin," which had corrupted mankind.

When practiced for the purpose of procreation, the sex act became miraculously purified. Practiced more frequently, it became unhealthful as well as immoral, although not dangerously so if restricted to monthly intervals. Intercourse caused a man to throw all his energies into an act which, for the time being, completely unnerves and prostrates him, and *accomplishes nothing,* without even a worthy purpose, he ought to feel ashamed; no wonder he seeks darkness and hides the deed.

Under such circumstances it might have been thought the lesser evil for the man to vent his sinful passions upon low women, rather than upon virtuous mothers. Lest the sons of Adam be led to such a sophistry, Providence had provided a slow horrible death for transgressors in the form of venereal diseases, known as "the fruits of sin" and "the awful harvest." Men were self-willed, and the best hope for a man was the love of a good woman, who would endure his lust until his harsh passions had been gentled by her patient forebearance. To the American mind, only Adam and the serpent had erred.

Fallen women, the most wretched of humanity, were the consequence of manly betrayal of maidenly innocence; but the girl who had allowed herself to be led into the path of shame had only herself to blame. She had forfeited the virtue which was natural to her sex. Piety, like purity, was the natural condition for women, and therefore, according to *Ladies' Companion,* "female irreligion is the most revolting feature in human character."

The woman maintained herself in American society by her moral rather than her legal authority, for American law accorded wives and mothers little protection. The Bible had instructed Eve that "thy desire *shall be to* thy husband and he shall rule over thee," and in America the law continued to recognize this ruling. It had been the case in the early national period that if a woman brought possessions to the marriage, these became the property of the husband to do with as he pleased. However, most states passed private property acts before the Civil War, giving wives the right to possess property in their own names. Even so, in the eyes of the law, according to an Ohio decision of 1879,

A husband has a pecuniary, a property interest in his wife. The law protects this right of property. . . . She has not property in her, is not entitled to her wages. . . . She relies upon his pledge and his promise, which the law will enforce, and she looks to that alone.

That women were morally superior to men and that the home was the "woman's sphere," where the mother's influence should be paramount, were conceptions which were by no means embodied in either the Bible or the common law. Nor were they subscribed to by the Englishmen who settled America in the seventeenth century. The colonial woman's place was emphatically in the home, but within the home she was considered to be morally as well as physically and intellectually subordinate to her husband. The husband was thought to be responsible for the continuing formation of her character, which was to be trained to correspond to his own. He even accepted responsibility for her religious instruction and was advised "to make it easy to her," in consideration of her weaker nature. The idea that women as a sex were superior to men in virtue was one that emerged chiefly in the late eighteenth and early nineteenth centuries.

American women in colonial times earned greater freedom and responsibility than was the lot of English women; and the heroic figure of the frontier woman who was creating a civilized home in the wilderness was one that came to stand for all American women in conventional thought, especially in rural America. Marriageable women tended to be in short supply, especially in the western regions, and the value placed upon them tended to rise accordingly. The husband remained the head of the household by law, but the wife was responsible for the home by a moral authority that had come to be recognized in the community and sanctioned by the churches.

The superiority of female virtue was a firmly established fact in mid-nineteenth-century America, but female domestic authority remained ambiguous. On the one hand, according to *The Token of Friendship, or Home, The Center of the Affections,* published in Boston in 1844, "Home is the empire, the throne of woman. Here she reigns in the legitimate power of all her united charms. She is the luminary which enlightens, and the talisman which endears it." Nevertheless, wives were instructed by the same authority to be "submissive to your husbands. There must be a head, and God has wisely vested the authority in the husband." In short,

> *The father gives his kind command,*
> *The mother joins, approves;*
> *The children all attentive stand,*
> *Then each, obedient, moves.*

Many American women were made restive by these injunctions to be submissive, coupled with these acknowledgments of their moral superiority to men; and this restiveness expressed itself in contradictory ways in the Woman's Rights movement on the one hand and the temperance movement on the other. Sarah Grimké spoke for the woman's rights advocates, who were chiefly upper-middle-class women, when she wrote,

In contemplating the great moral reformations of the day, and the part which they were bound to take in them, instead of puzzling themselves with the harassing, because unnecessary inquiry, how far they may go without overstepping the bounds of propriety, which separate male and female duties, they will only inquire, "Lord, what wilt thou have me do?" . . . To me it is perfectly clear that *whatsoever it is morally right for a man to do, it is morally right for a woman to do.*

Other women, who thought the suffragettes were brazen females, preferred to argue their rights on the basis of the superiority of women rather than on the basis of their equality with men. According to this argument, women should not unsex themselves by attempting to place themselves on an equal footing with men, as by engaging in politics; on the other hand, their responsibility for the home gave them a responsibility for society generally. They were responsible for seeing to it that the home atmosphere was maintained throughout the society in which they were raising their families. This argument led to the woman's temperance movement, which, in the long run, did far more for the cause of woman suffrage than the somewhat antagonistic feminist movement was ever able to do for its own cause.

The bottle and the saloon were the dread of women who wished to bring up decent families, and they were the concern of preachers who worked for the Kingdom of God on earth. American women did not organize against the sex evil in marriage, although that was certainly an aspect of the suffragette movement. Against the drink evil, however, women organized militantly and effectively.

Women had played a major role in the pre-Civil War prohibition campaigns, and in December 1873 in Hillsborough, Ohio, women gave the first idea of what they could do independently as active public reformers, when bands of women marched against saloons, drugstores, and hotels and forced the closing of liquor dispensaries. Led by Diocletian Lewis, noted temperance lecturer (and inventor of the beanbag), this band struck a spark which ignited organized fury among women throughout the Midwest and the East against the saloon.

The Woman's Crusade raged on—an unheard of phenomenon—for a period of from six to eight months, resulting in the closing of saloons by the tens of thousands. Then it subsided, and the saloons went back into business again. However, the movement did not pass without leaving changes in its wake, the most tangible of which was the formation in Cleveland in November 1874 of the national Woman's Christian Temperance Union.

The WCTU remained the one effective interdenominational temperance organization in existence for a generation, until joined by the Anti-Saloon League in 1896, and its activities did much to prepare the way for the successful rise of the Anti-Saloon League. Women had been active on behalf of woman suffrage for longer than they had been involved in the antiliquor fight; and in the cities, especially, women were organizing on behalf of their own rights. The woman suffrage movement, however, was nowhere near as influential in winning the vote for women as was the WCTU, which persuaded evangelical America, that, as WCTU President Francis Willard urged, a vote by a woman was a vote for the protection of the home.

Children could be put profitably to work at an early age on the farm; hence large farm families were the rule. These farm children were treated like uncompleted grown-ups rather than as boys and girls enjoying an interesting period of life characterized by distinctive qualities which were attractive in themselves. They were looked upon as limbs of Satan, terribly vulnerable because they were as yet incompletely formed, morally as well as physically. It was the parents' duty to keep them as much as possible from idleness and play. The farm offered opportunities to keep the young employed, and the large families provided a hierarchical system of control from the parents through the older sons and daughters to the younger ones.

Children in many rural communities went twice to church on Sunday, in addition to attending Sunday school, and also to prayer meeting on Wednesday night. During the week they might have to be in readiness at all times to repeat the "golden text" from the previous Sunday in response to neighbor ladies' requests. The revivalistic spirit was maintained in many rural communities under the ceaseless supervision of brothers and even more of sisters of the church, as well as by ministers.

In addition to church there were Christian Endeavor, Bands of

Hope, Loyal Temperance Legion, Epworth League, Baptist Young People's Union, and Sunshine Brigade activities. The women had their weekly meetings of the Ladies' Aid Society and the WCTU, in addition to various other formal and informal religious bees. This comprised much of the social life of the community. In many towns there was no other social life, except at weddings and funerals and among the men in the saloons, or within the individual families, where additional nightly family prayer was often customary.

Supervision tended to relax as the children grew older and themselves took part in the supervision of their younger brothers and sisters. Courtship in rural and small-town America took place at church socials, picnics, and dances, often without being very much chaperoned, and generally—from the perhaps dubious evidence of reminiscences—in an atmosphere of bucolic innocence. Girls were taught as early as possible that marriage was their destiny and that only nice girls were in a position to marry advantageously. The rule was nowhere as rigid where boys were concerned, but they were taught at least to distinguish between the nice girls and the others and to conduct themselves accordingly.

While primary responsibility for instilling virtue in the young remained with home and mother, the community as a whole had assumed an ever-increasing responsibility in this sphere with the emergence of the common school system in the nineteenth century. Most Americans who grew up in the latter part of the nineteenth century received the grammar school education considered necessary, in Horace Mann's words, to "save them from poverty and vice and prepare them for the adequate performance of their social and civil duties," and thus secure the safety of the Christian Republic.

New England had pioneered in state education; and down to the nineteenth century the New England Primer had been the basic textbook, which "taught millions to read and not one to sin." It was supplanted by Noah Webster's Spelling Book, written in 1782, which enjoyed widespread use for a century and more. To this "Blue-Backed Speller" was added in the early nineteenth century the readers, of which the McGuffey's Readers, beginning in 1836, were far the most successful.

There were six readers in the McGuffey series, which was revised five times, the last revision being made in 1901. Publication figures do not exist for the readers throughout their whole career, but more than 2 million copies were sold each year in 1888 and 1889, and the best estimate of the total sales of McGuffey's Readers, Primers, and Spelling Book is 122 million between 1836 and 1920. New England preferred its own readers. Otherwise probably a majority of three generations of Americans in 1900 shared a common American training based upon William H. McGuffey's Readers.

McGuffey, a college president, professor of moral philosophy and Presbyterian minister, had attempted "to obtain as wide a range of leading authors as possible, to present the best specimens of style, to insure interest in the subjects, to impart valuable information, and to exert a decided and healthful moral influence." The First Reader presented fables, tales, and verse, mostly in words of one syllable, with the moral attached. The Fifth and Sixth Readers, for the most advanced students, were composed of poetry, orations, and prose excerpts from 111 authors, including Shakespeare, Scott, Longfellow, Bryant, Irving, and Daniel Webster, to name those represented by three or more selections.

A tone of melancholy tended to prevail throughout the readers, the lessons in morality pointing to dreadful and irreparable consequences that followed from even minor misdemeanors. Pupils were continually reminded that life was short, death was certain, and God was loving but just.

> A little child who lives to pray,
> And read his Bible too,
> Shall rise above the sky one day,
> And sing as angels do;
> Shall live in Heaven, that world above,
> Where all is joy, and peace, and love.

Pupils learned that admission to heaven required church, Sunday school, and prayer meeting attendance, absolute obedience to parents and to elders generally, and abstention from alcohol and tobacco as well as from all intemperance of spirit, such as the coveting of wealth.

No notice was given in the readers of the coming of the railroad or the rise of the city, even in later revisions; and the absence of such contemporary subjects does not appear to have reflected against the readers, in the judgment of McGuffey-trained Americans of prominence who were questioned by Mark Sullivan. Judges, ministers, and trial lawyers, on the contrary, attested to the excellence of the readers in providing the mental and moral discipline necessary to cope with their own contemporary problems. They had, of course, been trained by McGuffey to believe it would.

....

It was the church, far more than the school, however, that was relied upon outside the home to maintain society in a condition of virtue. Tocqueville wrote, "Religion in America takes no direct part in the government of society, but it must be regarded as the first of their political institutions; for if it does not impart a taste for freedom, it facilitates the use of it." Owing to sectarian divisiveness, a tax-supported national church had been out of the question for the United States from the outset, and the First Amendment to the Constitution declared that "Congress shall make no law respecting an establishment of religion." At the same time, it had been understood that the United States was a Christian republic; and although the states ceased to deny Catholics the right to vote, as had been done in colonial times, there was tacit agreement that the national religion would take the form of privately supported Protestant denominationalism.

By 1900 the Catholic Church had become the largest of the American religious denominations, claiming jurisdiction over 12 million people; but that did not change the prevailing attitude toward the character of American religion. Americans who took religious instruction from the Catholic Church were separating themselves in their religious life from the national religion, which continued to be Protestant denominationalism. The Catholic Church, itself, after vigorously debating the matter for several generations, came in effect to accept this point of view in the post-Civil War period, when it decided upon a comprehensive separate system of education for American Catholic children. By 1900 there were 4,000 Catholic parochial schools in operation.

The American alternative to a state church was unique, because America's sectarian character was unique, and the solution was accepted as a necessity and therefore not requiring any philosophical justification. Religious rationalists like Jefferson, Madison, and George Mason, who were the strongest advocates of the First Amendment, were themselves convinced that religious faith was essential to a free society. It was a favorite argument of these men that all of the major religions were in agreement on the existence of God and a divinely ordained moral order, and that this area of religious agreement should be established and accepted as common creed.

The doctrine of complete separation of religion and state was therefore a defensive measure rather than the expression of a clear-cut principle, even where men of the enlightenment like Jefferson, Franklin, and John Adams were concerned. However, the declared purpose of the government of the Constitution was to provide for the general welfare; so the government was not unconcerned in moral matters. The government assumed responsibility for maintaining order in the nation, presumably including moral order, which was what Jefferson had in mind in advocating basic religious instruction in the public schools.

For the organized sects, which would be kept completely separate from the federal government, however, acceptance of the constitutional principle was tantamount to conceding limits to the authority of their religious beliefs. As Sidney Mead has pointed out, in accepting the doctrine of separation of church and state

they also accepted by implication the typically rationalist view that only what all the churches held and taught in common (the "essentials of religion") was really relevant for the well-being of society and the state. Obversely this meant that they accepted the view that whatever any religious group held peculiarly as a tenet of its faith must be irrelevant for the general welfare.

Civilized mid-nineteenth-century Americans prized elevated sentiments above enlightened ideas. They valued the decorous mysticism of Emerson and the nondenominational moralism of Longfellow as the finest expressions of the religious spirit and the surest guides for right thinking. Religious aspiration was in the direction of universal uplift, accompanied by ecumenical harmony and good riddance of needless doctrinal disputation.

This was the high road to the good Christian life and the brotherhood of man. The low road was by way of the revival meeting. That was the road that had been most busily traveled during the first half of the century and the one that led to the religions which were characteristic of Jacksonian democracy, chiefly the Methodist and Baptist churches but also the Millerites, Campbellites, and Mormons and also the revivalistic and perfectionist tendencies within the Congregational and Presbyterian churches.

At the time of the Revolution the American churches in the order of the number of their congregations had been Congregational, Presbyterian, Baptist, Anglican, Quaker, German and Dutch Reformed, and Lutheran, the Catholics following next with fifty congregations. By 1850 the order of denominations had changed drastically to positions that were to remain fairly stable thereafter. The Catholic Church was the largest, followed by the Methodist and then the Baptist, the two of them together making up half of all the Protestants, followed by Presbyterians, Congregationalists, Lutherans, Disciples of Christ, Episcopalians, and Mormons.

The Methodists, like the Catholics, had hardly more than existed at the time of the Revolution; and during the Revolution they had been, like the Anglicans, on the Loyalist side. Yet in the generations that followed, the Methodists became not only the most numerous American Protestant sect but also the most influential in impressing its most distinctive doctrines upon American thought generally. Methodism had differed from most American sects at the time of the Revolution in holding to the Arminian belief that Christ had died for all mankind and that salvation was therefore open to all who sought it.

Also distinctively Methodist was the doctrine of perfection: that the experience of spiritual rebirth would bring assurance of God's grace and that society itself was perfectable through the agency of personal conversion. The revival meeting, although not exclusively Methodist in origin, was associated particularly with the Methodist approach. These characteristics of Arminianism, perfectionism, and revivalism were all distinguishing qualities of American religion in the mid-nineteenth century.

The revival meeting was not a forum for doctrinal discussion. It appealed for united faith in Gospel fundamentals, and its tendency was to obliterate doctrinal distinctions. The consequence of its widespread acceptance by the evangelical sects might have been their fusion into one great evangelical sect, except for institutional loyalties, which continued to reinforce minor doctrinal distinctions, and other loyalties—ethnic or sectional or class-related—which were represented by particular churches.

In 1900 the religious results of the sectional conflict between North and South persisted chiefly in the persistence, as separate denominations, of the Southern Baptist Conference and Methodist Episcopal Church, South. The Congregational Church remained the church of New England, even where it had extended itself across the nation. The Episcopal Church was the church preeminently of the Anglo-Saxon ruling classes, and where it was not in existence the Presbyterian Church tended to stand in its place, or in some areas the Lutheran. Presbyterianism remained somewhat Scotch-Irish in character and Lutheranism remained North European. The Baptist and Methodist churches remained the dominant denominations of rural and small-town Anglo-Saxon America.

Rural religion continued to be revivalistic and unquestioningly literalistic. It was the conviction of every sincere evangelical believer that everything that happened in the world occurred according to the purposes of God. God's ways were inscrutable, as when He took away little babies or virtuous persons who were engaged in useful work; the only human recourse in the face of these mysteries was faith and prayer. Church congregations prayed for rain as the Indians had before them and then accepted whatever happened as divinely ordained.

Revivalism was emotional and anti-intellectual, resting its belief upon the unintelligible experience of salvation and demanding rote acceptance of biblical stories and injunctions which, when taken literally rather than metaphorically, did not make sense in terms of modern life and scientific knowledge. By the same token, dedicated evangelical Protestants, by affirming belief in this literalistic form, were given strength to deny the validity of changes in society which threatened, or at least unsettled, the life for which experience and training had equipped them.

In concentrating attention on the saving of souls and dismissing all else as secondary, the evangelicals assumed an attitude of indifference to social reforms other than those, like prohibition, regulating individual conduct. Social reform for them meant soul-saving and nothing else.

The Protestantism of upper-class, educated America had ceased to be thoroughly literalistic, but in relatively subdued and dignified ways it was nevertheless also fundamentally emotional and anti-intellectual in its arguments. Emersonian transcendentalism had elevated intuition above intellect and had lifted religion above the sphere of theology. Emerson's pantheism had been generally admired as literature and as coming from a moral and high-minded man, but it had not generally been seriously considered as religious doctrine. The Connecticut Congregationalist minister Horace Bushnell, however, remained within his church and developed a comprehensive argument in opposition to the evangelical tenets of biblical literalism and moral individualism. Bushnell was influential in the tendency—which was strong in the late nineteenth century in genteel America—toward religion that relied upon intuition rather than either on reason or biblical authority.

Bushnell taught that religious truth, by its nature, could be communicated only by poetic metaphor and that it could never be reduced to exact law. Biblical literalists, he argued, misunderstood the nature of biblical truth. The story of Adam and Eve was not a literal truth, and the child was not born in sin. It was Bushnell's most influential argument, in *Christian Nurture,* that the child could be raised in a Christian atmosphere and never know sin. Bushnell's argument placed minimum emphasis upon personal salvation and maximum emphasis upon the creating of a Christian environment.

One consequence of this direction of thought was the abandonment of any fixed scheme of religious beliefs in favor of changing standards of taste and the appeal to what was presumed to be the better feelings of the people. As to who should be the judge of standards of taste and feelings, no better environment existed than that of upper-class Protestant America, and therefore it was presumed to be the highest product of Christian nurture.

Henry Ward Beecher of Plymouth Church in Brooklyn, one of the wealthiest congregations in the nation, was widely regarded as one of the greatest men in America, and was the outstanding spokesman for this genteel Protestantism which sanctified feeling and abandoned doctrinal belief. Beecher and his followers could accept any social or intellectual development, such as Darwinian biology, as simply being God's way of doing things, without having to go deeply into the question of either divine will or evolutionary theory.

Robert Ingersoll, who rivaled Beecher as one of the best paid public speakers of the day, was the leading representative of agnosticism in America. Conservative politically and unexceptionable as to his moral standards, Ingersoll was much in demand both as a political speaker in support of the Republican party and as an agnostic in opposition to Christianity. His lectures against Christianity, such as "Some Mistakes of Moses," had the audience alternately laughing so that they could hardly hear him, and subdued to silence by the majesty of his utterances.

Influential in persuading many Americans to abandon Christian belief, Ingersoll was respected by devout professing Christians because he preached agnosticism as though it were another version of Christianity, and one which was, after all, not clearly distinguishable from the religion of Beecher or Lyman Abbott, Beecher's successor at Plymouth Church. Abbott gloried in the fact that at Plymouth Church "we do not ask what men believe," a sentence in which, as Sidney Mead points out, "care" might be substituted for "ask."

Beecher, in common with most Protestant ministers, preached the Gospel of Wealth: that wealth was the sign of God's favor as well as the evidence of a righteous life. Revivalists like Dwight Moody could reach the same conclusion through biblical literalism, but that entailed homely duties and narrow beliefs which Beecher and his followers were free of. Bushnell's argument regarding Christian nurture and against literalism was, however, more directly influential upon a different upper-class Protestant tendency, that of the Social Gospel, which advocated social reforms to improve the environment of society as a whole to turn it into a suitable environment for Christian nurture. Bushnell influenced the younger generation of liberal clergymen, including Washington Gladden, whose induction sermon at North Adams, Massachusetts, was delivered by Bushnell, and who became the leading figure in the Social Gospel movement during the next generation.

The Social Gospel avoided sectarianism and dogma and took as its text the Golden Rule. It was concerned with "practical philanthropy," as Washington Gladden said: "How to mix Christianity with human affairs; how to bring salvation to the people that need it most; how to make peace between the employer and the workman." It replaced the individual with the community and the power of self-interest with the power of altruism. It worked through institutional churches and in local and national political reform movements to create a Christian environment nationally. More than any other influence, it shaped the dominant ideology of the Progressive era.

The Protestant churches were filled with pride that the consequence of the doctrine of separation of church and state had been that the nation in its political life had become so infused with religious sentiment. There seems to have been little awareness on the part of the Social Gospelers or the Gospelers of Wealth or the Anti-Saloon Leaguers that American Protestantism, by involving itself so actively in the political life of the nation, might be overextending itself, especially where urban America was concerned.

....

There remained the challenge to the Protestant Republic of the unmanageably burgeoning, predominantly non-Protestant American city. The American city was just as shockingly sinful in reality as it was in the lurid imaginings of the farm woman whose son or daughter had left home for the bright lights of the metropolis. All cities supported their raging red-light districts, and until the nineties little thought was given to eradicating these, or even to seriously regulating them. They were taken for granted as manifestations of the dark side of man's nature; and many pious people took some satisfaction in viewing them as the continual working out of God's law that the wages of sin are death.

In some older communities, notably Boston and Philadelphia, a tradition of civic responsibility was in existence which to some extent provided guidance into the age of metropolitan expansion. It was true that all American cities were sinks of sin in the Gilded Age; and the Gas Ring, which controlled Philadelphia politics, was probably as corrupt and venal as the Tweed Ring, which controlled New York. Nevertheless, Philadelphians were justified in comparing their City of Homes favorably with most other large cities in the nation. And even in New York City the old tradition of civic responsibility was strong enough to send Boss Tweed to jail. Generally speaking, the worst-run cities in the nation were those that sprang up out of nothing in the nineteenth century; and the biggest and most flamboyant of these at the end of the century was Chicago.

Sprawling planlessly along the mud flats of Lake Michigan's southern shore, Chicago by the close of the nineteenth century had increased its population twenty times since the opening of the Civil War, to become the second largest city in the nation. The consequences of this disorderly growth were much in evidence. "A more lawless, uncivilized, uncontrollable settlement does not exist in the whole country," the Chicago *Tribune* had declared in the sixties. The city was destroyed by fire in 1871, inspiring sermons concerning God's judgment upon the wicked. It rose at once from the ashes, and no part of it more rapidly than the sections dealing in gambling and prostitution. More than 2,000 saloon licenses were issued within the year, at which time the police force for the entire city numbered 450, one for every 10,000 inhabitants.

The old red-light districts had been obliterated, but within a few years a dozen new ones had developed, scattered through the city. A reform administration was partially successful in bringing these areas under control between 1887 and 1891. It was followed by an administration dedicated to making Chicago a wide-open town in time for the world's fair of 1893, which it managed to do. A reaction toward reform followed once more, but the police force was never adequate to the task.

Conditions in Chicago were reputed to be somewhat worse than in other major cities, but the pattern was everywhere much the same, with some regional variations, as Herbert Asbury has demonstrated in his voluminous chronicles of immorality in Chicago, New York, New Orleans, and San Francisco. In New Orleans the French Quarter was distinguished by its Creole flavor, its speciality of quadroon beauties, and its reputation for Mardi Gras merriment. In actual fact, the New Orleans red-light districts, like those of Chicago, were mainly dilapidated hovels on muddy streets, infested with pickpockets, burglers, and muggers.

In 1897 an ordinance was introduced in the New Orleans City Council by Alderman Sidney Story, restricting prostitution to an area inside the French Quarter, and within a few years the area became nationally famous as Storyville, the most musical red-light district in the nation. In 1917, with America's entrance into World War I, Storyville was closed down by order of the Departments of Army and Navy, and jazz moved up the Mississippi to Chicago and then to New York.

More famous even than Storyville was the world-renowned Barbary Coast in San Francisco. (When John Masefield arrived in San Francisco, the first thing he is said to have said was, "Take me to see the Barbary Coast.") San Francisco's origins had been at least as lawless as those of Chicago, and unlike Chicago, San Francisco had successfully romanticized them into a municipal asset, a part of "the Paris of America" which remained the favorite American city for visiting Europeans. Beneath this aura of romance, San Francisco's vice districts differed little from those of other American cities, except that Chinatown offered opium dens and a system of prostitution based upon actual slavery.

In New York the brothels were crowded most thickly below Fourth Street and especially in the Bowery. The more affluent classes of the city were catered to in the Tenderloin district, where some of the best churches were also located, in the area roughly between Twenty-fourth and Forty-second Streets and Fifth and Seventh Avenues.

New York City possibly had fewer disorderly houses per capita than did San Francisco or Chicago or New Orleans; and if the number of saloons per capita was anything like the measure of community depravity that reformers often took it to be, then New York was three times more moral than San Francisco (although not quite as good as Philadelphia). New York was nevertheless more evil by far than San Francisco or any other American city, in the vile slums it maintained for most of its population and in the gang societies it fostered as a consequence.

Out of a population of 3,437,202 in 1900, the tenement—which was to say the slum—population numbered 2,273,079. It was most of this two-thirds of the citizenry to which Jacob Riis was referring in his classic study *How the Other Half Lives* (1890). It lived, as he abundantly demonstrated, under miserable circumstances. New York, as the nation's chief port of entry, had absorbed a larger share of three-quarters of a century of immigration than had any other American city. As these immigrants had moved in, native Americans had tended to move uptown or else out of the city altogether, leaving the newer groups to fight among themselves for living space. Fourth Street south to the Battery was their main area of concentration; but they carved out uptown enclaves, such as Hell's Kitchen, and occupied Harlem. The first to arrive, the most numerous and, relatively speaking, the best-off were the Germans and the Irish. Then, more or less in order of squalor and poverty, came the Italians, the Bohemians, the Jews from Russia and Poland, and the Negroes. Among these, the Negroes were arbitrarily restricted by landlords as to where they could settle, and they were even more viciously overcharged for rent than were the other groups.

Density of population of New York, at 31,000 per square mile in 1880, was probably greater than that of any other city in the English-speaking world. It pressed most heavily upon the Negroes, Bohemians, Italians, Jews, and those who rented lodgings by the night for from 3 to 15 cents in the Bowery. In the Jewish Tenth Ward on the lower East Side, people were crowded together at a rate of 276, 672 per square mile, or about twice that of the most congested areas of London. Health officials were inclined to make it appear less crowded than it was by listing as a "family," for instance, the father, mother, twelve children, and six boarders, who together shared two rooms.

Such crowding was commonplace, but the average for tenements on Manhattan as a whole was two rooms for a family averaging 4.31 persons. Out of 255,033 tenement apartments examined in one survey, 306 possessed bathrooms. By the end of the century, tenement builders were supposed to meet minimum standards, but most of the housing still consisted of older buildings that had been cut up into cubicles and added on to. It was estimated that rents more often than not were fixed to realize for the landlord 30 to 40 percent per annum and sometimes as much as 100 percent. In only a small fraction of cases could the cost of living, under these circumstances, be met by the head of the family without the assistance of wife and children.

The tenement districts of Manhattan were overrun with crime and violence, the pattern being set principally by ethnic origins of the community. Riis thought the Bohemians best on this count and the Chinese worst. He placed the chief responsibility for crime, however, with the native American offspring of the Old Immigration from northwestern Europe, who mainly made up the neighborhood gangs. Gangs were organized in a great endless chain around the city, from the Battery to Harlem.

In no other major American city were housing conditions as bad as they were in New York for as much of the population. Best among the major cities in this respect was neighboring Philadelphia, where single-dwelling homes rather than tenements were the rule, and where the average occupancy per dwelling, counting the tenements in, was 4.91 persons. The expansion of housing facilities was being energetically undertaken in Philadelphia, to keep pace with population expansion. Philadelphia was the model for reforms in housing conditions and in municipal housing laws, which were among the most significant reforms undertaken in the nation during the Progressive era.

The United States Commissioner of Labor made a survey of 2,567 families of workingmen, a large number of whom were union men and therefore more highly paid than the national average. With average family earnings of $768.54, they were not limited to bare necessities. As against $326.54 for food and $122.92 for rent, these families spent, according to their statements, $9.49 for religion, $17.44 for amusements, $24.53 for liquor, and $17.44 for tobacco. The saloon, the dance hall, and the "cheap theater" were the chief forms of amusement. The New York dance halls were attended by a quarter of a million during the week, mostly by men and women between the ages of 16 and 30, for an admission charge ranging from 5 to 50 cents. These dance halls were commonly operated in conjunction with saloons, and the guess may be hazarded that, as the family grew, the one came to use up a smaller part of the budget and the other a larger one.

The saloon remained, beyond all comparison, the main center for the men's entertainment and the main family expense for entertainment. It was supposed that the figure arrived at in the Commissioner of Labor's average budget for liquor was much too low, for the reason that the housewives had probably not wished the interviewers to know how much was being spent in the family on that item.

Wives in most industrial workers' families were not expected to contribute to the family income. They were expected to stay home and take care of the family. This usually included handling the family expenditures, the husband turning over his paycheck to his wife and then going to her for money when he needed it. It might appear from this that the workingman's wife was the true head of the house, but such was not generally the case. Workingmen as a whole appear to have looked upon their wives much as the law did. It was commonly true that, from the beginning, there was little love to be lost between man and wife. He earned the money, she kept the house and was available to satisfy his sex demands; and no pretense was made by either that there was anything more than that to the arrangement.

If the interviewed housewives put too low a figure on the amount spent for liquor, it is probably also true that they gave the investigators too high a figure for the amount spent on religion. Except among the Irish and the Jews, organized religion does not appear to have played a major role in the lives of industrial workers. According to the careful estimate of a minister in one of the largest New England industrial towns, not one man in fifteen among the Protestants ever attended church. In the entire area of New York City south of Fourteenth Street in 1890, where about half a million people lived, there were only 111 places of worship of all kinds, as compared to more than 4,000 saloons.

....

Above the sins and smells of the dangerous classes, late nineteenth-century upper-class urban America comported itself outwardly according to a Victorian code of behavior which was fastidious to a high degree. Such moral niceties were observed as earlier American gentries would have laughed out of living room.

In America as in England, Victorianism and the rise of industry were related developments. The industrial revolution had provided an ugly, smoky, smelly means to affluence and leisure for many—especially for many women and children—such as formerly had been known only to the few. What was to be done with this new affluence and against this new ugliness? To have asked the question would have been to have answered it. The one must be used to seal good society off from the other.

New developments in architecture were among the results of this line of thought. For the very rich, the simple and balanced Georgian architecture of the eighteenth century was supplanted by big and bulging dwellings, sometimes with oriels and turrets and gargoyles and sometimes hung inside with tapestries. Middle-class American houses were refined by fretwork and scrimshaw and filled with knick-nacks and waxed flowers under glass, and horsehair sofas with antimacassars. Only for the rich could the bathroom faucets be made of gold, but for everyone from the middle classes on up, it was the age of the flush toilet, and an age that was characterized by a greater delicacy of behavior than had formerly been known.

It has always been important to know how to behave in polite society, and never more so than in the Victorian age, especially in America, where people were moving up in the social ranks more generally than they were anywhere else. Instruction was needed, and under pressure from the women, instruction was taken. Silas Lapham had very clear ideas of his own about the kind of house he wanted to build when the Laphams were in a financial position to move into an upper-class neighborhood, but between his wife and her architect he was talked out of all of them. Lapham did not develop the airs and graces his family would have wished, but they tried to remake him. Some said that good manners came only from breeding and not from books; but many etiquette books were published in America, and their directions were followed.

Europe, especially England, provided the pattern for upper-class American manners and morals in the late nineteenth century, as Americans sloughed off some of the country customs that even the well-to-do had practiced early in the century. The chaperon took the lead in this development. Young couples had gone about unescorted even in New York City in the early years of the century, and this continued to be the case throughout the century in some of the interior cities. In New York, however, and in other cities that were conscious of supporting a Society the chaperon came to be a social must, beginning around the middle of the century. "Of late, for instance," *The Rag-Bag* declared in 1855,

it is not considered *Fifth-Avenue-able* for an unmarried young lady to ride unattended in an omnibus—nor to be seen on Broadway without a carriage or servant—nor to go unchaperoned to the play with a young gentleman—all of which newly forbidden things, and others of the same kind, were considerable and innocent privileges of the restrained sex.

A generation later the chaperon had become an unbudgable fixture. Mrs. John Sherwood wrote of her in 1884:

She must accompany her young lady everywhere; she must sit in the parlor when she receives gentlemen; she must go with her to the skating rink, the ball, the party, the races, the dinners, and especially to theater parties; she must preside at the table, and act the part of a mother, so far as she can; she must watch the characters of the men who approach her charge, and endeavor to save the inexperienced girl from the dangers of a bad marriage, if possible.

In a revised edition of her book, Mrs. Sherwood wrote even more strongly on the matter.

Nothing is more vulgar in the eyes of our modern society than for an engaged couple to travel together or to go to the theater unaccompanied, as was the primitive custom.

Daisy Miller was probably more popular with the American reading public than anything else that Henry James ever wrote; and among the upper classes it was read as a warning to young ladies that the wages, not alone of sin, but also of bucolic innocence, were death. "Daisy Millerism" became a phrase to describe the wholesome and disingenuous young American lady whose social gaucheries were a discredit to her sex and nation.

The last word on how a proper young American lady should comport herself, *The Well-bred Girl in Society,* was written by Mrs. Burton Harrison and published in 1904, "with the earnest hope that it may aid girls in the smaller as well as in the larger cities of the country to be in all things representative of what is best and loveliest in American womanhood." For Mrs. Harrison, form was nearly everything, although she cautioned insistently that it should never be carried to the absurd: "to wear gloves while playing cards seems an unnecessary affectation of elegance," and "just here, a word as to the addenda of theatre costume—fans, smelling bottles, and bonbonnières. All such things have been vulgarized by exaggerated display."

Modesty in manner and dress was much emphasized, but immodesty was to be insisted upon where the alternative would indicate "the lingering influences of Puritanism and provincialism." For example,

In all great capitals of the world it has been, since time out of mind, considered appropriate that women should appear on gala occasions, and by artificial light, in gowns with low-cut bodices, wearing such ornaments as they may possess. Queen Victoria, the most rigid of moralists, will not allow presentations to be made to her—and that in the garish light of day—of women wearing the ordinary high-cut gown.

On the other hand, "Exaggeration of this, as of any mode, is sure to be offensive and disgusting in the eyes of people of good taste."

Sex was the most important thing to watch out for, Mrs. Harrison cautioned. "Just what attitude a girl assumes in society toward young men is the crucial test," and if she erred in any direction, it was better to err in the direction of excessive prudishness. The question of the chaperon was, of course, discussed at length, the point clearly being made that no well-bred girl would be seen alone with a young man at the theater, in a restaurant, or anywhere else in public. Perhaps illogically, she might receive calls from that young man alone at her home.

To lay down any law of restriction or limitation for the American girl with regard to receiving calls without the presence of a chaperon in her own home, from a young man with whom she associates by her parents' sanction, would be to revolutionize a state of things firmly established long before the political liberties of our republic had been secured.

How a girl was brought up in the oldest and most genteel of American families may be seen in Eleanor Roosevelt's account of her own childhood, *This I Remember* (1949). Even as a small girl, her reading was uncensored; but when she came upon passages which she did not understand and asked questions, the books sometimes disappeared, as with *Bleak House,* which she searched for in vain for days.

Certain things my grandmother insisted on. On Sundays I might not read the books that I read on weekdays. I had to teach Sunday school to the coachman's little daughter, giving her verses to learn, hearing her recite them, and then seeing that she learned some hymns and collects and the catechism. In turn, I must do all these things myself and recite to my grandmother. . . .

I had grown fond of the theater . . . allowed to see some of Shakespeare's plays and occasionally to go to the opera, but my young aunts and their friends talked all the time of plays which I never went to see.

She was not permitted to play games on Sunday, but on weekdays she could do much as she pleased, until she reached her teens.

It would be difficult for anyone in these days to have any idea of the formality with which girls of my generation were trained. I cannot believe that I was the only one brought up in this way, though I imagine that I was more strictly kept to the formalities than were many of my friends.

It was understood that no girl was interested in a man or showed any liking for him until he had made all the advances. You knew a man very well before you wrote or received a letter from him, and those letters make me smile when I see some of the correspondence today. There were few men who would have dared to use my first name, and to have signed oneself in any other way than "very sincerely yours" would have been not only a breach of good manners but an admission of feeling which was entirely inadmissible.

You never allowed a man to give you a present except flowers or candy or possibly a book. To receive a piece of jewelry from a man to whom you were not engaged was a sign of being a fast woman, and the idea that you would permit any man to kiss you before you were engaged to him never even crossed my mind.

Wrote one New York gentleman, "Even when I was thirty years old, if I had asked a girl to dine with me alone, I would have been kicked down her front steps. If I had offered her a cocktail, I would have been tossed out of Society for my boorish affrontery."

English upper-class women, it was said, mixed more freely with men than was the case in America. American ladies were thought to be more absorbed with domestic matters and more ignorant of the worlds of business and politics than were their English counterparts, and demanding greater delicacy of expression in drawingroom conversation. It was Henry James's opinion that the separation of the sexes in America was "*the* feature of the social scene." At the same time, outside the drawingroom a much freer behavior was to be observed, if one is to lend the least credence to the gossip column of the highly popular New York weekly magazine *Town Topics*.

Week after week, the "Saunterer" in *Town Topics* reveled in tales of high society, adultery, incest, illegitimacy, abortion, transvestism, and nymphomania, giving broad clues as to the participants and sometimes coming right out and naming names. It may be doubted that all Saunterer's charges were accurate, but it may not be doubted that high society enjoyed them thoroughly. It would not have done to have been caught reading the magazine, but the Saunterer was avidly followed by the social set. According to the son of the social authority Emily Post, *Town Topics* "found its way into almost every cottage in Tuxedo Park, as it did into the cottages, villas, and mansions at Newport. It was read upstairs, downstairs, and backstairs."

Delicately handled prurience was the stock-in-trade of the writers of what were known as women's books in the nineteenth century. The most successful example was *Charlotte Temple,* a moral tale of seduction that eventually went through more than 150 editions. Among the most popular American poets of the late nineteenth century was Ella Wheeler Wilcox, who was a past mistress at presenting "Black sin" as "oft white truth, that missed the way." Her *Poems of Passion* (1884) dealt sympathetically with such human conditions as were experienced by the gentleman who, married to the "stately Maud," still recalled the warm and sweet Lisette and how he kissed her throat and "her shoulders nude." It included a gentleman who, upon being smiled at "in mad-tiger fashion" was incited to "clasp her with fierceness and passion / And kiss her with shudder and groan."

The women in these situations were not by any means the sort that the gentle reader would ever knowingly invite into her own drawing-room, but the men were. And decent women in Mrs. Wilcox's verse were permitted to indulge their passionate natures to the extent of thinking "a sin of the deepest dye," and privately glorying in the thought, so long as it was in no way acted upon.

Mrs. Wilcox knew that she was on thin ice, and she was careful to explain that "by the word 'Passion,' I meant the 'grand passion' of love. To those who take exceptions to the title of the book I would suggest an early reference to Webster's definitions of the word." Acknowledging that the volume had caused "much agitation throughout the entire country, and even . . . a tremor across the Atlantic into the Old World," she defended the poems that had been brought into question and pointed to the "other selections quite irreproachable in character."

Nearly everybody knew about the unmentionable goings-on which characterized urban America, and they did not exactly not talk about them. In the drawingroom conversations of Henry James's novels much shocking information is, in a muffled and circumlocutory and allusive manner, conveyed; and by the end of the century, Mrs. Burton Harrison notwithstanding, it was coming out more into the open.

Upper-class American society during the last quarter of the nineteenth century seems to have made a more determined effort to be modern in morals than previous generations had. Thomas Beer named his book on the 1890's, *The Mauve Decade* (1926), taking his title from James Whistler's definition of mauve as "pink trying to be purple." Beer wrote,

The Americans of the '90's achieved a frame of mind that was apparent even to small boys; when the ladies said "actress," they meant something else. . . . The decade became a little more liberal in conversation and in print. . . . "whore" came from its covert once or twice, rendered as "w - - - -," which deceived nobody but gave everybody a sense of daring. Children were told that it stood for "where" and didn't believe it.

These children who were raised in upper-middle-class homes during the nineties were themselves taking the leading part in a social revolution, which was causing alarm in some quarters, but which met with no effective resistance because it was taking place in the children's nurseries and was therefore nobody's business but the parents'. The revolution, which had been developing during most of the nineteenth century, consisted of treating little children as though they were angels of light instead of potential imps of Satan. This was a profound change; and it was followed by profoundly revolutionary consequences, which were most startlingly represented in the pre-World War I Greenwich Village revolt against American morality.

Seventeenth-century Puritans had thought it natural for parents to be inclined to coddle their children; but they had abhorred this paternal inclination, as they abhorred all natural corruptions of the flesh, and had guarded against it. "Spare the rod and spoil the child" was the rule, and it remained the rule two centuries later in Jacksonian America.

Religious tendencies of the Age of Enlightenment were away from unconditional insistence on the natural depravity of man, however, and by the early nineteenth century, the doctrine of infant depravity was being questioned even by respectable clergymen. Lyman Beecher, in "Future Punishment of Infants Not a Doctrine of Calvinism," in 1828 argued that children who died before conversion would not necessarily go to hell. Many thoughtful mothers were in advance of Beecher in their opposition to the doctrine of the natural depravity of children. Lydia H. Signourney, whose *Letters to Mothers* appeared in 1838, became their leading authority. She declared that the problem of nurture was 'how the harp might be so tuned as not to injure its tender and intricate harmony." Children were the "ark of the nation," and mothers should "feel with Rousseau" that "the greatest respect is due to children."

Horace Bushnell's *Christian Nurture* appeared in 1847, together with Lyman Cobb's *The Evil Tendencies of Corporal Punishment;* and both were summaries of current tendencies of thought rather than pioneer works. Even Bushnell, however, retained the idea of "tendencies to depravity" in children which required "weeding out." The "new realism in nurture," Bernard Wishy writes, "was largely first envisioned as a more effective means of fulfilling the child's destiny of obedience to the laws of God and the rules of moral righteousness."

Changing attitudes toward child nurture in the age of Darwin were most influentially conveyed in Jacob Abbott's *Gentle Measures in the Management and Training of the Young* (1871), which emphasized the need for "right development. . . . in harmony with the structure and characteristics of the juvenile mind." Mrs. Carl Schurz, wife of the German-born Senator from Missouri, introduced the kindergarten to America in 1855, and the kindergarten movement developed widely during the latter part of the century. Abbott's Rollo stories, appealing to the imaginations of children, had sold widely during the pre-Civil War generation in competition with the conventional, grimly moralistic literature, most prominently represented by the Peter Parley stories.

The last third of the nineteenth century is the classic age of modern children's literature: *Little Women, Little Men, Alice in Wonderland, Prince and the Pauper, Treasure Island, Wizard of Oz, Little Black Sambo, Jungle Book, Black Beauty, Mrs. Wiggs of the Cabbage Patch,* and, by far the most influential in its impact upon child care, Frances Hodgson Burnett's *Little Lord Fauntleroy.* The new sentimentalization of childhood, which this literature reflects, was a natural consequence of the relaxing of religious restrictions in genteel society. The same tendency was evident in middle- and upper-middle-class England and in Europe; but, in the view of foreign observers, it appears to have been more pronounced in America than elsewhere. This was related in their minds to the further observation, recorded in numerous travelers' books, that the woman, as Fredrika Bremer, the Finnish novelist said, was "the center and lawgiver in the home of the New World."

In America, as elsewhere, this sentimentalization of childhood was fostered by the increasing urbanization of society. Compared with farm children, urban middle-class children were nearly useless to their parents. On the farm, children could be put to chores at the age of four or five; and by the time they were seventeen or eighteen, their parents would very likely have been repaid for what it had cost to raise them. Urban children represented expenses which never were repaid in financial terms, and they took up room which was not as abundant as it was on the farm. These were among the reasons why families of ten and twelve children became uncommon among the urban middle classes. In 1900 the average was 4.5; it dropped to 2.8 a generation later.

As children came to be more a luxury than a utility, the value placed upon them began to change accordingly; and as they came to be reduced in number, there was greater opportunity for the parents, especially the mother, to devote individual attention to each one. Then, too, by 1900 there were servants available in middle-class homes to relieve mothers of many of their traditional tasks and to relieve them of the need to train their children in these tasks.

Catharine E. Beecher and Harriet Beecher Stowe turned their faces like flint against these new softening influences on children in their *American Woman's Home,* published in 1869. They urged that the children "be very early taught that their happyness, both now and hereafter, depends on the formation of *habits* of submission, self-denial, and benevolence." They wished to see the females among them trained like the "strong, hardy, cheerful girls, that used to grow up in country places, and made the bright, neat, New England kitchens of old times—the girls that could wash, iron, brew, bake, harness a horse and drive him, no less than braid straw, embroider, draw, paint, and read innumerable books." What they saw instead were "the fragile, easily fatigued, languid girls of a modern age," waited upon badly by "the raw untrained Irish peasantry," whom the American girls were incapable of training, not knowing how to do housework themselves.

Emerson, who had been an influential figure in this new tendency of thought, commented strikingly on the new attitude toward children in a Concord Lyceum address in 1880.

The ancient manners were giving way. There grew a certain tenderness on the people, not before remarked. Children had been repressed and kept in the background; now they were considered, cosseted and pampered. I recall the remark of a witty physician who remembered the hardships of his own youth; he said "It was a misfortune to have been born when children were nothing, and to live till old men were nothing."

In the 1890's the nation was plunged into the debate which has never ceased, between advocates of progressive education and the upholders of traditional educational methods and goals. By the turn of the century the new child-centered methods were winning wide and fervent acceptance. J. P. Monroe wrote approvingly in *Educational Review* in 1901 of "the ferment and even the wild license of this New Education," which, though "often an excessive reaction, against the old methods of compulsion symbolized by the rod," would secure for the child "his birthright of individual development, of self-expression, of sympathetic understanding and helpfulness from others."

The progressive educationists' concept of childhood was a radical departure from Mrs. Signourney's idea of childhood as "the ark of the nation," carrying civilization on through another generation, or as a harp which required delicate tuning by parents and teachers. The new idea was to create a condition whereby the natural harmony of the child would develop of itself, rather than being tuned arbitrarily, if delicately, to accord to preconceived harmonic patterns. Mrs. T. Birney advised in 1904 in *Childhood* to try with each child "to make out of each what the Almighty evidently intended him to be. What He intended is not always an easy matter to determine. The only way it can be determined is by carefully studying the peculiarities of each mind, heart and body with which every child is gifted." In the same vein, Charlotte Perkins Gilman, American feminist and reformer, argued that the question should not be whether the child was ready for God, but whether the God of our fathers ignored the God of our children. Religious training of children, she wrote, should be determined by what was fit for children.

The child, wrote William J. Shearer in 1904 in *The Management and Training of Children,* is "the tiny prophecy of future possibilities." In a world of visibly changing material conditions, a transition had occurred, as Bernard Wishy puts it, from the optimistic mid-nineteenth-century concept of the redeemable child to the optimistic turn-of-the-century idea of the child redeemer. That was not to say that the child was expected to lead the nation to a new and superior moral order, however. Rather, the idea seems to have been that the child would be entrusted with responsibility, in his lifetime, for guarding and improving the existing moral order under changing conditions.

Naturally enough, the children of the new educational philosophy viewed the role that had been assigned them from the standpoint of their own generation rather than that of their parents. The pre-World War I Greenwich Village revolt against puritanical morality and capitalistic ethics was led by sons and daughters of the upper-middle classes. It was an Ivy League movement of young people who had been nurtured in Christian homes to grow up without knowing sin. They showed the results of their upbringing by rebelling against their parents' generation at the very time when those Christian-capitalistic parents were succeeding, to their own way of thinking, in restoring morality to public life and social justice to the people in order to bequeath a morally rejuvenated nation to their children.

2.

Paths of
Righteousness
··

IF IT IS NOT THE MOST complex age in American history, the final third of the nineteenth century is certainly the most cumbersome period for the historian to deal with. It does not appear possible to reduce it to good comprehensive narrative order. It remains a prodigious mixed bag of Reconstruction and the New South; robber barons and political spoilsmen; transcontinental railroads, mining bonanzas, cattle kingdoms, Indian wars, and the end of the frontier; farm protest and labor unrest; the rise of big business and finance capitalism; the Catholic-Jewish New Immigration and urbanization; Anglo-Saxon race consciousness and the New Imperialism; and Darwinian evolution and the battle between science and religion in the emergent era of the engineer and the social scientist. It is an age distinguished neither for great poetry nor for great politics. It is a cross-grained and prosaic age, as well as a heroic and a creative one. It is not in any very important sense a Gilded Age, although more money was spent at being more genteel on a grander scale than ever before.

Then, at the turn of the twentieth century the nation achieved a momentary equilibrium, or the appearance of it, in the national sense of unity that prevailed, even among the anti-imperialists, following the Spanish-American War, and in the national prosperity and the semblance of economic order that accompanied the new consolidations of finance capitalism. It would be overstating the case to describe the Progressive era as the calm that followed the storm, but it was a quieter time than the nation had known for two generations or more. It would be excessively paradoxical to describe the Progressive era as an age of political and social reaction, following the revolution, but certainly Progressives were inspired by visions of free enterprise, republican responsibility, and national morality which they particularly associated with a golden age of the founding fathers.

Culturally the so-called Gilded Age was not as drastically unlike the Progressive era as the contrasting political climates would lead one to believe. The half century between the Civil War and World War I as a whole is characterized by the unremitting exertion of the forces of Protestantism to revive the nation spiritually, always encouraged by an optimistic faith in the destined moral salvation of America. Afterwards, in the Roaring Twenties, such a faith could no longer be widely sustained, even in the updated form of the Social Gospel. Until then, however, the Kingdom of God was never entirely out of sight, from the war to free the slaves to the war to make the world safe for democracy.

The Protestant Republic agreed that a great reformation could be accomplished, but it did not agree upon the design for the reformation. Many Americans accepted the Gospel of Wealth, others were converted to the Social Gospel, and still others remained steadfast for revivalism and personal conversion. This Revival Gospel placed emphasis upon the God of the Old Testament and concentrated its energies on the prohibition movement. The Social Gospel, emphasizing the New Testament and the teachings of Jesus, prepared the way for the Progressive movement.

The language of the Sunday sermon became the currency of politics during the Progressive era, in what appeared in retrospect to have been an abnormal inflation of the moral content of politics. It was followed after World War I by a deflation back to what President Harding called *normalcy*. Actually it was a moral deflation to well below normalcy, as measured by the corruption of the Harding administration and, more importantly, by the popular repudiation of "Protestant clericalism." Protestantism overextended itself in the Progressive era, and it suffered a severe loss of prestige as a consequence, much of which was never to be recovered.

••

The founding fathers had equated political parties with selfish factionalism, national disunity, and demagoguery; and upper-class Americans continued to share this distaste for the party system throughout the nineteenth century. That did not prevent them from becoming staunch party men, however, any more than it had prevented Hamilton and Jefferson from becoming party leaders. Something had to be done to defend the nation against the Jacksonian levelers, and men of breeding thanked God that Henry Clay or Daniel Webster or even William Henry Harrison was upholding the right. George Washington remained the model of what a President should be, and upper-class America continued to respect the Washingtonian conception of government by the best and wisest men chosen without regard to party considerations. Indeed, Harrison, the first Whig President, announced his intention of ruling above party; but, harried and abused by office seekers, he died of pneumonia during his first month in office.

Americans universally upheld the principle of separation of church and state. But the Bill of Rights said nothing about separation of church and politics, and during the election of 1800 Congregational ministers in New England had believed themselves to be particularly obliged to oppose the candidacy of a "howling atheist," as a Connecticut gentleman termed Jefferson. However, there was not again such an amount of religious partisanship for more than half a century. Whatever might be said against Jackson, he was a devout Presbyterian; and politics, which dealt with material interests, was widely considered not to be of direct religious concern in Jacksonian America.

With the rise of the Republican party and the coming of the Civil

War, however, a change occurred both in upper-class attitudes toward political parties and in general attitudes toward the relationship of church and politics. The Methodist Episcopal Church, South and the Southern Baptist Convention had already seceded from the national Methodist and Baptist churches, and northern evangelical religion joined the Republican party from its inception. The Unitarian Church, representing upper-class New England opinion, exchanged its implicit attachment to the Whig party as the party of relative respectability for a fervent attachment to the Republican party as the party of liberty and morality.

This moral attachment to Republicanism was qualified, even in Boston, by the thought of what southern secession would do to trade; but once the damage of secession was done, the merchants and the ministers tended to become of one mind on the matter. In New York City, where southern commercial connections were much stronger than in Boston, upper-class sentiment was much less responsive to Republicanism, and the national Episcopal Church survived the Civil War without separating into northern and southern denominations. In the North, as a whole, there was divided opinion about the Republican party throughout the Civil War among the upper classes and among the people generally; but the meaning of what came to be called the Grand Old Party changed almost overnight with the surrender of the Confederate armies and the assassination of President Lincoln.

In life, Lincoln had been accepted at the outset of his Presidency as the available man; and his reputation was never very high during the war, either in popular terms or in terms of the upper-class Republican consensus. In death, however, he was reverenced at once as the martyred savior of the Union and as the Great Emancipator. The Gettysburg Address and the Second Inaugural Address became spiritual texts for the Protestant Republic, equaled only by the Declaration of Independence. The Republican party became the party of Lincoln; and it remained the party of Lincoln, as an ideal separate from the reality, through the political squalor of the Grant administrations and after. It remained the party of the northern evangelical reformers, and only a few of them proved willing to leave it to join the newly formed Prohibition party in 1869. It also remained the party of the patrician reformers throughout the North, with the exception, to some extent, of the state of New York. The terrible beating that the Liberal Republicans took from the Stalwart Republicans in 1872 and their ostracism from high party councils thereafter did not change their transcendental attachment to Republicanism, even though they placed the mantle of their approval upon the Democratic President Cleveland in 1884.

Lincoln, whom the Liberal Republicans idolized, was by comparison to their other hero, Washington, quite unrepresentative of their political ideals, both in the matter of his origins and, more seriously, in the matter of his concept of constitutional government. Washington had been brought up to be a gentleman, and when duty had called, he had become the father of his country. He had ruled the new nation in the manner of a stern but just and loving father, who strove for harmony among the politicians and happy unity among the people. In his relations with Congress, he was father, and nobody doubted it. John Adams wanted to be such a President; John Quincy Adams announced his intention of being such a President and spent the next four years in very unseemly struggles with Congress; and in 1872 Charles Francis Adams was waiting in the wings in the hope that he might be chosen to restore the nation to Washingtonian righteousness.

On the other hand, Lincoln's humble log cabin origins never ceased to bother his genteel admirers, who never agreed upon the right attitude to take toward them. A good deal of genealogical effort was expended on the problem of discovering some blue blood in the Lincoln line to help account for his greatness. Some attributed Lincoln's greatness as a leader to divine intervention in the war against slavery. To others, Lincoln demonstrated that any American boy could become President; but that was dreadfully apparent anyway. Lincoln was therefore an inappropriate symbol of patrician righteousness. Neither was he well suited to the purposes of the evangelical reformers who also accepted him in the role of savior; for Lincoln's religious beliefs, however deep-seated and eloquently expressed, were not, to say the least, orthodox.

Worst of all for the purpose of the patricians, Lincoln the Great Emancipator was also Lincoln the party regular and friend to the spoilsmen. As he himself boasted during the Lincoln-Douglas debates, "In '32 I voted for Henry Clay, in '36 for the Hugh L. White ticket, in '40 for 'Tip and Tyler.' In '44 I made the last grand effort for 'Old Harry of the West.' . . . Taylor was elected in '48 and we fought nobly for Scott in '52." Party loyalty above nearly all else was a principle that was established in Jacksonian times and not originally in the age of Grant. Lincoln put loyalty to the Union above loyalty to party; but in the Civil War and its victorious conclusion, the Republican party was transformed into the party of the Union, and Republican politicians did not afterwards attempt to distinguish clearly between the two loyalties.

Lincoln's Whig party had been organized to combat the executive usurpations of Jackson; and Lincoln as President accepted the principle of congressional rule, even while vigorously extending his authority as commander in chief over the conduct of the war and terms of the peace. As President, Lincoln initiated no major domestic legislation other than that dealing with the war and reconstruction; and he signed every single bill that came to his desk with but four exceptions, three of them being of minor national concern and the fourth being the Wade-Davis reconstruction measure. The congressional bills he signed included, of course, innumerable pork barrel bills, in addition to those relating to tariffs, banking, contract labor, land grant colleges, and so on. Politicians, bureaucrats, businessmen, and soldiers were already deeply involved in the kind of corruption later known as "Grantism," most scandalously in connection with the illicit cotton trade, while Lincoln was still President. Consequently the Lincoln legend was better suited to the party-oriented righteousness of Roscoe Conkling, James G. Blaine, and Robert Ingersoll than to the upper-middle-class righteousness of Carl Schurz, Charles Francis Adams, and Henry Ward Beecher.

While patrician America felt a sense of kinship with the founding fathers, Liberal Republicanism was definitely tinged with foreign influences. Schurz, the German Forty-Eighter, was inspired in his twenty-year struggle for civil service reform by the example of the intelligent and dedicated Prussian bureaucracy; and E. L. Godkin, the Anglo-American editor of the *Nation,* attempted to apply the better standards of the British ruling class to the American situation. John Stuart Mill was the accepted philosopher of Liberal Republicanism, to some extent superseded as time went on, by Herbert Spencer. The Yale sociologist William Graham Sumner provided a native defense of "the forgotten man," as he called the upright middle-class and upper-middle-class American; but Sumner's Malthusian ethic tended to overshoot the mark, from the patrician point of view, and exalt the captains of industry as the fittest of all to rule the nation.

There was actually a better market for patrician morality in the party of disunion, because the Democrats necessarily had to present themselves in a positively upright and patriotic posture as the Republicans did not. In 1884 the Liberal Republicans supported the Democratic Cleveland against the Republican Blaine, and their influence was felt throughout both of Cleveland's administrations. Until Bryan captured the party in 1896 the Manchester liberalism of Cleveland was as advanced a liberalism as the Democratic party could well formulate on a national basis.

The Liberal Democratic-Republicanism of Cleveland, the Liberal Republicanism of Schurz, and the party loyalism of the seasoned professionals were all to some extent outmoded, anyway, when the captains of industry assumed political as well as economic stewardship of the nation at the end of the century. The Liberal Republicans resented this rise of the plutocrats; but Liberal Republican doctrine offered no good argument in opposition to their uncontrolled power as long as the plutocrats obeyed the laws which they, themselves, were increasingly in a position to make.

The transition from the spoilsmen to the business spokesman mainly took place in the 1880's. As Mathew Josephson, in *The Politicos* (1938), wrote,

The younger leadership rising through the Republican Party's transition, typified by the young Nelson Aldrich, now thought in terms of great economic groups, where the elder statesmen thought invariably in terms of geographical sections and political clans. . . . The oratory of the Elder Statesmen had played upon the swords and roses of war, the doctrine of universal liberty, the menace of rebellion in the South. The new men made speeches that bristled with facts; their heroes were pig-iron ingots and steel rails, matches, and mountains of glassware. From the outset certain of these young men, notably Nelson Aldrich, William McKinley, and Thomas B. Reed, determined to quit the hoary themes of Radical wartime Republicanism and devote themselves to studying the schedules of tariffs, the statistics of imports and exports, which were a mystery, a jungle, to the other statesmen.

These young men became in time the Old Guard against which the Progressives struggled; but they were joined in Congress by captains of industry themselves, who in many cases preferred to govern directly rather than through subordinates. They believed they had a right to rule and that the country would be better off if they did. The nickel magnate Joseph Wharton of Philadelphia spoke their mind when he declared:

I have supported and aided the Government more than it has supported and aided me. I am not a pauper nor a lawyer. . . . I am one of the men who create and maintain the prosperity of the nation and who enable it to survive even the affliction of wrong-headed and cranky legislators.

These men righteously bought their way into the Senate in the eighties and nineties until, at the turn of the century, the "Millionaires' Club" boasted at least twenty-five multimillionaires.

That, to their way of thinking, was just as it should be. Senator Hearst of California explained this in an afterdinner speech to a group of his senatorial colleagues.

I do not know much about books; I have not read very much; but I have travelled a good deal and observed men and things, and I have made up my mind after all my experience that the members of the Senate are the survival of the fittest.

There was nothing mealymouthed about the plutocracy, as there had been about the spoilsmen, in its professions of righteousness. The plutocrats believed that those who owned the country should run it, and they said so and did so.

Like Hearst, they had not acquired their learning through books; and their conviction that they represented the survival of the fittest came, not from reading Herbert Spencer or William Graham Sumner, but from experience and from what they had been taught at home and in church. The robber barons were typically church-going men who had practiced the Protestant ethic and who considered that they had been rewarded by God accordingly. "The success cult took its texts from the Bible," writes Irvin Wyllie, "not from writings of Darwin and Spencer. It preached no warfare of each against all, but rather a warfare of each man against his baser self."

Americans had been taught from earliest times that, as one Methodist minister of the Gilded Age put it, business "is sacred. It is a means of grace. It is a stewardship. It is building up for eternity, and laying up treasures in heaven." Businessmen ought to be honest in their dealings, and it was argued by some that honesty was necessary to great success in business; that, as Bishop William Lawrence of Massachusetts said, "in the long run, it is only to the man of morality that wealth comes."

Bishop Lawrence did not make clear what he meant by business morality, but he presumably accepted the standards of the day, which were very broad and liberal by comparison with the exact business standards of seventeenth-century New England. Business standards had relaxed during the more worldly eighteenth century. Benjamin Franklin was tolerant of, and himself practiced, sharp dealings that John Winthrop would not have tolerated. Franklin's cracker barrel business philosophy continued to be the approved way to wealth in the late nineteenth century, when sharp dealings, beyond keeping the competition on its toes, had come to affect the lives and fortunes of millions of bystanders. Business standards were redolent with religious injunctions to be sober, prudent, thrifty, and tirelessly devoted to work; but they were not bound by religious injunctions against usury, chicanery, and covetousness, as had once been the case.

Social Gospel ministers were preaching that businessmen should abide by the Golden Rule, but the robber barons still enjoyed the majority support of the churches in their arguments for believing that they represented God's will on earth. The businessmen were not themselves of one mind about the Gospel of Wealth, but many of them were certainly as pious in church as they were practical in business. Daniel Drew spoke for these in declaring that "when a man goes to prayer meeting and class meeting two nights of the week, and to church twice on Sunday, and on week days works at his office from morning till night, his life is made up of two things—work and worship." Drew is remembered for both the colorful corruption of his business career and for Drew Theological Seminary, which he founded.

Drew's schedule did not allow time for a life of politics; those businessmen who did allow themselves time to sit in the Senate were more apt to do so for the honor of it than out of a sense of sacred duty. They were no less righteous about their stewardship for that, for they were conscious of their being the chosen of God and of their representing the true interests of the nation rather than those of irresponsible politicians claiming to represent "the people."

These plutocrats were looked down upon by men of more seasoned wealth, but there was nothing in the Liberal Republican social philosophy to dispute their claims to superiority. They were scorned for their lack of cultivation; some of them were barred from some of the better clubs, but the line was hard to maintain in the dynamic and unaristocratic society of America. Money always counted in the end, and the older gentry did not have the money to keep pace. It was new money that built the Metropolitan Opera House, to make the older New York Academy of Music, sponsored by Beekmans and Livingstons, look like small potatoes. Theodore Roosevelt declared that he was "simply unable to make myself take the attitude of respect toward the very wealthy men which such an enormous multitude of people evidently really feel"; although he was "delighted to show any courtesy to Pierpont Morgan or Andrew Carnegie or James J. Hill." He felt the same way about the big political bosses. He had to remain in a position of subordination to both for many years, however, before his opportunity finally came to assume top stewardship of the nation's welfare.

Charles Francis Adams, Jr., who chose business as a career, was removed from the presidency of the Union Pacific Railroad by crafty Jay Gould at the height of his career and driven into semiretirement and the pursuit of cultural activities. In his autobiography, Adams heaped contempt upon the entire class of American big businessmen: their success came "from a rather low instinct," and all of them whom he had known had been "mere money-getters and traders . . . essentially unattractive and uninteresting." Adams confessed that he himself would have liked to have amassed one of those vast fortunes running into the tens of millions of dollars; but in his case, he wrote, it would not have been the money he desired but the good he could have done with the money by giving it to Harvard, where he served on the Board of Overseers.

Unlike Adams, other men, such as Vanderbilt, Stanford, Carnegie, and Rockefeller, did amass vast fortunes; and however unrefined their motives may have been, many of them did just as Adams said he would have done if he had had the chance. Rockefeller said that God had given him the money he was giving to the new University of Chicago, and the statement has been subjected to ridicule ever since. But Rockefeller, true to the training of his Baptist mother, had been setting aside a portion of his income for Godly purposes since he had started out in life as a poor boy. However reprehensible his business methods may or may not have been, plutocratic stewardship was an office Rockefeller was honorably entitled to.

If plutocratic stewardship appeared obscene to the old upper-middle classes, that reflected against their own Federalist conceptions of patrician stewardship. It was with this in mind, or at least in the back of the mind, and without by any means forsaking the belief that their class was the best class, that upper-middle-class Progressives after the turn of the century became the righteous opponents of "class interests" and "class legislation" of all sorts.

....

The year 1873 has a bad name in American history. It is the year of Crédit Mobilier and other scandalous revelations of "Grantism," and it is the year of Jay Cooke and the Panic of '73. Twain and Warner's *The Gilded Age* appeared the next year, and the title stuck to the era. The year does not appear in histories as marking the beginning of a great national spiritual rebirth; yet that is how it appeared at the time to millions of morally earnest Americans. Amid depression conditions which continued throughout Grant's second administration and amid continuing revelations of more and more political corruption, evangelical moral forces confidently regrouped themselves and marched forward in shining confidence toward the Kingdom of Righteousness.

The year 1873 was the year of the Woman's Crusade against the saloon, which lifted the prohibition movement out of the doldrums and revived interchurch cooperation in the temperance cause. It was the year when Anthony Comstock gained national prominence and single-handedly arranged for the passage of the national antiobscenity law which he would vigorously enforce for the next forty-two years. It was the year when the former president of the Chicago YMCA, Dwight L. Moody, hired an organist and singer, Ira B. Sankey, and toured England and Scotland to start a new era of urban revivalism in the whole English-speaking world. In 1874 the leaders of the Woman's Crusade met in Cleveland to form the WCTU to rid the nation of the drink evil. Also in 1874 a Methodist adult education program was formed in Chautauqua, New York, and the Chautauqua movement extended itself throughout the nation. A national meeting in Brooklyn of social unions of Baptist churches in 1874 resulted in the Baptist Congress, which similarly thrived in the years that followed.

The Woman's Crusade occurred in rural and village America at the height of the Granger movement; it appears to have been to some extent an offshoot of the farmers' protest movement, in which women as well as men had participated. Similarly the Anti-Saloon League was to be founded a generation later at the height of the farmers' Populist revolt and to draw strength and inspiration from the dry-minded agrarian reformers. As a political reform movement, Grangerism actually had substantially exhausted its possibilities by the time of the Woman's Crusade; and it was perhaps true that as faith in the power of politics declined, the spirit of militancy was redirected to a renewed preoccupation with the power of prayer.

Similarly the rise of the Chautauqua and the formation of the Baptist Congress were related to the Granger crusade. The origins of the Granger movement were in the Patrons of Husbandry, organized for social and educational purposes by Oliver H. Kelley, a clerk in the U.S. Department of Agriculture. The Methodist Chautauqua and the Baptist Congress represented continuations of these activities at a time when Reconstruction and the plight of the freedman had ceased to be a major concern of northern evangelical religion. On the other hand, the rise of Anthony Comstock was an urban phenomenon, Comstock's main support coming from the New York City YMCA, and Dwight L. Moody becoming nationally important in the United States only after experiencing two years of spectacular success in the major cities of the British Isles.

The strength of resurgent revivalism in the seventies remained in rural America; but the focus of its attention and the sources of its financial strength were in the cities, where men of wealth contributed generously to Moody in particular. Moody's active supporters included George Armour, Cyrus McCormick, and Marshall Field in Chicago; John Wanamaker in Philadelphia; Amos A. Lawrence in Boston; and Cornelius Vanderbilt II and J. P. Morgan in New York. These men were attracted to urban revivalism as a means of instilling salutary habits of thought and conduct among the lower orders of society. Charles Loring Brace's *The Dangerous Classes of New York* appeared in 1873, and at the time of Moody's triumphant return from England, the problem of the poor was disturbing the minds of the rich.

There was substantial agreement among men and women of wealth that, as Henry Ward Beecher put it, "No man in this land suffers from poverty unless it be more than his fault—unless it be his *sin,*" and "If men have not enough, it is owing to the want of provident care, and foresight, and industry, and frugality, and wise saving." From this point of view, urban revivalism appeared to be the one practical means of reforming the terrible conditions in the cities. For themselves, the rich enjoyed their own more liberal and plushy religions apart from the masses. Beecher observed that "our churches are largely for the mutual insurance of prosperous families, and not for the upbuilding of the great underclass of humanity."

Nevertheless, Moody found the rich men more responsive to his sermons than the members of the underclass. Although the conversion of the working man was the primary object of urban revivalism, middle-class Americans were the ones who filled the tabernacles night after night, together with Moody's sincerely pious plutocratic sponsors. Writing of the hymns that the congregations sang to Sankey's accompaniment, including Moody's favorite—"Dare to be a Daniel! Dare to stand alone!"—William G. McLoughlin, Jr., observed that "it is difficult to imagine J. P. Morgan or Phillips Brooks singing these verses, but they did."

The dangerous classes did not seem beyond hope of reformation to many in the seventies. The New Immigration from southeastern and central Europe was still in the future, and the nativist sentiments of the Know-Nothing party in the fifties had subsided. The Irish and the Germans had fought on the Union side in the Civil War, and in that way they had earned their American nationality, to the thinking of many old-stock Americans. The Irish would undoubtedly continue to practice Roman Catholicism and vote Democratic; but there remained plenty of unchurched Protestants among the working classes, and it was hoped that the reformation of these would lead to a reformation or improvement of the whole. When even these were found to be unreachable, national prohibition came to seem the only means of achieving national morality.

Both in his style of presentation and in his message, Moody represented a departure from the earlier revivalism of George Whitefield and Charles Grandison Finney. His emphasis was on the love, rather than the wrath, of God. His sermons were sentimental and anecdotal, and the music of Sankey's organ and of the choir and of the congregation was all blended into Moody's gospel message. It was, said one minister, "that tender weeping power in dear Mr. Moody that is so overwhelming"; and another observed, "I have heard the sound of his weeping as he pled with God for perishing men, while in the intervening pauses I could distinctly hear the weeping of the people."

Victorian sentimentalism was the dominant chord of Moody's revivalism, and Victorian decorum accompanied it. Moody refrained from inciting his audiences to emotional outbursts such as had always previously characterized American revivalism; if a member of the audience did become overwrought, the ushers removed him. Hell awaited all unrepentant sinners, but Moody believed that "where one person has been converted under the sermon, a hundred have been converted in the inquiry room." For Moody, religion consisted of learning truth from the Bible and seeking salvation and escape from eternal punishment through faith and repentance. He avoided theological controversy, and he did not much concern himself with the religious controversies arising out of the challenge of Darwinian science to biblical literalism. He held to biblical literalism without argument.

Moody, who was never ordained a minister, remained the most influential figure in American Protestantism until his death in 1899. His was a collateral doctrine to the Gospel of Wealth; and he epitomized the age of big business in his dynamic, efficient, large-scale organizational methods. However, though he denied the Social Gospel, Moody no more took part in political controversies than he did in theological ones; and the extended revivals in specially built tabernacles which rich men financed for him in New York and Boston and Philadelphia and elsewhere were dedicated to general spiritual purposes rather than to particular political and economic ones.

The case was otherwise with Moody's most influential successors, Samuel P. Jones and Billy Sunday, both of whom employed the emotionalism of what came to be known as the old-time religion. Jones, who began his career as a big-time urban revivalist in Memphis in

1884, appealed to conservative business interests by attacking labor unions and political reformers. In 1897 Jones was brought to Toledo to campaign against Samuel M. "Golden Rule" Jones, who was running for mayor on an independent reform ticket against both Democratic and Republican candidates. The argument of Reverend Jones against candidate Jones boiled down to the assertion that a mayor who tolerated one open saloon was immoral. However effective this argument no doubt was with many voters, "Golden Rule" Jones won more than twice as many votes as the combined opposition in the election.

Billy Sunday achieved greater national prominence than any other revivalist of the Progressive era. He was widely regarded as one of the greatest living Americans; but he was more evidently a crowd-gatherer and rabble-rouser, appealing to popular prejudices, than he was a spiritual leader. Sunday represents the nadir in the history of American revivalism when the militant crusade for "fundamentalism" was furiously counterattacking the conquering force of what was coming to be called "modernism."

Moody was a premillennialist, who believed that while salvation was open to all, society as a whole was irredeemably corrupt and doomed to destruction. This pessimistic interpretation of the Book of Daniel was widely held by evangelical Christians in the Civil War and post-Civil War years, against the contrary postmillennialism of the Social Gospel. The belief that society was irreversibly corrupt did not absolve Christians from their obligation to fight Satan and all his works, however, especially where impressionable minds of young people might be affected. It was to this charge of defending youth from sexual temptation by censoring the obscene that Anthony Comstock dedicated his life.

Comstock grew up in rural Calvinist surroundings; he was nurtured on hell-fire religion and taught the crying need for repentance, as was the case with Moody and with a host of other Americans of their generation. "If I could but live without sin," the young Comstock wrote in his diary, "I should be the happiest soul living; but Sin, that foe is ever lurking, stealing happiness from me." Moving to New York City after the Civil War, Comstock was aghast at the visible temptations that surrounded him. He brought suit against booksellers under an antiobscenity law which the New York YMCA had steered through the state legislature but which the legislature had not attempted to enforce. At Comstock's urging, the YMCA formed a Committee for the Suppression of Vice. In 1872 a federal antiobscenity law was passed; and in 1873 the scandal of the century occurred in Brooklyn—the Beecher-Tilton adultery case—and Comstock entered history.

In the course of four years of titillating revelation and altercation ending in a split decision of the jury of the Brooklyn Municipal Court, Henry Ward Beecher, perhaps the most prominent American minister of his day, was revealed as a sanctimonious adulterer and bombastic perjuror. The injured party was Theodore Tilton, editor of a leading national religious periodical, whose own moral character was brought into serious question in the course of the trial. And the scandal was given a public airing in the first place by Victoria Woodhull, spiritualist, stockbroker, newspaper editor, and champion of woman's rights and free love, who published the gossip about the affair, as told to her by Elizabeth Cady Stanton, who had heard it from Susan B. Anthony, who had heard it from Tilton's mother.

Comstock brought suit against Mrs. Woodhull and her sister, Tennessee Claflin, under the new federal antiobscenity statute, after the district attorney had refused to take action under the state law. The sisters were taken to Ludlow Street jail, where they remained for four weeks, refusing to accept bond, pending their trial. Eventually they were acquitted on the grounds that the federal law did not apply to newspapers, but Comstock had made his name known throughout the nation.

Following his contest with "The Woodhull," as the vivacious editor was called in the press, Comstock went to Washington, D.C., and quietly and quickly piloted through Congress a new antiobscenity act, which also prohibited the advertising of quack medicines and contraceptive information in newspapers and provided the legal foundation for his own activities as special agent to the postmaster general for the next 42 years. The law was very ambiguous, failing, among other things, to define what obscenity was. As defined in the courts, however, obscenity was that which might "deprave and corrupt those whose minds are open to such immoral influences"—a criterion which, as Judge Learned Hand pointed out in a 1915 decision, was such as "to reduce our treatment of sex to the standard of a child's library in the supposed interest of a salacious few."

An earlier law had given the Customs Office authority to prohibit the importation of works of obscenity. In the Comstock era both the Customs Office and the Post Office enforced the laws with sweeping authority, banning works by Balzac, Flaubert, George Moore, Anatole France, Voltaire, Boccaccio, Apuleius, Aristophanes, Ovid, and on and on. As the nation's cultural capital, New York was the center for censorship activity. But Boston, with its Watch and Ward Society, was particularly noted for genteel narrow-mindedness. In 1881 a Boston publisher withdrew a new edition of *Leaves of Grass,* under threat of action by the city prosecutor; and Boston continued to distinguish itself as a place where books were banned.

Comstock died in 1915 of a cold contracted while serving as an American delegate to the World's Purity Congress in San Francisco. The Comstock era was already passing by that time, in the sense that obscenity was ceasing to be clearly definable in law as anything that might conceivably corrupt youthful minds. But to the day of his death Comstock continued to be feared and obeyed by publishers and others who might offend him. This was testimony to Comstock's tenacity and resourcefulness, but more fundamentally it was testimony to the lack of resolute moral opposition to him in the nation. The cultural leadership of Progressive America as represented by W. D. Howells and Brander Matthews was more appreciative than Comstock was where contemporary world literature was concerned; but it tended to agree with Comstock that "art is not above morals," and "when the genius of art reproduces obscene, lewd and lascivious ideas, the deadly effect upon the morals of the young" justifies rigorous suppression. Evangelical America, of course, agreed with Comstock without qualification.

Victorian America opposed sin in the flesh as well as in print. But the problems involved in closing down red-light districts were of a different order of magnitude from the policing of publishers and booksellers, and the objection was always advanced that antivice crusades only served to publicize the unmentionable. Such crusades were sporadically organized in most major cities at various times, only to end in embarrassment, acrimonious dispute among the moral forces, and absolute failure. In Chicago, following the Great Fire of 1871, a Committee of Seventy, made up of businessmen and ministers, set out to suppress vice and crime and promote legal reforms. It soon came to be dominated by prohibitionists, however, who narrowed its campaign to the closing of saloons on Sunday. It was followed shortly by a Committee of Twenty-five, made up mainly of businessmen and dedicated to doing something about the fact that "the city is infested by a very large number of professional thieves, burglars, prostitutes and roughs." It also was subverted by the prohibitionists and faded away. In Los Angeles a good government crusade was launched in the late eighties, followed by a Citizen's League in 1893, a League for Better City Government in 1896, a Committee of Safety several years later, a Municipal League in 1901, and a Voters' League in 1905. All were led by ministers, and all tended to become dominated by the prohibitionists.

In 1878 a Society for the Prevention of Crime was founded in New York under ministerial leadership. It drifted along until 1891, when the Reverend Charles H. Parkhurst of the Madison Square Presbyterian Church was elected its president. Parkhurst attacked the city officials as "polluted harpies . . . a lying, perjured, rumsoaked, and libidinous lot." After he had been called before the grand jury and rebuked for speaking without evidence, he hired a private detective to take him around town and show him the evidence. He then drew up 248 bills of particulars, which became the basis for the colorful Lexow Committee investigation, authorized by the state legislature.

The spectacular success of the Lexow hearing was mainly due to its chief counsel, John W. Goff, who mercilessly browbeat or deftly disarmed a continuous procession of police, prostitutes, madams, politicians, businessmen, and gamblers. Both Goff and Parkhurst emerged as heroes, and a political slate of municipal reformers was swept into office. With the end to the investigations, however, gamblers and madams returned to town, and the red-light districts went back into full swing. In 1897 Tammany Hall returned to power to the victory chant of "Well, well, well! Reform has gone to Hell!" In 1901 the New York legislature appointed a new committee to investigate corruption in the metropolis, and the city elected another reform administration.

Chicago was aroused to righteousness in 1894 by an Englishman, William T. Stead, who published a book, *If Christ Came to Chicago,* in which he described the city's red-light districts block by block, together with the system of police bribery which made them possible. He published a blacklist of people, many of them prominent citizens, who either owned or occupied property that was being used for criminal purposes, and he analyzed the corruption that surrounded city hall. Stead's exposé resulted in the forming of the Civic Federation of Chicago. Concentrating on gambling, the Federation hired forty Pinkerton detectives, who were temporarily successful in closing the gambling houses.

What, if anything, had been accomplished by Parkhurst, Stead, and the rest of the antired-light agitators? By anybody's standards, their campaigns had proved ineffectually misdirected. To evangelical reformers, particularly, these campaigns struck, not at the root of the evil, but merely at its blossoms. Increasingly these evangelical reformers became convinced that liquor was the root of the evil and that prohibition of the manufacture, sale, and consumption of alcoholic beverages was the answer to it. From the formation of the Anti-Saloon League in 1895 to the passage of the Eighteenth Amendment, prohibition was pursued as the one main road to righteousness by all of evangelical America.

....

Originally Maine had shown the way to the dry millennium with the first statewide prohibitory liquor laws, but from the Woman's Crusade to repeal of the Eighteenth Amendment, Ohio was the center for the nation's prohibitionist activity. Ohioans had launched the Woman's Crusade in 1873. The Woman's Christian Temperance Union was founded in Cleveland in 1874. The Ohio Anti-Saloon League was founded at Oberlin in 1893, setting an example which other states followed; and the national Anti-Saloon League, formed in 1895, established its headquarters in Columbus, Ohio. Evidently there was something about Ohio which made it unusually productive of dry enthusiasm.

Ohio is in some respects unique among the states of the nation in its territorial history. It came into the Union on the same general terms as did the other states of the Old Northwest. But it was the first of these to be settled and the first to be admitted, and its settlement served special purposes: the original states during the period of the Articles of Confederation owed back wages to soldiers of the Revolution, and Ohio land was at first used primarily to satisfy some of these claims; Virginia had good title to all of Ohio, and, upon relinquishing its claim, it had reserved military lands in the southern part of the territory to distribute among its veterans; Connecticut had a color of claim to the northern part, and it had established the Western Reserve for the same purpose. In addition, the Ohio Company was formed by New England Revolutionary War veterans and received a large grant of land from Congress.

Settlement of Ohio was therefore more orderly than was the case with other western states, many of its early towns being patterned on the New England communities from which the settlers had migrated. At the same time, the wilderness environment served to revive the old spirit of primitive Puritanism. Ohio was New England's closest connection with the West, and it became a favorite area for New England missionary activity. One result of this is that Ohio has more good small private colleges than other Midwestern states, most of them founded as missionary ventures. Among them, Oberlin College in the 1830's became the most important training center in the nation for the abolitionist clergy, as it later became the birthplace of the Anti-Saloon League.

Ohio abolitionists had had a house of their own to clean. Although slavery had been prohibited in the state from the time of settlement, strong proslavery sentiment naturally existed in the southern part of the state on the old Virginia military land. Oberlin had become a hotbed of abolitionist activity as a result of an exodus from Lane Theological Seminary in Cincinnati, where students and faculty members had rebelled against the temporizing of President Lyman Beecher and the proslavery sentiments of the trustees.

Cincinnati was also the bastion of error for the Ohio prohibitionists in the late nineteenth century, with its Burghers and Biergärten and gemütliche Sonntage. The German-Americans of Cincinnati served to rouse up the Ohio drys as the French-Canadian lumberjacks had roused up the drys of Maine. There were more drys per capita in Kansas than in Ohio, but by the same token there was not as much of the drink evil within the state for the Kansas drys to sink their teeth into.

The father of the Anti-Saloon League was Howard Russell, who had left the legal profession at the age of 28 to devote his life to the temperance cause. He later recalled this decision in an address before the League's national convention in 1913.

Then came to me that mysterious change when the human will despite its stubbornness, was subdued by the mighty power of God, and I gladly laid aside personal aims and political ambitions to devote my life to the gospel ministry. For the period of preparation I found myself at Oberlin. It is very plain now that it was the hand of the Most High that turned my course toward that historic seat of reform.

Russell had observed drunkenness as a newspaperman, had delved into its effects on families as a lawyer, and had experienced it personally in his relations with his own alcoholic brother. It was clear to him in retrospect that God personally had been guiding him through his period of training.

At a Conneaut, Ohio, church in the winter of 1893 a pastor, introducing me to his congregation, said: "There was a man sent from God whose name was John; it is equally true there was a man sent from God whose name was Russell!" In the awed silence of my heart, I was compelled to believe the statement was true.

The movement was shot through with this messianic strain, and there were many messiahs on the national, state, and local levels, each of them as convinced as Russell that he was the particularly chosen of God. This must have created a lot of hard feeling in the councils of heaven, but it also produced a phenomenally effective leadership on all levels in a struggle which everywhere seemed almost hopeless at the outset.

Righteous zeal and unremitting exertion were not enough, as League leaders well knew. Russell did not suppose that in his own Ohio, dry-mindedness was shared by more than a third of the population. The other two-thirds would have to be tricked into prohibition for their own good. (God self-evidently sanctioned that kind of benign chicanery.) Russell asked the Oberlin faculty to suggest a student who could handle himself in politics—"tireless, tactful, optimistic, resourceful, a good speaker, a good mixer, a loving-spirited, self-sacrificing soul"—to become the League district manager. They gave him Wayne B. Wheeler, who rose to the position of legislative superintendent of the National League in Washington, D.C., to become the most powerful figure in the League.

Always a farm boy at heart, Wheeler was the king of the country slickers and for a generation the most powerful lobbyist in the nation's capital. It was Wheeler more than anyone else who made the dry vote in Congress the one immediate national objective of the League. Over Russell's objections, he cultivated wet politicians in Ohio and later in Washington, with an eye to future favors. He attended distillers' and brewers' meetings and once, it was said, even wrote a speech for a man whom he met on a train who hadn't decided what to say to the wet meeting he was scheduled to address. Wheeler, and therefore the League, didn't care how much a congressman drank but only how he voted.

The League spoke of itself as the organization by which the Protestant churches of America united themselves in the antiliquor fight, and it did command the support of all major Protestant churches with the exception of the Episcopalian and the Lutheran. Similar interdenominational antiliquor organizations had been tried on local and state levels since before the Civil War, but they had not worked out as well. The League's success evidently owed much to the continuing Catholic immigration, which gave the Protestant sects a common enemy. Many Anti-Saloon Leaguers were aflame with the conviction that they were defending their homeland against the ragged armies of the Pope. Even so, interdenominational unity was always difficult to maintain on all levels.

By singling out the saloon for attack, the League was choosing a target as wonderfully big as a barn door. To be sure, the saloons were the poor men's clubs that provided workingmen with the only bright and comfortable and festive surroundings they would be likely to experience in their entire lives. To be sure, also, saloonkeepers were good scouts, who found a fellow a job or a place to stay and who lent him money when he was down on his luck without requiring security or interest.

That same saloonkeeper was continually taking in money that otherwise would have been spent on food and clothing for ragged undernourished families, just as the prohibitionists said he was doing. The drunkard's doom was an everyday occurrence in every part of the country; and when the drunkard was finally down and out, friendliness and generosity were no more forthcoming from the saloonkeeper than they were from anybody else.

Saloonkeepers were notoriously contemptuous of the law, even in the smaller communities. They were always in with the police and the politicians, and everybody helped everybody else. Increasing, and increasingly confusing, bodies of laws were passed locally and on a statewide basis, especially from the time of the Woman's Crusade; but down to the end of the century they were widely ignored. In the larger towns and in the cities liquor was openly dispensed whenever there were customers, in violation of the curfew and Sunday closing laws. Little children "rushed the growler"—fetched beer home in a bucket—from saloons which displayed prominently the admonition that minors were not allowed on the premises. Saloonkeepers frequently manufactured their own liquor, and customers sometimes died of poisoning or were blinded as a consequence.

Politically the saloons were centers of corruption. Their political strength increased after the Woman's Crusade, since thereafter they felt obliged to organize in earnest. Socially, as the prohibitionists asserted, saloons were a corrupting influence. One social-drinking antisaloon man argued that "morally the liquor the saloon sells is usually the least part of the harm it does. The whole saloon atmosphere is opposed to ideals of every sort, moral, civic, and social. . . ." This was one reason why the League was able to turn law-abiding social drinkers against the saloon and then lead them methodically from local option to statewide prohibition to national abolition of alcoholic beverages.

In 1913 the League successfully sponsored the Webb-Kenyon Act, prohibiting interstate commerce in alcoholic beverages where state or local laws were violated as a consequence. In that same year it caused to be submitted in Congress a constitutional amendment providing for national prohibition. In 1917 American entrance into the war was used to advantage by the drys, who called for prohibition to conserve grain for the war effort and who asserted that the profits were sent to Germany, where they were used to make bullets to kill American boys. In December 1917 both houses of Congress approved the prohibition amendment by more than the necessary two-thirds majority, and it went to the states to be acted on by the rural-dominated state legislatures.

Congress enacted a war prohibition law in November 1918, ten days after the armistice was signed, and the nation went dry in July 1919 under its provisions. Then on January 16, 1920, the Eighteenth Amendment became a part of the Constitution. In June 1919 the

World League Against Alchoholism had been organized in Washington, D.C., to help make the world safe for democracy. "America," the Reverend A. C. Bane had declared, "will 'go over the top' in humanity's greatest battle, and plant the victorious white standard of Prohibition upon the nation's loftiest eminence."

Then catching sight of the beckoning hands of our sister nations across the sea, struggling with the same age-long foe, we will go forth with the spirit of the missionary and the crusader to help drive the demon of drink from all civilization. With America leading the way, with faith in Omnipotent God, and bearing with patriotic hands our stainless flag, the emblem of civic purity, we will soon . . . bestow upon mankind the priceless gift of World Prohibition.

The Anti-Saloon League appointed a seven-man committee to attend the Versailles Conference and write temperance reform into the peace treaty. The State Department denied the delegates passports, however, apparently upon the request of the British and French governments. The League thereafter abandoned the struggle for a prohibitionist world revolution, as it became increasingly absorbed in the task of establishing prohibition in one nation-state.

· ·

By the time the Anti-Saloon League was winning its fight to abolish poverty and sin in the nation through the abolition of the liquor traffic, those Americans who were directly engaged in the problems of poverty and sin—the social workers, philanthropists, sociologists, and many of the urban missionaries—had arrived at the conclusion that they had been wrong in the importance they had attached to intemperance as a cause of social distress. More broadly, they were coming to reject the formerly all-but-universal American assumption that poverty was the consequence of moral weakness; that the slums were monuments to moral sloth. Increasingly they were arriving at the conclusion that the reverse was more nearly true: that poverty bred sin, and that the harvesting of souls would be more effectively carried out by reforming slum conditions than by eliciting innumerable individual repentances from slum sinners.

Down until the late nineteenth century there had been little sympathetic understanding for the problems of the poor, even on the part of those whose lives were devoted to attending to those problems. Robert M. Hartley, who served for more than thirty years as secretary of the New York Association for Improving the Condition of the Poor, was probably the most important figure in the American Charity movement at mid-century; yet he held what he called "the debased poor" in contempt. "They love to clan together in some out-of-the-way place," he explained, "are content to live in filth and disorder with a bare subsistence, provided they can drink, and smoke, and gossip, and enjoy their balls, and wakes, and frolics, without molestation."

This contemptuous attitude was evident in the annual reports of the New York Society for the Prevention of Pauperism for the years 1818 to 1824. On the basis of its observations during these years, the society listed the main causes of pauperism as (1) ignorance, (2) idleness, (3) intemperance, (4) want of economy, (5) imprudent and hasty marriages, (6) lotteries, (7) pawnbrokers, (8) houses of ill fame, (9) gambling houses, and (10) the numerous charitable institutions of the city. It evidently did not occur to those most intimately involved with the problem of poverty that there were important contributing factors that had nothing to do with moral weakness, such as starvation wages and depressions, diseases and accidents, and the near impossibility for many slum children of learning anything outside the slum experience. The parallel between those who grew up in slums and those who grew up in slavery was at least as meaningful as the parallel between slavery and intemperance, but this apparently did not suggest itself as urgently to the evangelists of the abolitionist-prohibitionist cause.

As cities grew larger and depressions became more severe and longer-enduring, charitable institutions proliferated, and became more clamorous for contributions. It was widely thought by those who were being dunned for contributions—and with good reason—that their money was being inefficiently spent. Agencies overlapped one another in their activities, and far from cooperating in a common cause, often divided on sectarian or other grounds and involved themselves in mutual sniping and backbiting. Furthermore, they developed no rational plans for the dispensing of charity, making no systematic investigations into the needs of the families and individuals to which they distributed aid.

Scientific philanthropy developed in the late nineteenth and early twentieth centuries in response to the demand on the part of donors and taxpayers that a dollar's worth of service be rendered for a dollar spent in charitable activity. Intellectually the most significant result of the scientific research into poverty which followed was the finding that moral weakness did not result in poverty as surely as poverty served to disintegrate morality.

John Barleycorn had been the grotesquely genial personification of evil for generations of Americans. In the mid-nineteenth century the Sons of Temperance blamed him for most of the ills that society suffered, and in the early twentieth century the Anti-Saloon League charged him with almost single-handedly filling the prisons and hospitals of the nation and with reducing tenement dwellers to their condition of cruel want.

Scientific philanthropy reduced John Barleycorn's role to that of one of the supporting players. In the 1830's Joseph Tuckerman, a leading New England philanthropist, estimated that drink caused 75 percent of American pauperism. In the 1890's Amos Warner, author of the influential *American Charities, A Study in Philanthropy and Economics*, blamed alcohol for an obviously very roughly estimated 5 to 22 percent of poverty cases. By that time social workers were coming to dismiss any such statistics as unrealistic, in simplistically assuming that any one factor could be singled out as the cause of poverty.

Amid the righteous hullabaloo of the dry campaigns, social workers in the early twentieth century were striving to replace moral with scientific principles. They sought to define poverty, and they did so in terms of inadequacy of living conditions rather than in terms of degree of dependency on charitable institutions. Approached from this point of view, the problem of poverty was one to be solved by reforming the rich, who paid inadequate wages, rather than the poor, who could under no circumstances live decently within the existing system.

Scientific philanthropy also attacked the comfortable American assumption that poverty, where it was not the result of sinfulness, was a wholesome condition, favorable to the development of the simple virtues and stimulating to individual initiative. It was the conclusion of a monograph published by the Russell Sage Foundation, for instance, that poverty "does not kill perhaps but it stunts. It does not come as an overwhelming catastrophe; but steadily it saps the vigor of the young as well as of the old . . . With the less fortunate, poverty takes the form of a slow, chronic contest against everlasting odds."

Social welfare reformers went after the facts about slum conditions and about working conditions in factories, especially where women and children were involved. The more hopeful of them were convinced, with Charles R. Henderson of the University of Chicago, that "light is a very effective moral disinfectant. Information about abuses is often the only remedy that is required." All of them were convinced, with W. E. B. Du Bois and Augustus Granville Dill, that "there is only one sure basis of social reform and that is Truth—a careful detailed knowledge of the essential facts of each social problem." The result was, as Walter Weyl wrote, "The beautiful industrial idyls" of the nineteenth century had given way "to a very wide bookshelf on the influence of evil industrial conditions upon the virtues and vices of the industrial classes."

Factual exposure of the nation's social ills became the stock-in-trade of journalists writing for *McClure's* and other popular magazines during the first decade of the twentieth century. Theodore Roosevelt named these writers muckrakers, after the man with the muck-rake in *Pilgrim's Progress*, "whose vision is fixed on carnal instead of on spiritual things . . . who in this life consistently refused to see aught that is lofty, and fixes his eyes with solemn intentness only on that which is vile and debasing." The muckrakers did cater to a national interest in the seamy side of American life, and the moral of their story usually was that the real sinners were those supposedly upright members of the respectable community who controlled the slums and the sweatshops.

In the colleges, moral philosophy had been replaced by the social sciences, as part of the same intellectual revolution that was reordering religion-oriented charity into scientific philanthropy. The new disciplines of sociology and economics, during their early stages of development, did not, however, altogether divest themselves of the religious character of the parent discipline. When the American Economic Association was founded in 1885, a large part of its membership was made up of clergymen. The association made it clear that its purpose was not to discover economic laws that would rationalize the status quo but to use economic ideas as the means to improve the condition of society.

These new social scientists found the conditions of society to be bad, and they tended to place the blame with people who thought of themselves as belonging to the respectable classes. The sociologist E. A. Ross, in *Sin and Society,* was not concerned with "sex sins," which had long since been "recognized and branded," but with "prosperous evil-doers that bask undisturbed in popular favor" because "their obliquies lack the brimstone smell." Economists, like Richard T. Ely in his *Social Aspects of Christianity,* became theologians; whereas clergymen, like Washington Gladden in his *Working People and Their Employers,* became economists—dedicated in either case to the betterment of society as a whole through the use of religion and the social sciences.

Moral philosophy in the colleges also gave way in the late nineteenth century to various kinds of philosophical idealism, all stressing the idea that the individual, of himself, was nothing; that he gained meaning only as he made himself a part of society. Josiah Royce, the most influential American philosophical idealist, transformed German idealism, which tended to exalt the state over the individual, into an American idealism, which exalted the community over the individual, sanctifying it as an aspect of God Himself.

Standing outside both the academic and the religious communities, Henry George, with his *Progress and Poverty,* was by far the most influential figure in this trend toward humanizing religion and treating all men, including those in slum society, as a part of the greater community. George's single-tax theory was completely accepted by relatively few; but his argument did much to convince millions that poverty was the result, not of moral weakness, but of a vicious system of capitalism by which the working masses were methodically robbed of the fruits of their labor. Inveighing against the capitalists in language of biblical eloquence, George was influential in preparing minds for the Social Gospel and then for Progressivism.

In 1900 the National Federation of Churches and Christian Workers was founded to express the point of view of the Social Gospel. In 1908 the Social Gospel gained more powerful expression in the Federal Council of the Churches of Christ in America and its Commission on the Church and Social Service. Between 1890 and 1904 the number of benevolent institutions in urban America approximately doubled; some of those that had originally been organized for the purpose of soul-saving alone tended to be drawn mainly into practical social work. The YMCA, with its increasing concentration on physical fitness and clean, inexpensive living facilities, in addition to varied social programs, was the outstanding example of this transition from heaven to earth.

During the late nineteenth and early twentieth centuries, hundreds of sentimental Social Gospel novels were published on this theme of the change of heart which made society over into a heaven on earth. The most successful among them, and one of the best sellers of all time, was Charles Sheldon's *In His Steps*. In the same vein, but generally somewhat more ambitiously conceived, were the utopian novels, at least 47 of which were published in America between 1888 and 1900, beginning with Edward Bellamy's *Looking Backward*, which set the style and which was, again, one of the nation's best sellers of all time.

Looking Backward exerted a strong influence on American intellectuals, including John Dewey and Charles Beard, as well as a popular influence which was measured by the organization of Bellamy clubs throughout the nation to discuss the work and consider its implications for the society of the time. It is not too much to say that Bellamy's conception of the city of Boston in the year 2000 fairly well represented the ideal society toward which American reformers were striving in the Gilded Age and the Progressive era. It is therefore also not too much to say that Progressive idealists—including perhaps even Dewey and Beard—were themselves implicitly looking backward, as Bellamy was, to some golden age of the Patriarchs in the very distant and somewhat biblical past, as a vague model for their ideal machine-age society.

Bellamy's Boston of the year 2000 is a push-button Garden of Eden, where mechanization serves to provide comfort and leisure for all in a society characterized most fundamentally by "the solidarity of the race and the brotherhood of man." All receive equal recompense for an equal amount of labor, whatever the nature of the work, and one's occupation is determined entirely by one's capabilities. Technological improvements have advanced to the point where the simple and gracious amenities of life are available to all on the basis of minimal labor. Society has learned to live according to the true moral law, so that no further change is necessary in the general scheme of things. However, bright young men and women, impelled by creative curiosity rather than by competitive materialism, continue to devise ingenious technological improvements, particularly in the field of labor-saving devices, to further increase leisure time. The same goods and services that are available in Boston are equally available in the surrounding villages and throughout the nation.

Retirement age is set at forty-five, but, though the rest of one's life is free for self-improvement or recreation, the retiree voluntarily becomes active in a supervisory capacity and in what remains of the nation's political affairs. "We always continue honorary members of our former guilds," Dr. Leete of the year 2000 explains to the hero, "and retain the keenest and most jealous interest in their welfare and repute in the hands of the following generation."

In the clubs maintained by the honorary members of the several guilds, in which we meet socially, there are no topics of conversation so common as those which relate to these matters, and the young aspirants for guild leadership who can pass the criticism of us old fellows are likely to be pretty well equipped. Recognizing this fact, the nation entrusts to the honorary members of each guild the election of its general, and I venture to claim that no previous form of society could have developed a body of electors so ideally adapted to their office, as regards absolute impartiality, knowledge of the special qualifications and record of candidates, solicitude for the best result, and complete absence of self-interest.

Society in *Looking Backward* is conceived of as an industrial army, and "the line of promotion for the meritorious lies through three grades to the officer's grade" up to "the general of the guild, under whose immediate control all the operations of the trade are conducted." Above this are the generals of the grand divisions, who form a council for the general-in-chief, who is the President of the United States. The ten generals of the grand divisions are also elected by the "old fellows" in the honorary guilds, and the President is elected from among the ten by the members of the industrial army as a whole.

Needless to say, this military analogy was not intended to convey a spirit of militarism. The very reason Bellamy was able to apply military terminology to his conception of society without fear of being misunderstood was that the United States hardly possessed a real standing army in the 1880's, and there was no immediate reason to think it would ever need one. On the other hand, the patriarchal order of this Progressives' ideal society is fundamental. Patriarchy was the appropriate form of government in the perfect and therefore changeless society, where the new generations could be taught all they needed to know by the old fellows who had already been through it.

It may be objected that this would be the case with any utopia, but Bellamy's utopia is one that has been and continues to be revolutionized in the technological sector. There is no indication that Bellamy thought that this would make much difference, except in terms of increased comfort and leisure, to the character of society; and his readers do not appear to have thought about this either. What they and he saw in *Looking Backward* was the final achievement of the moral order that had been divinely ordained at the beginning of time and that had been expedited by labor-saving devices.

Progressivism encompassed conflicting opinions concerning many economic and social questions, but it represented a broad concordance of outlook such as the nation had not manifested since before the Civil War. The age was vibrant with moral indignation, but it was also vibrant with the sense of a sudden acceleration of progress in all the main areas of national life. Everybody was conscious of momentous changes in the business life of the nation, and everybody was aware of dangers to democracy or to economic soundness or to social health or to spiritual or cultural values. But the main tendencies were onward and upward: this was the all-but-universal assumption among the middle classes and upper classes.

This happy breakthrough of national confidence followed upon the demoralizing Panic of '93, with its Populism and labor warfare. The McKinley-Bryan campaign of 1896 had sounded more like class warfare than any previous election campaign in the nation's history. Then good times came again for farmers as well as workers. On top of that, the nation went to war with Spain to free the Cubans from oppression and emerged, to nearly everybody's surprise, as one of the great powers of the world. And finally, finance capitalism emerged during the immediate postwar years, in what appeared to contemporaries to be the final consolidation of the national economy in the hands of the titans of Wall Street, representing at one and the same time extremely dangerous and extremely desirable tendencies. These events, following in quick succession, contributed to the suddenly realized national sense of careening forward with dangerous speed toward the better world of tomorrow.

The election of 1900 found the depression-oriented Bryan without a convincing domestic issue to argue; he chose instead to campaign on the issue of imperialism, denouncing the acquisition of the Philippine Islands. McKinley returned to his front porch in Canton, Ohio, and doubled the margin of his earlier victory. Unlike free silver, imperialism was an issue that tended to unify the nation rather than divide it. Those on both sides of the question thought of themselves as having the welfare of their "little brown brothers" in mind as well as the welfare of the nation; and there was a mutual tolerance of opposing positions as compared to the deep suspicions of the free-silver controversy because the imperialism issue did not appear to involve the fundamental well-being of the nation as the free-silver issue had seemed to do. America as a whole evidently enjoyed the new role of colonial stewardship over "lesser breeds," from the Caribbean to the Orient. The nation seemed to be momentarily enveloped in a warm moral self-esteem. The readiness of southerners to volunteer for the conflict was a heartwarming surprise to northerners.

Economic nationalization in the form of finance capitalism, which completed mergers at a spectacular rate from 1898 to 1904, was not heartwarming; but its effect on the nation was nevertheless essentially a unifying one. On the one hand, within the business community, a new vision came to be shared of freedom from unlimited competition in a new age of corporate cooperation. This vision was not to become a substantial reality until World War I and the postwar decade, but the giants of the business world assumed a more responsibly conservative appearance than the robber barons had. The organized expression of this new appearance was the National Civic Federation—in which Samuel Gompers as well as Morgan, Hanna, and Belmont participated during the "honeymoon" between business and organized labor which lasted through the critical period of consolidation.

On the other hand, the "trustbusting" point of view that typified Progressivism was qualified by a general acceptance of big business as the inevitable shape of the better world that was to come. Bellamy had written in *Looking Backward* that "the solution came as the result of a process of industrial evolution which could not have terminated otherwise." Trustbusting was an overblown term for government activity based upon the belief that competition should be maintained where possible and that monopoly, as well as competitive business, should be held accountable to law. Progressives believed that economic progress presented a challenge to the nation to see to it that moral standards were maintained amid rapidly changing conditions. It was the permanent moral order that concerned the Progressives primarily, rather than the evolutionary economic order, whose details nobody understood well and whose general evolution was admittedly beyond human control.

McKinley of the McKinley Tariff and the Full Dinner Pail and the front porch in Canton, Ohio, was a man who believed in God and progress and the national destiny; but McKinley put his trust in the stewardship of wealth and he believed in letting events take their course without much executive direction. His manner of presiding over the nation helped to create an air of quiet and solidity during exceptionally dynamic times. Then in 1901 McKinley was assassinated, Theodore Roosevelt took office, and the Progressive era began.

At the time Roosevelt had entered New York State politics in 1881, he had been looked upon by other members of his social world as entering a degraded profession; while professional politicians and the press, unless they had reason to value his support, had tended to dismiss him as a "young squirt of a dude" who was hopelessly out of place in the world of wardheel politics. Although Roosevelt was never especially careful about his dress, he appeared as a dandy in the early political cartoons of him, which also featured, of course, the pince-nez glasses.

During his early career Roosevelt enjoyed the political company of his patrician associate in politics, Henry Cabot Lodge, but for Lodge Massachusetts provided a more genteel setting for a political career than New York. Lodge broke with the Liberal Republicans and supported Blaine in 1884, just as Roosevelt did, but Lodge remained something of a provincial aristocrat in politics. Roosevelt was the more energetically active campaigner in partisan politics, and he operated in a state where his family connections did not do him as much good as Lodge's did in Massachusetts.

Although Roosevelt got away from the "dude" image, he probably never would have advanced in the political ranks as far as governor of New York, except that the popularity arising from his exploits in the Spanish-American War virtually forced his nomination upon the New York Republican machine. Then, as governor, he was so energetically disturbing to the machine that the machine in turn forced him upon Mark Hanna as McKinley's running mate, to get him out of New York politics. A gentlemanly Liberal Republican in all but his professional insistence on party regularity, Roosevelt, as President, broadened and enlivened Liberal Republicanism, or Mugwumpry, as it was also called, and transformed it into Progressivism.

This was the chief substance of Roosevelt's political achievement, for, except in the field of conservation, it can be argued that he instituted no major reforms of great and enduring practical consequence. His spectacular settlement of the United Mine Workers strike and his startling attack on the Northern Securities railroad merger were both isolated episodes early in his Presidency that attracted attention without establishing new governmental policies. The distinction he made between "good" and "bad" trusts was hardly the basis for a practical program of business regulation, and the extension of government power in this area during his administrations was not such as to antagonize dominant business interests in the nation.

Yet Roosevelt became the most popular President since Jackson; and the basis of this popularity, as Mark Sullivan wrote, "was that he had, in the plain sight of the common man, presented spectacle after spectacle in which business, capital, corporate power, took off its hat in the presence of the symbol and spokesman of government." Roosevelt was concerned with vindicating the righteous authority of the people, vested in his office, rather than with reforming a business system whose mechanics he never pretended really to understand. This was the authentic voice of Progressivism. A flurry of reform went on throughout the nation, on state and local levels, and Roosevelt provided the national leadership that gave it coherence.

Roosevelt presented himself to the American people as a red-blooded American moralist. The real need in American public life, he declared, was *"the fundamental fight for morality,"* and his ingrained tendency to see political issues in moral terms was a matter for comment even among some of his close associates. Elihu Root declared that Roosevelt acted as though he imagined that it had been he who had discovered the Ten Commandments. "My problems are moral problems," Roosevelt commented shortly before leaving office, "and my teaching has been plain morality."

Robert La Follette conceded bitterly that "Theodore Roosevelt is the ablest living interpreter of what I would call the superficial public sentiment of a given time, and he is spontaneous in his reactions to it." It was Roosevelt rather than La Follette, however, who represented national Progressivism. He had rescued the Presidency from the democracy of the spoils system and had invested it with a moral authority that recognizably expressed the national will, or at least the will of the national middle classes. Neither he nor the nation he represented saw the need for sweeping economic changes in prosperous times, other than natural evolutionary changes. The moral order was the fundamental order to most Progressives, and with Roosevelt the moral order was obviously in good hands.

The standard-bearers of Democratic Progressivism—Bryan and Wilson—were in considerable contrast to each other, as well as to Roosevelt, in backgrounds and personalities and policies; but as Progressive Democrats from rural America, they shared much in common also. Wilson's education included a doctorate of philosophy from Johns Hopkins, whereas Bryan had attended an obscure college in Chicago. The ideas of both, however, were grounded in the philosophy of that other Presbyterian college president, William H. McGuffey, and his Readers. Both Democratic leaders were consciously Jeffersonian in outlook—the emphasis on states' rights initially being more marked in Wilson's case, and the emphasis on agrarian virtue being more pronounced with Bryan.

Both were Presbyterians, although Bryan had been raised in the expectation that he would be a Baptist minister, and both were the sons of ministers. Both, like Roosevelt, looked upon government as basically a system of morality. "The great political questions," Bryan declared, "are in their final analysis great moral questions, and it requires no extended experience in the handling of money to enable a man to tell right from wrong."

Both Wilson's father and maternal grandfather were Presbyterian ministers; and Wilson's stewardship as President, unlike Roosevelt's, was formal and austere, and even ministerial. He fixed his stamp of morality upon the government at once by canceling the traditional inaugural ball, and in his inaugural address he declared:

The Nation has been deeply stirred, stirred by a solemn passion, stirred by the knowledge of wrong, of ideals lost, of government too often debauched and made an instrument of evil. The feelings with which we face this new age of right and opportunity sweep across our heartstrings like some air out of God's own presence, where justice and mercy are reconciled and the judge and the brother are one.

Then in April 1917, America entered the World War to fulfill the larger moral purpose, as Wilson viewed it, of making the world safe for democracy. "The force of America," Wilson declared, "is the force of moral principle . . . there is nothing else that she loves, and . . . there is nothing else for which she will contend."

Frederic C. Howe, in his *Confessions of a Reformer* (1925), observed how comprehensive and fundamental this force of moral principle was in American culture.

Early assumptions as to virtue and vice, goodness and evil remained in my mind long after I had tried to discard them. This is, I think, the most characteristic influence of my generation. It explains the nature of our reforms, the regulatory legislation in morals and economics, our belief in men rather than in institutions and our messages to other peoples. Missionaries and battleships, anti-saloon leagues and Ku Klux Klans, Wilson and Santo Domingo are all a part of that evangelistic psychology that makes America what it is.

Progressivism had sought to reaffirm traditional, preindustrial American assumptions of goodness and evil and to hold the machine age accountable to them. The Progressive movement was led by well-educated men who were aware that old values were being challenged by new ideas as well as by new circumstances; but these men had no thought of replacing traditional Christian moral absolutism with Darwinian, not to say Freudian, relativism. At the same time, however, they thought of themselves as modern men and women; and as modern parents, they characteristically subscribed to the modernistic methods of Christian nurture. They sent their sons and daughters to progressive schools in many cases and then to colleges where the traditional mental and moral philosophy courses had given way to psychology, biology, and the evolutionary social sciences.

This younger upper-middle-class generation of the Progressive era was therefore trained, as no previous generation had been trained, to believe that progress represented evolution away from the eternal verities of their parents, rather than closer conformity with them. They were trained to believe that in a progressive society it would always be the children who knew best for their own generation. Pre-World War I Greenwich Village was the most striking manifestation of this breaching of the old moral order by the offspring of Progressivism.

THREE

Fruit
of the Tree
# of Knowledge

3.

The Evolutionary Outlook

....

EARLY IN 1860 D. APPLETON and Company published the first American edition of Darwin's *The Origin of Species,* which the New York diarist George Templeton Strong found "a shallow book though laboriously and honestly written." The recently established science of geology had already disproved the Bible story of the creation of heaven and earth in the minds of educated Americans, and Darwinian biology would similarly influence the minds of the young in the coming generations against belief in the special creation of man, the immortality of the soul, and the eternal moral law.

Most educated Americans evidently did not abandon belief in divine providence. Nevertheless the actual Adam was gone, together with the actual Garden of Eden; and since man apparently was not created in the image of God, the conception of God-the-Father lost something of its patriarchal meaning. In the college classroom and laboratory, man was studied in terms of his reflexes and instincts and social attributes, with no longer any mention of his soul. Truth became a pragmatic rather than an absolute concept, and morality became the product of social conditioning. Outside the classroom, some intellectuals tentatively accepted Marxian Socialism beginning in the first decade of the twentieth century and eagerly converted themselves to Freudianism during the next decade.

In a nation that was undergoing a tremendous urban, industrial, and technological revolution, the evolutionary concept presented itself as the key to knowledge. In response to the needs of industry and to the changing intellectual requirements of the age, a revolution occurred in higher education away from the traditional classical and moral orientation and toward the sciences—the applied sciences and the new social sciences—which were reclassifying man and society in evolutionary terms. In general, the concept of education from kindergarten to graduate school was reoriented from the teaching of a fixed body of knowledge to the teaching of methods of inquiry to be applied to the continually changing facts of existence.

Progressive education taught children to create their own world, rather than to accept without question the world of their elders, and the newly reconstituted institutions of higher learning provided the necessary methodology. Professors of the social sciences stopped short of teaching Marxian Socialism; and professors of literature excluded from consideration the controversial contemporary European literature of realism and naturalism and decadence, but inquiring minds were led to this literature in a university atmosphere of ostentatious dedication to free inquiry.

Campus radicalism did not result from this atmosphere to any significant extent, but postgraduate radicalism in Greenwich Village did. It was among these Greenwich Villagers that the phenomonen of the younger generation as a self-consciously reformist force in American society made its first major appearance. Greenwich Village recruited only a very small proportion of the college graduates of the day, however, and the main social impact of what Thorstein Veblen sarcastically termed "The Higher Learning in America" was felt below the level of the mind in the region which came to be known throughout the nation as "college life."

College life by the eve of the First World War was associated in everybody's mind with coeducation, fraternities, sororities, football, the "dance craze," and, in general, the opportunity for young people of the upper-middle classes to go away from home and broaden their outlook before marriage. The reconstituted higher education was a revolutionary social force in American life, but it was a revolutionary force that remained thoroughly middle class in orientation. Its revolutionary consequences were manifest primarily outside the world of political ideology in the Jazz Age and Dollar Decade aspects of the 1920's. From the prewar Greenwich Village point of view this was not radicalism at all, but it proved in time to have been nothing less than the revolutionary beginning of a new world order in the age of the technological filiarchy.

•••

During colonial times scientific investigation had been looked upon as an act of worship. Ministers had been eager, as with Cotton Mather, to celebrate through Newtonian science, "the Works of the Glorious GOD in the *Creation* of the World. . . . that He may be glorified in them. . . ." The evangelical churches that took the lead with the opening of the nineteenth century abandoned this avenue of worship, however. They ignored the science that did.not get into the farmer's almanacs and thought it sufficient to learn of the works of God from sermons and Bible readings. This became more emphatically the case in the face of the development of geology as a new science that was in direct conflict with the Scriptures.

Geology established itself as a recognized science with the publication of Charles Lyell's *Principles of Geology,* the first American edition appearing in 1837. Continuing the work of earlier scholars, Lyell found the earth to have been created, not in six days, but over many hundreds of millions of years. Until the publication of Lyell's work the most respected scientific opinion in America had accepted the Book of Genesis as authoritative. Benjamin Silliman of Yale, the nation's leading academic scientist, had written an account of the creation and the flood for use in colleges which had concluded that "Respecting the deluge there can be but one opinion . . . geology fully confirms the scripture history of that event. . . ."

It was a position that Silliman found impossible to maintain. His prize student and son-in-law, James Dwight Dana, published a textbook in 1837, *System of Mineralogy,* which incorporated the work of Lyell. That book established Dana and helped to establish modern geology in American colleges, and educated men ceased to believe in the biblical account of the creation of heaven and earth and in the story of Noah and the flood. This theological adjustment was brought about without great commotion. On the one hand, biblical literalists continued to believe the Book of Genesis word for word. On the other hand, religious liberals had long since ceased to believe that the Bible in its entirety was absolutely and literally authoritative on scientific matters.

Dana was a devout Christian whose attitude toward the pursuit of science was in the same tradition as that of Cotton Mather. A generation later, Asa Gray, who became America's leading botanist and foremost exponent of Darwinian evolution, was similarly in the tradition of Mather. Like Dana, Gray reconciled the scientific findings of his day with Christianity, and he assumed the responsibility for convincing his countrymen to do likewise in the case of evolution. Among educated Americans he was bound to be successful in the long run because educated Americans from Puritan times had faithfully accepted scientific truths as religious truths.

The idea of God's special creation of all species of plant and animal life had increasingly been brought into question by scientific investigation during the first half of the nineteenth century. Various theories of evolution had been advanced, including the influential Lamarckian theory of changes in species brought about through the transmission of acquired characteristics. Herbert Spencer argued a theory of evolution in *Social Statics,* which appeared in 1850. He continued his argument in his voluminous later writings, and from the beginning he attracted American followers. John Fiske, a leading American popularizer of evolution, was converted by reading Spencer before he became familiar with Darwin's *Origin of Species.*

Clerical censure of Spencer was inevitable, but Spencer's thesis in *Social Statics* concerned the evolution of man in social rather than biological terms, and his theme of human progress was particularly well suited to the American frame of mind. That man, along with everything else, had emerged from the original nebular mass was an aspect of Spencerian evolution which, to Fiske and other American followers, was incidental to the grand theme of human progress as manifested in universal law. *Origin of Species,* however, was a scientific treatise devoted specifically to replacing the Christian hypothesis of special creation with the evolutionary hypothesis of natural selection.

There were no such things as independently created species, Darwin declared. Species were only strongly defined varieties. Those variations that accidentally proved adaptable to their environment survived, while the less adaptable were crowded out. *Origin of Species* was followed by *Descent of Man* (1871), which traced the stages by which man had evolved from lower forms of animal life through the accidental process of natural selection. *Origin of Species* had already explicitly included man in the general evolutionary process, and both books received wide attention in America as elsewhere immediately upon publication.

Darwinian evolution substituted the law of the jungle for the beneficent and rational moral order, but there was a beauty and mystery to Darwin's jungle which romanticists had felt the lack of in the clear and mathematical moral order of the Enlightenment. Darwin captured this romance of evolution in his famous reflection in *Origin.*

It is interesting to contemplate a tangled bank, clothed with many plants of many kinds, with birds singing on the bushes, with various insects flitting about, and with worms crawling through the damp earth, and to reflect that these elaborately constructed forms, each so different from each other, and dependent upon each other in so complex a manner, have all been produced by laws acting around us. . . . There is grandeur in this view of life, with its several powers, having been originally breathed by the Creator into a few forms or into one; and that, whilst this planet has gone cycling on according to the fixed law of gravity, from so simple a beginning endless forms most beautiful and most wonderful have been, and are being evolved.

Asa Gray had been associated with Darwin and with Darwin's work prior to the publication of *Origin of Species,* and he was informally appointed to be Darwin's chief American defender. In defending Darwin's thesis, Gray was obliged, because of his own strong religious beliefs as well as those of his American audience, to go beyond Darwin into the question of God's intentions and His means of carrying them out. Darwin had solved that question for himself by moving easily, without anguish, from Christianity to agnosticism; but that was not possible for Gray or for America. Gray was confronted with the instinctive reaction among educated Americans which James Russell Lowell expressed when he declared that "such mush seems to me a poor substitute for the Rock of Ages. I am conservative—with God as against evolution."

The two most effective—almost the two official—defenders of Darwinian evolution were Gray and the English scientist Thomas Huxley; and the two men pursued two distinct lines of argument. Huxley believed in God, just as Gray did, but he argued that science should be kept separate from theology and that evolutionary theory should be supported purely on a scientific level in scientific terms. Gray, while he based his defense of Darwinian evolution on the scientific evidence before him, became associated from the first with the argument that evolution was the working out of God's design and was compatible with Christian orthodoxy.

Gray conceded that evolutionary biology could be used to support atheism, but so, also, he pointed out, could physical theories generally be used, including the nebular hypothesis and Newton's theory of gravitation. Evolution was the means by which God carried out his mysterious designs. It was not given to man to know what God's purposes were, but evolutionary theory at least provided insights into the mystery. With this in mind he went on to add: "While the physical cause of variation is utterly unknown and mysterious, we should advise Mr. Darwin to assume, in the philosophy of his hypothesis, that variation has been led along certain beneficial lines."

Gray's argument was taken up by influential religious liberals like Henry Ward Beecher and Lyman Abbott, who were politically conservative, and also by Washington Gladden and other Social Gospelers, who were striving to reform society along "certain beneficial lines." John Fiske, who had been a storm center at Harvard in the sixties because of his defense of Spencer, lived to become the nationally respected mediator between science and religion with the message that "evolution is God's way of doing things."

There remained the nagging difficulty of man's immortal soul and at what time in the evolutionary process it had entered into him and how and why. Immortality had always been an unfathomable mystery, but now the difficulties became concrete and apparently insurmountable. Max Eastman put these difficulties as they presented themselves to American intellectuals two generations later: "The idea of immortality for the innumerable billions of human beings going back to the Stone Age, and then the absurdly exact line to be drawn between human and animal, make the conception almost inaccessible to a factual mind."

For the college generations that emerged after the Civil War, evolutionary science replaced religion and literature as the main source of intellectual excitement. "Ten or fifteen years ago," Whitelaw Reid declared in a Dartmouth College address in 1873, "the staple subject here for reading and talk, outside study hours, was English poetry and fiction. Now it is English science. Herbert Spencer, John Stuart Mill, Huxley, Darwin, Tyndall, have usurped the places of Tennyson and Browning, and Matthew Arnold and Dickens."

For the colleges themselves the Civil War had been a mortally debilitating experience which made them the more vulnerable to the revolution in higher education that followed. For a generation before the war there had been widespread complaint against the impractical standard curriculum of classical languages and literature and natural, mental, and moral philosophy. Following the war, Cornell University, which started new in 1868 as a part land grant, part private institution, introduced a new curriculum of science, social science, engineering, modern history, and modern languages. In 1869 Charles Eliot, a chemist and not a clergyman, began his forty-year career as president of Harvard, where he moved energetically to increase the flexibility of the system and to make it more responsive to the practical needs of the students and the national community.

Scientists replaced clergymen in other of the older institutions, and were hired to launch new enterprises, including Clark University, Johns Hopkins, and Stanford. These and other new institutions of higher learning, such as Vassar, Vanderbilt, and the University of Chicago, were founded on the basis of endowments by businessmen; and the prestige of the business community, along with its money, was counted on the side of science-oriented higher education against clerical opposition.

From the seventies on, there was ruthless competition among college presidents for top faculty members, for there were not enough American scholars to go around, who had the training and competence to meet European standards. In order to entice these scholars and then keep them, it was absolutely essential to give them academic freedom. Students at the good American universities at the turn of the century were therefore exposed to an authorized freedom of expression such as was entirely new to their experience.

Led by Johns Hopkins, the new university graduate schools turned out scholars with doctor's degrees to meet their own demands. Initially, European training was considered almost essential for top appointments; but by the turn of the century American-trained scholars, especially in the social sciences, had already established the reputation of the American Ph.D. degree. Among the remarkable early group of graduate students at Johns Hopkins were John Dewey, Frederick Jackson Turner, John Franklin Jameson, Woodrow Wilson, John R. Commons, Josiah Royce, Charles M. Andrews, and Albion Small.

Although prestige was highest in the physical and biological sciences, progress was less impressive in these areas than it was in the social sciences and in philosophy and psychology. There were a few great names in American science—J. Willard Gibbs at Yale, Henry A. Rowland at Johns Hopkins, A. A. Michelson at the University of Chicago, and Theodore W. Richards at Harvard—and there was an ambitious subdividing and proliferation of the sciences into more and more specialized departments. Nevertheless, American universities at the turn of the century were very inferior in the sciences to European universities, and they were only beginning to achieve a status of respectable comparison with the European universities by the First World War.

Widespread acceptance of evolutionary biology led to widespread discussion of theories of morals, which some thought could now be placed on a scientific basis. Darwin himself, in *Descent of Man,* took up the subject of ethics, attributing the moral sense in man to man's social instincts, which man shared with other animals. Where man acted against this instinct, he experienced a sense of dissatisfaction. These experiences, "organized and consolidated through all past experiences of the human race, have been producing corresponding nervous modifications, which, by continuing transmission and accumulation, have become in us certain faculties of moral intuition."

Herbert Spencer considered the same question in *Data of Ethics,* published in 1879, and he arrived at an ethical system which subordinated morality to his great principle of life, "survival of the fittest." Survival is the main purpose of life, Spencer argued, and improvement in society as well as in species results from this struggle. Therefore good conduct is that which promotes survival, and bad conduct that which hinders or destroys life; "and in so implying that life is a blessing and not a curse, we are inevitably asserting that conduct is good and bad according as its total effects are pleasurable or painful." Spencer's argument was naturalistic, but it was accepted by some religious writers with religious emendations.

Evolutionary biology most obviously led to the absolute rejection of morality as having no possibility of existence in a world where actions were no more than processes of nature. "No man's conduct is his," wrote Antonio Llano in the *Philosophical Review* in 1896. "It is simply a manifestation of the way in which the universe exists and moves." Among the naturalistic philosophers who opposed their ideas to this blanket rejection of morality, John Dewey emerged at the turn of the century as the dominant figure.

It was impossible, Dewey argued, to observe the endlessly marvelous universe, including man, with his ability to observe the past work toward the future, as the result either of chance or of necessity. This did not, however, lead him, as it led Asa Gray, to the conclusion that it all must be the result of design. Such an argument failed to account for the wastefulness of nature, and for the fact that useless variations are "sifted out simply by the stress of the conditions of struggle for existence."

Philosophy had always been grounded upon the belief in the existence of absolutes, which were assumed to be superior to the impermanent and changing conditions of life. Evolutionary biology, however, demonstrated the impossibility of perceiving these absolutes, even if they might exist. Dewey pointed out that

to idealize and rationalize the universe at large is after all a confession of inability to master the courses of things that specifically concern us. . . . But if insight into specific conditions of value and into specific consequences of ideas is possible, philosophy must in time become a method of locating and interpreting the more serious of the conflicts that occur in life, and a method of projecting ways for dealing with them: a method of moral and political diagnosis and prognosis.

The business of the moralist is to solve problems, not to seek truths; and man is provided, by his possession of historical knowledge, with what Dewey called the genetic method. History "is a process that reveals to us the conditions under which moral practices and ideals have originated. . . . In seeing where they came from, in what situations they arose, we see their significance." The good way of doing things to achieve desired ends for society may be constructed from past experience. Distinguishing his ideas from those of the deterministic naturalists, Dewey explained that "the empirical method holds that the belief or idea is generated by a process of repetition or cumulation; the genetic method by a process of adjustment."

Darwinian biology, Dewey pointed out, had taken morals off "the track which it dared not leave for nigh twenty-five hundred years: search for the final good, and for the single moral force." Dewey's alternative genetic method for solving moral problems might be viewed as conservative in its reliance upon past experience; but it was natural that to young intellectuals emerging from college at the opening of the twentieth century, the appeal of Dewey was based less upon his historical method and his emphasis upon responsibility to society than it was upon the liberation which Dewey proclaimed from blind duty to obey traditional morality and particular class codes of conduct.

Pragmatism is the term which is used to identify the philosophical school of which Dewey and William James were the leading spokesmen. These two men were not in entire accord, however, either with each other or with still others who were more or less grouped within the same school. Dewey chose to separate his philosophy under the title of instrumentalism, whereas James distinguished his as radical empiricism. It was not that the two philosophies conflicted, but rather that they operated on different levels, Dewey thinking characteristically in terms of society and James in terms of individual.

As a philosopher, James was concerned with the nature of truth and especially the nature of religious truth in a world devoid of absolutes. Himself a trained scientist and at one time professor of anatomy, James derived his concept of truth from the scientific experimental method. An idea was provisionally true or false according to whether the use of the idea was followed by the intended consequences. Truth was not inherent in the idea itself. Truths were always provisional. *"Theories thus become instruments, not answers to enigmas, in which we rest."*

James made much of the tough-mindedness of the pragmatist, who "turns towards concreteness and adequacy, towards facts, towards action and towards power . . . as against dogma, artificiality and the pretense of finality in truth." James was motivated, however, by a tender-minded concern for the spiritual well-being of men and women, and almost all of his philosophical writings are concerned to some extent at least with religious problems. He was as deeply respectful of the mystical experiences arising out of seances and ghost-haunted surroundings as he was with those that followed from conventionally accepted religious practices. For him the test of the truth of a religious experience was in all cases the same.

If theological ideas prove to have a value for concrete life, they will be true, for pragmatism, in the sense of being good for so much. For how much more they are true, will depend entirely on their relations to the other truths that also have to be acknowledged.

The great store that James placed on spiritual well-being made him welcome among many religious leaders, but others failed to see the advantage of accepting his left-handed assistance. They were not willing to be grouped with mediums and astrologers, nor to accept the test of a pudding as applicable in the realm of religion. By his pragmatic method of argument James was reducing the church to a public utility and faith to a creature comfort. Dewey was even worse, from the orthodox religious point of view, in treating Christianity as a transitory phenomenon which was already passing away.

In transforming man from the image of God to a member of the animal kingdom, the theory of evolution converted psychology from a branch of theology to a branch of the biological sciences. In the United States, psychology was founded as a laboratory science by William James at Harvard in the 1870's, and James's *Principles of Psychology,* which appeared in 1890, was a very influential work with a wide audience. More influential from the point of view of American psychology as an academic discipline, however, was the experimental laboratory founded by Wilhelm Wundt in Leipzig in 1879, where a number of American scholars received their training. For Wundt, psychology was the study of the conscious mind, chiefly by means of introspection and experimentation. Wundt represented the self-conscious scientism of a discipline that was combating theological claims to authority over human psychology on grounds, which Wundt would not accept, that the immortal soul was involved.

G. Stanley Hall trained with Wundt in experimental psychology, at the time Wundt organized his laboratory, as well as with Helmholtz in physics and Ludwig in physiology. On his return to America he accepted a position at Johns Hopkins, where he taught a number of leading scholars of the next generation. Hall was too independent-minded to become Wundt's recognized disciple in America, however, and that position was assumed by Bradford Titchener. An English student of Wundt's, Edward Bradford Titchener, became director of the psychology laboratory at Cornell in 1892, and from that time until his death in 1927 he served as the acknowledged guardian of experimental psychology in its most pedantic and old-fashioned form against deviators in its ranks. Titchener rigidly limited the area of investigation to the generalized operation of the human mind, and he relied upon his mechanical equipment to measure sensation and perception. He was determined to maintain psychology as a pure science dealing with the central nervous system in isolation. "There is," wrote William James, "little of the grand style about these new prism, pendulum, and chronograph-philosophers. They mean business and not chivalry." They therefore did little to interest or influence society at large.

The history of psychology as an academic discipline has been that of one long running battle between structuralists and functionalists, pure and applied scientists, human and animal psychologists, animists, behaviorists, gestaltists, and Freudians, and then within the groupings, neobehaviorists and neo-Freudians, and so on. The first major struggle was between the structuralists, led by Titchener, and the functionalists, who were centered in the University of Chicago and spoken for chiefly by James R. Angell and John Dewey.

The functionalists rejected the idea that the mind or consciousness could be studied in isolation. Conscious thought, or stimulus, was not an entity separate from the accompanying action, or response. The boy who sees the apple and picks it up is not performing two separate processes: the sensory one of seeing and the motor one of picking up the apple. The whole activity is one continuous process. This conception of continuity between thought and action took psychology out of the laboratory and into the world. It was an argument for applied psychology which Dewey demonstrated in practice in his laboratory school. It led to the rise of social psychology, and—to the considerable disgust of its formulators—it led directly to the rise of Watsonian behaviorism.

The functionalists had prepared the way for behaviorism with their repudiation of the idea of consciousness as a distinct entity. William James wrote that consciousness "is the name of a nonentity, and has no right to a place among first principles. Those who still cling to it are clinging to a mere echo, the faint rumor left behind by the disappearing 'soul' upon the air of philosophy." The functionalists had eliminated the distinction between mind and matter; Watson got rid of the mind altogether.

Behaviorism began with animal psychology, and the leading pioneer figure in American animal psychology was James's student, Edward L. Thorndike of Columbia, whose *Animal Intelligence* appeared in 1898. Thorndike interpreted the behavior of animals, not in terms of ideas, but in terms of stimulus and response. He experimented in strengthening the bonds between specific stimuli and responses through application of the laws of exercise and effect. The one law calls for frequent and vigorous exercise of the bond between stimulus and response; the second affirms that bonds are strengthened or weakened according to whether the responses lead to satisfying states or to the opposite. Thorndike extended the application of his thesis to human intelligence, and amid continuing controversy, he remained the leading advocate of mechanistic educational methods.

John B. Watson, founder of the behaviorist school, received his doctor's degree in psychology in 1903 from the University of Chicago, where he had studied under Angell and Dewey. He became a professor at Johns Hopkins, and in 1915 was elected president of the American Psychological Association, in spite of the fact that his research had been mainly in the area of animal psychology, which was looked somewhat down upon in the profession and which was ruled out of psychology altogether by Titchener. Watson asserted that all psychology, so far as it was a legitimate science, was animal psychology, whether it dealt with men or mice; and in the 1920's he was hugely successful in persuading literate Americans out of their conscious minds, just as many had already been persuaded out of their immortal souls.

Watson presented his own particular views in 1913 in two articles: "Psychology as the Behaviorist Views It" and "The Image and Affection in Behavior." In the latter article he incorporated images into his system as implied language responses and reduced human affection to reactions controlled by tumescence and detumescence of the genitals. His book *Behavior* (1914) was a plea for the validity of animal psychology. His *Psychology from the Standpoint of a Behaviorist* (1919) extended the principles of animal psychology to human psychology and declared them to be the only valid principles of psychology. In 1925 his *Behaviorism* discarded heredity as a factor in psychology and largely dismissed instincts from consideration. It also paid greater attention to the practical applications of psychology than his earlier studies had. In 1919 Watson was asked to leave the Johns Hopkins faculty, and he had since then been employed as vice president of a major advertising firm.

Man, the increasingly messianic Watson said, is a machine and nothing more. All human functions, including thinking, are capable of being observed and controlled scientifically, and all can be interpreted scientifically in terms of stimulus and response. It was a practical possibility so to control the training of a child as to determine exactly the adult he would become. Watson boasted that he could take babies, regardless of hereditary background, and bring up one to be a doctor, another a lawyer, another a salesman, and another a sailor by special training patterns suited to each occupation.

....

Titchener said that what Watson was doing might be interesting, but it was not psychology. Watson said that Titchener's psychology was pseudoscience. A. A. Roback, Harvard psychologist and historian of American psychology, described Watson's behaviorism as "Psychology Out of Its Mind," and was revolted by the obligation to treat it historically as a branch of psychology. These quarrels were nevertheless all in the family, at least until Watson left university life for the advertising business. They were the arguments of academicians over conflicting interpretations of what all of them agreed was a branch of knowledge, to be investigated through experimentation and lectured upon in the classroom.

In 1909, however, a stranger joined the family circle when Sigmund Freud traveled to America to deliver a series of five lectures on psychoanalysis in commemoration of the twentieth anniversary of the founding of Clark University. Psychoanalysis—Watson called it demonology—was not only a concept alien to all American schools of psychology; it was no laboratory science at all; yet its impact upon American psychology, as upon almost all areas of American thought, was swift and profound.

Very surprisingly, Freud received his first academic recognition in what he called "prudish America." He had originally declined the American invitation, which included only traveling expenses, with the typically European comment that "America should bring in money, not cost money." When the occasion for the lectures happened to be postponed to a time more convenient for him, however, he accepted. His host, G. Stanley Hall, founder and president of Clark University, appears to have been hardly more aware of the importance of the event than Freud was. Hall, while thoroughly familiar with and influenced by Freud's work, was not a Freudian. He simply appreciated Freud as a brilliant and original investigator whom American scholars would do well to know more about. Hall also invited Freud's colleague, Carl Jung, as well as leading American scholars in associated areas, including the psychoanalyst A. A. Brill, the neurologist James J. Putnam, the anthropologist Franz Boas, and the psychologists William James and Bradford Titchener.

It was a full-dress affair; and the much impressed Freud, in thanking the university for conferring an honorary doctorate upon him, noted the fact that "this is the first official recognition of our endeavors." The five lectures he delivered for the occasion did much to make Freudians of American intellectuals. Freud never did know what to make of this landmark in his career. On the one hand, he declared, "America is a mistake; a gigantic mistake, it is true, but none the less a mistake"; on the other, "Who would have known that over there in America, only an hour away from Boston, there was a respectable old gentleman waiting impatiently for the next number of the *Jahrbuch,* reading and understanding it all, and who would then, as he expressed it himself, 'ring the bells for us?' "

Two outstanding reasons are sufficient to account for the rejection of Freud's theories by the European scientific fraternity up to the time of his American lectures, aside from the startling novelty of them. To begin with, they were ideas that Freud had developed simply on the basis of his experience in dealing with emotionally disturbed patients for a quarter of a century. They had not been arrived at by scientific methods of investigation, and they were not subject to the experimental method of proof. They were ideas involving intuition and subjective judgments, which could not be communicated as could other scientific ideas. "I naturally cannot foretell what degree of understanding of psychoanalysis you may gain from my lectures," Freud declared, "but I can at least assure you that by attending them you will not have learnt how to conduct a psycho-analytic investigation, nor how to carry out a psycho-analytic treatment."

Then there was the ugly head of sex, rearing itself in the unconscious mind, and repudiating civilized values. "Society," said Freud, "can conceive of no more powerful menace to its culture than would arise from the liberation of the sexual impulses and a return of them to their original goal." It was therefore natural, he concluded, for society to resort to diverting attention from these impulses, refusing to admit the omnipresent evidence of their existence, and branding the revelations of psychoanalysis as aesthetically offensive, morally reprehensible, or dangerous.

Most shocking of all to Americans was Freud's contention that the root of the evil was in the repression by civilized society of sexual impulses of infants, which were thus driven to lurk in the unconscious mind in a perpetual state of frustration, feverishly desiring to get out and cause trouble. It was sound American doctrine that infants were imps of Satan, but the idea of them as being impelled by sex urges directed toward their parents was not. Homosexuality was at the time openly being lampooned in the *Police Gazette,* but the idea of homosexual tendencies as being normal characteristics of adolescence was new to Americans.

Freud introduced his American listeners for the first time to the idea of the unconscious libido, forever striving against the conscious mind and against a censor that intervened between the two. He introduced them to the idea of the significance of dreams as symbolic expressions by the unconscious libido, of ideas the conscious mind had repressed. "The theory of repression," Americans learned, "is the main pillar upon which rests the edifice of psychoanalysis."

Freud's colleague, Carl Jung, in the years after he and Freud traveled to the Clark celebration together, became the leading deviationist from Freud's circle. Rejecting sex as the one overridingly important unconscious impulse, Jung posited in its place a generalized vital force, formed out of the universal and primitive experience of the race. Jung was chiefly influential among Americans for his concept of two psychological types: the extrovert and the introvert—the one directed predominantly by his feelings, and the other by his thought. As popularly interpreted in Jazz Age America, the extrovert was an emancipated and therefore admirable being, although this was not quite the meaning Jung had in mind.

Freud's Clark University lectures were published in English in 1910, and in 1913, A. A. Brill began to translate Freud's major writings for American audiences. Young American intellectuals went Freudian as fast as they could go. According to Alfred Booth Kuttner, who translated Freud's *Interpretation of Dreams,* there were not a half dozen qualified analysts in America in the early years, but there were hundreds in New York City alone who were convinced they were qualified for practice. Kuttner introduced Walter Lippmann, just out of Harvard, to Freudianism, in time for Lippmann to incorporate the new ideas into his *Preface to Politics* in 1912. Lippmann introduced A. A. Brill to Greenwich Village intellectuals, who were eagerly interested and already well informed.

According to Floyd Dell, by 1914 there were about a half dozen of the Greenwich Village group "who knew a good deal about psychoanalysis, and a score or so more who were familiar enough with the terms to use them in bandinage. . . . Everyone at that time who knew about psychoanalysis was a sort of missionary on the subject, and nobody could be around Greenwich Village without hearing a lot about it." The wealthy Bohemian Mabel Dodge went expansively from the psychiatrist Bernard Sachs to the psychoanalysts Smith Jelliffe and A. A. Brill, but that was much more than her Village acquaintances could afford. Max Eastman, after a period of treatment under Jelliffe, turned to self-analysis; others like Dell and Hutchins Hapgood read what they could find and went into self-analysis from the first. Hapgood later recalled that

psychoanalysis had been overdone to such an extent that nobody could say anything about a dream, no matter how colorless it was, without his friends' winking at one another and wondering how he could have been so indiscreet. Freud's scientific imagination certainly enriched the field of psychology and was a great moment in our knowledge of the unconscious. But every Tom, Dick, and Harry in those days was misinterpreting and misapplying the general idea underlying analysis.

Freud was accused of fostering sexual license; but the cause of sex freedom owed little to Freud so far as the Greenwich Village intellectuals were concerned. They were already familiar, at least at second hand, with the writings on sex of Havelock Ellis and Richard von Krafft- Ebing; Ellen Key's appeal for free love, *The Century of the Child,* was published in America in 1909 and Edward Carpenter's *Love's Coming of Age* in 1911, both of them reaching a wide audience.

Comstock had been effective in suppressing books on sexology; but prior to the Comstock law, books on free love had circulated openly, such as *Cupid's Yokes,* sponsored by the reformer D. M. Bennett, whom Comstock had sent to prison for distributing the book. *The Truth About Love, A Proposed Sexual Morality* had appeared in 1872, arguing that sex "is the great overmastering fact of all our lives, disguise it as we may," and that "amative passion is a healthful act, and therefore, speaking physically, a moral act." It called upon America to "recognize as legitimate the polyandry and polygamy of the nineteenth century," and argued for a state where "women who follow the business of prostitution are regarded as satisfying a great social need, and are pursuing a vocation as legitimate as that of milliners."

Sex freedom was already an article of faith for Greenwich Villagers at the time they became aware of Freudian psychology, but Freudianism provided lovers with an intellectual basis for their relationship and a system for discussing it objectively. More than that, Freudianism provided the young rebel against the Protestant Republic with a system of rules to clarify the nature of his or her alienation from father, mother, church, and society. It was an infallible means by which the young rebel could intellectualize himself to his own satisfaction, and it provided a lingua franca that admitted him to an esoteric band of rebels against the Protestant Republic.

Unlike Marxism, which only a few young old-stock American intellectuals managed to get any real feeling for, Freudianism found ready acceptance among the descendants of Puritans, being appreciated as a deterministic countersystem to Calvinism. Freudianism was taken up by many besides Bohemian intellectuals, including a good many ministers, who incorporated aspects of it into their own Christian doctrines. Psychologists, like ministers, accepted aspects of it selectively, and so did sociologists and social workers and artists and writers. Freud's influence upon American thought was pervasive and almost immediate. Darwinian biology had been accepted by many as a refutation of the traditional Christian concept of man; Freudian psychology was grasped as an alternative conception that replaced the soul with the id and provided a naturalistic substitute for religious belief.

....

At the time of the Darwinian revolution in higher learning the field of history had enjoyed high prestige in America as a branch of literature. Included among America's outstanding men of letters were the historians George Bancroft, Francis Parkman, John Lothrop Motley, and William H. Prescott. These scholars enjoyed international reputations, as well as a wide following among the well-educated reading public. They dealt with history as narrative, to be read for pleasure and for general knowledge, rather than as a subject to be studied in the classroom. They were nonacademic men.

As an academic field of study in the reconstituted science-oriented curriculum of the late nineteenth century, history was accorded equally high prestige in America. Scientific historians, trained in the German seminar system, returned to take up their duties in the American universities—Herbert Baxter Adams at Johns Hopkins, John Burgess at Columbia, Henry Adams at Harvard—and to train a generation of American scholars in the scientific method. The American Historical Association, founded in 1884, was the first professional organization among the social scientists, followed a year later by the American Economic Association. Literary history was condemned by the scientific historians as lacking in adequate scholarly standards, and its day in America was over. The AHA, meanwhile, became the nursery of the social scientists, until economics, anthropology, sociology, and political science branched out on their own. The American Sociological Society was not founded until 1905.

There were, however, serious disadvantages to the scientific discipline of history from an American point of view, which were related to the German orientation of American historical scholarship, and these disadvantages tended to prevent scientific history from commanding the influence in American society that literary history had formerly enjoyed. Scientific history had emerged in Germany in the context of German national aspirations. Scientific history was, by definition, the study of the political development of nations—a development that was conceived as an organic evolutionary development. The German nation did not exist as a unified political entity, but Germanic political institutions existed together with a racially deterministic germ theory to explain them. In America, scientific history became burdened with this Germanic germ theory.

The germ theory held that the political character of every folk or nation was racially determined and that the Germanic folk, in particular, possessed a strong racial propensity for self-government. German historians traced the origins of self-government to the tribal system of the ancient Germans, and they traced the dispersion of these germs of self-government as they were carried away from the Germanic forests: the Angles and Saxons carried them to Britain and eventually to America. Most American historians at the turn of the twentieth century accepted the germ theory to some extent.

The germ theory was an extremely pessimistic and reactionary doctrine to hold in America at the opening of the twentieth century, when old-stock Americans were fast falling into a minority position in the nation as a whole, amid the New Immigration from southern and eastern Europe. The second generation of American scientific historians did not repudiate the germ theory, but they tended to ignore it. The evolutionary frontier environmentalism of Frederick Jackson Turner was more acceptably American than were those deferential academic comparisons with institutions of ancient and medieval Germany.

The Turner thesis was actually an American variation of the germ theory, which took the racial assumptions of the germ theory for granted and concentrated all of its attention on the American forest environment. The frontier community that Turner described remained essentially an American Markgenossenschaft, peopled by English, Scotch-Irish, German, and Scandinavian settlers, who were recognized as being descended from those same Germanic tribes which centuries earlier had worked out similar institutions along the Germanic forest frontiers. No thought was given to attempting to apply the Turner thesis to non-Germanic frontier societies in Latin America or in French Canada.

The American wilderness was the real hero of the Turner thesis, rather than the settlers who were shaped by it into a democratic society; and the thesis appealed particularly to Americans of Turner's own native Middle West, who, according to the thesis, had enjoyed the maximum advantage from the democratizing forest environment. Historians from Harvard and Yale were comparatively reluctant to accept Turner's argument (even though Harvard hired Turner away from Wisconsin). New England historians preferred to explain American institutions of self-government in terms of the English and Puritan and perhaps, but not necessarily, Germanic origins. But under any circumstances, the Turner thesis, like the original Germanic germ theory, was a pessimistic doctrine to hold at a time when, as Turner himself pointed out in his original essay on the subject, the forest environment that he was glorifying was in rapid process of being replaced by the urban environment of the machine age.

The historical profession as a whole tended to disapprove of such theorizing as Turner engaged in, and it tended increasingly to insist that scientific history must be limited severely to the collection and proper arrangement of historical facts in the form of monographs. This narrow view of history deprived it of any practical or theoretical purpose outside the profession, to the dissatisfaction of scholars in the allied social sciences as well as of some historians.

Henry Adams taught his seminar at Harvard according to the orthodox German scientific method, but, finding it unreasonably confining, he gave up his teaching to seek a more intellectually satisfactory basis for history as science. Abandoning biology for physics as the scientific basis for history, Adams arrived at a "Law of Acceleration" to give meaning to the course that history had taken in modern times.

"After 1500," Adams wrote, "the speed of progress so rapidly surpassed man's gait as to alarm everyone, as though it were the acceleration of a falling body. . . . Suddenly society felt itself dragged into situations altogether new and anarchic—situations which it could not affect, but which painfully affected it." After 1840 power derived from coal had doubled roughly every ten years. Scientists assumed that such acceleration could not last, but "radium fairly wakened men to the fact, long since evident, that force was inexhaustible."

By 1900, Adams continued, the pace of technological development already far outdistanced man's understanding, based upon experience. Adams disclaimed any responsibility, as a historian, for dealing with the problem, for "he had never been able to acquire knowledge, still less to impart it; and if he had, at times, felt serious differences with the American of the nineteenth century, he felt none with the American of the Twentieth." For this "new American—the child of incalculable coal power, chemical power, electric power, and radiating energy, as well as of new forces yet undetermined—the historian asked no longer to be teacher or even friend; he asked only to be a pupil and promised to be docile."

Perhaps because he had no children of his own, Adams was an early discoverer of this essentially twentieth-century phenomenon, this "new American," the representative of the younger generation of the moment, who has already learned from his own fresh experience many things that his older teacher will never come to understand.

History for Adams had become the conceptualization of his sense of alienation from society, and on this basis, Adams' autobiography, containing his theory of history, particularly influenced the Lost Generation of the 1920's when it was posthumously published after World War I. Meanwhile, younger historians who remained within the academic profession became restive against the academic science of history, which was content to be so irrelevant to its own time. What these historians proposed as "the new history" was progressive history in the same sense that what Dewey was advocating in education was progressive education. Truly scientific history, Carl Becker and James Harvey Robinson and Charles Beard and others argued, was not merely the chronology of events of the past, however systematically researched and arranged in order. Truly scientific history consisted of the application of what Dewey called the genetic method, the study of present social problems as well as political institutions by discovering their origins and their development to the present.

By far the most influential work of the new history was Charles Beard's attack on the founding fathers, *An Economic Interpretation of the Constitution*. Beard's monograph consisted principally of an impressively interminable list of the private holdings of each member of the Constitutional Convention in money, public securities, manufactures, and shipping. He concluded that "the members of the Philadelphia Convention . . . were, with a few exceptions, immediately, directly, and personally interested in, and desired economic advantages from the establishment of the new system," and that "the Constitution was essentially an economic document based upon the concept that the fundamental private rights of property are anterior to government and morally beyond the reach of popular majorities."

So far as American historiography is concerned, Beard effectively laid the basis for economic determinism and for the theme of class struggle in American history. The key to the enduring influence of his *Economic Interpretation of the Constitution* was his use of the scientific historical method to present his evidence without committing himself to the causal relationships that the arrangement of his evidence implied. Marxism was unacceptably un-American, and Beard himself rejected it, but his own similar approach has proved a viable alternative to Marxism down to the present generation of "New Left historians."

The disciplines of the social sciences were still loosely defined, and Beard was probably more accurately classifiable, on the basis of his *Economic Interpretation,* as a political scientist than as a historian. Certainly the activist nature of his writings allied him with the nonhistorians, for among economists and sociologists and anthropologists there was an increasing criticism of the nonanalytical and nonactivist orientation of the scientific historians.

The American Economic Association was founded by John R. Commons, Richard T. Ely, and others explicitly as a vehicle for evolutionary economic reform against the conservatism of classical economics. Similarly the American Sociological Society, founded in 1905, represented the reform Darwinism of its first president, Lester Ward. These economists and sociologists were moralistic evolutionists, seeking to guide a continually changing society according to humanistically defensible purposes.

The field of cultural anthropology was established by Franz Boas, whose most significant research was with immigrants and the children of immigrants, demonstrating by the extraordinary physical contrasts between the generations the importance of environment to physical characteristics. Boas's research established the impossibility of defining race scientifically by cephalic index, skin pigmentation, kinkiness of hair, or any other physical trait offered by the racial theorists. Boas also pioneered in research in the cultural anthropology of the American Negro. He was the most influential intellectual of his age in combating racist doctrines, and his students—including Ruth Benedict, Margaret Mead, and Melville Herskovitz—continued to extend the influence of Boas in this area after his death.

Among the social scientists of the age, none has been more enduringly influential than Thorstein Veblen and none is more difficult to classify as to professional discipline. As was true of the one of his teachers who most evidently influenced his thought, the conservative Social Darwinist William Graham Sumner, Veblen was at the same time an economist, a sociologist, and an anthropologist. Where Sumner's style was blunt and didactic, however, Veblen's was convoluted and noncommittal. Whether Veblen was a reformer or a cynic or a disinterested scientist is not altogether clear from his writings. It is, however, clear from his writings, that he was among the most thoroughgoing environmental and biological determinists of the Darwinian era. Henry George, Edward Bellamy, and Henry Demarest Lloyd, had all shared an unquestioning faith in technology as the way to man's salvation; and the leading critics of Veblen's day, including Beard and Dewey and Herbert Croly, and all the muckrakers, continued to share this faith in technology while denouncing the evils of business. The first American work of any considerable influence to question this American faith in technology was Veblen's *Theory of Business Enterprise,* published in 1904.

The controlling principle in an industrial society, Veblen argued, was the "machine process," which applied not only to the operation of factories, but also to the materials that went into them and the finished goods that came out of them. "As regards the mass of civilized mankind," Veblen wrote, "the idiosyncracies of the individual consumers are required to conform to the uniform gradations imposed upon consumable goods. . . . Machine production leads to standardization of services as well as of goods. . . . So, also, amusements and diversions, much of the current amenities of life, are organized into a more or less sweeping process."

Different industries were necessarily interrelated, and therefore solidarity of management as well as standardization of products became essential. Not only did the workman have to conform to the machine process; his intellectual life also became standardized in terms of the mechanical process as well. "The machine throws out anthropomorphic habits of thought" and replaces them with the mechanical metaphysics of direct cause and effect. The skilled mechanical class bore the most "unmitigated impact" of the machine process; but the intellectual and spiritual training of the machine was widespread, leaving but a small portion of the community untouched.

The machine process, Veblen argued, promoted consumption in place of saving among those whom it controlled, while "the acquisition of property is ceasing to appeal to them as a natural, self-evident source of comfort and strength." The mechanical classes lacked the ability to express themselves in terms of new conventions or myths or to adapt old ones to their spiritual needs. "Nor do they instinctively feel themselves to be sinners by virtue of a conventional hereditary taint or obliquity. . . . They are in danger of losing the point of view of sin," in the course of serving a master who "is no respecter of persons and knows neither morality nor dignity nor prescriptive right, divine or human."

If Veblen was to be believed, an evolution in morals was occurring, marked by a "weakening sense of conviction, allegiance or piety toward the received institutions" of home, church, and state. By Veblen's reasoning it was hopeless to expect the schools to strengthen the allegiance of youth to "the received institutions," because the schools were functional agencies of the machine process. Veblen was not to be believed by Progressive America, however, for the conviction prevailed among idealistic educational reformers that the future would be won or lost in the public schools of the nation.

....

It was somewhere around the turn of the twentieth century that the younger generation made its appearance in American history as the vanguard of the future, rather than simply as the young people who were being brought up to follow in their parents' footsteps. For moral absolutists urging a return to the ways of the fathers as well as for moral relativists awaiting a brave new world, youth acquired a significance it had never had before. Reactionaries as well as radicals were conscious that the world was changing before their eyes, and few could any longer believe that the lessons of the past were entirely adequate for life in the present and the future. Those who were most zealously opposed to change and adamant against evolution found themselves driven to endorsing novel expedients, prohibition and fundamentalism, to achieve the continuation of the "Bands of Hope" to the future. Education of youth consequently came to be seen in a new light as the battle field for the future.

American civilization, being a business civilization, public education has always, to some extent, been a reflection of business needs. As Jane Addams wrote in her *Democracy and Social Ethics* (1902),

> The business man has, of course, not said to himself: "I will have the public school train office boys and clerks for me, so that I may have them cheap," but he has thought, and sometimes said, "Teach the children to write legibly, and to figure accurately and quickly; to acquire habits of punctuality and order; to be prompt to obey and not question why; and you will fit them to make their way in the world as I have made mine!"

Horace Mann was an idealist who created a public school system in order to form a sure basis for democracy and morality, but he was also a realist who secured his system by attaching it to the interests of the business community.

During the late nineteenth century the public school system expanded together with the expansion of industry; and to the extent that it developed an articulate philosophy, it was the philosophy of the U.S. Commissioner of Education, William T. Harris. Harris was a Hegelian idealist who conceived of the public schools as serving the purpose of national progress, which, in America, was business progress. As a practical matter, this duty involved meeting business standards that were, in the area of education, rigid and not high. Even after the business world had come to feel the need for trained engineers and scientists, its overall needs continued to be answered by a labor pool with an average mastery of McGuffey's Fourth Reader at the most. In the cities the additional need was increasingly felt to train immigrant children to be good Americans, but this was treated as a matter of simple indoctrination. Primary education was considered to consist of the traditional reading, writing, and arithmetic, which normal students could be expected to absorb and which would equip them for the normal occupational pursuits.

In 1892 *Forum* magazine published a series of articles exposing American public education as consisting of sterile memorization and recitation. The age of progressive education may be said to date from this series. Dedicated and influential reformers had been active in the field before them, but now, with this series, national attention was for the first time focused on the problem. This national interest continued through the Progressive era and resulted in sweeping and permanent revisions in American public education as a whole.

Progressive education was characteristically child-centered rather than course-centered; and it characteristically considered education to be a part of the evolutionary social process rather than merely a specific series of skills to be acquired by everybody everywhere, generation after generation. Society being in a continual state of change, it was the responsibility of the school to prepare the oncoming generations to adapt to changing conditions, and, democratic progress being an avowed objective of public education, the students should be taught to think for themselves and not be indoctrinated.

Among leading figures in the early history of progressive education, the most rigorous evolutionist was the Johns Hopkins professor and later president of Clark University, G. Stanley Hall, who was also the most forcefully effective spokesman for the argument that the needs of the child, both in terms of his environment and in terms of the condition of childhood itself, should determine the character of his education. It should not be the responsibility of the child to adapt to the arbitrary standards of the school, Hall argued; it should be the responsibility of the school to adapt to the special needs of the child and the community. "The shift," writes Lawrence A. Cremin,

was truly copernican, its effects, legion. On the one hand, it hastened the acceptance of academic studies long barred from the school by reason of traditions, custom, or simple apathy. On the other hand, it opened the pedagogical floodgates to every manner of activity, trivial as well as useful, that seemed in some way to minister to "the needs of the children." Reformers had a field day, as did sentimentalists, and American schools were never the same again.

Hall subscribed to the theory that the child, in the course of his development, recapitulates the evolution of the race from presavagery to civilization, and he believed that children should be given the opportunity to express these different stages of their development.

Their lives should be full of activity, and in the course of their development they should be under the disciplined instruction of someone who is trained to cope with the developmental needs of the child. Hall specialized in the study of adolescence; his voluminous two-volume study, *Adolescence,* which appeared in 1904, remained the basic source for the next generation. More than any other scholar, he created a national awareness of adolescence as a crucial stage in human development.

For Hall, as for other educational reformers, urbanization was the great challenge the schools faced, and Hall's own rural background united with his acceptance of the recapitulation theory to predispose him against the city as a favorable environment for childhood. "Increasing urban life," he wrote in *Adolescence,*

with its temptations, prematurities, sedentary occupations, and passive stimuli just when an active, objective life is most needed, early emancipation and a lessening sense for both duty and discipline, the haste to know and do all befitting man's estate before its time, the mad rush for sudden wealth and the reckless fashions set by its gilded youth—all these lack some of the regulatives they still have in older lands with more conservative traditions.

He added that he was, nevertheless, optimistic about the future, "not merely because an evolutionist must hold that the best and not the worst will survive and prevail," but also because "the very fact that we think we are young will make the faith in our future curative," in encouraging the better preparation of youth "for helping humanity on to a higher stage." Typical of his time and place in equating evolution with human progress and in the racial orientation of his ideas, Hall was unusually perceptive regarding the actual process of social evolution which was occurring in urban America of his time and which, he argued with striking originality, was chiefly occurring in each generation during the period of adolescence.

And although he was the most thoroughgoing of evolutionists among the educators, that did not lead him to the conclusion that the adaptation of youth to urban conditions represented evolution, and therefore progress. To Hall, social evolution encompassed the entire history of the human species, and urban life was a shock to a human system that had been in gradual course of development for hundreds of thousands of years. Hall's racial ideas have served to lessen his standing in mid-twentieth-century America, and the originality and pertinence of his social ideas as well as his great influence on America have been insufficiently appreciated. Hall was both an influential pioneer in the "Century of the Child" and a realistic analyst of social ills inherent in the urban, youth-oriented America of the future.

John Dewey remains the most famous name in progressive education; but his influence was greater with intellectuals than with educators, and his practical influence on American education was not commensurate with his prominence as a scholar. His brief *The School and Society*, which established his name in the field of education when it appeared in 1899, indicates why this was so. Although based upon Dewey's own practical experience in directing the University of Chicago laboratory school, it is a philosophical rather than a practical discussion, for all of its use of practical examples from Dewey's laboratory school experience. The essay was prepared in the first place as a series of lectures for the parents and patrons of the laboratory school; and Dewey's influence continued to be with the intelligent reading public rather than particularly with teachers and school administrators, in spite of later official endorsements by educators.

Like Hall, who had been Dewey's instructor at Johns Hopkins, Dewey was critical of traditional education for placing the "center of gravity outside the child" and for failing to relate education to the life of the community which the child shared. With Dewey, progressive education became children-centered rather than child-centered. The school should be an "embryonic community," which would reflect the life of the larger community. But unlike Hall, Dewey argued that the embryo community should be more "worthy, lovely, and harmonious" than the society which produced it, and that it should serve as a positive instrument of progress to raise the level of society as a whole. This theme was carried through Dewey's later writings, including his major work, *Democracy and Education*, which appeared in 1916. The task was no less than "to shape the experiences of the young so that instead of reproducing current habits, better habits shall be formed, and thus the future adult society be an improvement on their own."

This view of education "as a constructive agency of improving society" associates Dewey's thinking with that of his behavioristic student, John B. Watson, who argued that "the universe will change if you bring up your children, not in the freedom of the libertine, but in behavioristic freedom. . . . Will not these children in turn, with their better ways of living and thinking, replace us as society, and in turn bring up" superior children, who would in turn bring up . . ., and so forth. Watson's line of argument represents the reduction to absurdity of Dewey's conception of education as an instrument of innovative social progress. This was the least defensible and most appealing aspect of Dewey's educational theory for Progressives.

Fulfillment of democracy was an abiding concern for Dewey, and so, therefore, was the struggle for a truly universal public educational system in an increasingly urbanized society. His own middle-class and rural background and optimistic nature appear, however, to have restrained Dewey from making a truly realistic appraisal of the problem. Ideally, he wrote in *School and Society,* "the school building has about it a natural environment. It ought to be in a garden, and the children from the garden would be led on to surrounding fields, and then into the wider country, with all its facts and forces." This natural setting from Dewey's ideal school in the industrial age indicates less willingness to confront the major social forces of the time than Hall exhibited.

By common consent, the most successful early practitioner of progressive education was Francis W. Parker, who developed a nationally renowned school system at Quincy, Massachusetts, in the 1870's and then transplanted it to the Cook County Normal School in Chicago, where it thrived from 1883 to 1899. He was the "father of progressive education" according to Dewey, while Hall made annual visits to Chicago "to set my educational watch," as he wrote Parker. Of his own system, Parker wrote, "I repeat that I am simply trying to apply well established principles of teaching. . . . The methods springing from them are found in the development of every child. They are used everywhere except in school."

In Parker's system, geography started with walks rather than maps, arithmetic with games rather than numbers, and reading with words and sentences rather than letters. Routine was avoided, and progress was maintained through the stimulated initiative of the students, in a school which was, as Parker wrote, "a model home, a complete community and embryonic democracy." Dewey was, of course, thoroughly familiar with Parker's Cook County School when he established his own laboratory school; and Dewey's educational theory became substantially the argument of an evolutionist for the methods employed by the transcendentalist Parker, whose sources of inspiration had been the European apostles of romantic childhood: Pestalozzi, Froebel, and Herbart.

The progressive school system that attracted the greatest attention during the Progressive era was that at Gary, Indiana, where a former student of Dewey's, William Wirt, was afforded the opportunity of creating an entirely new system for an entirely new industrial city, following the decision of U.S. Steel to build its main plant in the area southeast of Chicago. The Gary System was not only widely discussed but also copied in whole or in part by at least 200 other school systems in the nation. It combined students of all grades into embryonic communities that emphasized learning by doing rather than by classroom work. Its appeal to school boards around the country rested, in good measure, on its claim to making more efficient use of the entire plant than was possible in traditional systems.

With the close of the Progressive era, the interest of liberal intellectuals in progressive education declined, and the support of professional teachers' organizations increased; and with this change there was an increasing emphasis on efficiency and system. Nevertheless, the controversy that it started has continued ever since, and the contending forces have continued to be those who stand for objective morality on the one hand and those who believe, on the other hand, that times change and that moral standards must adjust to the changing conditions. What is always particularly at issue is that ever-oncoming younger generation, which emerged as an innovative force at about the time that progressive education became an issue and which has gone on since that time to play an increasingly disturbing and influential role in American society.

....

While the advocates of progressive education were attacking the prevailing pattern of public education as being little more than basic training for the armies of industry, advocates of reform in higher education were in some respects going in the opposite direction, and with much greater success. During the late nineteenth century the leading American colleges and universities had consciously divested themselves of their traditional and quasi-theological character and assumed the character of centers of scientific scholarship and of learned service institutions for an evolving industrial society.

The students had not been instrumental in bringing these reforms about, and their wishes and interests had not been the primary concern of the reformers. The European concept of academic freedom for students was not considered as valid for the American situation as was the European concept of academic freedom for professors, which was emphasized. Students were permitted to select some of their own courses as electives, and their courses went beyond mere memorization in most cases. But the master principle would always be as it had always been—that the college or university was *in loco parentis* to the student.

It was therefore serendipitous that one of the most significant outcomes of the revolution in higher education turned out to be the twentieth-century phenomenon, known as "college life," when the younger generation of the upper-middle classes discovered the opportunity on men's and women's and coeducational campuses of taking the lead in the revolution in morals that reached its climax in the 1920's.

In the mid-nineteenth century college life was not much to write home about and probably not much not to write home about. Class work was routine and undemanding, and authorized extracurricular activities consisted mainly of daily chapel attendance. Students as a group took part in sophmore-freshman tugs of war and a variety of larks and brawls which almost inevitably involved infractions of college rules. A comprehensive network of rules regulated college life, and among the commonest of student activities were those of trying to "bend" the college regulations as far as possible, without being disciplined.

Disciplinary action at Harvard and elsewhere in the mid-nineteenth century included the subtracting of points a student had earned for his classroom work. Class standing was thus based upon deportment among other things. This situation was naturally not permitted to continue when the religious orientation of the college curriculum was replaced by a more nearly scientific one. The revolution in higher education at the close of the century gave scholarly students much more to think about with respect to their class work, and it tended to give all students greater freedom to do as they pleased outside the class. American students responded to this greater freedom by developing extracurricular college activities into a major cultural influence nationally.

Intercollegiate football is registered by sports annalists as having been born with the Princeton-Rutgers game in 1869, at the time Charles Eliot became president of Harvard and Andrew D. White started Cornell. White turned down an invitation from the University of Michigan to participate in a football match, declaring by telegram, "I will not permit thirty men to travel four hundred miles merely to agitate a bag of wind." Within twenty years, however, Cornell was playing football with a dead earnestness that is indicated by the fact that it appointed as its team captain a man who had been the coach of the Syracuse team the year before. It was during the nineties, when Americans became noticeably more sports-minded generally, that football became big-time in the colleges.

Although football had been no part of the plan of the university-makers, it was in harmony with the ideal of soundness in body as well as mind. In some ways it helped out wonderfully from the administrative point of view. It was an extraordinarily effective means by which the old college try could be turned outward, away from the contest with college regulations and with the faculty. It also proved to be, past all comparison, the most effective means by which alumni support for the institution could be kept alive.

Intercollegiate athletics became officially recognized by American colleges in the nineties, and special regulations were drawn up among colleges, including rules limiting the number of professional players per team. In 1893 the Yale-Princeton Thanksgiving Day game jammed the New York hotels and threw the city into an uproar. Religious services were shortened in liberal churches that day to accommodate the fans. When women put in what appears to have been their first general attendance at football with the Yale-Princeton game in New Haven in 1885, football established itself as a heterosexual spectator sport.

The college girl appeared on the American scene simultaneously with the rise of college football. Coeducation had been begun by Oberlin and Antioch before the Civil War, and female seminaries had abounded, but Vassar in 1861 was the first women's college that was comparable in its academic standards and financial backing to the better men's colleges. Wellesley and Smith followed in the next decade, and Wisconsin and Michigan and other state universities went coeducational. Cornell was coeducational from the outset, while Harvard and Columbia fostered Radcliffe and Barnard, respectively, in the eighties.

The women's colleges were victories for the woman's rights movement, dedicated in general to making equal educational opportunities available to women and in particular to training teachers of future women and mothers of future generations. While higher education for men was becoming more practical in purpose, women's colleges were being instituted for purposes other than to train girls for the manly professions of law, medicine, engineering, or business. Their course offerings were more traditionally classical than those of the men's colleges, placing emphasis upon literature and the fine arts. The maintenance of culture in the nation was a responsibility the women's colleges assumed, but the dominant purpose was to do good in the world.

More than 70 percent of the first generation of Wellesley graduates became teachers, most of whom remained spinster teachers. Of all women college graduates to 1895, fewer than 30 percent were married, as compared with about 80 percent for the adult female population as a whole. These women were mainly from the upper-middle classes, in which spinsterhood was more prevalent than in the nation at large; they came with what they considered a higher purpose than motherhood in mind, even though no such higher purpose than motherhood was conventionally thought to exist. During the early years of coeducation, the sexes tended to keep their distance from each other. All authorities agreed that the effect of coeducation on the young men was a civilizing one, but the young men were said to resent the restraints that the presence of women placed on their conduct.

The Progressive era witnessed a transition in coeducational college life toward a greater intermixing of the sexes in a campus life that was influenced by Progressivism and by the woman suffrage movement and also by sororities, fraternities, weekend parties, football parties, the arrival of the automobile, and the outbreak of the "dance craze"—from the fox trot to the grizzly bear. By that time college, rather than finishing school, had become absolutely the thing for the well-bred girl to do if she showed any symptoms at all of serious-mindedness. And serious-mindedness in young women was more acceptable to college men in Progressive America than it had been in the Mauve Decade of the nineties; for it was a seriousness of purpose which much of the college generation of both sexes shared together: to liberate society, themselves certainly included, from the ancient regime of their Progressive parents.

Randolph Bourne explained how this college generation felt about its parents in an article, "This Older Generation," written for the *Atlantic* in 1915. Specifically he attacked "the mothers and fathers and uncles and aunts of the youth of both sexes between twenty and thirty." He derided their "devout belief in simple goodness" and their "belief that social ills may be cured by personal virtue." He observed that the older generation "never speaks of death—the suggestion makes it uncomfortable. It shies in panic at hints of sex-issues. . . . It seems singularly lacking in the psychological sense." In its secret heart the older generation continued to admire the notorious Victorian era. "How well we know the type of man of the older generation who has been doing good all his life! How his personality has thriven on it! How he has ceaselessly been storing away moral fat in every cranny of his soul! His goodness has been meat to him."

Hopefully, Bourne concluded, the same criticisms would not in turn be leveled at the generation for which he spoke, by the generation which it would raise. He believed that it might possibly not be so, for "it shall be given to us to lighten, cheer, and purify our 'younger generation,' even as our older had depressed and disintegrated us." Bourne's younger generation was confident that they could have it both ways: liberating themselves from their parents on the one hand and on the other, enjoying the satisfaction of seeing the younger generation that they would raise accept their now parental ideas of liberty as the eternally right ideas.

G. Stanley Hall had warned that "coeducation in the middle teens tends to sexual precocity. This is very bad, it is one of the subtlest dangers that can befall civilization." This statement of Hall's was cited in Ernest Earnest's history of college life, *Academic Procession,* written in the early 1950's to indicate how old-fashioned even expert opinion could still occasionally be in the early years of the century. If Hall's dictum may have seemed old-fashioned fifteen years ago or more, it does not seem so at the close of the 1960's.

The evolution of younger generations since Randolph Bourne's time has not been the cheerful progress toward greater purity that Bourne had hoped for. The tendency toward sexual precocity has made for earlier rebellion, earlier marriage, and a shorter interval between younger generations. The accelerating descent of man from generation to generation ceased to be meaningful in evolutionary terms when it took the form in the twentieth century of the permanent revolution of the younger generation, fired not only by the energies of adolescence, but by the knowledge that they had the latest word on life, which the older generation, since it has to ask, is never going to know.

4.

American Bohemianism

··

ADA CLARE, ACKNOWLEDGED queen of the American Bohemians during the 1860's, explained what one had to be, to be a Bohemian. An affinity for the arts and a cosmopolitan attitude, unruffled by rules and customs, were the elementary requirements. It was not necessary, as "worldlings" supposed, that the Bohemian "must be poor, that he must take pleasure in keeping his boots and his cheese in the same drawer," or that he must drink to drunkenness or live in a garret. The Bohemian was at ease in whatever world he found himself, guided (but notice how Ada Clare's American upbringing seems to betray her here) "by the principles of good taste and feeling." He was an original among originals, stepping over the metes and bounds of society "with an easy, graceful, joyous unconsciousness."

He was a thoroughly un-American type—everybody agreed about that—and not only the term but also the way of life itself had to be imported to America from the Left Bank of Paris. In 1848 Henri Murger's *Scènes de la Vie de Bohème* had been published in France, popularizing the term "Bohèmian" in European literary circles. Murger had declared in his study that Bohemia could exist nowhere except in Paris. But his book created Murgerites who founded their own Bohemias. In 1858 a journalist from Nantucket, Henry Clapp, on arriving in New York from Paris, declared himself a Bohemian and collected a group about him which W. D. Howells characterized as "a sickly colony, transplanted from the mother asphalt of Paris, and never really striking root in the pavements of New York." Then Ada Clare returned from a sojourn in Paris and took up residence with Clapp's group as America's first Bohémienne.

The next decade or so seemed to bear Howells out. The movement hardly survived the Civil War. Bohemianism revived in the nineties, however, and Greenwich Village became its national capital in the early years of the twentieth century. Then, until blighted by the war, and again afterwards more broadly and gaudily in the twenties, the Bohemianism burgeoned and bloomed which those two undeservedly little remembered people, Henry Clapp and Ada Clare, had first planted in the pavements of New York more than a half century earlier.

Bohemianism did strike root in the pavements of New York, but by the time it reached full bloom in Greenwich Village in the early twentieth century, it had become an unmistakable American variant of the Paris phenomenon. "As Arthur Bullard used to say," wrote Max Eastman, "New York had an ethical, where Paris had an aesthetic, Bohemia." What started out as a flippant and profane defiance of the American moral order developed into something like a crusade for a new moral order based on socialism, sexual freedom, sex equality, and cultural progress for all of the people.

This crusade was ruthlessly dealt with during World War I, and the Greenwich Village liberation movement of the 1910's became part of the Lost Generation of the 1920's. It had been the first major movement in American history which had combined filiarchal Bohemianism with revolutionary radicalism; and it was not until two generations later, with the Beat Generation, the Hippies, and the New

Left that radical-Bohemian filiarchy again appeared on the American scene as a nationally important happening.

....

Clapp's circle met in Pfaff's cellar, which was situated under the sidewalk of Broadway near Bleeker Street. Its holy martyr was Edgar Allan Poe, who had died in 1849, and its chief genius-in-residence was Walt Whitman, who was on hand almost every night of the week when he was in town and whose poetry appeared in Clapp's *Saturday Press* (as did, incidentally, some of Howells' early writings, for which Howells was never paid). Whitman got on the nerves of some of the Pfaffians, and there were those who argued that he was not *really* Bohemian. The Bohemianism of Poe, who antedated the movement itself, was above suspicion.

Son of an actress and of the black sheep of a good Virginia family, and a foundling at three, Poe had been raised by a Richmond businessman to be a Virginia gentleman. He was schooled in England, privately tutored, and sent to the University of Virginia, which he left under a cloud, burdened with heavy gambling debts that his foster father refused to pay. Enlisting in the army to avoid starvation, he used what influence he could muster to become a cadet at West Point. He afterwards invented romantic tales of life in Europe to cover the period when he had served as an enlisted man, which the nervously snobbish Poe was ashamed to have done. Events and continuing quarrels with his foster father made life intolerable for him at West Point, and he systematically violated regulations, in order to be cashiered out and have time to devote himself to making his name in American letters.

After an editorial stint in Richmond and another in Philadelphia, Poe took up residence in New York, which was the main arena for new writers and a vicious one for those who were willing to do combat. Journalism in mid-nineteenth-century New York was contentious, slanderous, and litigious—and rough-and-tumble was a form of journalism which Poe learned all about. He was a loner, however, emotionally unstable and uncontrollably self-centered. He therefore often unintentionally alienated colleagues and patrons who might otherwise have eased his career. At the same time, he was repeatedly placing himself in predicaments, where he desperately needed help.

Poe was fiercely determined to make his mark in literature, and to do so he made himself excel at literary devices that were currently fashionable: Gothic tales of horror, journalistic hoaxes, sentimental poetry, biting criticism, and literary burlesques. Absorbed to the limit in his writing, he lived a personal life of continual horror, which he instilled into his writings.

There were aspects of Poe's personal life, mainly occasional drunkenness, which did not meet the moral standards of the day; but probably his amoral literary theory contributed to his somewhat shady reputation during his lifetime more than his private conduct did. Poe attacked moralism in literature, and he chose the ultrarespectable Longfellow as his main target. He charged Longfellow with debasing his genius by using it for didactic purposes, rather than for the sake of beauty, which was the true purpose of poetry. At the same time, Poe was careful to disavow the idea "that a didactic moral may not be well made the undercurrent of a poetical thesis," asserting only that the poet should not make it "the prevalent tone of his song," as Longfellow did.

Poe's own poetry left questions of morality totally out of account, as being unrelated to his purpose. For this reason, and because of Poe's attacks on poetic didacticism in the cases of Longfellow and others, James Russell Lowell was forced to conclude that, granting the man's genius, Poe "seemed wanting in the faculty of perceiving the profounder ethics of art." The Bohemian Whitman was even more severe, in his famous statement that "almost without the first sign of moral principle, or of the concrete or its heroisms, or the simpler affections of the heart, Poe's verses . . . probably belong among the electric lights of imaginative literature, brilliant and dazzling, but with no heat." It had been difficult for Whitman to overcome his distaste for Poe's poetry, desiring, as Whitman did, "the strength and power of health, not of delirium."

The decadence of Poe's poetic theory was dramatized by his own romantic life, as the details of that life were grossly falsified, first by Poe himself and then by his blackhearted literary executor, Rufus Griswold. Poe died as terrible and mysterious a death in Baltimore as any decadent Bohemian could have desired for him. Then Griswold made a career of besmirching his name, resorting extensively to forgery to do so. In France, in the meantime, Baudelaire had translated Poe's writings into French and had written an influential appreciation of Poe from a French decadent point of view.

Together, Griswold and Baudelaire conjured up the phantom Poe: drunkard, drug addict, seducer of women, falsifier, and defaulter; also flamboyant genius, reckless amoralist, defier of society, and intense experiencer of life. The involuntary Griswold-Baudelaire collaboration resulted in a Bohemian hero for Pfaffians and for American Bohemianism ever afterwards.

Poe's writings were popular during his lifetime and continued to be widely read, the moral objections to him extending only to his literary theory and his personal reputation. In the case of Whitman, it was the poetry that was considered objectionable, rather than the man; although genteel critics of Whitman seem to have been willing to believe the worst of the man as well.

Whitman remains a literary mystery, in a way that is not true of Poe. The development of Poe's literary genius from early childhood to death is in evidence and is substantially explainable in terms of the literary currents of the day and Poe's personal problems and literary opportunities. No such literary development is recorded for Whitman. A competent newspaperman and an incompetent conventional versifier until his middle thirties, Whitman abruptly presented the world with *Leaves of Grass* in 1855, generally conceded to be one of the great original works in the world's literature.

The American reading public was not remotely ready to accord generous recognition to Whitman for the apparently formless and endless sprawl of writing in which he engaged. Whitman knew that this would be so. "No one," he wrote, "will get at my verses who insists upon viewing them as a literary performance." With great strength of character, combined with much journalistic savvy, he set forth vigorously to cultivate his reputation. He needed all of this and great endurance too; for without it, it is quite likely that he would have been altogether forgotten about and perhaps not rediscovered later.

The blatant sexuality of Whitman's lines was where he went completely wrong morally in the eyes of contemporaries, and he was insistent upon doing it.

> *Urge and urge and urge,*
> *Always the procreant urge of the world.*
> *Out of the dimness opposite equals advance, always*
>   *substance and increase, always sex,*
> *Always a knit of identity, always distinction, always*
>   *a breed of life.*

The most notorious lines, because the earliest such to appear in the volume, were

> *I mind how once we lay such a transparent summer morning,*
> *How you settled your head athwart my hips and gently*
>   *turn'd over upon me,*
> *And parted the shirt from my bosom-bone, and plunged*
>   *your tongue to my bare-stript heart,*
> *And reach'd till you felt my beard, and reach'd till*
>   *you held my feet.*

At the outset Whitman enjoyed a wonderful stroke of good fortune upon which he capitalized. He was rewarded for sending copies of his book to leading literary figures with a reply from Emerson which Whitman promoted into some of the most famous lines Emerson ever wrote. Emerson declared,

Dear Sir:

I am not blind to the worth of the wonderful gift of *Leaves of Grass*. I find it the most extraordinary piece of wit and wisdom that America has yet contributed. . . . I give you joy of your free and brave thought. . . . I greet you at the beginning of a great career. . . .

Not even such an endorsement as this from such a man as Emerson was sufficient to win an appreciative audience among the respectable readership. Lowell decided that Whitman would not do, just as he decided that Darwin would not do, a few years later. "When a man aims at originality," he declared of Whitman,

he acknowledges himself consciously *un*original, a want of self-respect which does not often go along with the capacity for great things. The great fellows have always let the stream of their activity flow quietly—if one splashes in it he may make a sparkle, but he muddies it too. . . . Homer, Plato, Dante, Shakespeare, Cervantes, Goethe—are they not everlasting boundary-stones that work the limits of a noble reserve of self-restraint . . . ?

Whitman printed Emerson's letter in the Second Edition of *Leaves of Grass,* together with a lengthy reply of his own, which finally got to the sex matter.

Infidelism usurps most with foetid polite face; among the rest infidelism about sex. By silence or obedience the pens of savans, poets, historians, biographers, and the rest, have long connived at the filthy law, and books enslaved to it, that what makes the manhood of a man, that sex, womanhood, maternity, desires, lusty animations, organs, acts, are unmentionable and to be ashamed of, to be driven to skulk out of literature with whatever belongs to them. This filthy law has to be repealed—it stands in the way of great reforms.

That was hardly Emerson's own cup of tea, however, and among leading American writers Whitman fought it alone for the rest of his life. His magnetic, and at the same time warmly engaging, personality attracted to him a small band of articulate followers who set out with considerable skill to build Whitman's reputation. His place in American letters was still being debated at the time of his death in 1892, but he had by then become "the good gray poet." Some said he was one of the world's great poets, and even those who thought he was not were willing to agree that he deserved well of his country for the services he had voluntarily rendered in army hospitals during the Civil War.

It was in the course of the generation that followed Whitman's death that he came to be widely acknowledged, not only as the greatest, but also as the most representative of American poets. He had confidently predicted that such would eventually be the case, and meanwhile, during the early years of his new career, he had been able to relax and enjoy the company of admiring Bohemians in

> *The vault at Pfaff's where the drinkers and laughers*
> *meet to eat and carouse,*
> *While on the walk immediately overhead pass the myriad*
> *feet of Broadway.*

It would be difficult, on the face of it, for any group to dedicate itself to maintaining a devil-may-care attitude without becoming serious about it, but the Pfaffians appear to have managed it well enough, until the Civil War dispersed some and forced moral sobriety on others. Genius did not burn as brightly among them as might have been wished; but they enjoyed sex and liquor and good talk, and they were sustained by the genuine originality, so far as American culture was concerned, of their anti-Victorian outlook.

They not only ate, drank, and were merry like Parisian Bohemians, but they died like them also. Albert Parry, the court historian of American Bohemia, made a tally of these fatalities and concluded that

as organized group Bohemians go, the pioneer Bohemia of New York had a record in the best of traditions. From 1854 to 1875 it saw eight spectacular deaths, namely, two suicides, one death by pneumonia in a leaky garret, one of lockjaw as a result of a battle wound, one of paralysis ascribed to dissipation, one of lungs and nerves shattered by hasheesh and opium, one of rabies caused by a performing dog's bite, and one by alcoholism. And as behooves real Bohemians, six of the eight died young.

Clapp, the founder of America's first Bohemia, was the last on this list, having purposefully drunk himself to death in 1875, after subsisting for years, according to observers, on tobacco and coffee. Beginning his adult life as a Sunday schoolteacher and temperance lecturer in New England, he ended it as the subject of a temperance lecture in an obituary. "What memories must have haunted him," declared one account of his death, "of the young men who used to meet him at Pfaff's and whom he had educated to believe that drink and infidelity were the marks of literary genius!" Clapp took a severe drubbing in the press when he died, but Whitman's memory of him may well have been a just one: "Henry in another environment might have loomed up as a central influence . . . he had ability way out of common. . . . Henry was in our sense a pioneer, breaking ground before the public was ready. . . ."

According to the drama critic William Winter,

Clapp was an original character. We called him "The Oldest Man." His age was unknown to us. He seemed to be very old, but, as afterward I ascertained, he was then only forty-six. In appearance he was somewhat suggestive of the portrait of Voltaire. He was a man of slight, seemingly fragile but really wiry figure; bearded; gray; with keen, light blue eyes, a haggard visage, a vicacious manner, and a thin, incisive voice. He spoke the French language with extraordinary fluency, and natives of France acknowledged that he spoke it with a perfect accent. He had long resided in Paris, and, indeed, in his temperament, his mental constitution, and in his conduct of life, he was more a Frenchman than an American. . . . Such as he was,—withered, bitter, grotesque, seemingly ancient, a good fighter, a kind heart,—he was the Prince of our Bohemian circle.

Clapp discovered Pfaff's shortly after it was first opened by a genial German-Swiss named Charles Pfaff with hardly more equipment than a few kegs of beer. Clapp soon filled it with young writers and artists, reserving a kind of cave under the street with a long table in it for himself and his followers. His *Saturday Press,* for which a number of them wrote, "attacked all literary shams but its own," according to Howells, "and made itself feared and felt."

Ada Clare was the ornament of Pfaff's who gave it its most brilliant notoriety. There was nothing new about a group of men, literary or otherwise, hanging around a saloon; but there was something new to America about Ada Clare, who was permitted to treat Pfaff's as though it were her salon. She fit no available American classification, being neither a woman of the streets nor an "actress," as that word was understood when in quotation marks. Nor was she a champion of women's rights and free love in the crusading manner of Victoria Woodhull. She took care to be light and feminine and carefree and also sentimental, especially about her love affair with the world-famous concert pianist, Louis Moreau Gottschalk.

Whitman thought she had been the New Woman, arrived early. She attracted national attention for more than a decade; and since she seemed to be having a wonderful time, she must have set many young women to thinking. Some of them even joined the group at Pfaff's. The spine tingles at the thought of what must have passed through the minds of many American women when, during the height of the Woman's Crusade, Ada Clare died in agony from the bite of a rabid dog.

Like Poe, an orphaned but gently reared southerner, Ada Clare, whose real name was McElhenny, was raised in Charleston with her cousin Paul Hamilton Hayne, the poet, who influenced her in her own desire to become a poet. She was also determined to become an actress and, supported by a small independent income, she launched herself on both careers in New York, but with indifferent success in each field. She also launched herself—just as purposefully and with much better success—upon a grand affair of the heart. Selecting Gottschalk, to whom she had once been introduced, she wrote him, while he was staying in New York: "If you feel that a visit from an old friend might cheer you up, I should be very happy to call."

Always working for Ada was her striking beauty. "She is," wrote John Burroughs, "really beautiful, not a characterless beauty, but a singular, unique beauty!" Gottschalk responded to the note, and a child resulted. Afterwards, when she and her child met new people, she customarily introduced herself as "Miss Ada Clare and son." Her affair with Gottschalk continued for several years, accompanied by protestations of love which she composed for the press and which gave Gottschalk that national reputation as a great lover which he had not previously enjoyed.

Ada went to Paris in 1857 and wrote articles for New York newspapers about the impressions of a young woman traveling abroad by herself. When she returned to New York, she found Pfaff's already organized by Clapp and awaiting her. She involved herself publicly in new love affairs, while continuing her grand passion; for this she was severely rebuked in the press and strongly supported by members of the circle and so continued as a national figure. She was described as quiet in dress and dignified in manner, except that she chain-smoked cigarettes and drank large quantities of beer and indulged in off-color remarks. The poet E. C. Stedman admired her appearance, as most men did, and he was especially taken by her delicate, "tip-tilted nose," which, to his mind was just "the right nose for a trim little person with a past."

Pfaffian Bohemianism was fostered by the Panic of '57, which brought students and writers into the cheap boarding houses in the area and put some writers out of jobs, temporarily imbuing them with a scorn for society. Alarmed at this situation, *The New York Times* recommended

any sort of regular employment, than to become refined and artistic only to fall into the company of the Bohemians. They are seductive in their ways, and they hold the finest sentiments, and have a distinct aversion of anything that is low or mean, or common or inelegant. Still, the Bohemian cannot be called a useful member of society, and it is not an encouraging sign for us that the tribe has become so numerous among us as to form a distinct and recognizable class.

The Pfaffians supplanted the staid Knickerbocker school of writers in New York; but it did so at a time when Boston, rather than New York, had asserted itself as the literary capital of the nation. So far as any concrete thing stood for what the Pfaffians were against in America, it was the city of Boston. The young Howells was taken aback by the display of this phobic hatred that he experienced in the offices of the *Saturday Press*. "I had found their bitterness against Boston as great as the bitterness against respectability, and as Boston was then rapidly becoming my second country, I could not join in the scorn thought of her and said of her by the Bohemians."

Others joined the Pfaffians only to depart as soon as society gave them respectable employment and recognition. Thomas Bailey Aldrich, assistant editor on the *Saturday Press,* after three years of rejection notices from the *Atlantic,* received a letter of acceptance from its editor, Lowell, beginning, "My Dear Sir: I welcome you heartily to the 'Atlantic,'" and Aldrich put Bohemia behind him, eventually to become himself editor of the *Atlantic* and the leading spokesman in the nation for the cause of genteel literature.

The Civil War divided Pfaff's into northerners and southerners, and those who remained cynically and flippantly indifferent to any wartime cause. The belligerent Irish poet and short-story writer Fitz-James O'Brien got into fights over the war issues and then volunteered and was killed. Ada Clare's southern sympathies were disturbing to the life she had created for herself, and in 1864 she escaped to San Francisco, followed by Gottschalk. There was already a lively literary community in San Francisco; and others joined it who had been associated with Pfaff's, including the celebrated author of *The Hasheesh Eater,* Fitz Hugh Ludlow; the humorist Artemus Ward; and the poetess and actress, Adah Menken, world-famous as "the Naked Lady," for her American and European performances of the male role of Mazeppa in tights.

San Francisco was something new to America's experience. It was not just another boom town; it was a mining metropolis, with a nearly immediate population of tens of thousands from around the world. It was a rich city from the first, with an unusually large literate element for a frontier region, and with all the local color a writer could ask for. By 1850 there were fifty printers at work in the city, and in the course of the next decade more books were published in San Francisco than in all the rest of the trans-Mississippi West. With the discovery of the Comstock Lode in 1859, rich and roaring Virginia City added more wealth and local color to this novel development in American culture.

Numbers of literary magazines crowded the market, but the *Golden Era* dominated the field throughout the fifties and into the sixties. The height of its success was reached in 1863 and 1864, when its writers included Mark Twain, Bret Harte, Ina Coolbrith, Charles Warren Stoddard, Prentice Mulford, and Joaquin Miller—and the Pfaffians Ada Clare, Adah Menken, Ludlow, Ward, and Charles H. Webb. The Easterners had been eagerly awaited. San Francisco writers, while thumbing their noses at Eastern culture, were respectfully aware of Pfaff's Circle. Bret Harte had acknowledged this by calling his *Golden Era* column "The Bohemian Feuilleton."

Unhappily it turned out that East was East and West was West, and not even Twain could combine the different styles of irreverence. Bret Harte was a proper young married man to whom "Bohemian" was hardly more than a word that was current in literary circles. Nobody ever enjoyed a dirty story more than Mark Twain, but not in front of the ladies. When Artemus Ward gave his first San Francisco lecture, some of the newspaper reviews were troubled by the fact that his humorous remarks had served no moral purpose.

The Pfaffians were out of place in the West and most of them returned home. Then the best of the Western writers began to feel out of place also, and they too went East, although not to Pfaff's. Once in the East, or better yet in London, they could profitably rough themselves up before polished society, where in San Francisco they had been inclined to try to polish themselves and to be self-conscious about the crudities of the society in which they lived. On the whole, the Pfaffians had injured the morale of the Westerners by making them feel like country cousins, and then those Pfaffians, upon returning East, had learned that they themselves could not go home.

It was Balzac in his "Prince of Bohemia" in 1840 who coined the term Bohemian to describe the cultural outcasts of Paris, and it was a fine idea. It had been an inviting word to begin with, and its attractiveness was enhanced when it took on its new meaning. The word conjures up pleasant and romantic associations: laughing gypsies, apple-cheeked, full-breasted Bohemian girls, peasants in the field, the Iron Cross of Bohemia, and Good King Wenceslaus on the Feast of Stephen.

Quite evidently the word attracted Americans when it was introduced in its new dress by Clapp, and it went on attracting them. The Pfaffians, interesting as they were in themselves, would not have excited as much attention in the nation as they did, had they been known only as Pfaffians or the Pfaff's Circle or Clapp's Group. As Bohemians, they were the American incarnation of a cluster of ideas, some of them inadmissibly daring but others wholesome and even uplifting. Ada Clare was no better than she ought to be, but she certainly lived an interesting life. Mothers might well think twice before pointing her out to their daughters as an example of what might happen to them when they grew up if they didn't mind.

The word "Bohemian" was as attractive as Ada Clare was, and it was a word that did not have to go as far as Ada had gone nor quite in that direction. When the Pfaffians went to their reward, they relinquished their claim to the term, and it was at once appropriated by others all over the country, without the least thought, in most cases, of doing as Ada had done, or as Fitz Hugh Ludlow or Henry Clapp had done.

In New York, the self-conscious successor to Pfaff's was the Tile Club of artists, which was, according to Albert Parry, "exclusive to the point of snobbery. It was the Four Hundred of New York's Bohemias." Its members called themselves Bohemians and played practical jokes on one another and told off-color stories; but there was a limit, as the wife of one of them made clear, when she observed disapprovingly that one member was a "real" Bohemian. Salons were in vogue in the eighties, and Tile Club men ornamented them, together indicating a French influence upon society, carefully domesticated.

More durable and influential than the Tile Club was the Bohemian Club in San Francisco. Organized as a drinking man's press club in

1872, the Bohemian Club gradually expanded and prospered into a general social organization run by jolly rich men and their wives. In 1880 a group of artists and writers resigned after making a formal protest and formed a separate club under the slogan "None of Your Silk Plush Imitation Bohemia!" But this revolt came to nothing. It was left to the poetess Ina Coolbrith, who had served as librarian of the Bohemian Club, to take the lead in what was probably San Francisco's first authentic Bohemian movement—which included Ambrose Bierce, Jack London, Joaquin Miller, George Sterling, and George Cram Cook—at the turn of the century.

Bohemian magazines mushroomed. In 1893 the *Bohemian* appeared in Buffalo under the motto "I'd rather live in Bohemia than in any other land," and observing that its title whispered "of babbling brooks . . . the songs of birds . . . of tender pathos, of sentiment . . . the sum of human enjoyment that a fond fancy imagines to lie embosomed in the classic vales of Bohemia!" There was a Boston *Bohemian,* a San Antonio *Bohemian Scribbler,* a Cincinnati *New Bohemian,* an Oakland *Amateur Bohemian,* which published Jack London's earliest writings, and in San Francisco both an *Illustrated Bohemian* and a *Bohémienne.*

Short stories and novels on the theme went well. *The Bohemian, A Tragedy of Modern Life* appeared in 1878 about a group of writers and artists who "to a man, claimed to be Bohemians, and were proud of the name." The author, Charles de Kay, was the brother-in-law of Richard Watson Gilder, of *Century,* who with his wife held a salon in his luxurious home, "The Studio," to which Tile Club men were sometimes invited.

The Bohemians that de Kay wrote about were a bad, hypocritical lot; but in 1893 the ones in W. D. Howells' *The Coast of Bohemia* were so engagingly harmless that hypocritical would really be too unkind a word for them. His heroine "aimed to be a perfect Bohemian . . . uncertain of the ways and means of operating the Bohemian life," and her indulgent mother gave her free reign. No harm was done, for the reason that Bohemianism was little more than a fancy. Many parents in real life in the nineties, perhaps viewing the Bohemian fad in this light, were similarly indulgent with daughters.

Hutchins Hapgood came to know a number of these daughters of indulgent middle-class parents during the nineties as reporter for the

New York *Commercial Advertiser,* and the ones he knew were not the sort to be condescended to in the manner of Howells' novel. "These and many other young women of the day," he wrote, "enjoyed the same spirit as the young men; they suggested the French Bohemia of Murger, and yet were the equals of their men-friends; the poor little girls of the quarter in Paris in *La Vie de Bohème* were slaves."

These young women in New York, with the sense of economic liberty, were still deeply held by the traditions of womanly restraint and by the unconscious belief that the ceremony was a necessary condition to love-affairs. They provide a marked contrast to a generation of girls following them; their light and joyous spirit was changed, deepened, and made somber by elements of revolt, in the field of labor and in the suffrage fight, in marriage and the relations of the sexes in general.

In 1894 there occurred the *"Trilby* craze" over the Frenchman George du Maurier's novel about the lovable artist's model in the Parisian Latin Quarter who came under the hypnotic sway of Svengali. As it appeared in serial form in *Harper's Monthly,* it was avidly followed. When it came out in book form, the early demands were impossible to fill. Libraries could by no means keep up with the demand. The Chicago Public Library purchased twenty-six copies, and it was estimated that ten times that number would have been needed to meet the call for it. The Mercantile Library of New York put one hundred copies in stock. *Trilby* was performed in theaters throughout the country. Trilby songs were written, and "Scenes and Songs from Trilby" occupied the nation's concert stages. There had been nothing like it since before the Civil War. *Trilby* was a kind of *Uncle Tom's Cabin* of sex.

The success of *Trilby* in the circumspectly gay nineties was the outstanding example given in Thomas Beer's *Mauve Decade* of "pink trying to be purple." The naked artists' model was presentable to the reading public, because she was clothed in romance and was living during a past time and in a foreign country. American writers were still expected, as Howells approvingly put it, to "concern themselves with the more smiling aspects of life, which are the more American." Dreiser's *Sister Carrie,* as a novel about a contemporary American girl, was not weighed on the same moral scales that had been used for

Trilby, when it became the center of controversy in the following decade.

••

James Gibbons Huneker, who had studied in Paris and who was an exemplar of American Bohemianism, said that *Trilby* gave a false picture of life in Montmartre. A generation later, Huneker himself wandered down memory lane, as du Maurier had before him, to present a fictional account of Bohemian life as he had known it in New York at the time of the *Trilby* craze. Huneker's *Painted Veils* dealt with free love, both blasé and frenetic, and its plot was complicated by lesbianism. It recounted a dinner party where the waitresses were naked, and it described a Holy Roller meeting that had turned into a sex orgy. Huneker insisted that he himself had taken part in both events, but it appears from other evidence that his memory of the dinner, at least, was livelier than life. There was still Comstockery, if not Comstock himself, to worry about when *Painted Veils* appeared in 1919, but, published in a limited edition, it went almost unscathed.

Huneker was the nation's most influential critic of the arts. He made all of the seven arts his province, and while many of his colleagues excelled him in scholarly knowledge of one art form, he was unrivaled in his comprehensive and detailed familiarity with the cultural world of his day. In this respect, there has probably never been another one quite like him in the history of criticism in America. The impact of his wit and erudition upon his fellow connoisseurs has been breathlessly attested to by a number of them, as, for example, Benjamin De Casseres, recounting his first meeting with Huneker.

What a night. I had met the most extraordinary talker America has ever produced. . . . The dawn peeped in through the window. Huneker had abolished time. He raced on: Chopin, Spencer, Roosevelt, Brillat-Savarin, Howells, Goya, Ireland, Cellini, Rembrandt, Lincoln, Culmbacher, Paracelsus, George Ehret, Poe, Harry Thaw, Renoir, William Penn—I know not.

Beginning his career during the 1880's, in the most provincial period of American cultural history, Huneker made it his purpose in life to let his fellow Americans know that there was a lot going on abroad in the artistic world which they would enjoy if they knew about it. He was the most cosmopolitan of Americans and the most cosmopolitan influence in America of the Progressive era. As Van Wyck Brooks said, he "shoveled into the minds of the young precisely what they did not learn in college." Others concurred, including Floyd Dell, Ben Hecht, Kenneth Burke, Malcolm Cowley, S. N. Behrman, Edmund Wilson, George Jean Nathan, and Henry L. Mencken. "If a merciful Providence had not sent James Gibbons Huneker into the world," Mencken wrote, "we Americans would still be shipping union suits to the heathen, reading Emerson, sweating at Chautauquas and applauding the plays of Bronson Howard. In matters exotic and scandalous he was our chief of scouts, our spiritual adviser."

Huneker grew up in Philadelphia, and it was fitting that his father had been a friend of Poe, who had lived in the same neighborhood. Whitman still lived across town in Camden, and the young Huneker paid him a visit and showed Whitman a picture of his girl friend. She was a large girl, who, Whitman told him, would be the mother of ten at least. Huneker's father was a musician, and his mother was an intellectual who "could have dominated an 18th century salon," according to his actress-sister. Huneker became absorbed with culture and, to the distress of his parents, with little else except girls and Pilsner beer. He married and then went to Paris to study—he does not mention taking his wife with him—returned to study law fretfully, and then in 1886 left his wife to take up his Bohemian career in New York.

Luchow's Restaurant served somewhat as a Pfaff's for Huneker, but Huneker established no real permanent headquarters, ranging instead through the city's cultural purlieus and its demimonde. Artists, journalists, scholars, and art patrons predominated in his circle of friends, but there was no real Huneker Circle. He remained a genial one-man campaign for the pleasures of the arts and against the forces of Comstock.

More than anyone else, Huneker was instrumental in making Americans aware of the plays of George Bernard Shaw; but he criticized Shaw, as Poe had criticized Longfellow, for Shaw's incorrigible didacticism. "The real Shaw," he wrote in 1914, was a "kindly, humorous fellow—a reactionary chock-full of old fashioned notions and exuding sentiment and prejudice of the approved British variety," who contented himself with writing "country lyceum discussions punctuated by clownish humor," instead of "real plays." In Huneker's opinion *Pygmalion* was not a play, but the libretto for a comic opera, "fairly begging for a musical setting." Huneker's attacks on morality were often delightful to the Greenwich Villagers of the pre-World War I period; but when it came to criticizing moral uplift of the Fabian-Shavian sort, most of them primly parted company with him.

The mild tendency toward intellectual decadence in the *Trilby* era was captured fleetingly in three short-lived magazines. The *Chap-Book,* which two Harvard students had taken to Chicago, published pieces by Henry James, Hamlin Garland, H. G. Wells, Max Beerbohm, Robert Louis Stevenson, and W. B. Yeats. The *Lark,* in San Francisco, gave the world Gelett Burgess's "The Purple Cow," and in New York *M'lle New York* was started by Huneker and his friend Vance Thompson. Thompson was a minister's son and Princeton graduate, who had studied at Heidelberg and had returned to America, according to Huneker's biographer Arnold T. Schwab, "with a Ph.D., yellow gloves, long paddock coats, the most English Lincoln and Bennet toppers, and a monocle." He had married an actress and, like Huneker, had gone in for art, drama, and literary criticism for the press, and for gargantuan beer drinking.

The *Lark* was the earliest and most original of these magazines, lasting for two years and eliciting from the reformed Pfaffian and staid dean of the New York drama critics, William Winter, the comment that the *Lark* was "one more hysterical magazine—from the realm remote from the moorings of intelligence." The magazine quit while it was ahead, because, according to its editor Gelett Burgess, "I had done what I wanted, I wanted it to die young and in its full freshness, it was paying, yes—it would have made money. But I wanted to come East."

Of *Chap-Book* it was said that "a place exists in the minds of those who love it. . . . A place where kindred virtues have fled for refuge, and where Mrs. Grundy has no sway"; but the physical premises were vacated after a four-year stand. *M'lle New York* was dead after eleven months.

That American literature of which Mrs. Grundy disapproved was

able to find its way into print at all during the nineties and through
the first decade of the twentieth century was very largely owing to the
good offices of the remarkable Colonel William D'Alton Mann, publisher and editor of *Town Topics* from 1891 on and also publisher of
Smart Set, which he founded in 1900 and controlled until 1911.

Even though he apparently robbed only from the rich, Colonel
Mann, as a professional extortionist, was a scoundrel by American
standards; and probably for this reason his name has arbitrarily been
expunged from the historical record. *Smart Set* has received recognition for the role it played in advancing American letters, but its
achievements have not been associated with Colonel Mann. H. L.
Mencken and George Jean Nathan have been given credit for it,
although they did not go to work for the colonel until 1908 and did
not take over management of the magazine until 1914, after its
period of unique importance was over and it was on the decline in
circulation as well as literary importance. By that time a number of
other magazines were in the field, where the colonel's publications
had formerly stood alone.

Town Topics was always primarily a magazine concerned with
society scandal, and an important source of revenue for Colonel
Mann continued to come from rich people who faced the alternative
of exposure in the gossip column, "Saunterings." At the same time,
Colonel Mann insisted that *Town Topics* was principally a magazine
of criticism—and its columns of criticism were the liveliest, most
knowledgeable, and most sophisticated of any periodical in the nation. Huneker was its music critic for five years, beginning in 1897;
he was joined by Charles Frederick Nirdlinger as drama critic and
Percival Pollard as literary critic.

Mann started *Smart Set* as a literary magazine that catered to New
York's "400" and invited contributions from aspiring writers in the
Social Register. The magazine, much of which was given over to
sentimental tales of love among the yachting set or romance in far-off
places, did extremely well in terms of circulation and also in terms of
the excellence of much of the literature it published. Its contributors
included Gelett Burgess, William Rose Benét, Edwin Markham, Sara
Teasdale, Vance Thompson, James Branch Cabell, Jack London,
O. Henry, Damon Runyon, Theodore Dreiser, Sinclair Lewis, and
Carl Van Vechten.

The list included also those who were to be most prominently associated with the new Bohemia of Greenwich Village in the immediate future, including Floyd Dell, Inez Hayes Gillmore, Susan Glaspell, Harry Kemp, Louis Untermeyer, and Mary Heaton Vorse. Most of these writers were unknown to the general reading public at the time that *Smart Set* accepted their material at the inflexible rate of a penny a word.

Smart Set had achieved a circulation of perhaps 165,000 by 1905. Mann launched on another cultural venture with *Transatlantic Tales* in 1908 and sold *Smart Set* in 1911. He continued to publish *Town Topics* until his death in 1920, as well as *Snappy Stories,* a pulp magazine which he started in 1917 and which did well at once. *Transatlantic Tales* offered stories written by the best contemporary French, German, and Russin authors and sold briskly on the American smut market.

Smart Set declined in circulation from its heyday under Mann to 23,000 when Mencken and Nathan sold it in 1923, after which it once again did very well, this time as a true-confession magazine under Hearst management. Mencken and Nathan, with their *American Mercury,* were to influence American thinking in the twenties in a way that had not been possible for them in the prewar and wartime years of *Smart Set*. Nathan had been wholly disinterested in politics, and Mencken was belligerently opposed to political reform, and was furthermore culturally pro-German at a time when America was at war with Germany. Prewar Greenwich Village Bohemianism was Bohemianism with a serious social message; and by the time Mencken and Nathan took over the magazine, the Village Bohemians were speaking their minds, not so much in the frivolous *Smart Set* as in the essentially sobersided *Masses*.

....

Bohemianism and political radicalism simmered up and simmered up during the first decade of the new century, amid the dominant moral righteousness and moderate reforming temper of Progressivism, and then the new ideas came to a boil around 1912. The year 1912 was also a banner year for Progressivism, when Roosevelt bolted the Republican party to run Progressive against Wilson, the prophet of the New Freedom; yet the Hoosier Socialist Eugene V.

Debs pulled close to 900,000 votes out from under them. The Supreme Court ordered the Standard Oil and American Tobacco Company trust to dissolve themselves. But Emma Goldman was ordering the federal government to dismantle *itself,* and the more she was denounced, the more she attracted the sympathetic attention of intellectuals.

Labor radicalism erupted to disturb Samuel Gompers in his cautious and successful program of labor advancement through the American Federation of Labor. Somebody blew up the Los Angeles *Times* building. The Industrial Workers of the World were raising Ned out West, and in 1912 they went East to organize the textile mills at Lawrence, Massachusetts, and Paterson, New Jersey. That gave young men and women in the land of the Ivy League a chance to learn at first hand about class warfare, and Greenwich Village intellectuals did not have to think twice to know which side they were on.

The age of the New Woman was at hand. Jane Addams seconded the nomination for Roosevelt at the Bull Moose Progressive convention—a million women had the vote by then—and Alice Paul, the militant Quaker jailbird, took over the Congressional Committee of the American Woman Suffrage Association from the socially prominent Mrs. William Kent. For some women, social prominence, itself, was going out of style. In 1907 Mrs. Gertrude Vanderbilt Whitney remodeled a stable in MacDougal Alley in the Village and launched herself on a career in sculpture. Helen Stokes, sister of the wealthy socialist J. G. Phelps Stokes, also went downtown to the Village, to work for radical causes. Mabel Dodge turned her drawingroom into a salon for artists and revolutionists. In 1910 Dorothy Arnold asked her father for permission to take an apartment by herself in Greenwich Village. He refused, and she left the house and never was heard from again.

"When the world began to change," wrote Hutchins Hapgood, "the restlessness of women was the main cause of the development called Greenwich Village, which existed not only in New York but all over the country. . . ." Young women took the lead in Bohemia, and young men followed. Harriet Monroe started *Poetry* magazine in Chicago in 1912; and Margaret Anderson started the *Little Review* there two years later, organizing the Chicago Bohemians into her group. Ina

Coolbrith was still the mistress of the house for Bohemians on the West Coast; but the artists and writers she brought together then tended to go East, as they had done before in the post-*Golden Era* days. In Greenwich Village it was Henrietta Rodman, high school English teacher, socialist, sometime nudist, and dedicated feminist, who chiefly founded the Liberal Club in MacDougal Alley and organized the Village Bohemians.

In Chicago, Bohemia rose from the ruins of the world's fair of 1893, artists and writers taking up residence in the vacant buildings at the edge of the fair grounds. Chicago was proud of itself intellectually at the turn of the century. Wealthy women of the community, such as the McCormicks and the Palmers, were bringing culture to the Midwest, and the University of Chicago was founded in 1891. Culturally, Chicago was the aggressive underdog to New York City, so the Chicago Bohemians were on its side.

Chicago Bohemians sang praises to America and worshipped their adopted city, with its stockyards, its factories, and its whorehouses, as the heartbeat of America. The Chicago spirit was expressed in the rough verse of Carl Sandburg and in the newspaper reporter's cynicism of the "Pagliacci of the fire escape," Ben Hecht. "And I came to love Chicago," Margaret Anderson wrote,

as one only loves chosen—or lost—cities. I knew it in every aspect—dirt, smoke, noise, heat, cold, wind, mist, rain, sleet, snow. I walked on Michigan Boulevard on winter afternoons when the wind was such a tempest and the snow so icy that ropes were stretched along the buildings to keep pedestrians from falling.

There was a regular soiree conducted by the wife of Floyd Dell, the literary editor of the Chicago *Evening Post,* where Dreiser, Sherwood Anderson, George Cram Cook, Susan Glaspell, and Margaret Anderson, among others, argued. Then there was the Dill Pickle, a raucous hangout, where newspapermen predominated and where bearbaiting sports were followed and hoaxes were pulled off, such as inviting a female antitobacconist in to lecture and answer questons. As against Greenwich Village social consciousness, the Chicagoans tended to believe in art and sex each for its own sake, rather than as means to a better world. It was true that Margaret Anderson had "heard Emma Goldman lecture and had just time to turn anarchist before the presses closed," and that she had continued to favor anarchism thereafter—it agreed with her taste in poetry—but, on the other hand, she found socialism as grim as she found her mother's Christian Science.

Margaret Anderson thought the conversations of the New York Bohemians were second-rate intellectually, compared to those of the Chicago Bohemians; and she later found Paris second-rate in that respect, when compared to New York. She nevertheless left Chicago for good in 1917, taking the *Little Review* to New York, and a good many of her earlier Chicago friends were already there to meet her. Floyd Dell had gone in 1913, after breaking up with his wife, and had become an editor of *Masses*. "I had been happy in Chicago," Dell wrote, and it would never "seem to me a gray and ugly city. I loved the Lake, Michigan Boulevard with its open vista and its gleaming lights. . . . It had been a generous city to a young man"; but it was still the second city in the nation.

Dell arrived in New York at the time when Henrietta Rodman was organizing the Liberal Club above the restaurant operated by Polly Halliday in the Village. Various cliques of artists, writers, and social reformers already existed in the Village, but Henrietta Rodman helped to bring them together as a distinct and organized group. Dell described her as "a very serious young woman, who had an extraordinary gift for stirring things up."

Incredibly naive, preposterously reckless, believing wistfully in beauty and goodness, a Candide in petticoats and sandals, she was laughed at a good deal and loved very much indeed, and followed loyally by her friends into new schemes for the betterment of the world. She was especially in touch with the university crowd and the social settlement crowd, and the Socialist crowd; and it was these, many of whom never actually lived in the Village, who, mixing with the literary and artist crowds in the Liberal Club, gave the Village a new character entirely, and one which was soon exploited by real-estate interests; it was not any longer a quiet place, where nothing noisier happened than drunken artist merrymaking; ideas now began to explode there, and soon were heard all the way across the continent.

The Village did acquire a new character in the history of American Bohemia—a typically American character, full of the sense of high moral purpose. Villagers dedicated themselves to the task of breaking the capitalistic and Puritanical chains that bound them. They advocated the new ideas of the Marxists and the Freudians. They were reckless in their talk about revolution and casual in their sexual conduct; or as reckless and as casual as they could manage, given the conventional middle-class upbringings of most of them and the sense of dedication.

Crystal Eastman, attending New York University Law School and earning her living in social work, wrote that she loved New York, "for the people there and the thousands of things they think and do . . . especially the radicals, the reformers, the students—who really live to help, and yet get so much fun out of it." They were happily pursuing their duty, to find out what civilization really was so that they could bring it to the Anglo-Saxon Protestants of the nation, which included most of the Village Bohemians themselves.

The Liberal Club was organized for the purposes of arguing and poetry reading and one-act-play performing and listening to agitators, especially those who were able to come fresh from jail to the club. There were other similar meeting places, including the Mad Hatter and the Purple Pup; but the Club gave the Village its unity, also staging elaborate dances, such as the masquerade Pagan Routs. "But even in this new dancing," wrote Lawrence Langner, a Club member who later founded the Theater Guild,

there was, so to speak, a spirit of revolt against the older more formal dances, such as the Boston and the old-fashioned waltz. . . . As you clutched your feminine partner and led her through the crowded dance floor at the Club, you felt you were doing something for the progress of humanity, as well as for yourself and, in some cases, for her.

Max Eastman's *Masses* was the *Saturday Press* of the Village Bohemians, just as Polly's was their Pfaff's, and in the contrast between these two radical papers the comparative softheartedness of the Pollyans in contrast to the cynicism of the Pfaffians is marked. *Masses*, operating always on a shoestring, soon gained an international reputation, printing original contributions from Romain Rolland, Bertrand Russell, and Maxim Gorky, in addition to those from new American writers. "Our magazine," Eastman wrote, "provided for the first time in America, a meeting ground for revolutionary labor and the radical intelligentsia. It acquired, in spite of its gay laughter, the character of a crusade." Floyd Dell wrote that the problem it solved was no less

than the "co-operation between artists, men of genius, egotists, inevitably and rightfully, proud, sensitive, hurt by the world, each of
them the head and center of some group, large or small, of admirers
or devotees," and all of it brought off with good humor.

The keynote of earthy wisecracking radicalism was struck by
Eastman in his first issue, with a double-page cartoon portraying the
"capitalist press" as a brothel. This cartoon brought him letters of
remonstrance from his Progressive friends Oswald Garrison Villard
and George Foster Peabody, containing such phrases as "vulgar beyond anything" and "in sorrow and in friendship" and "distinctly
injurious." "These fatherly admonitions did not bother me greatly,"
Eastman wrote, "for I had committed myself now to revolution and
was glad to break the ties still binding me to what I called reform."

The statement of policy of the *Masses* came to be taken as the
classic statement of Village ideology, socially as well as politically:

A revolutionary, and not a reform magazine; a magazine with no divi-
dends to pay; frank, arrogant, impertinent, searching for the true causes;
a magazine directed against rigidity and dogma wherever it is found;
printing what is too naked or true for a money-making press; a magazine,
whose final policy is to do as it pleases and conciliate nobody, not even its
readers—there is room for this publication in America.

●●●

Greenwich Village affiliated with both upper-class salons and proletarian meeting halls. Mabel Dodge conducted the most important
salon just off Washington Square; and Emma Goldman, the dominating figure in the American anarchist movement, had established her
headquarters nearby. The dancer Isadora Duncan never stayed long
in the Village or any other one place in the world, but she had her
Village friends and she played a dramatic role in Village thinking.
These three women were three outstanding titanesses of sex, to bor-
row Thomas Beer's term, in the age of the New Woman.

Mabel Dodge was one of the idle rich, and she was living "in
accordance with the fixed determination I had acquired to be broad-
minded and without social taboos." Moving with her husband to New
York, where she knew virtually nobody, she took an apartment on
Fifth Avenue near Washington Square, put herself under the care of a
psychiatrist, and began collecting colored glass while seeking something more recherché to collect. One day her husband, trying "to find

diversions to take me out of myself," brought the artist Jo Davidson home to meet her. Then "Jo brought others, like a child trailing strange bright rags of seaweed gathered on some shore whose waters spread to far neighborhoods."

Soon Mabel Dodge was presiding over a nightly "Evening," attended by members of the Village group, as well as by actors and newspapermen from uptown and by anarchists and Wobblies from the orbit of Emma Goldman. Her husband had "become the obstacle between me and my continuing life," and she persuaded him, through her psychiatrist, to go away for the sake of her mental health. "It was ironic," she wrote, referring to the part her husband had played in starting her salon, "that Edwin, in his effort to help me, launched the boat that sailed away and left him behind."

There were limits to her broad-mindedness. Alexander Berkman, the anarchist and would-be assassin of Henry Frick, was unsuccessful again when he made a pass at Mabel in a taxi; and there were similar misunderstandings involving others. In spite of such occasional *faux pas*—her peyote party put one poor girl in an insane asylum—her "Evenings" were extremely successful. They were successful for many people who simply wanted nothing so much as a good argument. Max Eastman thought that Mabel Dodge had the power to create

a magnetic field in which people become polarized and pulled in and made to behave very queerly. Their passions become exacerbated. . . . And they like it—they come back for more . . . from Walter Lippmann, representing the drift toward respectability, to Alexander Berkman, representing revolt *in excelsis*.

Mabel Dodge's deepest interest was in "sex expression," and a good part of her appeal to the Villagers and others was evidently the aura of silken sensualism with which she invested her apartment. As she herself wrote of the Liberal Club room "there was nothing very attractive about it; no place to sit, no place to eat, and only useful, really, for meetings or lectures." The anarchists' Purple Pup can hardly have been much more comfortable; and in those romantic days, even anarchists appear to have accepted the possibility of having the best of all worlds for the moment.

According to Mabel Dodge, it was Margaret Sanger, the birth control advocate, who really taught her the true art of sex expression.

Margaret, she wrote, "made love into a serious undertaking—with the body so illumined and conscious that it would be able to interpret and express in all its parts the language of the spirit's pleasure." Margaret laid down the principle for her.

Not just anyhow, anywhere, not promiscuity, for that defeated its own end if pleasure were the goal; not any man and any woman, but the conscious careful selection of a lover that is the mate, if only for an hour—for a lifetime, maybe.

Mabel Dodge selected the writer John Reed, successfully for a considerable period of time, and then the artist Maurice Sterne, with similar success for another period of time. In time she became "empty of my love for Maurice," however, and then "an emptiness was all I experienced." She tried reading a book on mysticism, then dabbling in psychic phenomena, then resting on a remote island off the coast of Maine with Sterne, then Jungian analysis, then Freudian analysis with A. A. Brill, and then a Dr. Bernard, who "was a mixture of a Medicine Man in a country circus, and an East Indian Yogi," then marriage to Sterne, and finally life in Taos among the Indians.

Emma Goldman appealed to another side of the Villagers. They put Emma on a pedestal, without, in most cases, accepting her anarchism, but still believing that she was a noble and persecuted woman. The one quality that was totally admirable about her to them was the fact that she was the direct opposite of bourgeois; for if there was one thing they could agree upon, it was that the term *bourgeois* had negative value. Thus with Margaret Anderson:

Emma Goldman had written how much she appreciated my article on anarchism. Now she wrote again that she was passing through Chicago and would like to see me.

I was exalted. To know the great martyred leader! I thought the lake and the empty apartment would be soothing to her so I asked her to stay with us while she was in Chicago.

She answered, thanking me graciously, but explaining that she never visited families, that she couldn't adapt herself to bourgeois life even for a few days. I replied that we weren't exactly bourgeois perhaps—that we ought to be very congenial to her, being without furniture.

The two women met and got together at once. Margaret found that Emma was "entirely reassured as to my unbourgeois nature, and eager to see the empty apartment. . . . She relaxed when she saw the apartment."

Regardless of the merits of anarchism, Emma Goldman was great in the role of a martyred leader. She was a magnetic speaker, a dedicated idealist, and a warmly loving person—"motherly" was the frequently given description of her, and *Mother Earth* was her publication—and she was subjected to (and resolutely invited) violent harassment everywhere she went. To join in defending her against the hysterical attacks that vollied forth from pulpit, press, and police was to do a chivalrous deed and at the same time to give the stodgy upholders of the status quo a righteous raspberry. For those who did not wish to go deeper into her cause, freedom of speech was sufficient reason to support her. It was the conclusion of the civil liberties leader Roger Baldwin that in the service of that cause, "Emma Goldman fought battles unmatched by the labors of any organization."

In addition to advocating anarchism and free speech, Emma was among the doughtiest of fighters for women's rights. Since she dismissed woman's suffrage as a fool's errand, however, she put herself directly at odds with the movement. Furthermore, she particularly opposed the evils of enforced marriage and involuntary conception, which most suffragettes did not view as evils, to be corrected publicly. To the extent that the suffragettes held an official position on free love and birth control, it was probably the one presented by Charlotte Perkins Gilman in *Women and Economics,* which praised chastity, rebuked "over-sexed" women, and warned that "excessive indulgence in sex-waste has imperiled the life of the race."

Margaret Sanger had been arrested in 1914 for publishing *Woman Rebel,* which advised birth control both for married and unmarried women, and advised women to face the world with a "go-to-hell look in the eyes." She avoided the possibility of imprisonment for the time being by going abroad, where she introduced herself to Havelock Ellis and became his devoted companion. (Mrs. Sanger's husband was, parenthetically, also arrested.)

Emma Goldman, who had influenced Margaret Sanger to take up the cause originally, decided that she "must share with them the consequences of the birth-control issue"; and she proceeded to try to do so. She was unsuccessful in Oregon in August 1915, when a circuit judge set aside her conviction, commenting that, "the trouble with our people today is that there is too much prudery." It was not until February 1916, after a year of transcontinental birth-control campaigning, that she finally achieved arrest in New York and was convicted. She chose fifteen days in the workhouse instead of a $100 fine and went to jail for the first time in more than a decade. At the end of her sentence, the Birth Control Meeting to Welcome Emma Goldman from Prison, held at Carnegie Hall, was a big success.

The persecution Emma Goldman had suffered had been disappointingly mild, and she had probably not done much to advance the birth control cause. Margaret Sanger, who eventually returned and won her case, thereafter made birth control preeminently her own cause, disassociating herself from Miss Goldman and limiting her appeal to the right of physicians to instruct patients in contraceptive methods. She did what she could to create a public image of herself, not as Mabel Dodge's instructress in dalliance, but as the guardian of the health and well-being of the mothers and children of America. Even so, she remained a Jezebel to millions of Americans throughout the Jazz Age.

Emma Goldman was far more successful in her practice of free love than Mabel Dodge was, despite the dark experiences of her youth. She had suffered a harsh childhood as the unwanted daughter of unwanted Jews in Russia, and, emigrating to New York, she had married a man who was impotent and who had visibly disintegrated under the strain of the marriage, which had lasted less than a year. Thereafter, however, she had settled into a life of comfortable sexual relationships with a series of men, apparently unbothered by the neuroses and unpunctuated by the disagreeable, or at least anticlimactic, aftermaths which other New Women suffered.

To Emma, according to her biographer Richard Drinnon,

free love meant the mutual, essentially private attraction of two responsible human beings to each other. It meant the tender and passionate feeling she had for Berkman, Brady, Reitman, Max Baginsky, Hippolyte Havel. . . . Paradoxically, given their number, her affairs of the heart were in the main built on lasting foundations of tenderness and mutual esteem.

Isadora Duncan became an advocate of free love at the age of twelve as a consequence of reading in George Eliot's *Adam Bede* of the shame of unwed motherhood. "I was deeply impressed by the injustice of this state of things for women," she wrote in her autobiography,

and putting it together with the story of my father and mother, I decided, then and there, that I would live to fight against marriage and for the emancipation of women and for the right for every woman to have a child or children as it pleased her, and to uphold her right and her virtue.

Isadora's parents had been divorced. Her mother was a musician and an agnostic. Quite a New Woman in her own right, she had been unable to take any nourishment while Isadora was in the womb, except iced oysters and iced champagne, again according to the autobiography.

Isadora's first affair was with a Hungarian who was playing the lead in Romeo and Juliet at the Hungarian Royal National Theater. When she returned to Budapest from a series of dancing engagements throughout the country, however, she discovered that her lover was now playing the role of Mark Anthony, and

all the passionate interest centered in the Roman populace and I, his Juliet, was no longer the central interest. . . . All joy seemed suddenly to have left the Universe. In Vienna I fell ill and was placed by Alexander Gross in a clinic. . . . From the experience of Budapest, for years after, my entire emotional reaction had such a revolution that I really believed I have finished with that phase, and in the future would only give myself to my Art.

Subsequent love affairs were not disastrous; but when all was said and done, they were not perfect because of the element of mortality in them. While in the throes of passion, for example, she could believe that her lover, Gordon Craig, the son of Ellen Terry,

was not a young man making love to a girl. This was the meeting of twin souls. The light covering of flesh was so transmuted with ecstasy that earthly passion became a heavenly embrace of white, fiery flame.

There are joys so complete, so all perfect, that one should not survive them. Ah, why did not my burning soul find exit that night, and fly, like Blake's angel, through the clouds of our earth to another sphere?

It was not to be.

When two weeks had passed, we returned to my mother's house; and, to tell the truth, in spite of my mad passion, I was a bit tired of sleeping on a hard floor, and having nothing to eat except what he could get from the delicatessen, or when we sallied out after dark.

A child, Deirdre, resulted from this union and occasioned the welcome international reputation.

....

It was not thought essential, even in Bohemia, that the New Woman be accomplished in the art of sex expression or even bother with it at all. The emancipated Margaret Anderson, who appears to have been a sensible girl, even about her spontaneous enthusiasms, did not discuss her love life in her autobiography except to say that her first real love "was a great love—great in everything including disappointment."

Ina Coolbrith and Henrietta Rodman were similarly private about their romantic attachments. Ina Coolbrith, who was the daughter of a Mormon, was almost certainly demonstrating a distaste for polygamy when she changed her name. She had originally been christened Josephine D. Smith. At the age of seventeen she had married a player of the bones in a minstrel show, only to divorce him three years later when he charged her with infidelity and shot at her with his rifle. Rumors followed her in which various literary figures were mentioned; but she made no comment other than to refuse to write an autobiography, saying that if she were to write what she knew, the book would be too sensational to print.

Henrietta Rodman practiced nudism at home for a time but found it uncomfortable and gave it up. She was an earnest young woman for whom sex was no laughing matter, and on one occasion she went so far as to call a special meeting of the Liberal Club to protest a one-act farce which was put on for the club, called "What Eight Million Women Want."

Free love was accepted socially in Greenwich Village Bohemia to the extent that lovers who got married in some cases tried to hide the fact rather than flout public opinion. The Village was looked upon, Floyd Dell wrote, as

a refuge from Mother's morality. But it was not, except for some, a permanent refuge. One hoped to find out what one was like, what one could do happily in the way of work, and straighten out one's love life. Being free to have all the love affairs that one might wish, was a means to the end of finding one love affair that suited, that could be permanent. That was how some of us figured out Greenwich Village. To others it meant other things, of course.

Dell divided the Villagers into two classifications: highbrow and lowbrow, according to their sexual mores. According to the highbrow standard, which he applied to himself,

one's sexual impulses were indulged, not impulsively or at random, but in the light of some well-considered social theory, which might be of almost any kind but had to be thoughtful and consistent.

Lawrence Langner wrote that "the attitude of the young people toward sex was in the nature of a crusade, and when a young man and young woman decided to live together without benefit of clergy it was then called 'free love,' and books and essays and plays were written about it."

In cases where Villagers did marry, they were expected to employ the services of a justice of the peace rather than a minister and to edit the marriage service to remove the religious stigma and especially to delete the part concerning the wife's promise to obey her husband until death. Marriages were entered into on the assumption that they would be provisional upon the continued agreement of both parties, the bride sometimes retaining her maiden name, as with Ida Rauh, whose maiden name happened to be peculiarly appropriate to her troubled marriage with Max Eastman.

Villagers truly suffered for the cause of free love, and the men, generally speaking, appear to have suffered worse than the women. Hutchins Hapgood explained why.

The women of the [Paris] Latin Quarter were not equal with the men. They were "little" shop-girls, sweet creatures, intended by themselves and the men as playthings and tender conveniences. . . .

In Greenwich Village, however, the women were not victimized in any way . . . for the general situation put the man at a disadvantage. The woman was in full possession of what the man used to regard as his "rights," and the men, even the most advanced of them, suffered from the woman's full assumption of his old privileges. To be sure, man retained the same "freedom," or what was called freedom, that he had always had, but his "property" had been taken away from him, and no matter what his advanced ideas were, his deeply complex, instinctive and traditional, nature often suffered, a suffering the woman was relatively spared. From the emotional point of view, the man, rather than the woman, was the victim.

Dell, among others, certainly had a hard time of it, as his autobiography indicates, despite the devil-may-care figure he cut. It was not until his thirty-fifth year, following his second marriage (guiltily entered into, of course), that he managed to straighten himself out, to the point where, as he wrote in the concluding two sentences of his autobiography, "I can face the boy of eighteen that I once was, without shame. I have gained the courage to love."

Other outwardly bold lovers later confessed even more explicitly and in greater detail than Dell to similar inner anguish and timidity. Bawdy Ben Hecht confessed that in his mad escapades he was endeavoring to sever the silver cord that bound him to Mother and that the effort sometimes had almost strangled him.

Probably the most detailed testament of this often-savage American Bohemian struggle against Home, God, and Mother and for Woman is the one prepared by Max Eastman in his *Enjoyment of Living*. In the Foreword, Eastman explained that he was about to tell

the story of how a pagan and unbelieving and unregenerate and carnal and seditious and not a little adolatrous, epicurean revolutionist emerged out of the very thick and dark of religious America's deep, awful, pious, and theological zeal for saving souls from the flesh and the devil.

Nearly six hundred pages later the story ends at the age of 33 in the arms of what seemed at the time to be the right woman at last.

In each of us for the first time the ideal rapture and the physical achievement of love were so perfectly blended as to be indistinguishable. . . . Morally and intellectually too, I had come to a landing-place in my development. I find inscribed in a notebook of those days the statement: "My life began in January 1917!"

It had been a long and harrowing struggle up until then. Eastman was by birth almost uniquely disadvantaged for sexual emancipation. In addition to his father being a minister, his mother was Annis Ford Eastman, the most widely acclaimed woman preacher of her day. She was the dominant one of his parents and the one main formative influence upon the young Max. And it was nearly impossible for him to rebel against her, for she was not only a loving mother but she was also a New Woman. The curse of Puritanism, by the time it had descended through a long line of New England Puritans to his mother, had transformed itself into a unitarianism that was on the verge of agnosticism. Annis Ford Eastman, for instance, had gone so far in her willingness to accept modern alternatives to religion as to become one of A. A. Brill's early patients.

From adolescence on, Eastman agonized inconclusively over sex, as Hamlet agonized over death, through one unconsummated love experience after another; and one after the other, he later relived them in his autobiography. At the time he came upon the Village scene he was a handsome young man who fluttered the hearts of Village girls, but he was also a very nervous virgin. It was only with the greatest trepidation that he brought himself to marry Ida Rauh, who represented some, but by no means all, of the qualities he was looking for in a mate. The particular attraction she exerted upon him derived from the fact that she had been the one to convert him from Emersonian idealism to Marxian Socialism. "The choice," he wrote, "seemed merely intelligent," until he awoke the next morning "with a craving to escape as sharp and shocking as a cramp in the muscles."

For a time there seemed to be some hope of making the marriage work, despite Eastman's disturbing doubts and daydreams. But then Eastman was partially seduced by one of his wife's friends; and emotional wounds were inflicted in his wife when she learned of it, which never healed. His conscience did not permit him to conceal his infidelity, which under any circumstances should not have been considered by his wife as a betrayal of her, under the terms of their marriage vows. Nevertheless, Ida Rauh "was transformed into a vengeful animal" by his confession.

Seeking to save the marriage, Eastman submitted himself to psychoanalysis, resulting in the finding (as his analyst recalled it a number of years later) that

you weren't quite aware of the Oedipus situation, the hostility to the father working itself out in prejudiced radicalism. You were tied up also in a complex situation with your sister which made relations with your wife uncomfortable. There was a sister-identification, and through that identification a fundamental narcissistic cathexis or investment.

Concluding that psychoanalysis was for sick people, whereas he was merely bewildered and in need of common sense, Eastman went off by himself for several weeks to attempt self-analysis.

While he was away, but in extensive communication with his wife by mail, he received a letter from her, declaring that she did not "suppose any boy or man with your sexual make-up has ever really gone through his whole youth as you did before you met me without actual sexual and complete experience." She promised him, under those circumstances, to leave him free, within the marriage, "to have your loves whenever and wherever you want them." Eastman returned home immediately, only to find her "in despair—sobbing, and running round and round the subject of my kind of feelings for her and for other girls. There was no ray of light, no ray of interest in anything, even intellectual comprehension." They agreed to live separately but close by each other. He was in possession of his sexual liberty, but did not exercise it.

Then once again his wife, upon hearing that he was having an affair (which he was not, although he was thinking of it), declared that their present arrangement would have to be altered. Eastman's sister, meanwhile, had divorced her husband and married another man. That was the situation when Eastman met a girl at one of the balls sponsored by *Masses*. The girl was "twenty-one and was in exactly that state of obstreperous revolt against artificial limitations which I had expressed in my junior and senior essays at college." Further disagreeablenesses followed with Ida Rauh and then came the final break. Eastman and the girl from the *Masses* ball went off together, and he emerged "from a disease of conflict that for five-and-a-half years had dimmed and damped my soul."

Such, in capsule form, is the case history of one young intellectual's struggle for sexual fulfillment in the prewar Bohemia of Greenwich Village. Eastman's was a special case, as was every case, but he does not appear to have been unrepresentative of his place and time. Lawrence Langner was of the opinion that "the Liberal Club, in retrospect, became singularly successful in promoting matches, and many a happy couple now celebrating their silver weddings were led into marriage by the vehemence of their denial of its value as an institution." For others, however, it must have been the result of exhaustion rather than emotional communion. The experience of

Eastman and others of that day helps to explain why, in the twentieth century, the struggle for sexual freedom has to be fought all over again by each successive generation, after having been lost by each preceding one.

....

Among the prewar Greenwich Villagers, Randolph Bourne was the acknowledged philosopher of filiarchy. Bourne entered this vocation, as a 25-year-old sophomore at Columbia, by replying to a derogatory article, "A Letter to the Rising Generation," in the *Atlantic Monthly*. Bourne's reply, "The Two Generations," appeared in the *Atlantic* in 1911, and a series of subsequent articles by him were published together in 1913 as *Youth and Life*. After graduation, Bourne joined the newly founded *New Republic* as a contributing editor. He broke with the magazine when it failed to accept his antiwar position and joined the newly created *Seven Arts* magazine in 1917, which soon was suppressed by the government. He died in 1918 at the age of 32.

Bourne is vividly remembered in a description and appraisal of him by James Oppenheim, editor of the short-lived *Seven Arts*. "I shall never forget," Oppenheim wrote,

how I had first to overcome my repugnance when I saw that child's body, the humped back, the longish, almost medieval face, with a sewed up mouth, and an ear gone awry. But he wore a cape, carried himself with an air, and then you listened to marvelous speech, often brilliant, holding you spellbound, and looked into blue eyes as young as a spring dawn. His coming was the greatest thing that happened to the *Seven Arts*. . . . Bourne turned out to be the real leader, I take it, of what brains and creativeness we had at the time.

Raised in "an old, dull and very uncomfortable house" in Bloomfield, New Jersey, he was protected and indulged by his family; but as he grew up, he was "constantly confronted there by the immeasurable gulf between my outlook and theirs." He wrote a friend in 1915: "My relatives are quite hopeless, and I feel at times like a homesick wanderer, not even knowing where my true home is." Where other Greenwich Villagers, confident of their liberation movement, tended to view the older generation with a condescension which was good natured, at least to some extent, Bourne viewed the world of his elders with extreme bitterness. He was welcomed by less embittered Villagers as the most articulate spokesman for a Bohemian revolt of youth that promised to carry all before it. Later on, in the 1920's, Bourne became the martyred hero of the Lost Generation—the stilled voice of alienated youth.

Bourne's opening attack against the older generation in 1911 was specifically an attack against "A Letter to the Rising Generation," by Cornelia A. P. Comer. And since the lines of argument he martialed against Mrs. Comer's article remained basic to his subsequent thought on the subject, Mrs. Comer's influence upon his thought was evidently seminal. Her article has been dismissed as no more than a pretext for Bourne to express his philosophy; but, in fact, Bourne's arguments were carefully shaped to conform obversely to Mrs. Comer's most perceptive observations.

Mrs. Comer rightly observed that the rising generation of 1911 was different in kind from all generations that had preceded it. One basic difference was the religious difference. "Of the generation of your fathers and mothers," she wrote,

it may be generally affirmed that they received their early religious training under the old regime. Their characters were shaped by the faith of their fathers, and those characters usually remained firm and fixed. . . . You have the distinction of growing up with a spiritual training less in quantity and more diluted in quality than any 'Christian' generation for nineteen hundred years.

The dilution of religious indoctrination had been the unhappy consequence, in good measure, she wrote, of the battle between Darwinian science and religion in the seventies and eighties—the battle that had unsettled the old beliefs of the parents and had unfitted them to give effective religious instruction to the young. More fundamental than the challenge of science, however, had been the corrupting circumstances of the industrial revolution. She believed that the plain truth seemed to be

that the utmost which can be done for the child to-day is not enough to counterbalance the rapidly-growing disadvantages of urban life and modern conditions.

On the matter of modern conditions:

One wonders how Marcus Aurelius would have judged the moral possibilities of flats or apartment hotels? When one gets light by pushing a button, heat by turning a screw, water by touching a faucet, and food by going down in an elevator, life is so detached from the healthy exercise and discipline which used to accompany the mere process of living, that one must scramble energetically to a higher plane or drop to a much lower one.

Whereas former generations of children had been trained to a great extent by the circumstances of rural life, this generation was raised in circumstances which artificially produced idleness and self-indulgence.

The responsibilities of the schools for training youth in good habits had correspondingly increased, and "from the multiplied and improved machinery of education, it would seem that we must be far in advance of our fathers." And here Mrs. Comer launched into the comprehensive attack against progressive education, which appears to have been her main purpose for writing the article in the first place. In the "middle of an age of unparalleled mechanical invention and discovery," maturity was required as never before, and yet immaturity was prevailing, in the rising generation, as never before.

Scorning the "most obvious retort . . . that the world in which we find ourselves is in no way of our own making," Bourne began his reply with the "most obvious fact," which was "that the rising generation has practically brought itself up," for the very reasons Mrs. Comer had mentioned. "The two generations misunderstand each other as they never did before. This fact is a basal one to any comprehension of the situation." The schoolroom courses which former generations "gulped down raw," did not appeal to this self-directed generation. "The four years' period of high-school life among the comfortable classes is, instead of being a preparation for life, literally one round of social gaiety." However, "social virtues will be learned better in such a society than they can ever be from moral precepts." The artificial separation of the sexes disappears; and the girls, as well as the boys, "begin to chafe under the tutelage, nominal though it is, of the home," and take a serious view of life, as they, themselves, perceive it.

In a changing and increasingly complex world, Bourne argued, it becomes ever more difficult for men to avoid the alternatives of

being swallowed up in the routine of a big corporation, and experiencing the vicissitudes of a small business, which is now an uncertain, rickety affair, usually living by its wits, in the hands of men who are forced to subordinate everything to self-preservation.

The difficulty of finding activity which makes use of technical and creative ability had increased, and the younger generation had demonstrated a correspondingly greater initiative than former generations in preparing itself.

Our critics are misled by the fact that we do not talk about unselfishness and self-sacrifice and duty, as their generation apparently used to do ... It is true that we do not fuss and fume about our souls, or tend our characters like a hot-house plant. This is a changing, transitional age, and our view is outward rather than inward. ... We feel social injustice as our fathers felt personal sin. ... The religion that will mean anything to the rising generation will be based on social ideals. ... An unpleasantly large proportion of our energy is now drained off in fighting the fetishes which you of the older generation have passed along to us, and which, out of some curious instinct of self-preservation, you so vigorously defend.

In a subsequent essay, Bourne argued that

old men cherish a fond delusion that there is something mystically valuable in mere quantity of experience. Now the fact is, of course, that it is the young people who have all the really valuable experience. ... Very few people get any really new experience after they are twenty-five, unless there is a real change of environment. Most older men live only in the experience of their youthful years. If we get few ideas after we are twenty-five, we get few ideals after we are twenty. ... Youth, therefore, has no right to be humble. The ideals it forms will be the highest it will ever have, the insight the clearest, the ideas the most stimulating.

It is a tragedy of life that

youth rules the world, but only when it is no longer young. It is a tarnished, travestied youth that is in the saddle in the person of middle age. ... The dead hand of opinions formed in their college days clutches our leaders and directs their activities in this new and strangely altered physical and spiritual environment. Hence grievous friction, maladjustment, social war. And the faster society moves, the more terrific is the divergence between what is actually going on and what public opinion thinks is actually going on. It is only the young who are actually contemporaneous; they interpret what they see freshly and without prejudice; their vision is always the truest, and their interpretation always the justest.

Carl Van Doren wrote of that first truly filiarchal younger generation that

if Bourne was its philosopher, John Reed was its hero, Edna St. Vincent Millay its lyric poet, Eugene O'Neill its dramatist, Sinclair Lewis its satirist, Van Wyck Brooks its critic. . . . All these had been heard by 1920. In that year the Younger Generation put on new colors. Scott Fitzgerald was younger still. He had gone off to war from college, like E.E. Cummings and John Dos Passos and Ernest Hemingway and Laurence Stallings and Edmund Wilson. But Fitzgerald was precocious, found his voice before any of his contemporaries. . . . The name Younger Generation was fitted to whatever, in the early twenties, was rebellious, aspiring, experimental.

So the aging younger generation emerged from the bludgeonings of World War I to find a new younger generation in its midst—bright, inclined to be cynical, and not much concerned about what the older "real Greenwich Village" had had on its mind. In the opinion of the somewhat jazzy and socially irresponsible newcomers, as Malcolm Cowley wrote, the senior younger generation represented the oddly dressed remnants of the age that had just passed into history.

Apropos of this contrast between all generations in the 1920's, Carl Van Doren remarked upon the impossibility of communication between members of different generations, even in the most friendly and mutually tolerant spirit. Only when they have both advanced in age can members of two different generations share the same view of life, he argued, and even then they will be unable to communicate to each other what their different experiences of youth had been. This inability to communicate, which struck Van Doren, writing from the retrospect of the thirties, is a fact of life in filiarchal societies, or of any society that, as Bourne said, is characterized by a "new and strangely altered physical and spiritual environment." Pragmatic truth in filiarchal societies is not merely relative to changing circumstances; it is also multilateral according to generation. This has been a fact of life in the 1960's, as it was in the 1910's and 1920's.

FOUR

The
Technological
Order

5.

The Mechanization of American Society

··

BLESSED WITH A WEALTH of raw materials, driven by the American ethic and challenged by a shortage of labor, Americans early developed the "American System" of mass production, which Europeans admired in the nineteenth century but did not largely adopt until the twentieth. This American System had been fashioned by any number of hardheaded tinkers, who knew or cared nothing about speculative truths but relied instead on common sense and patient effort. With the age of electricity, beginning in the late nineteenth century, the system came to depend increasingly on scientists and engineers; but Americans of the Progressive era continued to believe in the story of the inventors and to conceive of technological progress in simple terms.

Believing in both the old values and the new technology, Progressive America blamed the disturbing social effects of mechanization on the trusts or the saloons and went on praying for both moral and material improvement. In the long run, however, the new machinery was bound to conflict with the old morality in ways too obvious to miss. The automobile was already creating some doubts about modern times in the prewar period. Then World War I came as the catalyst which separated American materialism from American idealism and opened the way for the Roaring Twenties.

Postwar demobilization, together with hundreds of major and minor strikes and the Great Red Scare, completed itself before the Republican and Democratic conventions met in the summer of 1920. The election that followed struck the keynote for the decade to come. Both parties nominated relative nonentities, the crowds cheered Babe Ruth, Cecil B. De Mille did box office business with *Male and Female* and *Don't Change Your Husband*, home radios and home refrigerators went on the market, annual automobile sales passed the two million mark, national prohibition became the permanent law of the land, women voted and Warren Gamaliel Harding won by the most collossal landslide in the history of the Presidency.

Nor did the pace slacken right up to the Great Crash. H. L. Mencken, who reported as much of it as he could follow, watched it, he said, with all the wide-eyed eagerness of a Methodist Sunday School superintendent touring the Paris peep-shows. Methodist Sunday School superintendents watched it also, and much of the fun for Mencken was the cacaphony of moral indignation that also continued ceaselessly to the Great Crash.

And then it seemed to be gone like a dream. Liberalism was regained, and the twenties came to be thought of as the decade of reaction between two eras of reform, as well as the decade of blatant mass culture—Babbittry—before the sobering onset of the depression.

This interpretation of the twenties, beyond being substantially false, leads to sweeping misunderstandings of American history and culture from that time to the present. The business civilization of the twenties was revolutionary rather than reactionary, unless private enterprise is to be considered reactionary simply by definition. And the managerial revolution that it accomplished survived the depression and the Second World War, to appear quite recognizably in the era of Eisenhower. Similarly the mass culture of the twenties continued through the thirties, even though it was overshadowed by the crisis of the depression; and it continues today with a blatancy that is very reminiscent of the twenties. Both for better and for worse, modern culture *is* mass culture, and the American Jazz Age was nothing less than the world premier of modern culture.

....

Dispensing with palaver, the American Philosophical Society, in the opening paragraph of the preface to the first volume of its published papers, spoke the mind of the New Republic on the eve of the first machine age: "Knowledge is of little use when confined to mere speculation: But when speculative truths are reduced to practice, when theories, grounded upon experiments, are applied to the common purposes of life . . . and, of course the increase and happiness of mankind promoted; knowledge then becomes really useful." Members would therefore confine themselves "to such subjects as tend to the improvement of their country."

To this inquiring but practical cast of mind was added the faith of the Declaration of Independence that all men are equally at liberty to pursue happiness and that they are endowed by their Creator with the ability to alter the forms to which they are accustomed for new forms, such as seem better suited to effect their safety and happiness. This right of the many to pursue happiness, which throughout the nineteenth century was a distinctively American right, led to American leadership in the manufacture of automobiles, home appliances, radios, phonographs and motion pictures, as well as parlor cars and safety razors, in the early twentieth century.

Among America's early inventors, the most prophetic for modern times, perhaps, was Oliver Evans, a Delaware farmer who, on the basis of an elementary reading knowledge of mechanical principles and evidently a good deal of reflecting and tinkering, originated for the world in 1783 the automated factory as a practical concept. Four years later, Evans completed the mechanized flour mill he had designed, and it worked. Grain, loaded into it from wagons or boats, was carried by endless belts and raised and lowered by screw conveyors and bucket conveyors, was cleaned and ground and bolted and made ready for packing, without human intervention.

An observer reported that "the whole contrivance was a set of rattle traps unworthy the attention of common sense." Nevertheless other mills borrowed from Evans' design, and sought from Congress "relief from the oppressive operation" of Evans' patent to do so. Jefferson, among others, agreed with the complainants that there was nothing new about the mill—that "the elevator is nothing more than the old Persian Wheel of Egypt, and the conveyor is the same thing as the screw of Archimedes." Evans' contemporaries could not conceive of the fact that he had invented, by his combination of anciently known physical principles, the revolutionary new system of the continuous production process which the twentieth century would associate with the name of Henry Ford.

Eli Whitney, the son of a prosperous Connecticut farmer, invented the cotton gin in 1793 while visiting in the South. One man, working the crank on the box of the machine that Whitney devised, could do the work of fifty in separating the cotton fiber from the seed. It made possible the rise of the Cotton Kingdom in the South—and it is a classic example of how a simple invention may be followed by unforetellably momentous consequences.

While operating a cotton gin factory in Hartford, Whitney thought up, or perhaps heard of, the idea of mass-producing firearms for the government by casting parts in standardized molds. The idea was not uniquely original with Whitney, for Jefferson had observed a similar system being unsuccessfully attempted in France in the 1780's, and Simeon North in Middletown, Connecticut, applied the system to the manufacture of pistols at the same time Whitney applied it to muskets. Whitney nevertheless rightfully won his second great claim to fame by successfully filling a large government contract—although he was years late in doing it—which brilliantly met the startling novel requirement of interchangeability of parts.

The first American textile factory to adopt the methods of the industrial revolution was built in Providence in 1791 by Samuel Slater, who had memorized English textile machinery and then emigrated to America where the information would be well paid for. From this beginning, many small yarn-spinning mills sprang up in New England in the next generation. Origins of the textile industry as a characteristically American development, however, are connected not so much with Slater and his successors as with the Boston merchant Francis Cabot Lowell and the Boston Manufacturing Company.

Lowell had made a systematic study of the British textile industry; and the War of 1812, by eliminating English competition for the time, gave him the opportunity which he, with a group of other wealthy Boston merchants, seized, to build the textile factory town of Waltham, Massachusetts. The originality of Waltham lay in its over-ail conception, rather than in specific methods, which were largely adaptations of English methods. The Waltham method was character-ized by an overriding emphasis upon standardization, integration, and mechanization of the processes. English factories were the results of the evolution of techniques from medieval times, and still tended to put out much of the work, such as weaving, to families in the area. In Waltham, the entire process was carried on in the factory by workers who were paid in money wages and who had been especially recruited and were housed on company property.

Concentrating on a low-cost, coarse weave of cloth and strongly backed by ample working capital, the Boston Manufacturing Com-pany weathered the postwar British competition and expanded to Lowell and other mill sites. Factory methods similar to those pio-neered by Evans, Whitney, North, and Lowell were applied in the following decades to clocks and watches and rugs and shoes and then to a host of other manufactures, operating according to what came to be called the "American System."

For many Europeans the first idea of the kind of machinery Amer-ica was beginning to use came with the Great Exhibition of 1851 in London. Congress had refused to appropriate funds for the American exhibit, which proved too meager for the space allotted it and which consequently drew a good deal of belittling notice from the British press. Then came the competition for prizes, and the grubby Ameri-can display transformed itself into the wonder of the day.

The outstanding stars of the show were the awkward-appearing grain reapers of Obed Hussey and Cyrus McCormick, which "chewed up wheat" with a speed and efficiency amazing to Europeans. The other American farm equipment made a profound impression as well. The draft plows did not find serious competition, and other agricul-tural contraptions and garden variety tools were of an order of excel-lence and originality not known about in Europe. American weapons were unrivaled, as were American locks. The sewing machines of Isaac M. Singer and others were enthusiastically admired. The vulcanized rubber of Charles Goodyear was on display, and something of its possibilities was seen at once.

A chorus of praise for the American display issued from the press, and a parliamentary committee pursued the task of investigating the sources of America's mechanical creativity and discovering ways in which England might benefit from the American example. "Great Britain," concluded one observer, "has received more useful ideas, and more ingenious inventions from the United States, through the exhibition, than from all other countries." Among American inventions cited admiringly by a British commission in 1854 were a peculiarly shaped screw auger; rope-spinning machinery; a new sort of trip-hammer; a new sort of steam tilt hammer; a machine for polishing lasts; a vertical saw for cutting irregular forms; and machines for sifting sand, cutting tiles, making casks, and packing up machinery.

In America, meanwhile, increasingly inhumane conditions were arising out of the factory system that had come into being. At the time when the American industrial revolution had been launched with the Waltham experiment, everybody involved, conspicuously including the work force, had benefited from the system, which had offered young women from New England farms the opportunity to earn some money of their own while living in wholesome and congenial surroundings.

Inventors of labor-saving devices, as well as proprietors of early factories, had not infrequently been motivated by an idealistic concern for the working man and woman. Once established, however, the factory, operating in a fiercely competitive system, tended, itself, to determine the conditions under which it would run—and a concern for human happiness was not one of its attributes. By the eve of the Civil War, conditions in the New England textile mills were as bad as they were in England, for a force of woman and child labor which increasingly was drawn from the growing ranks of immigrants.

Although these women and children occasionally rioted, they were in no position to organize effectively in their own behalf; nor would public sentiment have permitted it. The skilled mechanic was better situated in society than the factory workers were, however, and he possessed a clearer conception of his economic rights. In the new industrial world the skilled mechanic had actually made progress so far as his economic position was concerned, although his gains were not commensurate with the rapid increase in the value of what he produced. What he had lost, and what he bitterly felt the loss of, was the independent position in society the machine had deprived him of and the self-respect that had gone with the independence.

The journeyman who had received his training during the first decades of the nineteenth century had been brought up to believe that a community of interest bound the journeyman and his employer together in a joint enterprise. This journeyman had formerly worked with his own tools and at his own speed and had been paid for his finished product. He might have differences with his boss; he might even join a union and take part in a strike. He nevertheless had not lived with the idea that there was a logical opposition between capital and labor. This mechanic had not really been a wage earner in the way the word came to be used. He had been paid, not for his labor, but for his "price," that is, for the value of the product he had sold his employer, whether it had been shoes or coats or cabinets.

With the rise of the factory system, the craftsman ceased to make a complete product, but instead performed one or more operations in a mass production process for a fixed daily wage. He became a part of something which came to be complained of as "wage slavery." With the wage system came also the demand for the speeding up of production and the consequent tightening of discipline. Responsibility for maintaining this discipline was often delegated to a boss who was himself a hired man rather than the proprietor of the establishment, as had been the usual case before.

Against this new, impersonal, aristocratic factory system, the workingman made furious complaint. The shoemaker's trade journal, *The Awl,* complained in 1844 that

some of the shoe manufacturers seem to think that the jours [journeymen] are designed for no other purpose than to be their subjects. . . . They seem to think it a disgrace to labor; that the laborer is not as good as other people. These little stuck-up, self-conceited individuals who have a little second-hand credit. . . . You must do as they wish . . . or you are out of their books; they have no more employment for you.

And the National Typographical Society declared in 1850

it is useless for us to disguise from ourselves the fact that, under the present arrangement of things, there exists a perpetual antagonism between labor and capital ... one striving to seek their labor for as much, and the other striving to buy it for as little as they can.

Skilled workers during the forties and fifties organized into craft unions to defend their interests, demanding a ten-hour day, better wages, and generally better treatment respecting the dignity as well as safety and health of their persons. The depression of 1857 crushed them, however, and they did not recover during the period of Civil War and Reconstruction. It was not until the organization of the American Federation of Labor in 1886 that the modern labor movement began to develop on a national scale.

In 1876 Philadelphia hosted the first of the international exhibitions to be held in the New World, and admiring attention was again drawn to American mass production methods and American machinery and tools. "American production in this department," wrote a French observer,

is characterized by a wealth of practical new ideas, astonishingly clever adaptation to special requirements, accuracy of the component parts, and an increasing elegance in the outward appearance of the machine ... the American with quite new ideas has unsaddled the Englishman, and we must unhesitatingly follow the new system if we do not wish to fall behind.

A Swiss observer was similarly unstinting in his praise of the Americans for "the variety of special tools for every conceivable purpose," and the "amazingly automatic" character of many of them; and he saw in them the new world of the future.

If the human mind will quietly contemplate again the ideas and achievements of the wonderful American exhibition of machines, it will not fail to recognize the approach of an immense change. The productive power of automatic machines will rapidly develop and become magnificent, and will overwhelm all mankind with a quantity of products which, we will hope, will bring them blessing.

And a German visitor wrote,

The essential elements in the life of North Americans—the MACHINE —which has enabled them to replace laborious handwork, to mass-produce everything, and to acquire immense wealth in such a short time is over-whelmingly presented here. . . .

Wherever the eye turned, the constant effort to remove purely mechanical work from the human hand and to apply it only where artistic shapes and forms were required was obvious. Think of our nail-smiths: How soul destroying and how laborious is the work, and how little, perhaps 100 nails a day, can be manufactured by one worker. In America there are no more nail-smiths: the nail there is manufactured by the machine. The American auxiliary machines and machine tools which furnish all the needs of industry,—produce tools, make mortices, tenons, pegs,—are incomparable.

....

The late nineteenth century was a violent period in American industrial relations, punctuated by the Great Railroad Strike of 1877, the Homestead Strike of 1892, and the Pullman Strike of 1894, and accompanied by lockouts, court injunctions, and battles with scab labor and armies of police and Pinkerton men. In spite of this, no revolutionary proletariat emerged from the struggle until the small and scattered force of the Industrial Workers of the World, founded in 1905. Nine-tenths of industrial labor remained unorganized, but by the end of the century the American Federation of Labor had established itself as the dominant workers' organization in the nation.

Except for two major industrial unions, the Brewery Workers and the Mine Workers, the chief member unions of the AFL represented skilled crafts, and, despite efforts of Socialists to win control of the Federation, it continued to reflect the procapitalist position of its founder and long-time president, Samuel Gompers. It was Gompers' argument that "unions, pure and simple, are the natural organization of wage workers to secure their present material and practical improvement and to achieve their final emancipation. . . . The way out of the wage system is through higher wages." Evidently most non-union workers also accepted the capitalist system without question and counted on the machine to make a better world for them, just as the owners of the factories did.

But though the worker did not turn anticapitalist, there remained that antagonism between capital and labor which had arisen with the wage system—the employer tending to want as much work for as little pay as possible, and the worker tending to do as little as he could get away with for as much money as he could get. This was accepted as a fact of industrial life which worked itself out in practice, one way or another. Various schemes of incentive payments were known about and fairly widely used; but until Frederick Winslow Taylor developed scientific management, it was not supposed that a man could be operated like a machine. Taylor went far toward proving that he could be.

Scientific management as developed by Taylor was intended as the means of applying the Protestant ethic with mathematical precision. Brought up in a well-to-do Philadelphia family by a mother who was an active antislavery and woman's rights champion, Taylor chose to start his career as a factory hand and work his way up, when headaches and eye trouble decided him against college. Taking a job at Midvale Steel Company as a journeyman machinist, he rose to chief engineer in six years. It was an occupation he was well situated to observe objectively, for he was not dependent on his wages and did not live a workman's life after hours.

Taylor was imbued with the American belief in the virtue of hard work, and he put great store by "the real monotonous grind which trains character." He was disturbed by the lazy and sloppy work he observed at the factory. He argued that efficient working methods, by increasing productivity, would benefit the worker in wage raises as well as the company in profits, and he argued that it was the company's responsibility to see to it that these optimum conditions were achieved.

It was the business of management, he argued, to make studies of all of the work operations, to train the workers to know precisely how to carry out their tasks, and then to time their performances to determine whether objective standards were being met. Under these conditions, incentive pay for those who produced beyond the established norm would mean something. The norm would have been scientifically established and could itself be insisted upon. The benefits would be in profits and wages, and perhaps most important of all, in the spiritual condition of the workers, who would constantly be giving of their best.

The Taylor System, where it was introduced, supplanted the conventional "military system" of a chain of command from manager to foreman to worker. The planning department, operating through the instruction card clerk, relieved the foreman of much of his responsibility. Taylor had worked out his system in great detail and had tested it with great success at Midvale Steel Company when he delivered his first important paper in 1895 before the American Society of Mechanical Engineers on "A Piece-Rate System." His system met the opposition, first of management, which resented Taylor's never-ending disruption of routine at Bethlehem Steel and fired him, and next of labor, which suspected scientific management of being simply the scientific sweating of labor. Taylor's following increased, however, in labor as well as management, and the Taylor Society was founded in 1911 to forward the system.

Among those who joined Taylor in the crusade for increased efficiency, the most influential was Frank B. Gilbreth, working in co-operation with his psychologist-wife Lillian M. Gilbreth. The principal addition of the Gilbreths to the stop-watch methods of Taylor was the motion study. The Gilbreths broadened the area to include the psychology of work and problems of psychological contributions to worker fatigue, but the mechanical aspect remained in the foreground. "It is the aim of Scientific Management," Gilbreth wrote, "to induce men to act as nearly like machines as possible, so far as doing the work in the one best way that has been discovered is concerned." It was his finding that generally "it does *not* refresh a worker to use different motions. . . . Different motions each time require additional effort, a new mental process and a complete additional effort."

During the Progressive era, Taylorites joined the camp of the Progressives, who stressed efficiency in government, in the utilization of the nation's natural resources, and in the operations of business. Louis Brandeis gave scientific management the best national publicity it had yet received by using it to attack the railroads' rate-making policies. The concept suggested to President Wilson the idea of an "all-correlating moral adventure," while it led Roosevelt to observe that "the time, health, and vitality of our people are as well worth conserving, at least, as our forests, minerals, and lands."

Taylorites were given significant parts to play in the war effort, and after the war, they were enlisted in the fleetingly hopeful cause of "Industrial Democracy." Dishearteningly for some of them, however, scientific management came into its own during the triumphantly antiunion era that followed the defeats of the postwar strikes. During the twenties the ranks of the Taylor Society were swelled by staff members from General Electric, Du Pont, Western Electric, and A.T. & T.; and "human engineering" became part of the businessman's "American Plan."

In attempting to reform the steel industry, Taylor had been up against an industrial system that was already fairly set in its ways and resistant to change. The automobile industry, on the other hand, was just starting out in bicycle shops all over the country at the turn of the century. Rational methods of operation could be developed and maintained from the beginning. In the case of Henry Ford and his Model T, rational methods of operation were developed beyond anything the history of mass production had witnessed. Ford made himself the master of modern mass production, but his achievement went beyond even this. In addition to moving the world into a new stage in the machine process, he made himself the prophet of the democratic machine age. By the eve of World War I, Ford and his Model T had come to signify to millions of Americans what the American machine age meant.

Until 1907 Ford was only a very skillful mechanic and shrewd and successful businessman in an automobile industry around Detroit which had hardly been seriously thought of a dozen years before. Then against all of the best-qualified advice in town, Ford announced his mission to the world and became a figure of international importance.

I will build a motor car for the great multitude. It will be large enough for the family but small enough for the individual to run and care for. It will be constructed of the best materials, by the best men to be hired, after the simplest designs that modern engineering can devise. But it will be so low in price that no man making a good salary will be unable to own one—and enjoy with his family the blessing of hours of pleasure in God's great open spaces.

Ransome E. Olds had already pioneered successfully in making inexpensive cars; and all American manufacturers, to the extent that circumstances seemed to justify it, had turned to mass production methods, which were the typically American methods. Ford, however, at a time when the auto was still principally the plaything of the sporting crowd and the rather rich, thrust all of his considerable resources into the construction of one cheap, light, durable, ugly car for the common man, especially designed for the wretched rutted roads which the nation then provided.

Having set the task, which was generally thought possible as an engineering feat but hopelessly impractical from a business point of view, Ford built his factory at Highland Park and drove his work force toward the goal. The problem of combining durability with lightness was solved with vanadium alloy. The problem of persuading men to stay on jobs, which were at once hectic and monotonous, was solved by the five-dollar day, which was about double the going wage in the industry. And finally the master solution was the moving assembly line. Endless controversy has surrounded the subject of precisely what credit Ford deserves for his many specific innovations; it appears that these three main ideas were very likely suggested by others. The project as a whole was Ford's doing however.

The central conveyor belt was first installed in 1914, reducing the time it took to assemble a car to one-tenth of what it had formerly been. Then subassembly lines were joined to the central conveyor, so that the workers throughout the plant might stand, each at his station, before a waist-high moving belt and repeat one simple task. The completely assembled Model T moved off the line at a rate of one a minute in 1920 and one every ten seconds in 1925. Conveyor belts had been in use in America since Oliver Evans' grist mill; but there had never been an undertaking like Highland Park, where men and machinery were coordinated into one integrated machine. Production rose to 39,640 in 1911 to 342,115 in 1915 to 740,770 in 1917. In 1920 every other car in the world was a Model T Ford.

....

The idea that middle-class daughters might go out in the world and work for their livings was not a new one to Progressive America, because circumstances had often made this unavoidable in the past. In the nineteenth century, however, the genteel working woman had been a pity to her friends. This was still true to some extent in the Progressive era; but by that time the machine age was offering respectable and at the same time inviting jobs to young women, creating a situation which was more than the old moral order could cope with.

During the nineteenth century the most widely available occupation for genteel women was elementary school teaching, for long hours and low wages and under strict supervision by the community as a whole. It was not to be thought of that teaching should become an attractive alternative to marriage, but the position was recognized as at least a permissible alternative. To this was added, during and after the Civil War, a poorly paid and overworked but well-regarded female nursing profession. There were even some women who fought it out all along the line to become physicians and lawyers. They were few in number, but they were at least symbolically important.

It was the common office girl, however, and not the exceptional woman physician or lawyer, who ushered in the new era of freedom for young women; for the typist not only won her place in the business world against male competition, but she won it with ease. And with it, she won the decent working conditions and, in many cases, the freedom during off-hours that men holding comparable jobs received.

Office work had traditionally been considered a man's or a boy's job, until the invention of the typewriter, which was first marketed in 1873. Women became typists at the time when the typewriter itself was a novelty, and they successfully identified themselves with the new vocation at the outset. Courses in typing were provided for them in the eighties by the New York YWCA and Cooper Union, and by 1900, 85,000 women were employed, most of them single and under twenty-five. Together with clerks, copyists, bookeepers and accountants, the female office workers by then numbered 403,000 or one-twelfth of all gainfully employed women in the nation.

Moving confidently about the office among the gentlemen, businesslike in her black skirt and white shirtwaist, the office girl made herself an attractive and essential part of the business world. The ease and swiftness of her conquest was partly due to the fact that she was more tractable than most men would have been in the same situation—in positions which offered little possibility for advancement—and did not worry herself about advancement. It was also due to the fact that employers found young women more pleasant to have around in such positions than men, who rather pathetically remained as "the boy at the office," no matter how old they became. Office work provided young women with a respectable occupation in which they were able to use the appeal of their sex to advantage.

Henry B. Fuller's *The Cliff-Dwellers,* which appeared in 1893, is a novel about life in an eighteen-story office building in downtown Chicago.

The tribe inhabiting the Clifton is large and rather heterogeneous. All told, it numbers about four thousand souls. It includes bankers, capitalists, lawyers, "promoters"; brokers in bonds, stocks, pork, oil, mortgages; real-estate people and railroad people and insurance people—life, fire, marine, accident; a host of principals, agents, middlemen, clerks, cashiers, stenographers, and errand-boys; and the necessary force of engineers, janitors, scrub-women, and elevator-hands.

A minor heroine in the novel is Cornelia McNabb, who came to Chicago because "I couldn't make out that I was going to have any terrible great show there in Pewaukee." She worked for a while in the restaurant in the Clifton Building as head waitress and lied in her letters home that she was a ten-dollar-a-week clerk. (Her parents had not wanted her to go to Chicago at all.) She had gone to high school in Pewaukee, however, and had even taught a term in Waukesha County, and while working as a waitress she had taken a course in shorthand and typing at the Athenaeum.

With her new skill, Cornelia landed a job as a typist for several offices in the Clifton, easily sloughing off some of her small-town manners. "You needn't think the Pewaukee girls are jays," she explained. "They're too near Lakeside and Waukesha for that." She "dressed with a trim and subdued modishness. She had taken a good many cues from Mrs. Floyd, and she had not been above cultivating an intimacy with a girl who worked for the excessively dear and fashionable house that dressed Mrs. Ingles." She accepted dinner engagements with different men in the building, and she married Burton Brainard, son of the president of the Underground National Bank, which was situated in the Clifton.

Cornelia was a schemer, but she was no Becky Sharp. She had simply taken the modern opportunity the typewriter represented. The typewriter as a practical instrument had been invented by Christopher Latham Sholes. Toward the end of Sholes's life, his daughter-in-law had once said to him, "Father Sholes, what a wonderful thing you have done for the world!" and he had replied, "I don't know about the world, but I feel that I have done something for the women who had always had to work so hard. This will help them earn a living more easily."

Cornelia McNabb's high school education had placed her among the privileged minority in the nineties, but once she had shown what a high school education could do for a girl, almost all of the girls kept on through high school if they could. Between 1890 and 1924, public school enrollment in the United States increased twenty times more rapidly than the increase in the national population. In the twenties a junior high school education was considered sufficient for mail clerks and filers; but a high school education was needed for stenographers, dictating machine operators, bookkeepers, bookkeeping-machine operators, and office managers. A college education was generally required for a good secretarial stenographer's job.

Like Cornelia McNabb, these office girls expected to marry and settle down and put their office careers behind them, together with the apartment-house living which may well have been a part of the careers. They had entered the machine age as their mothers never had, however, and the modern outlook they had acquired would remain with them in marriage. And on the whole it would serve them well in marriage, because the American household was rapidly becoming more and more directly geared to the machine age.

The industrial revolution had started out, with the spinning jenny and Crompton's mule, as the housewife's boon; and it has remained at the housewife's service ever since, forever seeking new ways to lighten and brighten her domestic chores and appeal to her fancies. If the consequence has been to enmesh many American women in a mechanized, impersonal, and dreadfully unrequiting feminine mystique of modern living, that is not to deny that machinery has helped enormously with the housework. Nor is it to deny that the industrial revolution has served to raise the status of women in society generally.

Until the industrial revolution, women were considered to be comprehensively inferior to men, except for their ability to bear children. In machine age America, on the other hand, women came to be considered simultaneously inferior, superior, and equal to men, depending on the context. The woman's place in machine age society was never clearly determined, but it ceased to be limited to kitchen, church, and nursery. In one way or another, the industrial revolution in time delivered most women to some extent at least from the slavery of the family circle.

Respectable office girls were a sign of this incipient emancipation from the family circle during the Progressive era, and so were the rapidly increasing retail services, all ambitious to relieve the housewife of some of her burdens. Department stores such as Wanamaker's and Macy's and Gimbel's offered an almost infinite variety of manufactured household furnishings and apparel and whatnot. Montgomery Ward had started its mail-order service in 1872, Sears, Roebuck & Co. began in 1886, and during the first decade of the twentieth century, a large number of chain stores entered the field, such as J. C. Penney, Peoples Drug Stores, and A. S. Beck Shoe Corporation.

Nevertheless, middle-class American housewives in Progressive America continued to preside over households which were as yet unchanged by the machine age in any fundamental respect. Although bourgeois wealth came from the industrial revolution, bourgeois home life continued to belong to more traditional times. The Railroad Age was also the age of the trolley and the horse and buggy, and people did not think of moving about as they soon would with the coming of the automobile. Middle-class families did not ordinarily maintain their own carriages or keep a summer place or go on trips very much; and aside from expenses for college educations and perhaps boarding schools, the house the family lived in represented the one major family expenditure.

Normally, the lives of all of the members of the family centered around the home; and middle-class homes were sufficiently commodious to accommodate grandparents, maiden aunts, and other relatives on a permanent basis. Construction costs being as low as they were, middle-income housing at the turn of the century was more substantial than any but very rich people could afford to build two or three generations later. Upper-middle-class homes were typically three- and four-story buildings of from fifteen to twenty rooms, in addition to bathrooms and storage and utility rooms. These were built and kept up on the basis of $20,000 incomes, representing about five times that amount, very roughly, in mid-twentieth-century dollars. The mudsill of the middle class managed on a $1,500 income, which, with economies, could maintain a family in a two-story house on the best street in a town of 20,000. The economies would not include doing without a full-time maid, for this was essential to middle-class life and involved only a very moderate expense.

The servant situation was an important reason why middle-class households had resisted the machine age to the extent they had. The budget for the upper-middle-class household with fifteen to twenty rooms would easily afford a full-time cook, a gardener, a waitress, and a laundress, the latter two also doing the upstairs work. The total cost for this full-time help would be perhaps $17.50 a week; in addition, a seamstress would come in regularly, as well as, perhaps a cleaning woman at $1.50 a day, and a handyman for little more. The cost to the mudsill middle-class family for the full-time cook-maid would be about $4 a week, and the seamstress and handyman would help out there also.

This enormously favorable situation, which was perversely referred to in middle-class circles as "the servant problem," resulted mainly from the New Immigration from southeastern and central Europe, beginning in the mid-eighties, together with the northern migration of Negroes after the turn of the century. The New Immigration continued at a declining rate through most of the 1920's, and although the office girl better represented the spirit of the decade, the class of domestic servant remained the most numerous class of women workers. By that time, however, the machine age had revolutionized middle-class households, and prosperity was even beginning to extend some of the benefits of the machine age to members of the recent immigrant groups as well. And to the extent that lower-class families were experiencing some of the benefits as well as the worst of the burdens of the industrial revolution, the tendency was for them to approach the changing middle-class standards which were the recognized though changing national standards. To misappropriate a figure of speech from the Communist Manifesto, they were widening their existence as fractions of the middle class.

....

Where the Railroad era had run on coal, the Roaring Twenties was powered by gasoline and electricity. This, together with the new applications of chemistry to daily life, constituted the technological basis for the cultural revolution that followed the war. The chemical industry as a national cultural influence began during the war, when the government confiscated German patents and turned them over to American companies. The automotive and electrical industries, however, were far enough advanced by the eve of the war to indicate that a distinctly new era of some sort was at hand.

Automobile production had increased from 4,000 in 1900 to 573,-000 in 1914 to almost 1.9 million in 1917. Two million Model T Fords had been manufactured during those latter four years, and the day of the common man on wheels had come. Industrial power was 30 percent electric in 1914 as compared with 70 percent fifteen years later, and electric lighting, which only the fairly rich could afford at the turn of the century, had widely replaced gas lights in the cities before the war. Telephones had increased from 1.3 million in 1900 to 10.5 million in 1915. Movies were drawing crowds in theaters and barns across the nation, and the sale of phonograph records was rivaling the sale of sheet music. The new era was at hand, but the war in Europe was the major event of the day, demanding national concentration on Americanism and preparedness and then on mobilization for victory.

The new era belonged to engineers and business bureaucrats rather than to inventive mechanics and rugged individualists. The main difference technologically was the difference between the dynamo and the boiler room as sources for creative power. The potentialities of electricity could not be concretely visualized as the potentialities of steam power could, but required instead to be visualized in mathematical and scientific terms. A like change was taking place in the business world with the rise of finance capitalism. Henry Ford was an inventive mechanic and rugged individualist who successfully defied the laws of the new era down to his death in 1947; but Ford was the great exception, who rose to the top of a great industry during its primitive stage of development and after that just managed to hang on.

Ford, himself, believed that the technological progress of the age could be best understood as personified in the practical genius of his old friend Thomas Alva Edison. "It is the fashion to call this the age of industry," Ford wrote in *Edison as I Know Him*. "Rather, we should call it the age of Edison. For he is the founder of modern industry in this country." Edison was indeed the principal American founder of the world of electric lights, of phonographs, radios and motion pictures, and, as much as any other American of his time, of the potent and flexible force of the dynamo. Nor was he by any means forgotten by the age. He took care to keep himself in the public eye as "a simple, democratic, old man," and when the lights of the nation were turned on each evening, they went on in honor of Edison.

Edison's American reputation is that of the great inventor, the giver of light, and proof that what is worth doing in applied science mainly calls for the time-honored American qualities of common sense, native shrewdness, and stick-to-itiveness, and doesn't need all the frills of a fancy education. Norbert Wiener has argued, however, that Edison's

greatest invention was that of the industrial research laboratory, turning out inventions as a business. The General Electric Company, the Westinghouse interests and the Bell Telephone Laboratories followed in his footsteps, employing scientists by hundreds where Edison employed them by tens. Invention came to mean, not the gadget-insight of a shop-worker, but the result of a careful, comprehensive search by a team of competent scientists.

General Electric founded its research laboratory in 1900, and Du Pont followed two years later. Bell Telephone Laboratories were established in 1925, by which time American business had learned—in part from the German example, demonstrated throughout World War I—that pure science could pay off.

The transition from the freely enterprising industrialist to the organization man had been in progress since the depression of 1893 and earlier. Then, during the Progressive era, the trend was to some extent reversed, amid the emergence of new industries, such as the automobile and motion picture industries, which Wall Street bankers shunned as bad risks. World War I served to liberate American businesses from financial reliance on Wall Street by enabling businesses to accumulate capital through exorbitant profits, even after the payment of excess profits taxes. These widely distributed war profits enabled businesses to finance new ventures or to develop existing ones without having to apply to the conservative banking community for funds.

On the other hand, the war unified the national business community under government auspices in the common effort to mobilize for victory. The Council of National Defense, as initially created to coordinate the economy, was made up of a top executive from A.T. & T., the presidents of Sears, Roebuck and B. & O. Railroad, two scientists, the Wall Street broker Bernard Baruch, and Samuel Gompers. The most important of the subsequent wartime economic agencies, the War Industries Board, directed by Bernard Baruch, effected sweeping changes in the economy in the direction of simplification, standardization, and coordination. The major industries had developed trade associations before the war, and during the war, these associations became an important basis for industrial cooperation. Herbert Hoover served as Food Administrator during the war. Afterwards, as Secretary of Commerce in the twenties, Hoover vigorously supported the trade associations as the "industrial self-government" which, in his mind, was basic to American democracy in the machine age.

American business emerged from the war with more venture capital than ever before and with unprecedented experience in capitalistic coordination; the outcome of this was the business civilization of the twenties. Its arrival was heralded in innumerable ways in the immediate postwar period. One of them was the transfer in 1920 of 2.5 million shares of General Motors stock from William C. Durant to the Du Pont interests and the consequent assumption of control of GM by the Massachusetts Institute of Technology graduates Pierre Du Pont and Alfred P. Sloan, Jr.

Durant, a wheeler-dealer type of businessman, had followed as individualistic a career as Henry Ford had in the automobile industry, and until 1920 his success had been second only to that of Ford's. He had taken over Buick in 1904, incorporated General Motors in 1908, added Cadillac, Oldsmobile, Oakland, and Pontiac, lost control in 1910, developed Chevrolet to compete with the Model T, regained control of General Motors in 1916, and added the Fisher Body Company two years later. In addition, he had launched the home refrigeration industry with Frigidaire and had entered the tractor and farm machinery fields. These last ventures had proved too much for him, and a Du Pont-Morgan syndicate took up his stock.

In his *Adventures of a White-Collar Man,* Sloan observed,

Although I had become a vice-president of General Motors Corporation and had important responsibilities under Mr. Durant, our methods of approaching operating problems were entirely different. . . . General Motors had become too big to be a one-man show. . . . The future required something more than an individual's genius. In any company I would be the first to say that William C. Durant was a genius. But General Motors justified the most competent executive group that could possibly be brought together.

Sloan, who became president of the company in 1923, accordingly instituted a program of decentralization of management which was "analogous to free enterprise" in his mind.

After forty years of experience in American industry, I would say that my concept of the management scheme of a great industrial organization, simply expressed, is to divide it into as many parts as consistently can be done, place in charge of each part the most capable executive that can be found, develop a system of coordination so that each part may strengthen and support each other part; thus not only welding all parts together in the common interests of a joint enterprise, but importantly developing ability and initiative through instrumentalities of responsibility and ambition—developing men and giving them an opportunity to exercise their talents, both in their own interests as well as in that of the business.

This was the way of doing things which had been followed in the late nineteenth century by John D. Rockefeller with Standard Oil and by J. P. Morgan with the reorganization of railroad systems and the creation in 1901 of United States Steel. What was "analogous to free enterprise" to Sloan's way of thinking, had been unpopularly known a generation earlier as the "trustification" of business. Some of the new industries such as motion pictures, safety razors, automobiles, and photographic equipment had carried on for a time in the individualistic manner of the robber barons, and some, like Ford, managed to go on doing so. Ford paid a price for his individualism, however, by falling to third rank in the industry behind General Motors and Chrysler in an age when the man, however remarkable his genius, was no longer a match for the organization.

It was an article of faith of the organization man that by serving the interests of his company, he was serving the interests of the American people as a whole. He believed that the success of American business was founded upon the principles of individual initiative and competitive business conditions. He believed that these principles were not in conflict with his devotion to the principle of loyalty to group rather than to self or with the strategy of suppressing competition through trade associations for purposes of efficiency of operation.

There was no contradiction, Judge Elbert J. Gary, chairman of the board of United States Steel, told the annual banquet of the American Iron and Steel Institute in 1927, between perfect cooperation and perfect competition. He believed that the same legal protection of person was due a corporation as was due a living individual. He held to a credo which Thurman Arnold termed the folklore of capitalism, and until the system broke down in 1929 most of American society was willing to agree with him.

What made America believe in the wisdom of management was the wonderful new prosperity, which was expressing itself in all of the new products. The nation shared very unequally in this prosperity; but, even so, the general standard of living in the cities rose from 1923 to 1929 as it never had before, and as it increased, it simultaneously changed in terms of the new things that were becoming involved in what people understood the phrase "standard of living" to mean.

Among the most talked-about innovations of the twenties were the household appliances that operated on electricity. By the end of the decade, electric irons were to be found in most working-class homes and vacuum cleaners and washing machines in most of the homes of the middle-class families. The icebox was still widely relied upon; but the mechanical refrigerator, almost nonexistent at the opening of the decade in private homes, was standard equipment for the well-to-do ten years later. In the working-class homes that were unable to afford electrical equipment, the improvement in living standards was, comparatively speaking, equally marked, in the change from wood fuel to coal and from wood floors to linoleum and from fetching water by the bucket to tap water.

Nobody in the twenties was old enough to remember the age of homespun unless he had come from an isolated rural community; but most of America at the opening of the twentieth century had still been in the age of yard goods, the soap vat, the butter churn, and the cracker barrel, and when you "just spent your summer canning," as one woman remembered it. Foods and other household commodities were ever more widely available in packages and cans in the twenties, and fresh fruits and vegetables were in the stores the year around. Ready-made clothes, especially for men, had very generally replaced home-sewn, and, to a lesser extent, tailored articles. The twenties was the great decade of development for the commercial laundries. Home-baked bread became a thing of the past in the cities.

New materials of the age included Pyrex, Bakelite, cellophane, celanese, rayon, dry ice, and a vast variety of paints and cosmetics and medicinal preparations. New forms of mass media included tabloid newspapers, airplane skywriting, electric signs, sound movies, and radio broadcasting. Commercial radio began in November 1920, and two years later, 3 million homes possessed radio sets. Weekly movie attendance was 40 million in 1922 and 100 million in 1930. The output of automobiles increased year after year to 4.5 million in the peak year of 1929. By then there was one car to every five persons in America. Almost the ultimate in technological happiness had been accomplished by the end of the twenties in the air-conditioned movie theater wired for sound.

....

The impact of the increases in productivity was multiplied by the introduction of new products and new services and by the opening of the national market to local products and local brands, which took advantage of the development of the trucking industry. The purchasing power of the nation was also increasing at an unprecedented rate, but, even so, it was far from keeping pace with the expansion of goods and services. Henry Ford advocated increasing the national ability to consume by rigorously cutting prices and raising wages; but Ford was considered eccentric by other business leaders, particularly in his economic views. They considered their first duty to be to their stockholders, and they therefore believed themselves to be morally committed to stable prices and high profits.

But while the business community rejected Ford's utopian vision of a land of plenty at prices within the reach of all, some means obviously had to be found to accommodate the flow of production. Installment buying was one approach that was increasingly taken as the decade wore on, but credit had its limits also. The nationwide competition for the consumer's dollar came to be seen as the challenge of the decade to the business world. The primary response to this challenge was national advertising, and the wisest man of the day was thought to be the public relations counsel.

Retailers of products had relied on newspaper advertising from colonial times; and as national markets opened up in the Railroad era, national advertising kept pace in national magazines. By the turn of the century the public was becoming familiar with brand names, and the phrase "advertising psychology" was coined. Down to World War I, however, advertising was thought of as serving the purpose of informing the public about products and prices and substantially nothing more. By 1926 Calvin Coolidge indicated a new role that advertising had assumed when he asserted that "it makes new thoughts, new desires and new actions. . . . It is the most potent influence in adopting, and changing the habits and modes of life, affecting what we eat, what we wear, and the work and play of the whole nation."

In a rough-and-ready way, advertisers had always dealt in psychology; but in the age of human engineering they pursued psychology in a serious, scholarly way. The father of behaviorism, John B. Watson, had left the ivory tower for the advertiser's executive suite, and advertising agencies set about converting people into consumers who would uniformly respond to uniform stimuli. From the time the consumer of the 1920's arose in the morning and guarded himself against halitosis, B.O., and tooth decay to the time he retired for the night, after easing his aches and pains, preventing athlete's foot, and guarding against insomnia, he was continuously stimulated by advertising. "There is no detail too trivial," said Edward Bernays, the leading public relations counsel of the day, "to influence the public in a favorable or unfavorable sense."

Batten, Barton, Durstine & Osborne was among the leading advertising firms of the decade, and all four partners were apostles of the creed of national salvation through better advertising. Among them, Bruce Barton was the most effective in carrying the message to the people with his essay on Jesus, *The Man Nobody Knows,* which became a best seller of the mid-twenties. According to Barton, Jesus "picked up twelve men from the bottom ranks of business and forged them into an organization that conquered the world." Essentially

Jesus had been a salesman whose parables were "the most powerful advertisements of all time." Conversely Calvin Coolidge declared that "the man who builds a factory builds a temple, the man who works there worships there."

Sinclair Lewis's *Babbitt* appeared in 1922, and "Babbitt" and "Babbittry" went at once into the language, indicating both that the phenomenon it described was recognized as being typically American and that there were many Americans who were critical of the phenomenon. Babbitt, from the standpoint of his job of selling houses, thought of family life, including his own, as consisting mainly of the consumption of mass-produced and nationally advertised products. He was more immediately concerned with the brand of toothpaste his daughter used than with the college she went to, because he was part of the world of nationally advertised brands, and he was loyal to his world. His "god was Modern Appliances," and his ambition for his family was that it be up to date.

In former times the accepted duty of the father had been to transmit a traditional code of morals to his children, but for Babbitt this way of doing things was out of date. His parental responsibility was to see to it that his children got the same things and were able to do the same things the other children in their generation and neighborhood got and did, without being concerned much about inherited rules of conduct. Dependent for his livelihood upon his sociability and upon his success in adjusting to changing taste, Babbitt kept up with what was right and what was wrong through his associations with customers and with fellow members of the Elks, the Boosters' Club, the Chamber of Commerce, the Zenith Athletic Club, and the Outing Golf and Country Club.

Babbitt subscribed to the consumption-oriented message of national advertising, but he also gave lip service to the production-oriented belief in the virtue and necessity of hard work and thrift. This was cultural lag rather than conservatism; for he valued hard work and thrift without giving any thought to practicing it, just as he favored prohibition without giving any thought to practicing it.

Holding vestigial beliefs in the Protestant ethic, Babbitt subscribed absolutely to what William H. Whyte, Jr., has called the social ethic and has defined as "that contemporary body of thought which makes morally legitimate the pressures of society against the individual." Whyte divided the social ethic into three propositions: "a belief in the group as the source of creativity; a belief in 'belongingness' as the ultimate need of the individual; and a belief in the application of science to achieve the belongingness." By science, Whyte meant "social engineering," which Babbitt, being an independent real estate broker rather than a true corporate organization man, was not in a position fully to appreciate. And the private profit motive was naturally strong in Babbitt; yet the social ethic dominated his thought and conduct as it tended generally to dominate business thought and conduct in the twenties.

Others in Babbitt's world were more flamboyantly consumption-oriented than Babbitt himself, including the millionaire Charley McKelvey "and all that booze-hoisting set of his," and also including the Dopplebraus, whom Babbitt considered "Bohemian." Indeed, the Bohemian anti-Babbitts may be said to have been unwillingly in league with the advertisers on this question. It was the position of the Bohemians of the twenties, Malcolm Cowley wrote in *Exile's Return,* that "there must be a new ethic that encouraged people to buy, a *consumption* ethic." He noted that Greenwich Village ideas lent themselves well to this ethic.

Thus *self-expression* and *paganism* encouraged a demand for all sorts of products—modern furniture, beach pajamas, cosmetics, colored bathrooms with toilet paper to match. *Living for the moment* meant buying an automobile, radio or house, using it now and paying for it tomorrow. *Female equality* was capable of doubling the consumption of products—cigarettes, for example—that had formerly been used by men alone.

As Cowley ruefully concluded, "Everything fitted into the business picture."

Babbittry became the subject of renewed scholarly interest amid the return to prosperity after World War II; it was subjected to numerous analyses, most of which were explicitly scientific and implicitly hostile. Among these, probably the most influential in updating and revalidating the Babbitt image has been David Riesman's *The Lonely Crowd,* with its distinction between "inner-directed" and "other-directed" social types. Riesman, with his coauthors Nathan Glazer and Reuel Denney, wrote of the inner-directed type that

the source of direction for the individual is 'inner' in the sense that it is implanted early in life by the elders and directed toward generalized but nonetheless inescapably destined goals. [On the other hand], What is common to all the other-directed people is that their contemporaries are the source of direction for the individual—either those known to him or those with whom he is indirectly acquainted, through friends and through the mass media.

Inner-directed man, according to Riesman, was the characteristic product of the early stages of the machine age, when men's energies were devoted to the work of producing goods, the marketing of them being a secondary consideration. The other-directed man, on the other hand, is characteristic of later stages of the machine age, when overproduction becomes a problem, and energies are increasingly spent on persuading the public to buy more goods and services. The consequence, Riesman argued, is a social transition from "Morality to Morale" and from "Invisible Hand to Glad Hand." Furthermore, other-directed parents, lacking the self-assurance that inner-direction brings, permit their children to make their own rules; and their children become other-directed by their own childhood peers.

Critics of *The Lonely Crowd* have argued that Riesman underestimated the extent to which other-directedness characterized American society in the mid-nineteenth century and earlier. They have also pointed out that, as contemporary accounts by European observers indicate, American parents in that earlier period were already treating their children permissively by European standards. Tocqueville and other foreign travelers also observed tendencies toward conspicuous consumption among the Americans. What they did not observe, however, was anything approaching the pattern of consumption as it would be affected by later technology, for this was not apparent, even at the height of the Railroad era. Technological change in the Railroad era suggested the comparatively gradual evolutionary process such as could be explained in Spencerian and Darwinian terms. Technological change as it manifested itself in the twenties, however, was rapid change from decade to decade, from year to year, and from day to day. The sense of living in the age of the miracles of science was not a phenomenon of Tocqueville's America, which was still living in the old age of biblical miracles to a very considerable extent. The emergence of the modern age of miracles in American culture corresponds with the rise in the reputation of Thomas Alva Edison, and the 1920's was fully under the spell of its magic.

America in the twenties was a nation of avid, astonished, and somewhat aimless consumers amid movies and records and radios and appliances and cars and trucks and airplanes and on and on, ad infinitum. The decade itself produced the effect of passing before the people like a continual newsreel, featuring from one moment to the next Red Grange, Bill Tilden, Mary Pickford, Charlie Chaplin, Floyd Collins trapped in a cave, and Shipwreck Kelly setting the world record for flagpole-sitting. When these celebrities had done all they could do for the consumer, they would pass into history, which was to say, into the discard, along with the horse and buggy and the hand-cranked Model T.

It was not simply in terms of what the advertisements persuaded them to purchase that Americans of the twenties were consumption-oriented. In terms of experiencing the new phenomena of the gas and electric age, living standards went up for millions of Americans who did not improve their positions much economically. Similarly it was not simply in terms of Whyte's social ethic that Americans of the twenties were group-oriented, for the technological developments of the age placed the nation as a whole in one big continually changing mass medium. Tocqueville and others observed that social conformity was the rule in Jacksonian America, but that had been a comparatively simple age when inner-direction and other-direction tended to go in pretty much the same direction for most people. Other-direction in the twenties led, nobody knew where, but it led away from past practices and it rejected the past as being absolutely out of date.

Henry Ford expressed this rejection of history by technology in an interview. "I don't know anything about history, and I wouldn't give a nickle for all the history in the world. The only history that is worth while is the history we make day by day." And in another more famous interview, "History is more or less bunk. It is tradition. We want to live in the present, and the only history that is worth a tinker's damn is the history we make today."

In the twenties history was "debunked" by W. E. Woodward and others. The immediate past of Progressive idealism and Wilsonian internationalism was repudiated or forgotten by most Americans, while the nation concentrated its attention on what was coming up at the moment. It had been true that Tocqueville's America had lacked a deep sense of history by comparison with European nations; nevertheless it had been the America of Parson Weems, and what history it did have, it had made the most of. In the twenties, in spite of all the hot sentiment for "100 percent Americanism," there was less fili-opietistic interest in the American past than there had been a half century or a century earlier.

America in the twenties experienced the final crack of a revolutionary break between the old American world of the nineteenth century and the electric age of the twentieth. That is not to deny the persistence of old values in the new age or to deny that the new values bore family resemblances to old ones. Later on, under the impact of depression and then of war, older values that had seemed no longer useful would revive. But the story of creation, which the founding fathers had believed, had been revised by the 1920's into the story of continual re-creation of the world by the machine; and that revised version has gone without saying ever since.

Joseph Wood Krutch wrote in *The Modern Temper* in 1929 that modern science "does not seem, so surely as once it did, to be helping us very rapidly along the road we wish to travel." Not many months after Krutch's gloomy book appeared, the road took a sharp downward turn, and several years after that, Lewis Mumford warned in *Technics and Civilization* (1934) that machinery might prove to be the "means to a throwback to lower levels of thought and emotion which will ultimately lead to the destruction of the machine itself and the higher types of life that have gone into its conception."

Such pessimistic intellectual awareness that the machine process was on a humanly unpredictable course contrasted during the twenties with a popular awareness and, on the whole, a happy acceptance of, this situation, and with a corresponding reevaluation of American ideals away from old-fashioned belief in self-reliance and individualism. Technological determinism, as an inescapable aspect of the modern American way, has been an implicit American assumption from the twenties to the present, for all the rhetorical reassertions of the traditional, but now somewhat outmoded, moral and intellectual values.

The new technological condition of the twenties was to be a permanent condition. But the sensation of being caught up and carried along by the civilization of the machine was new to the twenties, and it created among Americans of the day, as Frederick Lewis Allen wrote, "a holiday mood. 'Happy,' they might have said, 'is the nation which has no history—and a lot of good shows to watch.' "

Women in the modern technological society of the twenties were still engaged in their ancient duties of housekeeping and child raising, but in the city, men did not work at their ancient duties of hunting and fishing and tilling the soil and defending their land against invasion. Their occupations did not call for what were traditionally thought of as manly qualities, and there was a very widespread uneasy awareness of this. Confronted in 1919 by soldiers returning from Europe, the men who had commanded the home front everywhere behaved bumblingly and mawkishly to everybody's embarrassment. American Legionnaires were to find to their surprise that they possessed almost magical influence, so far as little favors from the local business community were concerned, based entirely on the fact that they had once been in uniform.

If the technologically ordered world of the American twenties was not a woman's world exactly, it was even less a man's world. With secretaries and even businesswomen in on everything, the manly atmosphere of the business world had retired to the washroom. Away from the business world, women ran the house and overran the speakeasies, as well as most of the men's clubs. They were on the golf course and in the barber shop, and they were even likely to be found snooping around brothels on slumming larks. Only a few of the old male preserves remained sacrosanct, such as some of the rougher gymnasiums and some of the stuffier private clubs. It is in this context that the twenties became the golden age of professional and quasi-professional sports in America.

Rural America had always engaged in a variety of sports and pastimes, but these sports and pastimes had also been disapproved of as so many ways to waste time. It was when men were cut off from rural life that sports took on high positive value in American thought. As the President's Research Committee on Social Trends put it in 1933, "During the past thirty years the earlier prejudices against sports and amusements have been replaced by an almost equally intolerant belief in their value and necessity."

Hunting and fishing were looked upon as foremost among the

manly pursuits; an estimated 13 million people in the United States hunted or fished in 1929, millions of them with almost no success at all. Wildlife was nowhere nearly abundant enough around the populated regions of the nation to satisfy the desires of the armies of hunters and fishermen; and it was being further depleted in the face of timber cutting, forest fires, water pollution, drainage, farming and, of course, hunting and fishing. These outings became for many men simply the only known way to get away by themselves for a weekend or a week.

In the city there were facilities for men who wanted to work out at the gym or play tennis or go for hikes, but urban life was not very well integrated with participation in sports, except in the case of businessmen's golf, and it all went into the pedestrian category of physical conditioning, along with dieting. City conditions encouraged most men to live the strenuous life vicariously, and in the twenties they lived this vicarious strenuous life to the hilt.

That the twenties was the great age of American sport was widely asserted at the time, and it has been acknowledged ever since. There have been doubters, of course. Grantland Rice came upon one in the late 1940's who

offered the idea that sport today had just as many stars and just as many colorful competitors as the Golden Age ever knew.

I offered no argument in rebuttal. Age can argue with youth, but it can never win the argument. I might have mentioned just a few names—Babe Ruth, Jack Dempsey, Knute Rockne, Bobby Jones, Red Grange, Bill Tilden, Billy Johnston, Earl Sande, Tommy Hitchcock, Helen Wills, Man o' War, Exterminator, Rogers Hornsby, Frank Frisch, Charley Paddock, the Four Horsemen, Gene Sarazen, Glenna Collett—taking them helter-skelter in no set order.

What distinguished these athletes, to Rice's way of thinking, was that

they had something more than mere skill or competitive ability. They also had in record quality and quantity that indescribable asset known as color, personality, crowd appeal, or whatever you may care to call it.

In other words, the period was distinguished not so much by the skill of the athletes as by the record quality and quantity of the romanticizing of them by the American public.

Although baseball had been successful on a professional basis since 1869, the main ascendancy of spectator sports in America took place beginning at the turn of the twentieth century. Its progress was marked by the success of the first world series in baseball in 1903 and by the reorganization of college football two years later, following a scandalously brutal season on the playing fields. Then the war came, and with it a new public interest in physical fitness and training camps and combat, and the concentration of newspaper reporting on these matters.

During the 1919 season the home runs of Babe Ruth for the Boston Red Sox brought him to the national attention, and the Yankees bought him for $125,000. Tex Rickard staged the Dempsey-Willard fight in Toledo in July 1919, Bill Tilden and Bobby Jones were winning local tournaments, and Red Grange was starting out in high school football, mainly because the uniforms were free. The Great Red Scare was holding the national attention that year, but in 1920 the athletes came onto the center of the stage.

It is somewhat misleading to call the twenties the great age of spectator sports. Football attendance trebled during the decade, it is true, but the attendance at professional baseball games in 1930 was only about 10 million, or about 1 million more than it had been a decade earlier. The triumph of sport in the twenties was fundamentally a triumph of the sports media, mainly the newspapers and radio. The national sense of athletic prowess was by necessity a technological accomplishment in communications about all else.

The President's Research Committee on Social Trends, noting that baseball attendance had not kept pace with the increase in the population, predicted that football would replace it as the national game because football provided more action for the spectators. That prediction did not take into account the fact that the sport was being followed primarily in the newspapers and on the radio, and that baseball was in some respects particularly well suited to these media. It was a game in which individual player performances could be measured statistically in terms of batting averages, RBIs, HRs, and pitching averages and compared with performances of every other player of the century. In this respect it was preeminently the sport of accountants, the baseball statistics being themselves full of action for men who were accustomed to work with figures.

Track was the outstanding example of a field of athletics which had very little spectator appeal in the sense of drawing onlookers to track meets, but one that had great statistical appeal. Americans did not distinguish themselves in track in the twenties, but Paavo Nurmi, although Finnish, established himself as a major hero to Americans in the twenties. (Finland was the one European nation that was honoring its war debts to America, and Nurmi got credit for that.) The Englishman Sir Thomas Lipton was another foreigner who was a hero to Americans—in his case, because he demonstrated such good sportsmanship, as befitted an Englishman, while losing at yachting. A foreigner was required for that category of sports heroism, because, as the British observer D. W. Brogan has written, "In the United States, being a good loser is not as good as being a winner, good or bad."

The kaleidescopic sports world was perfectly suited to newspaper presentation. The American newspaper is not designed for reading in the sense of book reading. It's a jarring and distracting montage of unrelated pictures and news items and advertisements, all competing for attention and most of them immediately forgotten. In this respect, newspapers captured, as well as helped to create, a state of mind which was characteristic of the twenties, and of any section of the paper, the sports pages did it best.

American newspapers became increasingly standardized during the first quarter of the twentieth century, the same stories and columns being syndicated for the whole nation. At the same time a radical alteration occurred in the content of newspapers. An analysis of newspapers in 1899 and again in 1923 indicated that the space allotted to editorials was down 77 percent, to letters to the editor down 84 percent, and to society down 66 percent. General and political news was up 1 percent, business news up 4 percent, foreign news up 9 percent, sports news up 47 percent, and illustrations up 84 percent.

The newspapers of the twenties were of the yellow journalism school. *The New York Times* might pose as the newspaper of record, printing all the news that was fit to print, while the jazzy New York *Daily News* would make no such boast. The *Times* nevertheless devoted more than a half million words to the seamy Hall-Mills murder trial. By contrast the *News*, with its tabloid form and greater photographic coverage, limited itself to less than half as much lurid prose as the *Times* on that case. To a much greater extent than ever before or after, the national press in the twenties presented the world in terms of murder and divorce, football and boxing, flagpole-sitting and transatlantic stunt flying.

The newspapers wallowed in yellow journalism because they concluded that that was what sold papers. Newspapers were circulation-conscious in a more desperate way than had been true in the nineteenth century, because, with rising publishing costs, they were dependent on advertising as they had not previously had been, and the circulation of the paper was all that advertisers cared about. Joseph Pulitzer with the New York *World* and William Randolph Hearst with the New York *Journal* had shown the way to giant circulations during the era of the Spanish-American War, and during World War I, the national press as a whole had joined in, to its own large financial profit.

In 1919 the *Daily News* was launched as the first major successful tabloid, financed out of huge profits which recently had accrued to the Chicago *Tribune*. The *News* featured sex and crime and profuse photography, and within eight years it had become the first American newspaper to reach the million mark in circulation. It was soon joined by other tabloids: Hearst's *Daily Mirror* and Bernarr McFadden's *Daily Graphic*. Together the three papers cornered two-fifths of the metropolitan New York newspaper circulation. They did not cut into the circulation of the existing papers, but they frightened those papers into following the path of crime and scandal and succumbing on page one to the sports craze. This tendency was nationwide.

While pandering to vulgar public taste, the older newspapers continued to comport themselves on their editorial pages like anointed custodians of public morality. The Chicago *Tribune* spoke for the whole fourth estate in laying down the rule that the newspaper "must, like the parish priest, be guide, councilor and friend," and that "its real mission" was to approximate "the ideal of the clergyman in his ministration to his flock." Meanwhile, the ideal of the moment was to keep the news interesting and keep it moving and put it together with headlines and photographs that would sell it on the streets.

Commercial radio began in November 1920, and after a tentative year or so, radio hit its stride. In the fields of music and sportscasting, its magical potential was fulfilled almost at once. As a news medium it remained more circumspect than the press; more mindful of its family audience. It became a political force almost at once, but its real potential in that field was hardly realized until Franklin D. Roosevelt showed how public opinion could be mobilized in a "fireside chat."

According to surveys, radio gave children nightmares with its serialized adventures and taught them many new words and facts, making them generally more knowledgeable and perhaps more skittery than children had been before. It brought the tempo of the Jazz Age into the homes of the nation more surely than the phonograph had, and it created a new kind of national audience for sports events, as well as for a wide variety of music and drama. Radio has had the general effect on the national culture of standardizing speech and, with other mass media, synchronizing national interest and taste.

Housework no longer needed to be the never-ending activity it had once been and housewives found themselves with time on their hands. Some of them took outside jobs, others busied themselves with club work, and most of them took up reading. Women did most of the reading that was done in the twenties, and they read magazines rather than books. The saturation point for best-selling books was rather rigidly fixed at half a million, in a nation that daily purchased nearly one hundred times that many newspapers.

Magazines that enjoyed circulations running into the millions were of three kinds: the weekly family magazines—*The Saturday Evening Post, Liberty,* and *Colliers;* the monthly magazines for women—*The Ladies' Home Journal, Woman's Home Companion, McCall's, Cosmopolitan,* and *Good Housekeeping;* and the confessions magazines such as *True Story* and *True Romances,* and movie magazines.

Writing of Muncie, Indiana, in *Middletown,* Robert and Helen Lynd noted that "since 1890 there has been a trend toward franker 'sex adventure' fiction."

It is noteworthy that a culture which traditionally taboos any discussion of sex in its systems of both religious and secular training and even until recently in the home training of children should be receiving such heavy diffusion of this material through its period periodical reading matter. . . . In these magazines Middletown reads "The Primitive Lover" ("She wanted a caveman husband"), "Her Life Secret" ("Can a Wife Win with the Other Woman's Weapons?"), "How to Keep the Thrill in Marriage"

("Every girl on the eve of her marriage becomes again a little frightened child.")

While four leading motion picture houses were featuring synchronously four sex adventure films, *Telling Tales* on the Middletown news-stands was featuring on its cover four stories, "Indolent Kisses," "Primitive Love," "Watch Your Step-Ins!" ("Irene didn't and you should have seen what happened!") and "Innocents Astray."

There were also sex magazines for men, known as the pulps, including *Amazing Stories, Breezy Stories, Jim Jam Jems,* and *French Stories;* and there was burlesque, not to mention brothels. But women and children provided the main market for the sex-appeal magazines and the main audience for the sex movies.

The golden age of the silent screen was from *The Birth of a Nation* in 1915, which won the movies recognition as an art form, to *The Jazz Singer* in 1927, when Al Jolson sang the nation into the talkie era. By the end of World War I, Hollywood had gained ascendancy over the world market by means of the star system. Charlie Chaplin and Mary Pickford led the way, followed by John Barrymore, Rudolph Valentino, Ramon Novarro, Clara Bow, the "It Girl," Lillian Gish, Greta Garbo, and so on. Cowboy stories and slapstick comedy helped, but the main profits were being earned in what the trade called glamour—and the master of the form was Cecil B. De Mille.

In 1919 sin came to the silver screen on a grand scale when De Mille flooded the market with three sex films: *Male and Female, For Better, For Worse,* and *Don't Change Your Husband.* Under his direction, as his brother William wrote, "the art of bathing was shown as a lovely ceremony rather than a merely sanitary duty . . . underclothes became visions of translucent promise."

The scandals of the stars were publicized to help things along until 1922, when the Fatty Arbuckle rape case, in conjunction with exposés of murder, drug addiction, and some other out-of-bounds immoralities, aroused a storm of protest nationally. The terrified industry responded by forming the Motion Picture Producers and Distributors of America under Will H. Hays, Presbyterian elder and chairman of the Republican National Committee. The M.P.P.D.A., thereafter referred to as the Hays Office, was armed with absolute authority to censor the production of the member companies.

The Hays Office drew up a set of rules based upon the principle of "compensating values," that immorality must not go unpunished. As soon as the furor died away, the studios adapted glamour movies to the new rules by adding a catch-all sequence to the end of their films, during which just rewards were distributed as demanded by the code. There were also a job lot of specific prohibitions—such as a man and woman in bed together, and the interior of a female thigh—and these were stopped short of.

When women's clubs objected to this new prurience, De Mille outmaneuvered them with *The Ten Commandments* in 1923, putting his sex orgies in a biblical setting. Hollywood continued to do well with the westerns of Tom Mix and Hoot Gibson, with the comedies of Charlie Chaplin, Harold Lloyd, and Buster Keaton, and with the adventures of Douglas Fairbanks, and they also continued to do well with sex movies. In Muncie the big-name stars drew the largest crowds, and what were called sophisticated movies, such as *Married Flirts, The Daring Years, Sinners in Silk, Rouged Lips,* and *The Queen of Sin,* were next in popularity. The influence of these movies, as the Lynds pointed out, could only be inferred, except that they were a new source of sex education and stimulation for children and a dreamy diversion for adults, mainly women.

Americans of the twenties were living in radioland and movieland and in the tabloid world of sin and sports. But the technological society of the decade was very far from being a society of passive spectators. It was the age of gas as well as electricity. To the Middletown Sunday schoolteacher's question as to what the modern world had that the world of Jesus lacked, the child replied "Speed." The twenties had speed and it also had rhythm—and it was the children who set the beat.

6.

The Technological Filiarchy

··

THE SOCIETY WHICH seventeenth-century Puritans brought to America was, in theory at least, patriarchal. It conceived of God as the head of the household of mankind, handing down the law to all and entrusting to the eldest or best sons of successive generations the task of enforcing obedience to the law. As governor of Massachusetts Bay Colony, John Winthrop, with his magistrates, ruled the townships by virtue of an authority "such as hath the image of God eminently stamped upon it." As head of his own domestic household, Winthrop ruled his family by the same authority.

Wives, according to Winthrop's system, were made free by subjecting themselves to their husbands, "and whether her lord smiles upon her, and embraceth her in his arms, or whether he frowns, or rebukes, or smites her, she apprehends the sweetness of his love in all, and is refreshed, supported, and instructed by every such dispensation of his authority over her." Children and old maid aunts and other dependents in the family enjoyed this same absolutely subordinate relationship, except that the eldest or best sons were expected to assume some of the authority, under paternal guidance, which they would in time exercise in their own right.

For Winthrop, this system of heavenly, state, and family government was "the kind of liberty I call civil or federal; it may also be termed moral, in reference to the covenant between God and man, in the moral law." It has been called theocracy by some historians. In America it has been associated particularly with government and society in the colonies of Massachusetts and Connecticut. In most respects, however, it was in harmony with James I's theory of the divine right of kings, as well as with Roger Williams' argument for household democracy. It was already being written into law in Virginia at the time the Massachusetts Bay Colony was founded. It was what English men and women at the time of America's settlement understood to be God's will.

In the course of American history, two main influences worked against John Winthrop's patriarchal system. The first of these was the wilderness environment, and the second, the industrial revolution. The American wilderness had not been subdued under God's law as had the English countryside, and the head of the family often had to share his authority under new and trying circumstances, with the pioneer wife and with the children. Far more subversive than this, however, was what Frederick Jackson Turner called "the hither edge of free land," encouraging independence in boys and in girls as well. Hezekiah Niles observed in the early nineteenth century that "girls who behave as they ought, soon get married and raise up families for themselves. This is what they *calculate* upon, and it is this calculation that makes them 'saucy.' "

The industrial revolution created a growing middle-class urban society, in which the raising of children became separated from the process of making a living, and children were treated as children —lovable very likely, but certainly useless—rather than as working farmers and farm women in imperfect stages of development. Furthermore, it was less likely in the city than on the farm for the boy to follow in his father's footsteps, and it was less likely that the father would want him to. In an era of technological progress, it was expected that the sons and the daughters would enjoy advantages that the parents had not been able to enjoy, in a mechanically better world than the parents had known. This changed relationship between age and youth disturbed American society fundamentally in the 1920's.

America in the twenties was in the throes of a social revolution, the like of which the world had never seen. This was abundantly evident at the time, but what the social revolution was all about was not so evident. It was seen as a postwar phenomenon, to be sure, but that did not explain it away. Previous postwar periods in American history had been characterized by cynicism and fury and public and private scandal, but not by social revolutions. The Roaring Twenties, beyond being a postwar phenomenon, consisted of nothing less than the blanket repudiation of the traditional farm-oriented, church-oriented, somewhat patriarchal moral order of the Protestant Republic, and the crux of the revolution was the reversal of the order of authority in society from age to youth.

The twenties was a time when to be full of years and wisdom was to be out of it and a time when to be young was as nearly heaven as was conceived of by an essentially post-Christian machine-age society. This society was filiarchal rather than patriarchal in character. The youthful Lindbergh was made to stand for the ideals of this machine-age filiarchy; the youthful flapper was the embodiment of the age itself.

....

The appearance in respectable society of the adult female knee was among the most startling sights of the twenties, and its significance as a sign of changing times was far more profound than was realized by either those whom it scandalized or those whom it delighted. The new fashions represented a good deal more than novelty. They represented a departure from all previous civilized custom—a departure so abrupt and clear-cut as to suggest a basic alteration in the moral character of the nation. The remarkable fact is, that when American women exposed their legs in public, they violated a requirement of civilization which seemingly had been confirmed for all time by thousands of years of unbroken observance in the nonprimitive societies of the world, Oriental and Western.

Historically, standards of decency in dress have varied widely. In

Elizabethan England, for instance, women's breasts were exposed with propriety, while the baring of any part of the arm was cause for scandal. The French Revolutionists had been determined to free themselves from the tyranny of the Old Regime in their modes of dress as in other matters, and the fashionable ladies among them had garbed themselves daringly in translucent drapery. Still, they had felt compelled to wear pink or white tights underneath, and they had continued to be gowned to the feet.

American women of the twentieth century, on the other hand, raised their skirts from the floor to the knee, and they did so purposefully, yet in response to no revolutionary appeals or to any acknowledged appeals whatever. They did not do it in response to suffragettes, who had largely given up on radical dress reform long before, with the failure of the Bloomerite cause. A good deal had been said, but little done, about the need for more practical costumes for women who were active in the business world. Middle-class women were increasingly taking up tennis and golf and especially cycling at the turn of the century. These activities naturally suggested the need for costumes that offered greater freedom of activity, but little came of it. The divided skirt was devised for cyclists, but most women cyclists still kept to their dresses.

Neither did the dress styles of the twenties owe anything to the lead of the Greenwich Village Bohémiennes, who were in advance of their time in the shortness of their hair but not in shortness of skirts, as was also the case with the anarchist women. The flapper style was the result of a quarter of a century of changing fashions initiated by middle-class girls all over the country, with the approval and then the emulation of middle-class mothers. It was the reflection of a change in middle-class values; not a revolt against them.

The flapper is said to have striven to achieve a boyish figure by compressing the breasts into flat-chestedness, and to have epitomized flaming youth by displaying her legs. Such was hardly the case at all. Some flappers may have felt both boyish and flaming, but the reason they were able to go around town in short skirts without being arrested for indecency was that they represented something else to the middle-class womanhood which was responsible for the new style. To middle-class America the short skirt and the flat chest betokened little-girlhood, the state of preadolescence, which had become as much the object of veneration for twentieth-century worshippers of the future as ever old age had once been, or had sought to be, in the biblically-oriented patriarchal days of John Winthrop.

To her fond parents the flapper represented the little girl they had hoped would never grow up. Also, to many a flapper's mother, who was keeping up with the times too, the short dress represented the quality of youthfulness and promise a modern mother might share with a modern daughter. It was not license for loose living; it was license for youthful living. Grandmothers in short skirts were definitely out of place, but then grandmothers were out of place in modern America as a whole. That the short skirt was the literal expression of the emergence of a kind of American filiarchy is indicated in the history of how this fashion came into existence, by way of the evolving fashions in children's clothes.

The idea that children should be dressed differently from adults is itself relatively new to the world, and it is still largely limited to Japan and Western Europe, and especially to England and the United States. In all countries, until the eighteenth century, even upper-class children were dressed like their parents, down to corsets and bustles for little girls and swords and codpieces for little boys. That is the reason why children in paintings dating from previous centuries tend to look like adult dwarfs instead of like little boys and girls.

Out of the romantic movement, during the late eighteenth and early nineteenth centuries, with the sentimentalization of childhood, distinct styles of children's clothing came to be designed which were intended to be expressive of the idea of childhood, especially for dress-up occasions.

Catharine E. Beecher and Harriet Beecher Stowe opposed this trend in their *American Woman's Home* in 1869, just as they opposed the whole trend toward coddling the young. They opposed putting little girls into corsets, because they thought it unhealthy. Outwardly, however, the little girls were to appear as adults.

The proper way to dress a young girl is to have a cotton or flannel close-fitting jacket next to the body, to which the drawers should be buttoned. Over this, place the chemise; and over that, such a jacket as the one here drawn, to which should be buttoned to the hoops and other skirts. Thus every article of dress will be supported by the shoulders.

The Beecher sisters gave no advice on the clothing of boys, but they did have this to say:

Every boy is to be trained for his future domestic position by labor and sacrifice for his mother and sisters. It is the brother who is to do the hardest and most disagreeable work, to face the storms and perform the most laborious drudgeries.

It seems altogether likely, therefore, that they visualized these boys in workingmen's clothes.

Of incomparably greater influence than the *American Woman's Home* was Frances Hodgson Burnett's *Little Lord Fauntleroy,* which first appeared in 1886 when romantic tales of childhood were in full fashion. In a new edition published twenty-five years later, Mrs. Burnett was able to write, "The children who read it first are now men and women. Many of them have children of their own, and these children, it seems, are reading it also—or want to read it, or their friends wish to give it to them to read."

One fashion authority declared in 1894,

Mrs. Frances Hodgson Burnett was probably the first mother to exploit the decorative possibilities of children in the home. It was the golden curls and velvet doublet of Little Lord Fauntleroy that first gave young women with artistic instincts and pretty little children something to think of. . . .

This same authority thought it necessary to caution these young women with artistic instincts and pretty children against the extremes of Fauntleroyism.

Always resist the temptation to dress a child too finely. Elaboration does not belong to childhood. . . . The same caution applies quite as much to the dress of young girls in school, whose clothing should be tasteful and substantial, but simple to the verge of plainness.

A *Handbook of Dress and Childhood,* issued by the American School of Home Economics in 1906, suggested that "Dresses for little girls may have drawers made of the same material, thus permitting them the same freedom as boys. The life of the child is play. . . ." It was from the costumes of these playmates that the flapper's costume evolved, during the first quarter of the new century, as may be followed visually, step by step, in the Sears, Roebuck catalogs from the 1890's onward.

According to the reckoning of the Sears, Roebuck catalog, the life of childhood started at from four to six years of age and passed over into adulthood at fourteen or fifteen. In the mid-nineties, one single children's style served for this age group as a whole. At the turn of the century the same single category remained, but where girls were concerned its title had been changed to "Children's and Misses'."

For the girls at the "Misses'" end of the scale in 1900, the catalog offered to "supply a long-felt and needed want by the ambitious Miss just blooming into womanhood," in the shape of a Coronet Misses' Waist, "when her figure begins to take on the matronly form which this garment so beautifully displays." These girls were quite evidently on the very verge of losing childhood status and therefore of being obliged to lower their skirts to below their ankles like other women. In the meantime, they and their parents and Sears, Roebuck were all apparently agreed that there was still time for them to buy another Gretchen and wear their skirts at knee length a little longer.

By 1910, although the age group of the child had not changed, the appearance of the models in the catalog had, some of them being evidently older than the stated fourteen-year limit. Then, in 1912 a new category was added: "Junior Dresses" for thirteen- to seventeen-year-olds, with the hem at the calf of the leg, about midway between the knee-length skirts of girls and the women's skirts, which were by that time up to the ankle.

By 1916 the category of "Junior Misses" had been added, with this admonition: "Be Sure to State Bust Measure When Ordering." In 1918 a whole clutch of new categories were added, including "Misses' and Women's," "Stylish Dresses for Misses and Small Women," "Intermediate Dresses for Growing Girls," "Becoming Dresses for Juniors," and "Stylish Skirts for Girlish Figures." These dresses were all cut at the middle of the calf.

The year 1918 was the one when Sears, Roebuck, extremely conservative, always with its rural clientele in mind, at last openly invited all women, except, perhaps, the "Stylish Stouts," to the perquisites of girlhood. The catalog sort of explained how this had come about in the general introduction to the women's clothing section. "The trend of the times," it declared, "is toward simplicity. The lines this season are perhaps less pronounced than they have been for some time. It is a season when the predominating styles are suitable for young and old, to every figure."

At the same time that the skirt was rising, the high-topped woman's shoe was giving way to "Low Cuts." There seems to be no way of learning from the catalog what articles of apparel women were beginning to discard, but they were beginning to discard underthings at a rate that was frightening to the president of the New York Cotton Exchange. Recent changes in dress, the president of the exchange declared in 1912, had "reduced consumption of cotton fabrics by at least twelve yards of finished goods for each adult female inhabitant" in the nation.

The Sears catalog for 1918 included one further new category— "Dresses for Mourning and General Wear"—in recognition of America's entrance into the war, but as very few doughboys had reached the front lines at the time the catalog was being prepared, that sales item was not emphasized. In Europe, mourning dominated the styles for two years after the war. In America, hems may have dipped momentarily; but by 1921 they were up higher than ever, and from then on they kept climbing until in 1927 they reached the knobby-kneed apex immortalized in the drawings of John Held, Jr.

The dresses of this latter period did not have to use up very much more material than a pillowcase, and they were not necessarily much harder to make. The style was beginning to sweep England and Europe in 1922, and the fashion industries of two continents, reeling amid disaster, united in one vast coordinated effort to lengthen the skirts and sew extra materials on them. Fashion magazines and fashion designers in Paris, London, New York, and elsewhere designed longer dresses, and clothing manufacturers made these by the million. But the women either left them in the store or bought them and shortened them.

The industry continued in futile opposition to the women, until the knee was reached and, here and there, passed beyond. Then, for whatever reasons, women decided that that was enough of that. They lowered their skirts once again to their calves and, amid the sobering experience of the Great Depression, more or less left them there until World War II.

The children's dresses advertised by Sears early in the century were of substantially the same pattern for both six-year-olds and four-teen-year-olds, except that in some cases the hem was somewhat lower for the older girls. The dresses were worn differently by the models, however. The older girls belted themselves around the middle of the waist. The younger girls wore their belts below their waist, making the skirts appear even shorter than they were. It was the little-girl rather than the big-girl models that were copied by the flappers of the mid-twenties.

The flappers also took the little girl as the model for the flapper figure, rather than that big girl, "just blooming into womanhood," for whom Sears at the turn of the century had provided the "Misses' Waist." By 1927 one of the fastest-moving items in the women's section of the Sears catalog was "Our Famous Vanity V, Worn by More Thousands Than Any Other Garment Known to Corsetry."

> Gives a firm, youthful slenderness and imparts graceful body poise. . . . Upper part is a perfect fitting confirmer with shoulder straps. Cleverly designed to keep the flesh from protruding between the girdle and brassiere, a splendid feature.

Evidently that was a greater extreme of youthfulness than the women of the girlish twenties were willing to sustain for long. At the same time they lowered their skirts, they threw away their confirmers and reverted to womanhood. The age of the flapper was over, and the much less noteworthy age of the siren had begun.

....

Americans in the early twentieth century were in no hurry to get married. The right time for a girl was said to be about 24, before she reached her quarter century mark, and the right time for a young man was 29, before he entered his thirties. On the average, marriages were at a somewhat earlier age than that and the national trend was slightly toward still earlier marriages. But in 1920 the 15- to 19-year-old boys of the nation were 97.7 percent single; whereas fewer than a third of the 20- to 24-year-old males were married. One-sixth of the population never did get married, but the expected thing to do was to fall in love eventually and then marry as the romantic inclination directed. It was also expected that precious little joy would be found in most of these unions.

On matters relating to courtship, marriage, and the family, the nationally syndicated columnist Dorothy Dix seems to have spoken the mind of the twenties. According to Robert and Helen Lynd's

Middletown, in the twenties, Mrs. Dix was "perhaps the most potent single agency of diffusion from without shaping the habits of thought of Middletown in regard to marriage" and probably more representative of Middletown's own ideas on the subject than any other single source. She was discussed at Ladies' Aid meetings and quoted with approval by the minister who was considered the "most intellectual" of the town's clergymen. She was the first thing many women read in the newspaper and often the only thing.

The most striking characteristic of popular thought in the twenties, as revealed in the writings of Dorothy Dix, is the grimly fatalistic Darwinism which permeated it. Mrs. Dix was relentlessly biological in her interpretation of human behavior, bleakly convinced that men and women were in the grip of instincts over which they had little control and that their instincts bode them much ill and little good in life. This sturdy pessimism of "the little lady of New Orleans" probably struck a responsive chord in Calvinist quarters, but hers was a thoroughly materialistic world where God did not enter.

Dorothy Dix (*Dorothy Dix, Her Book: Every-Day Help for Every-Day People* [1926]) believed that girls, with few exceptions, were doomed to follow the course of "The Ordinary Woman."

Years and years ago, when she was fresh and young, and gay, and light-hearted, she was married. Her head, as is the case with most girls, was full of dreams. Her husband was to be a Prince Charming, always tender and considerate and loving, shielding her from every care and worry. Life itself was to be a fairy tale.

One by one the dreams fell away. The husband was a good man, but he grew indifferent to her before long. He ceased to notice when she put on a fresh ribbon. . . . He never gave her a kiss or a caress, and their married life sank into a deadly monotony. . . .

That is the way of the Ordinary Woman.

It was her opinion that "without doubt, marriage is a cruel and a bitter disappointment to nine-tenths of those who enter into the holy estate." This was especially so for women, but Dorothy Dix did not suppose that men were any more to blame for this than women were. It was their nature to behave as they did. Nature filled young people with romantic delusions, so that they would marry and have children, in the "blind faith that they are going to find it an earthly paradise." However, "A man marries to end romance . . . so that he will be free to give his undivided attention to his business," and "not one man in a hundred ever gives any real serious thought or makes any honest effort to make his marriage a success." And then, when a child was born of the marriage, the situation worsened.

"The first baby definitely and for all time puts the husband's nose out of joint." The wife neglects herself as well as her husband, as her maternal instincts take over. The husband wants his wife's companionship. "But she will seldom go with him, and when she does, she is no fun because she doesn't enter into the spirit of anything." The wise woman knew that "the first principle in treating a husband is to treat him as if he were your littlest baby." But women were rarely wise.

Instinctively, children, as they grow up, "bleed Father and Mother white for the things they want," and they keep on doing it after they, themselves, are married and have children. The parents, however, have nobody but themselves to blame, for it was they who brought the children up in the first place. They should not have allowed themselves to be imposed on. At the same time, they themselves should not impose on their children.

Most of us have a curious and naive belief in what we call "natural affection." We befool ourselves into thinking that people must love us because they stand in a certain relationship to us and because there are blood ties between us. Never was there a more fallacious theory.

Parental love is a one-way street. The careful parent will therefore have been "laying up affection" for his old age—and also money.

For in all the world there are no people so piteous and forlorn as those who are forced to eat the bitter bread of dependence in their old age, and find how steep are the stairs of another man's house.

Predestination and individual responsibility went hand in hand in the exhortations of Dorothy Dix, as they had gone hand in hand in the hellfire sermons of Jonathan Edwards in the eighteenth century. Every fallen woman "is what she is because her mother did not teach her self-control," and yet, "Look at the poor old people who are dependent on their children. . . . They had their chance of fortune."

Unlike Jonathan Edwards, Dorothy Dix held forth no hope of a better world to come, but only a temporarily better, although cruelly chimerical, world for the children coming after them. It was, of course, possible to avoid marriage altogether, and "the woman who espouses a career does not get the worst husband there is." But "work is the consolation prize," which fails to fulfill a woman's life; for while "it is a misfortune to a woman never to be loved, it is a tragedy to her never to love."

Although the happiness of young people was illusory, Dorothy Dix hoped they would make the most of it while it lasted. The ideal mother, according to her system, was a thoroughgoing Watsonian behaviorist, who, controlling her own maternal instincts, "begins when they are babies to teach them self-control, and thrift, and industry, and all the principles of right living." Once that has been accomplished, the daughter can be trusted to "jazz" around with the others of her age, the parents forcing themselves to remember how it had been with them when they were young.

How can a girl tell her mother that a boy kissed her, if mother represents herself as Miss Prunes and Prisms, and says that when *she* was young girls never skylarked, and never went on joy-rides or to cabarets, or held hands in the movies, but spent a pleasant evening sitting up in the parlor in the presence of their elders discussing improving topics?

Mrs. Dix advised young women to marry for love rather than for what were advertised as more practical reasons, because they would need all the love they could muster to get along with their husbands. In the meantime, they would do well to eat, drink, and be merry; and their parents would do well to let them, for the mating years were the best years of their lives, when nature allowed them to live for a time in a fool's paradise.

In one important respect, the women of the twentieth century were at a clear advantage over their ancestors. Jobs were open to them which freed them from the abject dependence upon fathers and husbands which formerly had been woman's state, and Dorothy Dix's advice was, "Learn a Trade, Girls." She listed several arguments in favor of learning a trade, but the nub of the matter was this:

Being able to make your own living sets you free. Economic independence is the only independence in the world. As long as you must look to another for your food and clothes you are a slave to that person. You must obey him. You must defer to him. You must bend your will to his.

But when you can stand on your own feet you can snap your fingers in the face of the world and tell it where it gets off. . . . You can support yourself, and you are free.

Divorce became an avenue of escape for the woman with a job. Dorothy Dix thought that the grounds of incompatibility, increasingly used and increasingly attacked as being immorally trivial grounds, probably came as near to justifying divorce as any that one could think of. "Missionary activities" outside the home also were avenues of release, she wrote, and "there is scarcely a movement in the world for the uplift of humanity or for ameliorating the sorrows of the poor and helpless that does not owe its existence to women." The fact still remained, that woman's basic purpose would always be to keep house and raise children, and if women would only be persuaded to do that job well, as indeed many were, they would be operating at their highest level of achievement. The high order of their performance would not be recognized, of course, owing to "the stupidity of a nation that believes that breeches and brains are synonymous," but that would not lessen the achievement.

This philosopher of animalism was followed approvingly by newspaper readers in almost every sizable community in the nation, and her views were warmly endorsed by many, including no less an authority on the "Ordinary Woman," than Faith Baldwin, who wrote, "Mrs. Dix, I assert, gives pretty sound advice. Her advice follows a conventional pattern, it has to, but it is delivered in a far from sentimental manner. . . . Of all the columnists I believe her to be the best."

....

The glorification of youth in the twenties was reflected in a marked shift in emphasis on the part of advocates of progressive education. During the Progressive era the intent of educational reform had been to train the youth of the nation to be useful members of a society that the youth of the nation would be responsible for further improving. This idea of education as a means to social reform was inevitably diminished in influence by the postwar reaction against social reform. During the twenties, progressive education tended instead to emphasize, in direct opposition to Watsonian behaviorism, the uniquely creative qualities of the individual child and the desirability of permitting the child free expression of these creative qualities.

In 1914 the Play School was opened by Caroline Pratt in Greenwich Village, with the support of Greenwich Village intellectuals. The Play School provided children with play materials, and the teachers placed the pupils in teaching situations which were as little structured as possible. So far as possible the children would learn by themselves in their own child's community. This form of progressive education thrived in the twenties. According to Harold Rugg and Ann Shumaker in *The Child-Centered School,* which appeared in 1928, "No educational discovery of our generation has had such far-reaching implications. It has a twofold significance: first, that every child is born with the power to create; second, that the task of the school is to surround the child with an environment which will draw out this creative power." In the twenties the school continued to be considered as "an embryonic community life," while the pupils tended to be given increased initiative to create these communities themselves.

Children had come to be institutionally cared for from kindergarten through high school, almost as a matter of course by the twenties. In *Middletown,* Robert and Helen Lynd noted that in Muncie, Indiana, the public schools took over the kindergarten in 1924, and public playgrounds were constructed for the children. A dean of women was appointed in the high school because, according to the local paper,

it was found impossible for mothers who worked during the evening to give proper time to the boy and girl in school. . . . It is the dean's business to help solve their problems along every line—social, religious, and educational.

The school was abetted in this by the YMCA, YWCA, Boy Scouts, Girl Reserves, and various churches, which, in the minds of some mothers, tended to be overly indulgent with the desires of the children. One mother complained:

What can we do when even church societies keep such late hours? My boy of fifteen is always supposed to be home by eleven, but a short time ago the Young People's Society of the church gave a dance, with the secretary of the Mothers' Council in charge, and dancing was from nine to twelve! And so few mothers will do anything about it. My son was eleven when he went to his first dance and we told him to be home by ten-thirty. I knew the mother of the girl he was taking and called her up to tell her my directions. "Indeed, I'm not telling my daughter anything of the kind," she said; "I don't want to interfere with her good time!"

The Muncie schoolboard in the late nineteenth century had declared that "the teachers shall often remind the pupils that the first duty when dismissed is to proceed quietly and directly home to render all needed assistance to their parents," and the school did not concern itself with extracurricular activities. In the 1920's, however, the high school newspaper repeated in each issue its purpose: "To support live school organizations," and "above all to foster the real 'Bearcat' spirit in all of Central High School." Friday night was basketball night for many of the townspeople as well as for the students.

Socially the most influential organizations in the high school were the fraternities and sororities, illegal by state law, but kept alive under different names by active graduate chapters. The high school organized Pep Clubs, and the YMCA and YWCA had their clubs, which were affiliated with the school, but one girl thought that "it's not much good to belong to a Y.W. club; any one can belong to them." Most students belonged to several clubs, which held their meetings in the evening.

What with these and with dates and other engagements, according to the results of a questionnaire, 55 percent of the boys of Muncie and 44 percent of the girls customarily spent fewer than four evenings out of the seven at home. One mother, who had considered sending her daughter away to school because of the hectic social life in town, said,

There is always some party or dance going on in a hotel or some other public place. We don't like the children to go out on school nights, but it's hard always to refuse. Last night it was a Hallowe'en party at the church and tonight a dramatic club dance at the high school. Even as it is, we're a good deal worried about her; she's beginning to feel different from the others because she is more restricted and not allowed to go out as much as they do.

According to the Lynds, where the older generation had customarily attended parties in groups, when they had been growing up, the adolescents in the twenties went in couples. The newspaper accounts of high school dances took care to list the escort of each girl. It was considered essential that the boy have the family automobile for the occasion; hence the automobile was a source of friction in the family for both boys and girls. Automobile parties were not exceptional, and movie dates were a regular thing. Sex confession magazines circulated widely among the students, and "sex films" were widely attended. The telephone provided boys and girls with a semi-private means of contacting each other. "Petting parties" were common, many—perhaps most—of the students taking part in them.

The boys did not dress or act much differently than they always had, by comparison with the girls, and they were not especially noticed in the twenties. They did little more to attract attention than wear raccoon coats and play ukeleles and get drunk in the parking lot at a dance, and here and there, wreck the family car and get in trouble with a girl. Boys were just being boys, but they were being led on by girls who were not just being girls.

The girls were running around with "practically nothing on," and their mothers were too. The *Journal of Commerce* in 1928 estimated that within 15 years, women had stripped away 12¼ yards of material from their average outfit, leaving only seven yards of cloth in addition to stockings; these garments were made of silk or the new rayon, rather than cotton or wool. Girls got rid of the old black cotton stockings after the war; a fairly low-income working-class wife told the Lynds that "no girl can wear cotton stockings to high school. Even in winter my children wear silk stockings with lisle or imitations underneath."

Corsets and brassieres were going out of style. A girl complained that boys did not want to dance with girls in corsets, and therefore at dances girls sometimes checked their corsets in the cloak room. The high school girls were wearing rouge and lipstick so that it showed, and some of them took to smoking cigarettes and drinking, as well as joyriding, and shimmying and petting and necking and whatever else went on.

As to what else went on, Judge Ben B. Lindsay of the Denver Juvenile and Family Court in *The Revolt of Modern Youth,* which appeared in 1925, depicted an adolescent world in which the rule among the more innocent was "that one could go automobile riding at fifteen; that one could drink freely when one was eighteen; that love making could begin at any time," and that, among nice girls, care should be taken not to be found out by the older generation.

Lindsay had an inexhaustible supply of illustrative stories to tell. He went on and on with them and then continued to tell more seamy stories in a second book, advocating "companionate marriage" as the solution. Judge Lindsay undoubtedly saw the worst side of the younger generation from where he sat, but he thought he had taken that into account.

According to an "ex-flapper" writing in 1922, there were two distinct levels of flappers. "There is the prep-school type—still a little crude. . . . She has not the finish of the college flapper who has learned to be soulful, virtuous on occasions and, under extreme circumstances, even highbrow. . . . But the after-prep and college girl emerges into something you can check up." The finished product, as described by the ex-flapper was a good sport, who liked to dance and swim and ski and who wouldn't knit you a necktie but would give you a lift in her car. She was frank and independent and would "be the mother of the next generation, with the hypocrisy, fluff and other 'hookum' worn entirely off."

An anxious discussion went on in the newspapers and popular magazines about necking and petting, complicated by the problem of distinguishing between the two terms, which meant different things in different parts of the country and in different people's imaginations. There was also disagreement as to how it had all got started, although it was agreed that the unsettled and emotional wartime conditions had had much to do with it. Eleanor Rowland Wembridge averred, "The sex manners of the large majority of uncultivated and uncritical people have become the manners for all." The upper classes had been infected because "the prudent lawyer's child has no idea of letting the gay daughter of the broad-joking workman get the dates away from her. If petting is the weapon Miss Workman uses, then petting it must be."

F. Scott Fitzgerald, who had pioneered in the new movement, explained that it had begun the other way around, with the social groups whose families were rich and kind enough to give their children cars.

As far back as 1915 the unchaperoned young people of the smaller cities had discovered the mobile privacy of that automobile given to young Bill at sixteen to make him "self-reliant." At first petting was a desperate adventure even under such favorable conditions, but presently confidences were exchanged and the old commandment broke down. As early as 1917 there were references to such sweet and casual dalliance in any number of the *Yale Record* or the *Princeton Tiger*.

Although runabouts could be bought for less than $500 in 1911, the democratic age of the automobile had not yet arrived. It had been Woodrow Wilson's opinion in 1907 that "nothing has spread socialistic feeling in this country more than the use of the automobile," which, to the worker and the farmer, Wilson said, was "a picture of the arrogance of wealth, with all its independence and carelessness." Motoring was hazardous and terribly time consuming in the upkeep and preparations that were necessary, and it was looked upon as a form of entertainment long before it came to be thought of as a practical means of transportation.

There were 2 million cars in the nation in 1914, and the automobile was becoming a serious matter. In 1921 there were 9 million, and five years later there were 18 million, or about one for every two families. The family automobile outing had established itself as an institution, and the family quarrel over who would get the car that evening had established itself as a regular subject for dinner conversation. At the outset of the twenties, most cars were open. Ten years later most of them were closed, and so had become "bedrooms on wheels," for the younger generation.

The "dance craze" had started at the same time as the Model T Ford, and together the rattle of the Ford and the jiggle of the fox trot set the tempo for the new era. Until about 1912 the waltz had held its popularity among young people, against the two-step, which had taken the field in 1890 to the tune of John Philip Sousa's "Washington Post March." Then, in the year when Woodrow Wilson was campaigning for his own sobersided "New Freedom" for the nation, Irving Berlin rocked the country with "Alexander's Ragtime Band" and "Everybody's Doin' It Now." The hobble skirt gave way to the slit skirt, and the dance craze was on, which continued without letup right through the Great Depression.

Ragtime dancing swept parents along with the children, but the young people went in for many different dance steps which older people often either couldn't or wouldn't do. These included, according to Mark Sullivan's list in *Our Times*, the horse trot, crab step, kangaroo dip, camel walk, fish walk, chicken scratch, lame duck, and the snake. Most popular among the more decorous dancers was the fox trot; while the younger set concentrated on the turkey trot (which, according to one authority, "deserved much of the abuse it got"), the bunny hug, and the grizzly bear. A song of 1912 contained the lines, "But mother said I shouldn't dare,/To try and do the grizzly bear." Nevertheless it was tried all over the country.

Ragtime gave way to jazz in the twenties, and the bunny hug and turkey trot gave way to the Black Bottom and Charleston, without changing the essential character of the dance form. Jazzy dancing alternated "hugging"—a key word both in the lyrics of the songs and in the condemnations of the dances—with frenetic individual activity "way out in space," as the lyrics to "Ballin' the Jack" described it. The president of the Christian Endeavor Society denounced it as "indecent dance," which was "an offense against womanly purity, the very fountainhead of our family and civil life." Many others were equally critical. But worst of anything in the minds of the morally concerned were the girls' clothes. According to the president of the University of Florida, "the low-cut gowns, the rolled hose and short skirts are born of the Devil and his angels, and are carrying the present and future generations to chaos and destruction."

Many of the older generation, without fearing actual chaos, were still distressed, especially with the conduct of the girls. And many were just bewildered. "Girls are far more aggressive today," one Muncie housewife told Robert and Helen Lynd. "They call the boys up to try to make dates with them as they never would have when I was a girl." Another declared, "When I was a girl, a girl who painted was a bad girl—but now look at the daughters of our best families!" Working-class mothers, polled by the Lynds for their study of Muncie, emphasized "strict obedience" and "loyalty to the church" from a list offered them of fifteen attributes to be most desired in children. Business-class mothers, however, rated "independence" and "frankness" above "loyalty to the church" and on a par with "strict obedience," one mother commenting that "strict obedience does not accomplish anything at all."

Middle-class mothers in Muncie were conscious of being modern themselves, and took pride in their modern children and in the liberal upbringing the children were receiving. These mothers were a part of the moral revolution they witnessed in their children. Indeed, they were its vanguard. They had been the young ladies who, beginning two decades before or thereabouts, had stripped off the extra petticoats, put away the high-topped shoes for dancing slippers, and abandoned the waltz for ragtime. By 1915 the new American woman had already advanced sufficiently for H. L. Mencken to herald her arrival and bestow upon her the name flapper.

Observe, then, this nameless one, this American Flapper. Her skirts have just reached her very trim and pretty ankles; her hair, newly coiled upon her skull, has just exposed the ravishing whiteness of her neck. ... Life, indeed, is almost empty of surprises, mysterious, horrors to this Flapper of 1915. ... She knows exactly what the Wasserman reaction is, and has made up her mind that she will never marry a man who can't show an unmistakable negative, ... is inclined to think that there must be something in this new doctrine of free motherhood. She is opposed to the double standard of morality, and favors a law prohibiting it.

Mencken's worldly-wise flapper was to be found in New York rather than in Middletown, but the girls in Muncie were doing their best to keep up with the styles. Ten years later, skirts were still on the rise, and Middletown mothers were busily adjusting their own hems as well as those of their daughters.

· ·

From the social point of view, American colleges and universities came into their own in the 1920's. Hundreds of new colleges of many sorts were started up during the decade and hundreds of thousands more students were enrolled in colleges than ever before. Where 3.04 percent of college-age youth had been enrolled in college in 1890, 8.14 percent were enrolled in 1920 and 12.37 in 1930. The one million mark was overtaken by the end of the decade. But enrollment figures only begin to tell the story of the increased impact of college life upon the national culture.

From the point of view of scholarship, World War I was an overwhelming disaster to American higher education. The leaders of the American university movement had been inspired by the German example in all their work. Abruptly in 1917 American colleges and universities converted to a wartime basis, and they began by ruthlessly eradicating whatever appeared to smack of German culture. Patriotism was the subject that was first of all to be taught in the classroom, and the colleges geared themselves so far as possible to the war effort.

Businessmen dominated the college boards of trustees, and if many of them had practiced noninterference with college activities before, they now believed that for the emergency their more practical experience was needed. The business community moved onto the college campus to cooperate with the colleges in seeing that everyone pulled together in the war effort. The tradition of university scholarship and academic freedom had been only a very recent one in American life, and it was slow to recover in the years after the war and the Great Red Scare of 1919. By the end of the twenties there were more than a thousand institutions of higher learning in the nation, and the new ones especially, narrowly vocational as they usually were in purpose, had little or no contact with the university ideals that had been fostered by Gilman and Eliot and White and others.

Higher education was bitterly attacked by intellectuals throughout the twenties for its business orientation; and presidents of leading colleges and universities, among others, agreed that the late nineteenth-century campaign to modernize higher education had overshot its mark. Speaking with great authority to this point was Abraham Flexner, director of the Institute for Advanced Study at Princeton, in his *Universities, American, English, German,* which appeared in 1930. An earlier critique by Flexner of American medical schools had resulted in sweeping reforms; he no doubt wishfully hoped for a similar influence throughout higher education generally.

Noting that "The term 'university' is very loosely used in America," Flexner did not "pause to characterize the absurdities covered by the name," but devoted his criticism to "the most highly developed and prominent of American institutions." For a few of these he had nearly nothing but praise. In general, however, he found that the " 'service' station" functions and the truly educative purposes of the colleges and universities had not been kept sufficiently distinct. He thought that this was the heart of the problem.

The problem of America is not "Main Street"; there are Main Streets in all countries. The hopelessness of America lies in the inability and unwillingness of those occupying seats of intelligence to distinguish between genuine culture and superficial veneer, in the lowering of institutions which should exemplify intellectual distinctions to the level of the vendors of patent medicines. So, too, there are Babbitts in all countries, not only in the United States; but "Babbittry" in the presidency of great universities is an exclusively—as it is widespread—American phenomenon.

There was much criticism by others in a similar vein, and some institutions responded by modifying the elective system to force upon all students some acquaintance with the arts and sciences. The general tendency in the colleges as a whole was not checked, however. The state colleges and universities, especially, were popularly looked upon as part of the public domain, financed by taxpayers to serve the purpose of shaping the new generation culturally and vocationally, to meet the desired needs of society at the moment and in the immediate future, as far as that could be predicted. They were also increasingly viewed as places where young people could have the good time they deserved to have.

For a time following World War I it seemed that too much could not be said in praise of American youth. There was a disposition to make large allowances for a generation of young men who had necessarily "seen Paree," so to speak, in the line of duty, and it was therefore not surprising that they acted with greater familiarity than formerly had been customary toward nice girls, who were expected to respond in kind as long as everything stayed within bounds. As to what the bounds were, the discussion was led off by F. Scott Fitzgerald with the publication of his *This Side of Paradise* in 1919, telling of a "vast juvenile intrigue" that was going on behind the parents' backs. This intrigue, so far as Fitzgerald dealt with it, was one that was going on among the sons and daughters of the rather rich and very rich in the Ivy League and its sister colleges. Somewhat lower down on the economic and social scale, other boys and girls were joining in at the state colleges and universities; but, altogether, the campus revolution in manners and morals directly included few outside the moderately substantial old-stock Americans.

Slightly more than 90 percent of American college students were of this old American stock, according to a very thorough nationwide survey of colleges published in 1927, and slightly more than 45 percent were put through college entirely by parents and guardians. It was expected that many students would take college jobs in order to help support themselves—and this was approved of socially, at least in the state universities—but for nearly half of the students it was not necessary.

For middle-class America, college had become a normal part of the process of "growing up." The renowned cartoonist of the American flapper, John Held, Jr., believed that there were basically only two reasons why the male American was sent to college.

The first is that the male parent went to this or that particular college, and his father before him. Therefore, the college is handed down from generation to generation, each going, only because his father went before him.

The second reason is that the boy must have an opportunity that the father never had; father, having to battle his way through life and climb the ladder of wealth without the assistance of a college education, always insists that his son will never have to overcome the obstacles that were in his path. Either boy does not go to college for education. They go so that they won't need to stammer and apologize when they are asked:

"What college did you go to?"

Employers in the business world held the same views as male parents, for they were the same people. Where a college degree had been widely looked upon as useless frippery in the age of the robber barons, it was honored and increasingly required for business advancement in the age of management. A bachelor of arts degree no longer signified much about the training of the recipient, owing, as a former president of the University of Michigan put it, to "the genial habit of using the name 'university' to describe many different types of units of the higher educational system in America." Businessmen had nevertheless come around to the view, expressed by the director of an employment agency, that "a college education is a good thing. It clears out the mind."

The number of girls who went to college to train for lifetime careers was undoubtedly small. Girls normally went to college to meet college boys and because the other girls they knew were going to college. For boys as well as girls, college was the parents' answer to the question of what to do with the child who was out of high school and who was thought too young to begin a career or to get married. Together the boys and girls were expected to learn how to behave so that they individually would not be out of things in an age when things were being done so differently than before.

Much of the same intellectual equipment that had been used in the prewar Greenwich Village revolt was put more widely and vaguely to use by postwar college men and women. Freudian explanations accounted for parental attitudes and disposed of parental arguments. The woman's rights argument, no longer needed for the woman's suffrage campaign, was enlisted in the cause of sexual freedom, as it had been in the old Greenwich Village days. Young men had always done as they were doing, and by doing it with young women of their own sort, the young men and women were together advancing beyond the barbarism of the double standard. Also, they were ridding themselves of the unhealthy hypocrisy of the Victorian era. The woman's rights movement had always been a two-edged sword, as the free-love feminist Victoria Woodhull had demonstrated, and in the twenties it seemed to be cutting with the nether edge only.

Prohibition gave college life in the twenties some novel characteristics not associated with prewar days of traditionally hearty chug-a-lugging of beer by the men. Bathtub gin took the place of beer, and the purple passion punches were designed for the coeds at least as much as for their escorts. The practice of cutting in at dances had been an old southern custom. In the twenties it was introduced everywhere on college campuses, where it changed girls' conduct at dances: girls were rated by the number of cut-ins they got, and they were therefore encouraged to dress and dance and behave accordingly.

Dorothy Parker remarked that if all the girls who attended a Yale prom were laid end to end, she would not be surprised. Others heard in detail of what actually went on, and were surprised indeed, as was the woman who was told of them by a woman friend and went to Christian Gauss, the dean of Princeton, with the news. Her friend had told her,

It was not merely a question of "petting" and "necking." She had cited instances of more shocking types of delinquency and insisted that certain scandalous practices were common. They would indicate that the attitude toward sex was ultra matter of fact, incontinence was the rule rather than the exception and the general code tolerated if it did not encourage a deplorable laxity. The old idea of chastity was no longer held, not even by young women. "Virgin" was a term of reproach and meant only a backward, unattractive, unsophisticated person in an age when sophistication was a virtue. Love and romance were fast disappearing and giving place to a sensuality which was no longer touched or sublimated by any appreciable degree of sentiment.

Gauss's dean-like comment was that "according to the proverb, everybody's aunt has seen a ghost," but that, while there was something in it, it was not just what the older generation thought. That was true, and it was also true that the older generation was not equipped by what it could remember of its own youth to understand what was going on among the young people, because the younger generation was growing up under conditions that were different from those experienced by its parents' generation. This had increasingly been the case since the end of the nineteenth century, and it was to continue to be the case. It is a situation which parents are aware of but one which children are much better aware of.

As far as premarital sexual experience is concerned, it was the conclusion of the exhaustive Kinsey reports of the 1940's that the pattern of behavior of college men in the twenties changed basically only to the extent that they were now more likely to have sexual relations with women in their own social class than formerly had been the case. The pattern of behavior of college women, by contrast, changed radically, petting being generally accepted by them for the first time as normal behavior, and sexual intercourse being not generally accepted but nevertheless occurring sometime during the college life of a good many girls. A maiden's virginity continued to be highly regarded by both coeds and college boys, but the loss of it in most cases ceased to be a matter of such gravity as it once had been.

Other studies before and since the Kinsey reports tend to agree generally with this conclusion concerning Protestant middle-class Americans and what happened to their attitudes toward sex and when. It appears that a marked change in attitude did take place among the generation that grew up during World War I, and that no equally marked change has taken place since then. The twenties experienced an attack against Victorian hypocrisy and the double standard in sexual morality, rather than an attack against sexual morality as a general principle. It represented the adoption of a moral code governing youth which reflected the point of view of youth and courtship, rather than, as formerly had been the case, the point of view of age and parenthood.

■■

John Winthrop's aged father, upon learning of his son's betrothal to Margaret Tyndal in 1618, wrote his future daughter-in-law this letter (I have altered the spelling and punctuation):

I am, I assure you (gentle Mistress Margaret), already inflamed with a fatherly love and affection towards you, the which, at the first, the only report of your modest behavior and mild manner did breed in my heart, but now through the manifest tokens of your true love, and constant mind, which I perceive to be settled in you towards my son, the same is exceedingly increased in me. . . .

. . . I doubt not, but I shall have just cause to praise God for you, and to think myself happy, that in my old age I shall enjoy the familiar company of so virtuous and loving a daughter and pass the residue of my days in peace and quietness. . . .

And therefore I assure you (good Mistress Margaret) that whatsoever love and kindness you shall vouchsafe to show hereafter unto me, I will not only requite it with the like, but also, to the uttermost of my power, redouble the same.

And for that I would fain make it a little part of your faith to believe that you shall be happy in matching with my son, I do here faithfully promise for him (in the presence of almighty God), that he will always be a most kind and loving husband unto you, and a provident steward for you and yours during his life, and also after his death. . . .

Your assured friend,
ADAM WINTHROP

The glory of well-attained old age was the crown and symptom of good society in Puritan England. It was intended that this should be so in colonial America also; and it became the case wherever English society established itself, whether the society was based upon the counting houses of Boston or Philadelphia or the plantations of Virginia or South Carolina. There was, however, that "hither edge of free land" to make sons bold against their fathers, and the rawness of American life, which was bruising to the dignity of age. Old age was at a disadvantage amid the commotion of the westward movement and later amid the building of an industrial society.

The industrial revolution produced conditions that simultaneously extended human life and put a premium on youth. In the case of the United States, the proportion of the population over 65 increased from 3.9 in 1890 to 6.8 in 1940. In nineteenth-century America, it was statistically improbable that both parents would survive to see the last child married off, because of the relative lateness of marriages as well as the relative brevity of life spans. The remaining statistical parent would live for only two years after all the children were married. Therefore, even though Americans individually did not marry and die according to the law of averages, there did not exist at the turn of the century an aged people free of parental responsibilities in America as a distinct social class.

Age, like childhood, was not as clearly defined and set apart in the nineteenth century as it came to be in the twentieth. In the factory as on the farm, children had been put to work as soon as they were able to do the job, and men and women went on working as long as they were able to, slowing down gradually as they aged.

This way of allowing things to be done was an offense not only to humane feelings but also to scientific management. When scientific management revolutionized American business methods during the first quarter of the twentieth century, it defined old age in terms of the loss of the capacity to work; and it separated old people from the rest of society arbitrarily at the age of 65. The percentage of the gainfully employed over 65 decreased during this period, while the percentage of people over 65 went up.

The idea of the elderly person in American society commands respect, but the idea of the elderly people does not. The rise of the city deprived old men and women of the place of honor in the home, and the rise of the factory and the mass production system rigidly classified them as inferior human material. It was not to be expected that they could keep up with the times, and for their own good as well as the good of everybody else, it was best that they keep out of the way.

The short skirt, along with the efficiency kitchen, served to super-annuate the older woman. Young mothers took happily to the fashions, but the styles were hard on women of indeterminate ages.

No corset, though I'm forty-odd,
And rank a stylish-stout—
Skirts to my knees, and rolled silk hose—
I dare not look about. . . .

Aging women were not expected to adopt the new fashions, and Dorothy Dix was harsh on those who tried, for "Old mutton never seems so old, and tough, and stringy as when it is dressed as spring lamb." She asserted that "the last lap of the journey of life has its compensations and its joys if we are willing to accept them," but they were miserably poor compensations as she described them.

Never had old people been such back numbers as they were in the twenties. As F. Scott Fitzgerald wrote of the Jazz Age,

there were entire classes (people over fifty, for example) who spent a whole decade denying its existence even when its puckish face peered into the family circle. . . . Silver-haired women and men with fine old faces, people who never did a consciously dishonest thing in their lives, still assure each other in the apartment hotels of New York and Boston and Washington that "there's a whole generation growing up that will never know the taste of liquor." Meanwhile their granddaughters pass the well-thumbed copy of *Lady Chatterley's Lover* around the boarding-school.

Organized religion, which had always exalted patriarchal authority, was little help to the aged in the twenties even though formal church membership was proportionally greater than at any previous time in the nation's history. The rural origins of American Protestantism had poorly equipped it to maintain its influence in the cities, and despite the achievements of the Social Gospel movement, the churches tended to abandon efforts at social control as the price of maintaining their congregations. The congregations tended to be made up of people who did not live in the same neighborhoods or engage in the same occupations. They associated together only for occasional religious and sociable purposes. Old ladies might complain to the minister, and he might make the young ladies cover their throats and shoulders and knees before attending services; but that was about all he could do, if he could do that.

One approach taken by churches in the twenties was to increase the young people's programs, which generally resulted in social activities reflective of the times, thereby tending to put members of the older generation in opposition to the church itself. Another approach was to reduce the requirements of religious beliefs to a common denominator low enough to allow the pews to fill up. As summarized for the 1930's by the secretary of the Commission for the Study of Christian Unity of the Federal Council of Churches, these requirements amounted to little. Referring to Americans of Protestant background, outside as well as inside the churches, he wrote,

They believe—in a shadowy way, to be sure—in God and in immortality. They respect and admire the good—though, as generally viewed, the impractical—Jesus. Of actual historical facts about him they are ignorant. About the theological Christ they know little and care less. In extreme emergencies they pray, almost to the last man.

He further noted that "sensational periodicals" were, by their statements, more favorable to orthodox Christianity than the so-called intellectual magazines, and that, therefore, "a magazine's orthodoxy is about in proportion to its unworthiness to exist at all!"

Those who remained dedicated to evangelical religious orthodoxy remained dedicated also to the corresponding doctrine of individual responsibility to make one's way in this world and to provide for one's own old age. This rural-oriented economic individualism had never worked well in American cities, where depressions and accidents had thrown men helplessly out of work and had wiped out lifetime accumulations of savings for old people. The Great Depression was much the worst depression the nation had experienced. The number of old people living on their accumulated savings was much greater than it had ever been before. In this situation, the disinherited aged of the nation banded together in the early years of the thirties to form themselves into a new American social class.

Among the Western nations, only in the United States were the old people forced to organize themselves independently of the existing political parties to bring pressure on the government to legislate in their behalf. In Germany, Bismarck had instituted compulsory national old-age insurance under pressure from the Socialists. In England, the Liberal party had enacted the Old Age Pension Law of 1908 under pressure from the Trade Union Congress and the Fabians. A similar course had been taken in other European countries, as well as in Latin America, under left-wing and labor auspices.

In America, on the contrary, the American Federation of Labor did not even endorse the principle of federal old-age pensions until its national convention of 1922; and, concentrating on obtaining immediate direct benefits for its own membership, it contented itself thereafter with lip service to the principle. Theodore Roosevelt had advocated old-age insurance in his presidential campaign of 1912; and Franklin D. Roosevelt, in the campaign of 1932, had said that he would look into the matter. That was almost the extent to which state-guaranteed security for the aged had impinged upon the American political reform tradition, at the time when Dr. Francis E. Townsend started his movement early in the New Deal. The American Association for Old Age Security had been organized in 1927, but the few state pension laws in existence were due primarily to the efforts of the Fraternal Order of Eagles.

Southern California, with its warm dry climate and cool sea breezes, became a haven for old people in the twentieth century, its population of people over 65 approximately doubling during the decade of the twenties. The depression naturally put old people out of work more readily than young people, and the banking crisis wiped out the life savings of thousands upon thousands of them. Their wails of anguish were heard by a number of organizers of social discontent, including Upton Sinclair, Huey Long, and Father Charles E. Coughlin, but their own particular messiah was Dr. Francis E. Townsend of Long Beach.

Townsend launched the movement by sending a letter to the Long Beach *Press-Telegram* in September 1933, outlining a program for recovery. The program consisted of retirement by the government of everybody who was 65 or older, on a pension of $150 a month, each payment to be spent before the next one was received. The pension program was to be financed out of a sales tax. The letter brought a tremendous response, the pension went up to $200, Townsend dropped everything else, and in January 1934 he incorporated with a real estate promoter-acquaintance as Old Age Revolving Pensions, Ltd. Townsend Clubs spread throughout the nation, and membership rose to about 1.5 million within two years.

Delegates to the first national convention of Townsend Clubs were described as "just folks . . . Methodist picnic people." They were of sturdy American stock and from rural and small-town backgrounds.

To them, the Townsend movement was rooted in the rural, cheap money, reform tradition of the Greenbackers and the free-silver Populists, and its mission was, not simply to enrich old people, but to rescue the nation from disaster. The aged American, although abandoned by his children, would now lead his children out of the depression.

> *The Townsend Plan is marching—*
> *It will cause all fear to cease—*
> *It will give us larger freedom*
> *And a greater sense of peace.*
> *Let us praise our God in heaven,*
> *And give glory to His name—*
> *His Plan is marching on.*

Until then the New Deal had not evinced much concern for the plight of the aged. The administration's Wagner-Lewis bill of 1934 dealt only with unemployment insurance; and in November, in a major speech, Roosevelt said, "I do not know whether this is the time for any Federal legislation on old-age security." Following the 1934 elections, however, he instructed the Committee on Economic Security that "we have to have it. . . . The Congress can't stand the pressure of the Townsend Plan unless we have a real old-age insurance system, nor can I face the country without having devised at this time . . . a solid plan which will give some assurance to old people of systematic assistance upon retirement."

In 1935 the Social Security Act was passed, providing for unemployment insurance and old-age pensions. Beginning in 1942 retired workers over 65 would receive pensions of from $10 to $85, per month, to be paid out of a fund created jointly by employers and workers, through a payroll tax. Because many were excluded from the benefits of the act, including farm laborers, domestic workers, and public employees, the Townsend Plan kept marching on. Subsequent administrations brought in additional categories of workers, however, and the Townsend movement faded away during and after World War II.

Old people were given no bed of roses to rest on during their declining years, but they had at least established the civilized principle for the nation that, as Eleanor Roosevelt expressed it, "the government has an obligation to guard the rights of an individual so carefully that he never reaches a point at which he needs charity." As the history of the subsequent fight for medicare demonstrated, however, the American filiarchy remains reluctant to waste its affluence upon those who are euphemistically referred to during elections as senior citizens.

What is perhaps most striking about the tight-fisted policy that America maintains toward its elders is the Spartan self-sacrifice it entails. To begin with, this policy burdened millions of young Americans with the personal responsibility for the support of their surviving parents; and when these burdens included heavy medical expenses, they often proved financially disastrous to the children. To end with, the children, themselves, had their own old age to look forward to, and it was only untimely death that could save them from it. A public policy that treated their parents harshly was also one that treated their own future lives harshly.

In a society based on reason, each generation will wisely provide for its own future by improving the lot of the preceding generation. In a technologically conditioned society it is the machinery of civilization which tends to become important and immortal, rather than the technicians who service it and improve it and, in their own brief time, know how to use its new improvements. Those who are actively engaged in maintaining and improving the machinery of society will be disciplined by it to sacrifice themselves doubly for it. They will spend their resources selflessly upon their children, who will succeed them as the engineers and enjoyers, and they will deprive themselves of the fruits of their own labors, as a generation, when they have passed the working years in the biological cycle and can no longer engage actively in the timeless and directionless tinkering with the machine process.

••

The spiritual aspect of the machine process revealed itself to the world overnight in May 1927, when Charles A. Lindbergh flew the Atlantic to become the hero of the world and the prophet of the mechanical filiarchy. Lindbergh's flight took place during the era of ballyhoo, when Americans eagerly followed Shipwreck Kelly's record-breaking flagpole-sitting, without reference to the possible practical uses to which flagpole-sitting could be put. Airplane stunt men who set records similarly attracted attention. Among them, Lindbergh in 1927 attracted all of the attention there was. His transatlantic flight, which was soon to be followed by many other transatlantic flights, might conceivably have been looked upon as simply the biggest stunt of them all. But it was not. It assumed instead a religious character, relating to the searchings of the new age for its salvation.

Lindbergh, from his youth in rural Minnesota, had been characterized by a soul-possessing interest in machinery and a brilliant skill in the handling of it, combined with a general disinterest in people, which always passed with some for shyness and with others for arrogance. In high school and at the University of Wisconsin his motorcycle absorbed his attention. The carefully calculated death-defying risk fascinated him, and he became master of it.

Lindbergh possessed attributes which one might associate with a mechanical man; this was true of his relationships with people as well as machines. His friendships were mainly with like-minded men, and he characteristically expressed his friendships in practical jokes, such as snipe hunts and pratt falls, designed to test the nerves, reflexes, and emotional endurances of the objects. His own nerves, reflexes, and endurance were remarkable even by the standards of the barnstorming confederates he soon joined.

Lindbergh left college in 1922 to learn flying and take up a barnstorming career as stunt man and parachutist for county fairs and the like. The next year he bought his own plane and was in business for himself. In 1924 he trained as a U.S. Army flying cadet, graduating the following year with a brilliant record. He returned to barnstorming, and then went on to airmail carrying, airplane testing, and instructing other flyers. Of his early flying experiences he later wrote,

When I think of the planes we flew, of the difficulties we all had in making a living in aviation, it seems to me that men and aircraft were more closely connected then than now; that the character of men, in those days, was almost a structural part of the aircraft.

The key to Lindbergh was his great ability to function as a structural part of the machinery he controlled and his natural tendency to make of the smoothly functioning machine the model for all of his social attitudes.

In 1919 a French-born member of the Aero Club of America offered a prize of $25,000 to the first aviator to fly the 3,600 miles nonstop from New York to Paris. The five-year time limit passed with no takers for what seemed an impossible stunt, and in 1926 it was renewed. The Alcock-Brown flight from Newfoundland to Ireland had been successfully made in 1919, but the distance was only 1,960 miles, and, according to Sir John Alcock, it had been "a terrible journey," and "the wonder is that we are here at all." (Alcock was killed six months later in an air crash.)

The renewed offer in 1926 came at a time when trimotor planes were being developed which airplane manufacturers and many pilots thought might manage the flight where a single-engine monoplane would not. Among those who were so persuaded was the greatest of the French war aces, René Fonck, who, on his first attempt, crashed his heavily loaded Sikorsky at takeoff, killing two of his crew. In March 1928 the French war aces Charles Nungesser and François Coli started from Paris for New York and disappeared over the Atlantic. In April Commander Richard E. Byrd, with a crew of three, crashed during a test flight preliminary to trying for the prize. Byrd returned to the contest, and so did Fonck, and a third crew, flying the prized Bellanca, prepared for the flight. In addition there were dark horses, including Lindbergh, "who plans to make the flight alone," according to a newspaper report.

The many tellers of the tale of what happened after that have all experienced the frustration of being unable to do the story justice, and they have also experienced a compulsion to explain the meaning of the story; for nothing quite like it ever happened before in the world's history, and just what could ever happen again to equal it is not quite imaginable. Lindbergh set out on the morning of May 20, 1927, in his little monoplane, the *Spirit of St. Louis,* despite weather conditions which discouraged the competition. And he flew perfectly, alone and by dead reckoning, to Paris, where 50,000 Frenchmen awaited his arrival at the airport, 33 hours and 30 minutes later.

He did not need the letter of introduction he carried with him to the American ambassador to France, but he did need the fifty-dollar limit he had specified to the clipping bureau whose services he had used to collect press notices of the trip. The departure of his plane from New York ignited a worldwide excitement without parallel in history—an excitement that did not die down after the event slipped into the past. Not only for America, but for the world, Lindbergh had made himself a unique symbol of the air age and of the machine age.

What the flight symbolized for Lindbergh, himself, is easier to determine than what it symbolized for the world. For Lindbergh, the flight was a mechanical achievement, pure and simple. Lindbergh's first concern upon landing in France was for his plane. His first request was for a mechanic. His anger at hero worshippers who had torn canvas from the plane seemed surprisingly excessive, since the plane was little damaged by it. He had intended to fly home around the world in the *Spirit of St. Louis;* hence, it was with great reluctance that he submitted to having his airplane crated up and to having the two of them, himself and the *Spirit,* shipped back separately on a warship sent by President Coolidge for the purpose.

He was remarkably at ease amid the endless waves of adulation, bearing himself with an enormously appealing air of self-confident modesty. When he told of what he had done, it was always "we," meaning himself and the *Spirit of St. Louis,* and never "I." He invariably treated his flight as a technical, and not a personal, accomplishment. A typical exchange between Lindbergh and his public was made at the welcome banquet given for him on his return to New York—the largest banquet, it was said, ever given an individual in history, consuming, among other things, three hundred pounds of butter.

The principal speaker at the banquet was Charles Evans Hughes, who declared in part: "This is the happiest day of all days for America, and as one mind she is now intent upon the noblest and the best. . . . We are all better men and women because of this exhibition in this flight of our young friend. Our boys and girls have before them a stirring, inspiring vision of real manhood." To which Lindbergh replied, in part, that "there is great room for improvement in the United States in aeronautics," and that "airports closer to cities" were particularly needed.

Lindbergh's later scientific association with Alexis Carrel resulted in the creation of a mechanical heart. He admired the machinelike in man and in society. His friendship for Nazis and his high respect for the virility and discipline of their system, as well as for the state of their airforce, led him to doubt that democracy would be able to prevail against them. In 1940 he therefore became the leading figure in the America First movement to keep the United States out of war with Germany.

His speeches became increasingly racist and vituperative, until it was altogether impossible for his fellow Americans to separate the hero from the Nazi admirer, as *Time* magazine had earlier attempted to do by commenting that ideology was not Lindbergh's forte. Staking his reputation on the struggle, Lindbergh destroyed himself as hero. His heroic flight apparently had not meant to the American nation what it had meant to him: the worship of the machine.

"In so far as a consensus was ever reached," wrote Lindbergh's biographer Kenneth S. Davis,

it would seem to be that Lindbergh's historic mission, however inadvertent on his part, was that of savior. . . .

The era appeared to many living in it as one of unparalleled lawlessness, sensationalism, political corruption and spiritually demeaning commercialism. It was also an era in which the individual person feared he was becoming steadily less important, being more and more an object of mass manipulation. He had begun to hear and talk a great deal about how "The Machine" was "crushing the individual life."

Then there flashed before the jaundiced public eye, unheralded, this slim, clean-cut single-minded youth who seemed to stand for everything in which the Jazz Age had lost faith. . . . And far from being crushed by The Machine, he used a machine as a means of self-expression. In his flight, and even more in his fame, he proved that personal heroism, decency, and dignity were yet possible in the world. Americans by identifying themselves with him could regain some of their lost self-respect.

To the world, perhaps, Lindbergh had used the machine as a means of self-expression. From his own point of view, Lindbergh had been "almost a structural part of the aircraft," using himself to help express what the machine could do. This was not sufficiently appreciated by writers about Lindbergh because they thought in verbal and in human, rather than in mechanical, terms.

Among many others, however, for whom the machine, as Veblen had put it, had thrown out "anthropomorphic habits of thought," Lindbergh was probably inarticulately admired in his own machine-made terms and not in the terms of libertarian humanism which flowed so freely from pulpit and press and which later felt itself so blatantly betrayed when Lindbergh applied his machine-oriented values to social questions. Again, in 1940 there were perhaps many who were instinctively in agreement with him—those in society upon whom the machine had borne with the most "unmitigated impact," on the assembly line, or in other machine-oriented areas of activity—who were, by the same token, without the ability or opportunity to express themselves in the medium of words.

The universal emphasis that admirers placed upon Lindbergh's youthfulness has been much commented on by psychologists and others. Lindbergh was a seasoned pilot, at the peak of his physical development, and he was well past thinking of himself as a boy. The world, however, insisted upon it. One important reason for this was the one Henry Adams had given: the technological age belonged to youth, because the age was constantly outdistancing the comprehension of those elders who, in preindustrial times, had been able to think of themselves as better. American society looked to youth for guidance, in the case of Lindbergh reverentially, in the age of the technological filiarchy.

FIVE

The
Melting
Pot

....

7.

Americanization and Counter-Americanization

··

DURING THE CENTURY AFTER WATERLOO, nearly 30 million people migrated to the United States, which increased in total population from under 9 million to 100 million. Immigration in the early years of the twentieth century was at a rate of almost a million a year. Somewhere around 1914 native Americans of primarily British descent ceased to comprise a majority of the nation. In order of size, the main composition of the non-Anglo-Saxon majority was African, German, Irish, Italian, Jewish, and Swedish in origin.

Outside of New England, Revolutionary America had already been ethnically mixed, especially in the western regions and in Pennsylvania. The French immigrant Crèvecoeur concluded that this ethnic mixture was forming itself into a new race. In his famous essay,

"What Is an American?" Crèvecoeur explained that an American was a composite European, made self-reliant by landownership and made tolerant by life among neighbors of different faiths and customs. New England, he observed, was the least American part of English America because it was the most thoroughly English.

New Englanders naturally tended to take the opposite view: they considered themselves the truest Americans, being freest from alien admixtures; and, being the most literate as well as the most homogeneous section of the country, they were in an unrivaled position to indoctrinate the nation in their Boston-oriented Yankee ideology. Yankee settlers carried the message to the Midwest and the Far West, and Yankee textbooks taught Plymouth Rock and Bunker Hill to southerners as well. Crèvecoeur's flattering theory continued to win acceptance, especially in the form of Frederick Jackson Turner's frontier thesis, but the Yankee image was a clearer likeness than Crèvecoeur's and Turner's composite American. Uncle Sam was still a Yankee in 1914, no matter how many non-Anglo-Saxons had been allowed in.

Anglo-Saxon concern over the New Immigration expressed itself in immigration literacy test bills, which Congresses passed and Presidents vetoed in 1897, 1913, and 1915. In 1917, amid the wartime campaign against "hyphenated Americanism," Congress passed a literacy test bill over Wilson's veto and pressed on, through the Great Red Scare, to the immigration restriction law of 1921. Nativist excitement continued to mount as the American Legion marched and the Ku Klux Klan rode, and in 1924, Congress passed the National Origins Act, limiting total immigration to 150,000 a year after 1927.

In 1924, however, nativism triumphant was nativism in tatters. The idea of the Anglo-Saxon world mission had achieved full expression in the "war to make the world safe for democracy," and it suffered for it in the postwar reaction against Wilson's war. German-America did not immediately rise again; but H. L. Mencken did, and so did a lot of others who had been damned during the war as hyphenated Americans, together with some intellectual Anglo-Saxons and many additional thirsty ones. Prohibition was the aspect of the Anglo-Saxon mission which met the most devastating defeat in victory. For that matter, immigration restriction, itself, resulted in the destruction of nativism as a movement, though not as a sentiment.

The decade of the twenties is not primarily significant for the fury of the reactionaries, but rather for the changes that were taking place which made them furious. In the twenties the old moral forces stood at Armageddon, and went down to defeat; then Hoover and the American System went down to defeat after them in the Wall Street crash.

The Great Depression ruthlessly continued the process of Americanization which had been fostered by the National Origins Act of 1924. During the thirties writers who concerned themselves with ragged hordes and huddled masses were no longer referring to immigrant hordes and masses but to Americans of every sort of origin. The depression was a great communitarian leveler for a large part of the population—a melting pot that was reshaping the national character.

In the election of 1928 Herbert Hoover, who ran against the Catholic Al Smith, had been made to appear the defender of Anglo-American civilization in spite of himself. Then Hoover and the American System were discredited by the Great Depression; and under the patrician leadership of the old-stock but non-Anglo-Saxon and Protestant but nonevangelical Franklin Delano Roosevelt, "a new deal for the American people" was undertaken. It was accompanied by the repeal of prohibition, which, to millions of Americans, signified more broadly the repeal of the Protestant Republic as the sovereign national ideology.

•••

No proudly held American ideal was ever more hollowly held for generation after generation than the traditional ideal of America as the land of welcome for the downtrodden peoples of the earth. The American policy of unrestricted immigration had, from colonial times, been accompanied by gargantuan evils and horrors, which Americans had never felt responsible for as a nation, except half-heartedly in the case of the Negro slave trade. America as a democratic nation did not take responsibility for the activities of the steamship agents, contract labor agents, and padrones who trafficked profitably in immigration during the nineteenth and early twentieth centuries. It did not even take responsibility for preventing Chinese girls from being sold into slavery in San Francisco's Chinatown brothels, at a time when "white slavery" was a national issue; nor did it prevent organ grinders in New York from enslaving small boys who had been kidnapped from Italy to be used as beggars, at a time when reforms in child care were occupying the mind of middle-class America. Social workers and Bohemian radicals assumed that America was responsible for these evils, but Progressive America as a whole was inclined to rest this responsibility with the various foreign elements involved and forget about it.

Immigration restriction in the form of a literary test bill first passed through Congress in 1897, only to be postponed for a generation by the vetoes of Presidents Cleveland, Taft, and Wilson—all in response to an idealistic tradition that the Statue of Liberty personified. However, these vetoes were also in response to the ever-increasing pressure of the immigrant vote, which was an inescapable fact of political life, particularly in all presidential elections.

Woodrow Wilson was a painful public example of the conflict between the old-stock ideal of racial purity on the one hand and the politically necessary ideal of the melting pot on the other. As a political scientist, Wilson had classified the New Immigration as inferior human material in passages in his *History of the American People,* which spokesmen for ethnic groups never allowed him to forget. As President of the American people Wilson, under relentless pressure from ethnic minorities, became the last defender of those immigrant groups against old-stock demands for an end to unlimited immigration. The fact that immigration restriction was ultimately achieved in an atmosphere of racial violence has served to disguise the other more important fact that the traditional policy of unlimited immigration had always been characterized by equivocal idealism and real human exploitation where native Americans were concerned.

Ethnic histories have naturally chosen to emphasize the contributions of immigrants to American democracy, but the preponderant influence of immigration throughout the century of the great European exodus was far from being a democratizing one. Quite the contrary, except for the institution of Negro slavery and the resulting Civil War, immigration was the most formidable antidemocratic force in American life during the nineteenth century.

The great European exodus to America, supplemented by an Asian immigration to California, provided the heavy labor for the American industrial revolution, as is always gratefully pointed out. It was also the means by which the dignity and security of American labor were continuously undermined, and it was the basis for a growing class system which became accepted on racial grounds against democracy.

Jacksonian America was the product of two full generations of freedom from mass immigration. The American Revolution, followed by the French Revolutionary and Napoleonic wars, had sealed America off from heavy immigration. Mass immigration did not occur again to unsettle American society until the 1830's; it did not take on the character of an onslaught until the Irish exodus from famine and the German flight from overpopulation and unsuccessful revolution in the late 1840's. It was of incalculable importance to American democracy that the political system agreed upon in 1787 was given these two generations in which to develop from Federalism through Republicanism to Jacksonian Democracy.

During the ages of Jefferson and Jackson, the servant problem was one that attracted much attention from foreign visitors, who were used to having things done for them by servants in the Old Country and having them done in a properly servile manner. Hezakiah Niles wrote that

Europeans, especially Englishmen, settling in the United States, who lived decently at home, have a universal complaint to make about the "impertinence of servants," meaning chiefly *women* and girls hired to do housework. . . . These girls will not call the lady of the house *mistress* or drop a *curtsey* when honored with a command; and if they do not like the usage they receive will be off in an instant.

And Tench Coxe noted that "no country of the same wealth, intelligence and civilization has so few menial servants (strictly speaking) in the families of persons of the greatest property" as the United States.

The influx of "the raw untrained Irish peasantry" changed that condition and by the eve of the Civil War, wealthy American wives and daughters were being waited on hand and foot by liveried servants. It was the opinion of one immigrant observer in 1865, after the experience of three years as a workingman in America, that "there is an untitled aristocracy both in New York and the other great cities of the Union, more haughty and exclusive than any within the region of

Belgravia"—an assertion that received substantial support from native American observers.

By the end of the nineteenth century, amid the influx of the New Immigration, the modest fortunes of the antebellum merchant gentry had been superseded by the great fortunes of the plutocracy, and private establishments of one or two hundred servants were an absolute must for those men and women of wealth who were truly serious in their intention of keeping up with the Vanderbilts. Middle-class housewives during the Progressive era kept one or two or three or more servants to help out around the house as a matter of course, and these were looked upon as inferiors who were lucky to hold the job, considering the numbers of girls and women who were seeking domestic service.

Native Americans did not tend to suppose that these immigrants were their equals, and race-consciousness increased under the impact of the New Immigration. How this racial doctrine came to be codified in the schoolbooks of nineteenth-century America has been summarized by Ruth Miller Elson.

Each race and its subdivisions—nationalities—are defined by inherent mental and personal characteristics which the child must memorize. ... The American, as the ideal man, is of the white race, of Northern European background, Protestant, self-made, and, if not a farmer at least retaining the virtues of his yeoman ancestors. As race becomes an increasingly significant way to think about human beings, the English are exalted to a position just below the Americans. ... Yet the American population is not identical with the English because the American environment sieved the English population. . . . The American is a distilled Englishman.

Immigrant children were taught from these same schoolbooks, unless they attended the parochial schools which multiplied during the last decade of the century.

Americanization in this form was a powerful influence in encouraging the development of ethnic patriotism among all the immigrant groups. The Germans, the Irish, and the Jews had been fully imbued with cultural self-awareness upon their arrival in America. But for most of the New Immigrants, ethnic patriotism was mainly a product of the American ghettoes: it was there that these Italian or Polish or Hungarian or Greek immigrants often first became conscious of

themselves as belonging to any distinctive social group at all beyond
the family and the village of their home country. They became
hyphenated Americans all at one time by simultaneously discovering
their identity as citizens of their adopted country and their other
identity as representatives of an ethnic group in Europe.

During and after World War I the chauvinism that welled up in the
United States was by no means confined to Anglo-Saxons, for all the
ethnic groups that the Ku Klux Klan opposed were themselves
afflicted with their own chauvinisms. German-American chauvinism
had been powerfully expressed and then most ruthlessly demolished.
Irish-Americans came violently to the support of the Irish rebels in
the rising of 1916; after the war they helped to defeat ratification of
the Treaty of Versailles because it had not served to secure the independence of Ireland. Polish-Americans organized in support of an
independent Poland. Italian-Americans organized in opposition to the
acquisition of Fiume by Yugoslavia. Zionism swept through the
American Jewish community as Jewish Israel came into existence and
as American anti-Semitism became an increasing matter for concern.
Black racism swept through the Negro ghettoes of the northern cities,
inspired by the Jamaican Negro Marcus Garvey and his Back-to-
Africa movement.

All of these non-Anglo-Saxon chauvinisms were directed toward
extranational objectives, however, and they diminished in fervor during the twenties, just as the drive for Americanism itself did. There
was much going on in America to distract ethnic minority groups
from distant concerns, and much going on to unite them as Americans. There was the unifying influence of the general rise in the
standard of living, accompanied by the greater availability of mass-
produced commodities. Automobiles and radios reshaped the living
habits and ideas and accents of recent immigrants along with those of
old-stock Americans, and in the same general way.

Progressive America had been unable to contain its anxieties about
race matters. While the New Immigration increased from year to
year, native Americans were, themselves, committing "race suicide"
—so it was more and more widely argued—by increasingly limiting
the size of their families. According to the widely accepted Germanic
germ theory, American institutions of self-government derived from
Germanic, which was also to say Anglo-Saxon, racial germs. If this

was true, the New Immigration was surely undermining the foundations of the Republic. Yet attempts to limit immigration were persistently frustrated by the political attractiveness of the immigrant vote, which was, in turn, annually increasing in importance. In 1907 the New Immigration reached an all-time high of nearly one million; in that year the German-American Alliance and the Ancient Order of Hibernians signed an agreement to oppose all immigration restriction, in order to protect continued German and Irish Immigration.

The only alternative hope was that the immigrants would become Americanized in the manner described by Crèvecoeur and Turner. But the frontier was gone, and Turner, himself, entertained doubts that the New Immigrant was racially as capable of liberty as the Old Immigrant had been. If he was capable of it, then the public schools would be the means of instilling the spirit of liberty in him. Some additional indoctrination was attempted by patriotic organizations such as the Daughters of the American Revolution, but responsibility was mainly left with the schools.

Outright enthusiasm for the melting pot idea in Progressive America was chiefly limited to spokesmen for the New Immigrants, themselves, especially those for whom America was the only main hope of escape from Russian persecution. Emma Lazarus, who wrote the verse inscribed on the Statue of Liberty, was a native American of Sephardic Jewish ancestry. Israel Zangwill, whose play *The Melting Pot* popularized the phrase, was an English Jew who had visited America briefly but who, as director of an emigrant society, had helped thousands of Jews to escape to America from Russia. Mary Antin was a Jewish immigrant to America from Russia, whose autobiography, *The Promised Land,* was the ultimate testimonial for the melting pot thesis. "I have been made over," she wrote. "I am absolutely other than the person whose story I have to tell."

The relatively few American social workers and intellectuals who defended the New Immigrants—like Jane Addams, Jacob Riis, Horace Kallen, and Hutchins Hapgood—were not motivated by faith in the melting pot idea. They were cultural pluralists, who argued that America was being culturally enriched by the new elements in its population. This was a line of argument that was a practical one in the context of settlement work; but it was not calculated to appeal widely to the American public.

In spite of political difficulties, immigration restriction of some sort was imminent, even before World War I came to influence nativist sentiments. The literacy test bill, directed against the New Immigration, would have become law in 1915 if President Wilson, who was, himself, a thoroughgoing racial determinist, had not felt obliged to honor campaign pledges to immigrant groups by vetoing it. By that time, however, Europe was deadlocked in the trenches, and as Anglo-America and German-America became emotionally involved in the conflict, ethnic anxieties in the United States came to be related to the Old Immigration even more than to the New Immigration.

The outbreak of war in Europe threw the United States into an ethnic paroxysm that revealed how essentially Anglo-Saxon the character of American nationality was. This came as something of a surprise to almost everybody. England had stood for tyranny in American history, and even the Boston-oriented Immigration Restriction League had indicated no preference for the English over the Germans or Scandinavians as immigrants. The concern of the evangelistic moral reformers had been with religion and drinking habits primarily, and although the Germans came off somewhat worse than the English on these counts, German nationality and language had not been a crucial issue.

Theodore Roosevelt, in his 1912 presidential campaign, appeared to accept the arguments of social reformers like Jane Addams and Jacob Riis, that America was being enriched by the addition of new cultures and that the American idea ought to be one of cultural pluralism. Then war came to Europe, loyalty became the paramount issue in America, and the chauvinistic Roosevelt found himself declaring that "above all, the immigrant must learn to talk and think and *be* United States." And in making this statement, Roosevelt had the German-American hyphenates particularly in mind. There must be an end to efforts to preserve German culture in America. For the sake of national unity, American culture must be an English-language culture exclusively.

If this discovery of the importance of English-language Americanism was new to many Americans of English ancestry, to Americans of German ancestry it came as a brutal and incredible blow. More than 8 million Germans and Austrians had settled in the United States since 1820. And in an age when German music, literature, and learning were preeminent in the world, these immigrants had not come primarily for the purpose of imbibing American culture; they would keep their own. Cincinnati, St. Louis, and Milwaukee were the outstanding urban examples of the successful transplantation of German culture to America.

The Germans had kept to themselves as much as almost any immigrant group had, but they had represented diverse interests and occupations, and they had made themselves actively a part of their adopted homeland. Refugees from the unsuccessful German Revolutions of 1848 had brought the spirit of liberal nationalism with them. In this spirit Carl Schurz had become an outstanding figure in American national politics. Francis Lieber and Hermann Von Holst had lectured Americans on liberty and democracy with impressive academic authority. The debt of American education to Germany was freely acknowledged. Thus, in spite of their clannish tendencies and their continental drinking customs and Sunday convivialities, the Germans had won the respect of Anglo-Saxon Americans. A Boston sociologist gave higher marks to the Germans than to any of Boston's other immigrant groups.

When the war broke out in Europe, German-Americans were confident that as good Americans of German background, they had a mission to perform—to preserve American isolation from the Machiavellian designs of the British. The Wilson administration was pursuing a policy of neutrality which permitted trade with the Allies and which was therefore not truly neutral. The German-American Alliance favored, instead, the old Jeffersonian formula of applying an embargo against all belligerents; in January 1915 every major German-American organization in the nation sent its delegates to Washington to join in an impressive representation of this position.

The American press was divided in its reaction to this demonstration, but the American English-language press was not. "Never since the foundation of the Republic," declared *The New York Times,* "has any body of men assembled here who were more completely subservient to foreign influence and a foreign power and none ever proclaimed the un-American spirit more openly." The German-language press replied indignantly for a brief while and then was shut down for the duration.

"Preparedness" was the watchword for both parties in the election of 1916, and that meant loyalty and national unity and an end to "hyphenated Americanism," by which was meant German-Americanism and Irish-Americanism and Italian-Americanism, and yet not English-Americanism. Americanism *was* English-Americanism. Americanism evidently spoke no other language.

Then the United States entered the war, and the Committee on Public Information massively indoctrinated the nation on the "Hun," assisted by powerful new private organizations led by the National Security League and the American Defense Society. Gone were the friendly, music-loving, hard-working, God-fearing German-American home folks. Gone also was the American racial debt to Germany for its institutions of self-government. A savage Asiatic strain was added to German blood, which caused the "Hun" to start wars and butcher babies abroad and put ground glass in bakery bread on the home front.

On the home front, de-Germanization was executed with thoroughness down to the neighborhood level. German music was banned from concert halls. German books were withheld from library circulation. Sauerkraut became "liberty cabbage," and dachshunds became "liberty pups," and Americans with German names or foreign accents were patriotically ostracized and terrorized. How thoroughgoing the Americans were about their Kulturkampf is indicated roughly in the fact that between 1910 and 1920, the number of German- and Austrian-born Americans decreased by 1.5 million.

Americanization was proceeding on other fronts as well, and the German menace increasingly came to be overshadowed by the Communist menace. The American Socialist party, which for a decade had been organizing German and East European foreign-language units, met in 1917 and voted not to support the war. Congress responded to the antiwar position of the American Socialist party with the Espionage and Sedition Acts and with the jailing of hundreds of antiwar Americans, including IWW leader Bill Haywood, the Socialist presidential candidate Eugene V. Debs, and the Milwaukee Congressman Victor Berger.

In Russia the parliamentary revolution gave way to the Bolshevik Revolution, and in March 1919 the Third International was formed. In the United States two distinct Communist parties were created: native American radicals, including John Reed and Benjamin Gitlow, founded the Communist Labor party, with a membership of about 10,000; the Communist party was formed, mainly out of the foreign-language groups of the Socialist party. The Communist party included about 60,000 members. The Socialist party retained only about 30,000 and continued to decline. Haywood joined the Communist party declaring, "Here is what we have been dreaming about: here is the IWW all feathered out," and the Wobbly movement was largely absorbed in the new organizations.

English-America had subdued the Germans, both at home and abroad. Now, without a moment's pause, it lunged ahead into what was conceived to be the fearfully developing struggle with the Red Menace.

In February 1919 the Seattle Central Labor Council, led by men with suspected IWW leanings, called a general strike throughout the city, in support of striking shipyard workers. In discussing the announced strike the official Labor Council newspaper appealed for quiet orderliness on the part of the citizens, promising that the strike committee would preserve the law and see that the sick were cared for and necessary businesses kept in operation. Then it concluded: "We are undertaking the most tremendous move ever made by LABOR in this country. . . . We are starting on a road that leads—NO ONE KNOWS WHERE!"

The peaceful end to the four-day strike was a great momentary relief to a nervous nation, but nobody relaxed much. A 4-million-man army was being disbanded as rapidly as possible. Corporate business, ensconced in the government by the war, had acquired new ideas about how the country should be run. Organized labor, pampered and protected in exchange for its no-strike pledge, was eager to test its new strength. These were muddy waters, and the Communists were optimistically stirring them up in their many new magazines and newspapers.

The Seattle general strike opened a year of wild melodrama. In April homemade bombs were mailed to leading businessmen and politicians, and in June bombs were set off in eight cities. A rumored national general strike failed to occur on July 4; but hundreds of strikes were in progress, and more were being called every day, climaxed by the steel strike in September 1919. At this time the Boston police also went on strike, and when Governor Coolidge of Massachusetts declared in a telegram that "there is no right to strike against the public safety by anybody, anywhere, any time," he received the national publicity that led to the vice-presidential nomination.

In Centralia, Washington, members of the Industrial Workers of the World fired on American Legionnaires, who had broken ranks during a parade and started for the IWW meeting house. In the national press it was "Radicalism Run Mad," and "An Act of War Against the United States." The American Legion, meeting in Minneapolis in national convention, declared Centralia to be "the shrine of the American Legion, hallowed by our first martyrs."

In December 1919 a shipload of alien radicals, including Emma Goldman and Alexander Berkman, were deported to Russia. On January 2, 1920, Attorney General A. Mitchell Palmer conducted raids in 33 cities across the nation, rounding up 4,000 suspects. There were not warrants for everybody arrested, and many were roughly handled, but the Washington *Post* argued that "there is no time to waste on hairsplitting over infringement of liberty."

Then the nation lost interest in the Great Red Scare. With every conceivable revolutionary leader under lock and key, Palmer's continued warnings ceased to be listened to. Businessmen and politicians continued to keep a sharp eye out for Communist agitators, but the employers' battle for the American Plan of open shop and company unions had already been largely won. The election of Harding in November was by the most enormous landslide in the nation's history, and from the business point of view, the nation appeared to be sounder than at any time since McKinley.

Out of the war against Germany and the defense against communism, the American Legion emerged as a quasi-official guardian of the resulting concept of Americanism. The Legion had been launched in February 1919 by Army General Headquarters in France as a conservative counterorganization to a newly created group, World War Veterans, which GHQ viewed as dangerously radical. Theodore Roosevelt had died a month earlier, and GHQ selected his son, Colonel Theodore Roosevelt, Jr., as the Legion's founder, and adopted TR's phrase, "one hundred percent Americanism," as its motto. During the months that followed, the Legion was more successful than any other veterans' organization in enrolling members; but it failed to attract more than one-fourth of the veterans and by 1923 it was down to one-sixth.

The rowdy conduct of the Legion's national conventions gave it a bad reputation with moral forces from the first, and its concentration upon bonuses and pensions soon brought it under fire from business groups. It therefore did not become an awesome power nationally; but locally, through the individual Legion posts, it was often in a position of authority. On this local, personal level, speaking in the name of the war dead in the "little Arlington" section of the cemetery, the Legion, with its message of Americanism, exerted an influence that had to be respected.

....

From the point of view of rural and small-town Americanism, the loyalty campaigns and the defense against communism, necessary as they were, had diverted the nation from the main defense against the cohorts of the Catholic Church. At the same time, the war had made possible the triumph of national prohibition, first through the wartime law, which went into effect in 1919, and then through the Eighteenth Amendment, which guaranteed the perpetuation of the dry millennium.

The triumph of prohibition, after three quarters of a century of struggle, was naturally a joyous time for all drys, but it was met with various reactions within the dry camp. Many rested confidently in anticipation of the good days ahead. Others, who had been trained to believe in the strength and resourcefulness of the saloon power and of the Catholic Church, observed the beginnings of prohibition with an attitude of anxious watchfulness. As the director of the California Anti-Saloon League pointed out, "In wet territory, the sight of a drunken man in the gutter brings the comment: 'See what the liquor traffic has done!' In prohibition United States a drunken man will bring the comment 'See what prohibition has done!' "

Prohibitionists, who were on the lookout not only for a resurgence of the Catholic saloon power but also for backsliding among their own people, were early justified in their suspicions. Flagrant violations of prohibition were soon in evidence, even in rural communities made up overwhelmingly of Anglo–American Protestants. It was imperative that these mockeries of the moral law, which was now the national law, should not go unpunished, and, providentially, the means to this end was at hand in the resurrected Ku Klux Klan. Beginning on a large scale in 1920 and fanning through the nation during the next few years, the Klansmen rode again, this time to usher in the Kingdom of God on earth.

Organized in Atlanta in 1915, a week before the Atlanta showing of the movie about the original Klan, *Birth of a Nation,* the new Ku Klux Klan was patterned on the post-Civil War Klan, as a dashing and mysterious fraternal order with an anti-Negro purpose. It failed to attract much of a following for that purpose, however; and although it adjusted its mission to include pro-Americanism during the war and anti-Bolshevism during the Red Scare, it still did not do really well. By that time it had added anti-Semitism and anti-Catholicism to its list of purposes, as well as, from the positive point of view, the protection of home, motherhood, strict morality, and exact obedience to the law on the part of other people.

There had been flare-ups of anti-Semitism on several occasions in the South. And in 1921 Henry Ford launched a nationwide campaign against the Jews, based upon the Protocols of the Learned Elders of Zion, forgeries that were being circulated in Europe as evidence of an international conspiracy of Jews. The KKK took up anti-Semitism officially, but only as a side purpose and one which was not clearly understood by most Klansmen. The Catholic conspiracy was what the Klansmen had been brought up on, and the defeat of Romanism and all its works became the Klan's main avowed purpose.

In practice, however, the Klan's strength was greatest in areas where white Protestantism predominated—Indiana and Ohio in the Midwest; Arkansas, Oklahoma, and Texas in the South; and Oregon in the Far West—and the Klansmen do not appear generally to have bothered themselves much with distinctions of race and creed where their victims were concerned. Evidently their most characteristic intention was to enforce morality in the community by vengeful retribution against all violators, although Negroes as a group certainly suffered the worst cruelties.

Deliberating importantly and mysteriously in their Klaverns, the Klansmen chose their intended victims, ostensibly by strict standards of justice, before riding forth at night to execute their hooded vengeance, whether by whip or fist or tar-and-feathering or acid burns or rifle or a flaming cross as a warning. It was often noted by victims afterwards that the nature of their transgressions against the Klan code had been carefully explained to them when the punishment was administered. They had been declared guilty of specific acts of boot-legging or bribe-taking or adultery or wife-beating or drinking or failure to provide for their family or any of a multitude of often minutely trivial infractions of the code of the community.

How this bottom-drawer Anglo-Americanism saw itself was explained by the Imperial Wizard of the Klan, Hiram Wesley Evans.

We are a movement of the plain people, very weak in the matter of culture, intellectual support, and trained leadership. We are demanding, and we expect to win, a return of power into the hands of the everyday, not highly cultured, not overly intellectualized, but entirely unspoiled and not de-Americanized, average citizen of the old stock. Our members and leaders are all of this class—the opposite of the intellectuals and liberals who held the leadership, betrayed Americanism.

The Klan reached the peak of its strength toward the close of 1923, with a membership of perhaps 3 million; although its fortunes varied greatly from state to state and although it remained a powerful force in some states, such as Indiana, throughout the decade. Everywhere involved in politics, it met its defeat in some areas by dividing against itself; in others by an aroused political opposition to it. Inevitably it became used by members for criminal activities, and prominent members were exposed in these as well as in sexual immoralities, which, for a Klan leader, was much worse than mere thievery. The Klan was a major issue at the Democratic national convention of 1924, and then it gradually died its various deaths, amid the raucous moral-holiday activities of the Jazz Age.

The immigration restriction act of 1924 left the already disintegrating Klan without a great cause, because prohibition was by then a hopeless mess and because immigration restriction was the only general answer to the Catholic Menace that the Klan could practically think of. Not even the presidential campaign of 1928, redolent as it was of the old hatreds and suspicions, was sufficient to revive the Klan.

The fundamentalist crusade had been launched against modernism by the Los Angeles Bible Institute with the publication of *The Fundamentals* in 1909. It had run into heavy weather within the evangelical churches themselves even before the war, however, and it was on the decline in the mid-twenties along with the Ku Klux Klan, with which it was being confused somewhat unjustly and very damagingly. From the point of view of many Americans, the Ku Kluxers and the fundamentalists were virtually one and the same thing; and in the Scopes trial in Tennessee in 1926 the religious faith of what H. L. Mencken called "the Bible-Belters" was openly attacked, to the satisfaction of millions of Jazz-Age Americans.

The Scopes trial arose out of "An Act prohibiting the teaching of Evolutionary Theory in all the Universities, Normals, and all other public schools of Tennessee," on pain of a $100 fine for a first offense. The act had been introduced into the state legislature in 1925 by one John Washington Butler, as his own private reform, and had been passed, with little discussion, 71 to 5 in the lower house and 24 to 6 in the Senate. Educational authorities in the state delicately avoided notice of it, while the governor, in signing the law, made clear that "nobody believes it is going to be an active statute." It was not intended as a control on teaching, he said, but rather as a "protest against an irreligious tendency to exalt so-called science."

Butler's bill had been an embarrassment to the governor and the legislature because, although it was not wanted, few politicians, if any, wanted to fight against it openly. The solution—to pass it and then forget it—was the most reasonable one from the Tennessee point of view. But the American Civil Liberties Union in New York did not intend that the State of Tennessee should get away with it that easily. The ACLU had come into being during the war and the Great Red Scare, in defense of traditional and constitutional civil liberties, and it had grown up in the fight against the Espionage and Sedition Acts, the exportation of aliens, the Palmer raids, and other legal infringements on individual freedom.

As soon as the antievolution bill was signed into law, the ACLU advertised in Tennessee newspapers for a plaintiff, and a Dayton high school teacher, John Scopes, was persuaded to cooperate. He was argued into it by a Dayton businessman, who thought the law was a bad one and also that the trial of it in Dayton would be good for business. Another Dayton merchant sought to make business even better by bringing William Jennings Bryan into the case on the side of the state; but before he could reach him, Bryan announced without urging that he would enter the case as representative of the World's Christian Fundamentals Association.

The ACLU favored staging a dignified trial for the principle of the doctrine of the separation of church and state. The kind of interest that was being aroused nationally by the case did not seem appropriate to such a trial, however, and then William Jennings Bryan's appearance in the case decided its course. It would be a battle between old-time religion and old-time agnosticism. Clarence Darrow inevitably offered his services and they were accepted without enthusiasm by the ACLU. Famous as a trial lawyer for underdogs and unpopular causes, Darrow was the exact opposite of Bryan on the question at issue. A Midwestern contemporary of Bryan's, he was as absolutely representative of traditional American village atheism in the public mind as Bryan was of village evangelism.

The protagonists presented the issue as each side saw it. "These Gentlemen," Bryan declared, ". . . did not come here to try this case. They came here to try revealed religion. I am here to defend it. . . . I am simply trying to protect the Word of God against the greatest atheist or agnostic in the United States." And Darrow replied, "We have the purpose of preventing bigots and ignoramuses from controlling the education of the United States and you know it, and that is all."

Darrow had the assistance of Dudley Field Malone, a society divorce lawyer who was Irish and Catholic and eloquent, and Arthur Garfield Hays of the ACLU, who had been the only leading figure in the ACLU to approve wholeheartedly of turning the case over to Darrow. Bryan, who was, of course, assisting the lawyers for the state, was perhaps not in his best form (he died in his sleep a week after the trial was over). The trial lasted ten days and the jury convicted Scopes, who was given the $100 fine, as anticipated. When the ACLU appealed the case, the higher court refunded Scopes the fine and so prevented the ACLU from carrying the case to the U.S. Supreme Court.

The Scopes trial settled no issues, nor did it serve to turn back a resurgent fundamentalist movement. The World's Christian Fundamentals Association had lost its momentum before the Scopes trial was thought of, and the fundamentalist movement continued forlornly, with some neither very welcome nor very effective assistance from former Klan leaders. Tennessee retained its antievolution law as a matter of pride, still without serious thought of enforcing it.

The trial had no measurable influence upon thought in Tennessee or in the United States. But the ridicule of Bryan and of fundamentalism by Darrow and Malone had been broadcast throughout the nation to attentive radio audiences, and Bryan had lost his case so far as the national audience was concerned. It could hardly have been otherwise, for most Americans, including those who taught science courses in Tennessee schools, had long since accepted evolution as scientific fact.

What the Scopes trial did that was new was to ram the truth of evolution down the throats of the fundamentalists in the actual listening presence of the entire nation. "For the state of Tennessee," declared the Little Rock, Arkansas, *Gazette,* "the Scopes trial has been a moral disaster. It will plague the citizen of Tennessee wherever he may go." That was putting it very strongly, but the state's reputation certainly was influenced adversely by the trial. Bryan, the Great Commoner, and more recently the Florida real estate promoter and defender of fundamentalism, was, in ignominious defeat and unheroic death, a pathetic symbol of a weakening and now widely criticized form of Anglo-Saxon-Americanism.

....

Among all of the ethnic minorities in America, the Irish were the principal threat to the Protestant Republic from the dry point of view. From the pre-Civil War days of the Know-Nothing party the Irish had represented the main threat of the Catholic Menace and also of the "saloon power." How they were viewed by the dry forces on the eve of the New Immigration is indicated in a Methodist conference temperance report in 1880.

About the setting sun of the nineteenth century there hovers a group of dark and portentous clouds. In these clouds there may be the brewing of a storm the strength and fury of which no man can either measure or foretell. . . . In this raging battle, that has only begun, the powers of hell are not alone organized, but they are intensely unified, and come to the fray with solid and unwavering phalanx. . . . The king of this black legion of devils is the saloon power. . . . He has taken possession of our municipal governments from New York City down to the country village. . . . Also, this saloon power has turned some of our legislatures into Saturnalian orgies.

Others besides the Irish were involved in the liquor traffic and in city politics, but the Irish predominated. It was also the Irish who had built up the Roman Catholic Church in America, and there was no question in the minds of dry leaders that the saloon power and the Catholic power were one and the same and that the Irish were the special shock troops of the Pope. Obvious anti-Catholic nativism had subsided during the Civil War and Reconstruction, when industry was shorthanded and Catholics were the main source of labor supply, but it remained a living thing in the evangelical churches and in the dry crusade. In 1928 Al Smith felt the force of an old American sentiment that had been nurtured since the landing of the Pilgrims.

More than 4 million persons emigrated from Ireland to the United States during the century after Waterloo. The climax of this immigration was during the generation after the Irish potato famines, which, beginning in 1846, drove the Irish peasants to America, impoverished and illiterate, to take whatever work they could get. They created the new servant class, they entered the sweated labor system in the New England textile industry, they did the heavy work building the canals and railroads, and they remained the backbone of the industrial revolution, until they were increasingly replaced after 1880 by the New Immigration. They crowded into the cities, where they added greatly to the problems of the police, the charitable institutions, and the political organizations. It came to be widely assumed that they were incompatible with law and order and decent society. The NO IRISH NEED APPLY provision in advertisements for certain types of employment became proverbial for the subordinate status of Irish-Americans.

As a society the Irish brought to America a spirit of conviviality which was associated with heavy drinking, a village tradition which encouraged active political life for the sake of politics, itself, a heritage of religious and economic oppression, and a general village suspicion of higher education, except for the priesthood. Within a generation of the outset of the famine, they had taken over political control of New York, Boston, San Francisco, and other large cities, and had entered the middle classes in large numbers. As Daniel Patrick Moynihan wrote of New York in the Gilded Age,

The Tweed ring was heavily Irish, but so was the group that brought on its downfall. The pattern persisted. The Irish came to run the police force *and* the underworld; they were the reformers and the hoodlums; employers and employed. The city entered the era of Boss Croker of Tammany Hall and Judge Goff of the Lexow Committee which investigated him; of business leader Thomas Fortune Ryan and labor leader Peter J. McGuire; of reform Mayor John Purroy Mitchell and Tammany Mayor J. F. "Red Mike" Hylan. It was a stimulating miscellany.

Politics was a way of life for Irish-Americans, but the Catholic Church was their mission in life as a people. The Irish, by coming to America, were delivered from a religious repression far more thoroughgoing than the Massachusetts Puritans had known in England; and America was for them a religious promised land as it had once been for the Puritans. The Irish captured the leadership of an American Catholic Church which had been Spanish and French in orientation and which was being augmented by the German, as well as the Irish, immigration.

In order to capture control of the Church and develop it as their faith dictated and retain control through the period of the New Immigration, the Irish-Americans were forced to make heavy sacrifices in terms of worldly objectives they might otherwise have pursued. They taxed themselves heavily to support a system of parochial schools which systematically disoriented Catholics from the dominant pattern of American life. They offered many of their most capable sons to a priesthood which was as parochial and puritanical as any major American sect, despite Catholic sanction for liquor, and which viewed with great suspicion the changes arising out of the industrial revolution.

Ambitious Irish-Americans were characteristically attracted to politics or to a religious calling more than they were to business or to the professions, except for the law. They were also attracted to the worlds of sports and entertainment—the worlds of John L. Sullivan and James Corbett, and of Victor Herbert and George M. Cohan. Through sports and show business, and even more through the saloon business, they did much to make a quality that was thought of as Irish into an integral part of the American character—one which the Anti-Saloon League intended to remove from the American character if it could possibly do so.

Peter Finley Dunne was uniquely influential in bringing the Irish quality of humor to American political life during the self-righteous times of the Spanish-American War and the Progressive movement, in his Irish-dialect newspaper column concerning the opinions of the bartender Mr. Dooley. He appears in retrospect to have been remarkably right in his judgments, and it was generally conceded at the time that he was right. He remained on excellent terms with his favorite target, Theodore Roosevelt; in a letter to Roosevelt he argued that "the ideal of the young Irishman of this country is the straight American character," and that this was truer of the Irishman than it was of immigrants from other countries. Dunne's Mr. Dooley was a nationally effective argument for this point of view.

Dunne was also effective in his attacks upon what he considered to be the snobbish and also slavish Anglophilism of upper-class Easterners. He was especially unkind in this regard to Joseph Choate, the American ambassador to England, who, when the king sent for him, according to Mr. Dooley, "came as fast as his hands an' knees wud carry him." When the war broke out in Europe, however, Dunne took a worse view of the Germans than he did of the English, and he campaigned editorially for preparedness, with the German threat in mind. He supported the war but not the war mood, which his fellow Irish-American and very "straight American" author of *Yankee-Doodle Dandy,* George M. Cohan, captured in his war song "Over There." During the twenties Mr. Dooley reappeared in a speakeasy, agreeing with Mr. Hennessy that there was less drunkenness under prohibition but adding that "what there is is a much more finished product."

During the twenties the American Irishman personified personal liberty in the struggle against prohibition, while the fighting Irish spirit was strong in the sports world. That was not the limit of Irish-American ambition, however, as the writings of F. Scott Fitzgerald, Eugene O'Neill, Philip Barry, George Kelly, and James T. Farrell demonstrated. Still, the fear of literature was stronger among Irish-Americans than among Anglo-Americans, and anti-intellectualism in the Catholic Church was the subject of bitter criticism by American Catholic intellectuals during the twenties.

Irish dominance of Eastern city politics was beginning to be challenged by the New Immigration in the decade after World War I, when Alfred E. Smith served an unprecedented four terms as governor of New York. Smith was the last Irish-American to rise from New York City politics to governor or senator. His political power in

New York was as great as it was because, in addition to commanding the allegiance of Tammany Hall and the Irish, he attracted wide support among non-Irish on the basis of his outstanding program of practical reform and his great administrative ability.

Then, in the 1924 National Democratic Convention the nomination was denied Smith, after 103 ballots, by the rural Protestant wing of the party, and Smith became the national leader of recent-immigrant America. In 1928 the nomination went to him on the first ballot, to avoid a repetition of the previous party-destroying conflict, and the ethnic bigotry that had dominated the 1924 convention floor was extended to the national presidential campaign.

On political issues other than prohibition, there was substantially nothing to divide Hoover and Smith, as Smith emphasized by choosing the financier and Du Pont executive John J. Raskob to be chairman of the National Democratic Committee. Even prohibition did not provide an entirely clear-cut issue, since Hoover would say no more for it than that it was an experiment noble in motive. Over Hoover's strenuous protestations the campaign was directed against Smith's Irish Catholicism, together with his wetness, his New York accent, his derby hat, and his city mannerisms. For many who remained unenthusiastic about Hoover, this was the point. "As great as have been my doubts about Hoover," wrote George Fort Milton, "he is sprung from American soil and stock. . . ." Smith was a third-generation American, but that impressed the Protestant Republic not at all.

There was a flurry of excited activity in old Ku Klux Klan circles and a massive anti-Catholic campaign by the Anti-Saloon League was launched, which "literally exhausted its resources in men and money to beat Smith," according to a League newspaper. In the South the Methodist bishop James Cannon led the fight for both Methodists and Baptists against Smith, ostensibly on the basis of his wetness, according to Cannon, "altogether apart from his religion, although I knew that he was the intolerant, bigoted type characteristic of the Irish Roman Catholic hierarchy of New York City."

The attempt to separate Smith's Catholicism from his wetness and to concentrate on the latter was unsuccessful. The Anti-Saloon League *American Issue* put the issue in its most fundamental terms when it declared that Smith "appeals to the sporty, jazzy, and liberal element of our population. He is not in harmony with the principles of our forefathers. If you believe in Anglo-Saxon Protestant domination; if you believe in the maintenance of that civilization founded by our Puritan ancestors, and preserved by our fathers . . . you will vote for Hoover rather than Smith." Hoover won by a landslide, and the Solid South was broken for the first time since the end of Reconstruction—the upper South, Texas, and Florida going to Hoover.

In 1932 the Democratic party professionals, looking for a candidate who would not be "an offense to the villagers," chose the patrician Episcopalian over the Tammany Catholic. But the triumph of Irish-Americanism over fundamental Americanism was by then an accomplished fact. It was validated by repeal of the Eighteenth Amendment in 1933 and annually celebrated on St. Patrick's Day thereafter. Among the non-Anglo-Saxon Americans the Irish-Americans, in particular, had carried out the missionary work to convert the Protestant Republic into the Judeo-Christian Democracy.

....

After the war German culture was welcomed back to the United States in the universities and the concert halls, and if German-Americanism did not immediately reassert itself in an organized way, it reasserted itself brassily and to great effect through the individual efforts of H. L. Mencken. It is hardly an exaggeration to say that when Woodrow Wilson's cause was lost, during and after the Versailles Conference, it was H. L. Mencken, of all people, who at once took Wilson's place among American intellectuals as the foremost authority on the American national spirit.

Evidently much to his own surprise, Mencken was swept up in the postwar reaction against Wilsonian idealism and then carried along in the reaction against the Anglo-Saxon moralism of prohibition. Mencken was one of those hyphenated Americans from the Old Immigration who had been spiritually dispossessed of their citizenship during the war. Specifically he was a Saxon-American, his grandfather having migrated to Baltimore from Saxony. In the postwar period Mencken became a Germanic Crèvecoeur of the machine age, reasserting Crèvecoeur's mixed brand of Americanism against the Anglo-Americanism of genteel Boston on the one hand and fundamentalist Dayton, Tennessee, on the other.

Brought up in German-American Baltimore, Mencken gained his main education working for the Baltimore *Sun*. He read rapidly, and nearly everything that came into his hands, but his preferences tended to be Teutonic, Nietzsche and Ibsen, and among American writers, Huneker, Dreiser, Untermeyer, Hecht, and Hergesheimer, in addition, to be sure, to Mark Twain and many other Anglo-Americans. In 1911 he was given his own signed column in the *Sun,* and there, setting out "to combat, chiefly by ridicule, American piety, stupidity, tin-pot morality, cheap chauvinism in all their forms," he developed against the "baltimoralists," the style of invective which was to make him practically the official voice of anti-Anglo-Americanism in the twenties.

His assumption with George Jean Nathan of responsibility for *Smart Set* in November 1914 was badly timed. He was belligerently pro-German, and on the *Sun* his comments concerning the "slobbering ethic" of President Wilson and the "pious beery slobbering over Belgium" by the American people lost him his column in 1915. After that he gave up praising Germany and the Kaiser in print, but he continued to express his pro-German sentiments to friends and acquaintances.

In the fall of 1917 a patriotic literary attack was launched against him. The reviewer of Mencken's *A Book of Prefaces* in the *Nation* found that

Mr. Mencken is not at all satisfied with life or literature in America. . . . Probably the root of our difficulty is that, with the exception of Mr. Huneker, Otto Heller, Ludwig Lewisohn, Mr. Untermeyer, G. S. Viereck, the author of 'Der Kampf um deutsche Kultur in Amerika,' and a few other choice souls, we have no critics who, understanding what beauty is, serenely and purely love it.

Mencken continued to find literary work during the war, but the going kept getting harder. "If necessary," he wrote his publisher, "I'll do a piece proving that William G. McAdoo is the Son of God." He went for walks in the country with his friend Theodor Hemberger, and they sang "Ich Hatt' einen Kameraden" together and waited for better times.

Better times came in a rush, with the publication of his *American Language* in 1919. Americanisms had been a matter for comment, usually unfavorable, since colonial times, and Mencken, who relished words, had for years been sorting out distinctively American words and tracking down their origins. An early column in the *Sun,* "The Two Englishes," had brought an enthusiastic response, and similar, somewhat scholarly columns became a stock-in-trade for him. In 1918, with little call for his services from editors, Mencken worked up these old columns into a book, together with whatever additional information he could find on the subject in the library.

Mencken was probably not much more hopefully ambitious for the success of the work than he pretended to be. It was, he explained, " a heavy indigestible piece of cottage cheese. . . . I thus purge my blood of inherited pedantry." To Dreiser he wrote, "My ambition is crowned: I have written a book longer than *The 'Genius.'* It will be at least five inches thick." The thicker the better. His publisher, Alfred Knopf, published subsequent printings on extra-thick paper to give it all the impressive weightiness possible.

The book was an immediate startling success. Bookstores ran out of copies—only 1,500 had been printed—and the price, for a time, more than doubled. The complaint that it was an attempt to "split asunder the two great English-speaking peoples" went all but unheard in the chorus of enthusiastic reviews and comments. "Never," *The New York Times* commented, "has the flourishing personality of H. L. Mencken been so happily exercised as in this big book on the living speech of America." Within a matter of weeks Mencken had accomplished an absolute metamorphosis from "a member of the Germania Männerchor," as the hostile *Nation* reviewer had called him, to the patriotic founder and Johnsonian judge of literary Americanism.

In the days after the Treaty of Versailles, Germanophobia swiftly evaporated. Inevitably the old Anglophobias were out again, and the hounds were running with Mencken. Mencken was invulnerable in the twenties, for the more he was denounced the more fun it was. The president of the Arkansas Advancement Association, believing Mencken to be an alien, wrote the federal government suggesting that he had "made himself sufficiently obnoxious to a majority of the American people to warrant deportation." But Mencken was 100 percent American; he simply was not English-American.

Mencken was essentially middle-class German-American in outlook, and he disapproved of much that was going on in the revolt against the old Anglo-America. He was against jazz, Freudianism, the morals of youth, and all reformers—from Progressives to Communists—but intellectuals read him for his attacks on Anglo-Puritanism and Anglo-genteelness, not caring at the time how seriously he meant it when he attacked what they might be for. He had become, according to the *Times*, "the most powerful private citizen in America," and according to Walter Lippmann, "the most powerful personal influence on this whole generation of educated people."

In 1926 Mencken spent ten days in Dayton, Tennessee, composing the classic contemporary account of the Scopes trial; then he entered Boston and challenged genteel Anglo-America in its stronghold. In Boston the Watch and Ward Society was exercising a degree of censorship over literature which made the phrase "banned in Boston" almost as familiar to readers of *College Humor* as "Yes, we have no bananas." In 1924 Mencken and George Jean Nathan had founded the *American Mercury,* and in 1926 the April issue was banned in Boston. Risking a two-year prison sentence, Mencken stood on Brimstone Corner in Boston and sold a copy of his magazine and was arrested. The judge, after reading the issue, found in Mencken's favor, but the secretary of Watch and Ward succeeded in having the issue banned nationally from the mails by the Post Office.

There was a Post Office hearing and additional hearings, and Mencken was granted an injunction against the postmaster of New York. Finally there was an appeal by the government. The authority of the Post Office was upheld and there the battle ended. It had been a defeat for Mencken, and one which was especially galling to him because of the abuse he had received in the press, which, he thought, might have been expected to have seen freedom of the press as the issue. Reform in censorship practices awaited the next decades, but Mencken had backed up his brag and was a hero to liberals and intellectuals.

That attack on Boston was the climax of Mencken's career against the English-Americans as the Sacco-Vanzetti case reached its climax the next year. Mencken's style was farce, after the fashion of his covering of the Scopes trial, and not tragedy, such as was now being acted out in the Sacco-Vanzetti trial in Boston. Mencken was not at his best when confronted with such deadly serious business. He was even worse two years after that when confronted by the stock market crash, and he was awkwardly out of place throughout the depression. Mencken's derisive *Notes on American Democracy,* which appeared in 1926, had been badly received. The nation was used to him, and the culture he was attacking was changing without his appearing to notice it.

The Klansmen rarely rode any more, the flapper was about to go out of style, and the methods of violating prohibition were becoming regularized and taken for granted. The defense of Dreiser against the censors had been one of Mencken's great crusades, but now Dreiser's *American Tragedy* was a best seller, and Hollywood had bought it. In 1927 Sinclair Lewis's *Elmer Gantry,* lampooning fundamentalism, was the top seller on the fiction list, a year after Lewis had been awarded the Pulitzer prize and had turned it down.

The Literary Guild was founded in 1927. Its first selection was the debunking biography *Anthony Comstock* by Heywood Broun and Margaret Leech. Mencken's *American Mercury* reached its peak circulation in that year and then went down with the stock market. The depression destroyed Mencken's vogue, because it was no joke. But Mencken's jokes were already wearing thin, partly because people had heard them before and partly because so many people had become so willing to laugh at them, including the very butts of Mencken's ridicule, that the ridicule had lost a good deal of its point.

The American "booboisie" put up with being ridiculed and criticized in the 1920's as never before in American history and never since, and so did the "Bible-Belters" once the Klan had quieted down. Mencken was surprised and disconcertedly well impressed by the friendly reception he received from the townspeople of Dayton, Tennessee, while he was covering the Scopes trial for the *Sun.* Also Dayton was altogether a more attractive town than he had imagined it would be. When he went to Boston to be arrested, he was warmly welcomed in the city and at a Harvard luncheon, and the judge and the courtroom crowd all turned out to be on his side.

This widespread willingness to take criticism is not one of the most striking characteristics of a decade overrun by Klu Kluxers and prohibition agents and Legionnaires; indeed it was barely noticed, if at all, by the outrageous social critics who benefited so greatly from it. It was present, however, and it was an essential and distinguishing quality of the twenties. During his long career as a journalist, from the 1890's to the 1940's, Mencken was a significant figure intellectually precisely from 1919 to 1929. Over the course of more than half a century Mencken's journalistic style flowed along without perceptible change. But as a major figure in American cultural life, he started and stopped with the one decade in American history which suffered criticism gladly—whether from wisemen or fools.

One reason why so many Americans of the Dollar Decade were willing to take instruction and to see the joke when it was on them was the general underlying confidence in the American Way as the solution to man's age-old struggle against poverty. Nobody thought to attack the idea that American business enterprise was a big success from a materialistic point of view; and that was the important point so far as the business community was concerned.

Another reason was the general sense of newness; the sense of abrupt and breath-taking arrival upon a new and unexplored plateau of civilization—in the age of cars, movies, phonographs, radios, electric appliances, apartments, flappers, bootleggers, speakeasies, gangsters, tabloids, Klansmen, canned goods, packaged breakfast foods, sex magazines, national parks, religious cults, Greenwich Village, professional sports, the debunking of Boston, the New Poetry, the New Criticism, the American theater, higher wages, new corporate welfare programs and, toward the end, the stock market going up and up and up.

The twenties was a *nouveau riche* decade, as all American postwar periods have been, and people were of the opinion that there was a lot they had to learn about how to behave. *Etiquette* by Emily Post was the best-selling nonfiction work in 1923, but it was not supposed that Emily Post had anything like the final answers to the new social questions. There was a vast willingness to be corrected, because there was a vast confidence in the soundness of American progress. America in the twenties was one big eclectic reader for a wide American audience, and Mencken was the liveliest lecturer on the subjects.

. . . .

The twenties is the decade of the Lost Generation; yet it is also the decade when the American reading and theater-going public at last achieved that cultural self-reliance which American writers had appealed for in vain since the early national period. American literary criticism came of age in the twenties, and American arts and letters not only flourished in unprecedentedly rich diversity but were also intelligently appreciated by American readers and audiences. Never before had American genius been so readily recognized and rewarded, without first requiring the approval of English critical opinion.

Yet never before had American writers and artists complained so loudly of neglect and spoken so bitterly of their alienation from American society. A case in point is Sinclair Lewis. *Main Street* appeared in 1920 and, along with *The Sheik,* it became the best seller on the year's list of fiction. The reading public waited impatiently for *Babbitt,* which appeared two years later, amid extravagant praise. These were followed by *Arrowsmith* in 1925, *Elmer Gantry* in 1927, and *Dodsworth* in 1929, all popular successes, and in 1930 Lewis became the first American author to be awarded the Nobel Prize for literature. Lewis made "The American Fear of Literature" the subject of his acceptance speech in Stockholm. The burden of his complaint was that America did not support its best writers, and that he and other writers of high merit were unfairly treated by critics and had not been asked to be members of the American Academy of Arts and Letters. This was the testament of the Lost Generation to a decade that had been notably hospitable to its creative artists.

The postwar decade had, for many, been written off as lost as soon as it was well started. For writers who, like Lewis, had begun their careers before the war, the postwar disillusionment tended to create a fixed frame of mind that gave the whole era an ugly shape. The prewar Greenwich Villagers had really believed in their utopian dreams, and their brave new world had ended in war, loyalty hysteria, the Legion, prohibition, the KKK, fundamentalism, and normalcy. In 1921 Harold E. Stearns edited *Civilization in the United States,* written by thirty leading intellectuals; it was a bitter blanket indictment of the subject. The contributors, Stearns wrote, were agreed on three main conclusions concerning American civilization: that there was "a sharp dichotomy between preaching and practicing" in almost every branch of life; that there was "emotional and aesthetic starvation" which manifested itself in "the mania for petty regulation . . . the secret society and its grotesque regalia"; and "that whatever else American civilization is, it is not Anglo-Saxon."

To the mind of the Lost Generation the decade of the twenties was an Anglo-Saxon monstrosity in an age when America had ceased to be a predominantly Anglo-Saxon nation. This was the indictment against the decade that identified the dilemma of the Lost Generation; for whatever else the thirty contributors were, most of them *were* Anglo-Saxon within their meaning of the term, and in addition to that, a third of them were Harvard men. They considered themselves to represent the mind and conscience of America, but they were nonplussed by the dilemma of how to liberate America from Anglo-Saxon provincialism without abdicating their cultural function to non-Anglo-Saxons.

This dilemma is illustrated by the kind of importance the literary critic Bernard Smith attributed to Van Wyck Brooks' *America's Coming of Age*. Smith noted that others, including "Boyesen, Peck, Pollard, Spingarn, Huneker and, above all, the *Masses* group led by Floyd Dell," had issued similar calls for freedom from cultural provincialism. "But Brooks was not a 'foreigner,' not a Catholic, not a Jew, not a Westerner, not a radical, not even simply a New Yorker corrupted by those alien influences. He was a Yankee of Protestant descent who had been graduated from Harvard. That was the important thing."

One escape from this dilemma of the anti-Anglo-Saxon Anglo-Saxon, and the one which Stearns and a good many others took, was to go to Europe. There, as Malcolm Cowley explained in *Exile's Return*, they hoped "to recover the good life and the traditions of art, to free themselves from organized stupidity, to win their deserved place in the hierarchy of the intellect." Once abroad, these expatriates, many of whom did not have a serviceable second language, formed a foreign colony, a Left Bank Greenwich Village. They also traveled about, however, and they gained European-oriented perspectives on America. Then they returned, and in some cases, as with Cowley, they carried back to the United States "a set of values that bore no relation to American life, with convictions that could not fail to be misunderstood."

While one did not need to be a Harvard man to enlist in the Lost Generation—or for that matter to meet any other educational requirements—nevertheless, Harvard men played a leading part in the development of the mystique of alienation, and Harvard, itself, became a significant symbol for the alienated. "In my time at Harvard," wrote Cowley, "the virtues instilled into students were good taste, good manners, cleanliness, chastity, gentlemanliness (or niceness), reticence and the spirit of competition in sports; they were virtues often prized by a leisure class." While Dayton, Tennessee, symbolized Anglo-Saxon anti-intellectualism, Harvard came to symbolize genteel bigotry for the Lost Generation. It was in this context that the Sacco-Vanzetti case came to assume its transcendent importance for American intellectuals in the late twenties.

Two of Boston's immigrants, Nicola Sacco and Bartolomeo Vanzetti, had been arrested in 1920 and convicted of a robbery-murder. The case was appealed, and it dragged on for years, until, in 1926, the Harvard Law School professor, Felix Frankfurter, brought it to the attention of American intellectuals in an article in *Atlantic Monthly*. This article, together with an editorial in the Boston *Herald,* was the basis for the forming of the Sacco-Vanzetti Defense Committee, which directed the campaign to save the two men.

The American Civil Liberties Union, directed by Harvard-educated Roger Baldwin, had long supported Sacco and Vanzetti quietly, and it now made an open fight for them. The case was finally referred by the governor to a special committee which included President A. Lawrence Lowell of Harvard, and Lowell voted for execution. When that happened, Harvard men like Walter Lippmann, Heywood Broun, Granville Hicks, John Dos Passos, and Malcolm Cowley came to see themselves as having a special responsibility toward the condemned men.

Whether or not Sacco and Vanzetti were guilty and whether or not they had received a fair trial, given the rough tactics of their defense attorney, the Lost Generation convinced itself of their innocence and of the corresponding guilt of Massachusetts, of Boston, and of Harvard. When the executions took place, amid worldwide demonstrations of protest, many American intellectuals tended to arrive emotionally at the conclusion expressed by a character in John Dos Passos' *U.S.A.*: "If the State of Massachusetts can kill these two innocent men in the face of the protests of the whole world, it'll mean that there never will be any justice in America again."

Sacco and Vanzetti were anarchists; but the intellectuals of the day were characteristically apolitical, and their indignation was not primarily based upon left-wing political sentiments, although it helped to

create a good many. To the intellectuals, Sacco and Vanzetti symbolized the great voiceless non-Anglo-Saxon majority in a nation ruined
by Anglo-Saxon rule. As to the legal merits of the case, David Felix
has demonstrated that the intellectuals who organized on behalf of
the two men were not adequately informed about the original trial or
about the subsequent legal developments down to 1926. They were
also inadequately informed, to say the least, about that non-Anglo-
Saxon majority that Sacco and Vanzetti symbolized and about the
ethnological changes that were in the process of reconstituting America's national character.

Oliver Wendell Holmes, Jr., commented, regarding the Sacco-Vanzetti case, on the habitual partiality of intellectuals for "Red over
Black" in defending victims of social injustice. Negroes were subject
to the worst injustices in America, and they were the largest non-
Anglo-Saxon group in the nation, but the intellectuals did not take
their plight as seriously as they took the plight of the white non-Anglo-
Saxons. The National Association for the Advancement of Colored
People, led by the Harvard-trained W. E. B. Du Bois, continued to
enlist white support; but no celebrated causes comparable to the
Sacco-Vanzetti case emerged from its activities in the twenties. This
inability to take Negroes as seriously as whites prevented American
intellec als from coping adequately with the problem of determining
what American civilization was, if it was not Anglo-Saxon, particularly in the Jazz Age.

What Edmund Wilson called "the higher jazz" of Paul Whiteman,
George Gershwin, Aaron Copland, and others was taken seriously by
intellectuals, together with Negro jazz, and so were Negro performers
on the legitimate stage, like Roland Hayes and Paul Robeson. Bohemian intellectuals appreciated the jazz culture of the Cotton Club
and the Broadway musical revues, as well as the literary Black
Renaissance in Harlem. They were keenly aware that Negro culture
was a lively force in American society, and expatriates returned to
America with an awareness of the impact of American Negro culture
on the European avant-garde. Nevertheless they did not think to
accept the Negro on the simply human terms which rendered Sacco
and Vanzetti appealing to them. They were no more race-conscious
than their ancestors had been, but their indictment against Anglo-
Saxon civilization in America did not logically permit them to retain

these old race prejudices at all. For most intellectuals, as for most white Americans, the Negro remained stereotyped and separate from white humanity, however warmly his talents were appreciated.

Other non-Anglo-Saxon Americans were somewhat similarly stereotyped and set apart in the minds of intellectuals as well as nonintellectuals. Until Sacco and Vanzetti were brought to the nation's attention, Italian-America had been most prominently represented by Big Jim Colosimo, John Torrio, and Al Capone. The American melting pot idea had been exemplified by Capone's rivals, the North Side gang, a low-class cosmopolitan group directed by Dion O'Banion and his lieutenants Hymie Weiss, Schemer Drucci, and Bugs Moran.

Being less socially conscious than the prewar intellectuals, the Lost Generation was less inclined to get out and get to know Greek-Americans and Polish-Americans and Hungarian-Americans personally. The one common bond that gave the Lost Generation a positive sense of identification with the non-Anglo-Saxon majority was prohibition. Prohibition remained the leading subject of controversy in America throughout the decade, and it was the only important issue which legitimately enabled the Lost Generation to think of itself as part of the brotherhood of the great unrespectable American majority. It was a low common denominator, however, and the Sacco-Vanzetti case was welcomed as representing a higher one.

When Alfred E. Smith ran for President against Herbert Hoover, he became the first candidate to represent the non-Anglo-Saxon majority, but it turned out that the Lost Generation did not much want him in spite of this. On the one hand, he was hardly less a supporter of the business civilization than Hoover; on the other, Walter Lippmann argued, "there is an opposition to Smith which is as authentic, and, it seems to me, as poignant as his support. It is inspired by the feeling that the clamorous life of the city should not be acknowledged as the American ideal."

Then came the depression, and in 1932 a manifesto of intellectuals was issued, declaring that, "if I vote at all, it will be for the Communists," and signed by John Dos Passos, Edmund Wilson, Malcolm Cowley, Lincoln Steffens, Theodore Dreiser, Sherwood Anderson, and Sidney Hook, among others. That was the final pronouncement of the Lost Generation before the opening of the political age of the

New Deal. The Lost Generation had not all gone Communist; it had simply not yet awakened to the idea, which would absorb its attention in the thirties, that the self-realization of the new national majority ought, for practical purposes, to be a political rather than a literary matter.

....

Herbert Hoover was a shining hero of Anglo-Saxon American business civilization, and it made a lasting difference that it was Hoover who presided over the coming of the Great Depression, rather than Al Smith. Hoover went on preaching the American System, while the system itself was creating shantytowns called Hoovervilles. Hoover consequently served to personify the great failure of the idea of business stewardship in America in a clear and memorable way.

In the face of rising unemployment, which eventually included from a quarter to a third of the national work force, Hoover refused to use federal funds to prevent mass misery until his final year in office. Then, while vetoing a more generous congressional relief program in July 1932, he signed a bill extending federal loans of $300 million to the states on the condition that the money should eventually be returned to the federal government.

In these matters Hoover continued to be controlled by his traditionally American assumptions: that federal handouts "would have injured the spiritual responses of the American people," presumably to a greater extent than those of private charities; that the end result of increased federal authority would be the creation of an authoritarian state; and that, under any circumstances, economy remained the chief concern of the government. "The urgent question today," he told Congress in 1932, "is the prompt balancing of the budget. When that is accomplished I propose to support adequate measures for relief of distress and unemployment."

In October 1930 Hoover declared, "As a nation we must prevent hunger and cold to those of our people who are in honest difficulties," and he created the Cabinet Committee on Unemployment and the President's Emergency Committee for Employment. He requested that the governors form "non-partisan committees of responsible men and women, in each state, these committees in turn to organize such committees in each municipality and county," and he announced that 3,000 such committees had been called into being "to see that no one went hungry or cold."

The burden of relief rested on private organizations: the Salvation Army, which started bread lines; the YMCA and YWCA; the Jewish Social Service Association; the Catholic Charities; settlement houses and local clubs—all of which initiated their own programs. The Community Chest had been created in 1918, and it extended its activities to relief work, although its main commitments were elsewhere. In New York City an Emergency Work Bureau was created under the direction of the chairman of the board of the Bankers Trust Company to raise funds. Similar emergency organizations were instituted by leading private citizens in communities across the nation to raise funds through organized pressure.

Most basically the burden rested with the family and friends of the unemployed to save them from having to apply for charity of any kind in the first place. This weighed especially heavily with those of old American stock who had identified themselves with the American System during good times. The process by which they were brought to apply for charity was summarized for a congressional investigating committee by a social worker.

. . . when hard times are prolonged, the great middle class is hit, the white-collar workers, the skilled laborers, the clerks, the doctors, and the lawyers. They become dependent; and you add to your chronic dependents and your marginal dependents those who never before in their lives have sought charity or assistance in any form.

The thing that happens here is that when the breadwinner is out of a job he usually exhausts his savings if he has any. Then, if he has an insurance policy, he probably borrows to the limit of its cash value. He borrows from his friends and from his relatives until they can stand the burden no longer. He gets credit from the corner grocery store and the butcher shop, and the landlord foregoes collecting the rent until interest and taxes have to be paid and something has to be done. All of those resources are finally exhausted over a period of time, and it becomes necessary for those people, who have never before been in want, to ask for assistance.

In October 1931 Hoover opened a drive for funds for private relief agencies and asserted once again that "this task is not beyond the ability of these thousands of community organizations to solve." He received widespread support for this contention from the leading citizens who chaired emergency relief committees, but the testimony of social workers and directors of relief agencies was to the contrary and more and more bitterly so. By 1932 the cities of the nation were themselves facing bankruptcy. Essential services were curtailed. In Chicago schoolteachers had gone unpaid for eight months. The policy that municipalities followed was summarized by a spokesman for St. Paul who said, "We are merely trying to prevent hunger and exposure," and by one from Scranton who declared, "We are holding taxes down and spreading relief thin."

New York under Roosevelt was one of the first states to allocate large funds for relief, the Temporary Emergency Relief Administration being created in September 1931, with a $20 million appropriation. Other states began to do likewise, but they were in some cases sharply limited by the terms of their state constitutions.

There was the question of what to do with men and women and children sleeping in parks and building shacks on city property. One such shantytown, "Hoover Valley," in Central Park, was condemned because of the lack of water and sanitary facilities, but others under other circumstances were permitted. The Chicago public welfare department reported that "no fewer than 200 women are sleeping in Grant and Lincoln Parks, on the lake front, to say nothing of those in other parks." Tramps of all ages, not being eligible for assistance from local relief agencies, wandered through the country, begging and stealing. Hunger riots broke out in Midwestern cities. The Farmers' Holiday Association organized throughout the farm states and withheld food from market in defiance of sheriff's deputies, in efforts to raise farm prices.

Faith in the American System appears to have survived best in the smaller cities of the East and Midwest. An investigator in one such city in 1932 found conditions to be bad but local opinion to be that "we'd be pretty well off if the banks hadn't failed." Robert and Helen Lynd returned to Muncie, Indiana, in 1935 to follow up their study of *Middletown* with *Middletown in Transition* (1937) and found that conditions had improved during the year and that middle-class opinion combined confidence in the future with hatred for the New Deal. There was economic suffering among the working classes in Muncie, but no development of militant labor solidarity. It was observed that throughout the nation people were enjoying the Schadenfreude of knowing that "someone is worse off than we are."

In June 1932 the Republicans met in convention and without opposition or enthusiasm renominated Hoover as their candidate. In July the resolutely unpolitical Hoover called out the National Guard against the pathetic "bonus marchers," World War I veterans who marched on Washington to demonstrate for immediate bonus benefits. In November Hoover was voted out of office by a landslide, and the Republican party became the party of the opposition.

The Republican party remained intransigeantly committed to Hoover's American System throughout most of the depression, and it also remained associated with the Anglo-Saxon bias that had been dramatized by the campaign of 1928. The Democratic party was able to disassociate itself from the American System, which it had fully supported in the twenties, and at the same time it benefited greatly from the continued contempt that Republicans displayed for the ethnic realities of American politics in the thirties.

Upper-class Republicans looked upon Roosevelt as "a traitor to his class," and some of the wealthiest among them helped to organize the American Liberty League to carry on a heavily financed and very clumsy campaign against him, effectively dramatizing their transformation into an obstructionist minority group. Roosevelt called them "economic royalists," and the label stuck. Middle-class Republicans outside the large cities were similarly obdurate in their opposition to all New Deal reform. For many old-stock Americans in the working classes, however, the New Deal appeared as a wonderful new dispensation. Economic pressures allied them with the recent-immigrant workers, especially after the rise of the CIO, against the privileged classes. They became fiercely loyal to the new cosmopolitan nationalism, against the predominantly Anglo-Saxon old regime.

In 1938 Richard Whitney, the very upper-crust president of the New York Stock Exchange, was arrested for grand larceny and sent to jail. Whitney's thefts were at first disbelieved by people of his class and then defended, as far as that seemed possible. It was widely argued that his sins had not really been great and that his greatest sin had been to get caught. Whitney was bad publicity for the old regime, and so was the defensive editorializing about him in much of the national press. Much as the Populists and the Progressives had, each in their own time, considered themselves to embody the conscience of the nation, so the New Dealers considered themselves to represent the conscience of the nation. The American Liberty League and Richard Whitney were a help to them in this.

Much old-time Progressive support, Republican as well as Democratic, flowed to the New Deal, which was permeated with the ideals of social justice of the earlier reform period. However, the moral certitudes of Progressives were largely discarded by New Dealers, many of whom shared the anticlerical outlook that had been fostered in the twenties by the fights against fundamentalism and prohibition. Roosevelt in his speeches retained much of the moralistic and even biblical tone of the earlier age; but at the same time he cheerfully and openly accepted such unrespectable support as the Kelly-Nash machine in Chicago and the Hague machine in Jersey City, where this support advanced the interests of his party and his program.

Roosevelt was himself an old-time Progressive from an old American family, and while he personified the new national spirit and was utterly at ease with it in public, the times were always somewhat in advance of him. He was every inch the patrician reformer, often appearing to bestow upon the people as largess, reform programs that had been dumped in his lap by more radical congressmen and bureaucrats or by more militant public sentiment.

Roosevelt's patrician status was, however, a huge national asset in the depression crisis. His social superiority was a part of the role he assumed as the founder of the new Americanism. He invested the ethnically mixed new nationalism with the prestige he derived from his social position in the old order, as when he addressed the Daughters of the American Revolution as "Fellow Immigrants." Roosevelt was practicing Tory democracy, but he was leading the nation toward a new ideal of social democracy; besides, most of the Tories were on the other side.

8.

A New Nationalism

THE NEW DEAL WAS A SOCIAL revolution, completing the overthrow of the Protestant Republic and establishing a new order based upon a modern American, ethnocratic doctrine of cosmopolitan liberalism. This cosmopolitan liberalism could legitmately claim to be in the enlightened tradition of Thomas Jefferson and the founding fathers; it could not, however, legitimately claim to be in the evangelical tradition of American democracy from Andrew Jackson to Woodrow Wilson. And although the founding fathers had professed belief in the cosmopolitan outlook of the enlightenment, there had been only one Catholic signer of the Declaration and no Jew. Theirs had been an academic cosmopolitan liberalism; the New Deal's was a practicing one.

The various ethnic groups all had their own ethnocentricities, they all had their own leaders, and they were all accustomed to being appealed to by the politicians, on an ethnic basis. But they all were also conscious of being American; more so than ever since immigration restriction had fixed the national constituency by law. New Deal politicians could not afford to ignore the ethnic pride of any immigrant group, from the Pilgrims to the Poles; but all were also appealed to alike in the name of the new Americanism, which was being newly reformulated on the old authority of the Declaration of Independence.

New Deal ethnocracy was essentially white ethnocracy. The Democratic party was a coalition that included the southern white supremacists, and racial equality for Negroes was not treated as an officially recognized moral issue by the New Deal. Negroes had done more than their share toward shaping the national culture, especially in the Jazz Age, but America had integrated Negro culture without integrating the Negro.

On the other hand, the New Deal was not characterized by the lily-white outlook that had been typical of Progressivism, both Republican and Democratic. As the most submerged part of the depression population, black America during the New Deal received substantial assistance from the federal government for the first time since Reconstruction, and in 1936 it left the Republican party for the Democratic. And it was within the liberal northern wing of the Democratic party that the civil rights movement established itself to work for the then-unforeseeable revolutionary achievements that became possible in the Cold War era.

....

At the time Roosevelt won reelection as governor of New York in 1930, Will Rogers had commented that the Democratic party had just nominated its President. Roosevelt was as yet not very well known nationally, but he proved Rogers right two years later at the Chicago convention, and then he went on to dominate American politics as no President had since Andrew Jackson. His leading out-of-state opponents at the Democratic convention had been John Nance Garner of Texas, who was a regional favorite son, and Newton D. Baker of Ohio, who was the choice of militant Progressives. The only possible candidate, aside from Roosevelt, who enjoyed a truly national appeal was Al Smith of New York, and Roosevelt won against the opposition of his fellow New York Democrat.

Barring some dreadful political accident, 1932 was destined to be New York's year in Democratic politics, and the rest of the decade was destined to be New York's decade in national politics generally. The nation looked to New York for leadership in 1932, and New York responded by giving the nation, not only Roosevelt, but most of the political makings of the New Deal as well. Roosevelt became the formulator of the New Deal—"Dr. New Deal," as he himself put it—but it had been New York's qualifications for national leadership, rather than FDR's own personal ones, which had originally won him the office, and it was New York's political ideology, rather than his own, which became the New Deal. New York is not America, as the saying goes, but during the New Deal era it came nearer to being America than ever before or since.

For more than a century New York had been the most populous state in the Union, with the largest city, and New York political machines had been the most highly developed in the nation. Nationally, New York had wielded correspondingly weighty political influence, but ideologically it had held no special national significance except for the significance that was attached to the name of Wall Street. Culturally, it had come to be recognized as the national metropolis, superseding the prestigious but undeniably smaller city of Boston during the Gilded Age; nevertheless this did not allow it to speak for the nation, either culturally or politically. Chicago had made itself the symbol of the American spirit with its Columbian Exhibition of 1893; New York City, by comparison, represented only the East, or the East Coast, in the national mind.

True enough, the Progressive era had taken on the personality of the New Yorker Theodore Roosevelt, much as the New Deal took on the personality of Franklin Roosevelt. Nevertheless, TR was obliged to share the stage with other Progressives, such as Robert La Follette, and then, worst of all, lose it to Woodrow Wilson; whereas, FDR had no rival pretenders until Wendell Willkie appeared in 1940. Fundamentally this was because, during the Great Depression, New York had no rivals among the states of the Union as the ideological heartland of post-Progressive American reform. In TR's time, on the other hand, numbers of states such as Wisconsin, Ohio, Nebraska, California, and New Jersey had developed reform programs of their own; these state reform programs had in turn developed national leaders.

New York's uniquely available status in 1932 was the achievement of Al Smith, to the extent that it was any man's personal achievement. Smith had been a brilliant reform governor—the only brilliant reform governor anywhere in the era of Coolidge Republicanism—and he had been the first representative of non-Anglo-Saxon America to win the leadership of a major party. The Great Crash, arriving in the middle of the Bootleg era, came as the ultimate defeat for the Protestant Republic, which was persisting a-religiously in the form of Hoover's American System. What the alternative to the American System would be, nobody knew, but the obvious place to look for it was in Smith's Democratic party and in Smith's state of New York.

In the urban and polyethnic America of the Great Depression, New York was basically in a good position for political leadership, anyway; but so were other states, such as Illinois and Ohio and Pennsylvania, which also boasted large urban and ethnically heterogeneous populations. They also all had their counterparts to Tammany Hall, but none of their political machines had supported reform politics comparable to Smith's Tammany-based New York Democracy of the twenties. Tammany Hall, itself, was no longer an instrument of political reform by the time Franklin Roosevelt became governor of New York. Had Tammany Mayor Jimmy "Beau James" Walker not been persuaded to resign in 1932, the scandals of Tammany Hall would have been a serious liability to Roosevelt at the Democratic convention.

Nor had Tammany, itself, been even remotely associated with reform politics in the nineteenth century. It was during the Progressive era that Tammany Hall developed its own non-Progressive brand of good government under the wisely paternalistic guidance of Boss Charles F. Murphy. Under Murphy the machine became a more orderly and less graft-ridden operation than it had been, and it supported reforms that were demonstrably popular with the voters. Murphy was in a position to do much as he pleased with his organization, without accounting to anyone, and the most remarkable thing he did was to advance the youthful reformers, Robert F. Wagner and Alfred E. Smith, to party leadership in the two houses of the state legislature, over the heads of their seniors in the Hall.

Boss Murphy's relationship to the Progressive movement has been recalled by Frances Perkins who began her career during the Progressive era as a New York City social worker.

Certainly there was nothing social minded about the head of Tammany Hall, Charles Murphy, whom I went to see when legislation on factory buildings was before the state legislature. I went to enlist his support for this legislation. I climbed up the stairs of old Tammany Hall on 14th Street in a good deal of trepidation. Tammany Hall had a sinister reputation in New York, and I hardly knew how I would be greeted, but, as I later learned, a lady was invariably treated with respect and gallantry and a poor old woman with infinite kindness and courtesy. Mr. Murphy, solemn dignity itself, received me in a reserved but courteous way. He listened to my story and arguments. Then, leaning forward in his chair, he said quietly, "You are the young lady, aren't you, who managed to get the fifty-four-hour bill passed?"
I admitted I was.
"Well, young lady, I was opposed to that bill."
"Yes, I so gathered, Mr. Murphy."
"It is my observation," he went on, "that that bill made us many votes. I will tell the boys to give all the help they can to this new bill. Good-by."
As I went out the door, saying "Thank you," he said, "Are you one of these women suffragists?"
Torn between a fear of being faithless to my convictions and losing the so recently gained support of a political boss, I stammered, "Yes, I am."
"Well, I am not," he replied, "but if anybody ever gives them the vote, I hope you will remember that you would make a good Democrat."

Al Smith secured Frances Perkins' vote for the party by appointing her to his administration; Roosevelt elevated her to commissioner on the Industrial Board and later to Secretary of Labor, when he moved his administration to Washington.

As a laboratory for urban ethnocracy, New York offered more ideology and reform activity than FDR cared to involve himself in, when he went to Washington in 1933, but it all contributed to the New Deal ideology anyway. Roosevelt's own range of political ideas at the time is suggested by the advisors he had gathered around him in New York, who continued to assist him in Washington. They included the political technicians from the Tammany machine, Edward J. Flynn and James A. Farley, together with Roosevelt's more intimate political advisors, Samuel I. Rosenman and Louis M. Howe. There were the social workers, Frances Perkins and the Iowan Harry L. Hopkins who had created the New York Temporary Emergency Relief Administration.

Bernard Baruch had introduced Roosevelt to General Hugh S. Johnson, who had worked with Baruch during World War I on the War Industries Board. There was that highly significant novelty, the Brain Trust from Columbia University, chiefly made up of Professors Raymond Moley, Rexford Tugwell, and A. A. Berle, Jr. Intellectually, the most influential of Roosevelt's advisors who was not directly a part of the New York scene was Felix Frankfurter of Harvard Law School, whose influence bore with increasing effect against the Brain Trust's New Nationalist emphasis on big government. Except from the social-work point of view, there was little in this group of advisors that was representative of "the forgotten man at the bottom of the economic pyramid," to whom FDR had appealed in the campaign.

The most effective congressional champion of the forgotten man at the bottom of the economic pyramid throughout the New Deal period was Murphy's old Tammany protégé, Senator Robert F. Wagner of New York. Senator Wagner was the author of FERA, CCC, NRA, and the Social Security and National Labor Relations acts. He was the outstanding proponent in the Senate of minimum-wage legislation, the leading advocate of those health and public housing measures which remained as key objectives in the Fair Deal, the New Frontier, and the Great Society, and the chief spokesman in the upper house for measures sponsored by the NAACP. Wagner, who was, himself, from the bottom of the economic pyramid and who had only the New York constituency to worry about, was consistently in advance of Roosevelt in his reform programs. This was so with the Wagner Labor Act, which received little White House support in the legislature but which became the mainspring of the Second New Deal once it went into effect.

Wagner, the German immigrant, was evidence of the willingness of Murphy's Tammany Hall to open its ranks to others besides the Irish-Americans who were its main strength. By the 1920's New York Jews were receiving increasing recognition by Tammany, with Herbert Lehman becoming lieutenant governor under Roosevelt and then governor after Roosevelt. In the ethnic crazy quilt of New York City politics, however, this was about as far as the Democratic party appeared to be willing to go in the direction of ethnocracy. In addition to being the largest Irish city and the largest Jewish city in the world, New York had also become the largest Italian city in the world by the 1920's. This Italo-American population was represented in politics by Edward Corsi and others; but it was expected, for the most part, to accept the authority of the Irish machine as well as of the Irish church, and for the most part it did so until the rise of Fiorello La Guardia in the Republican party and La Guardia's defeat of Tammany Hall in the New York mayoralty election of 1933.

Measured by the order of his fiscal responsibilities, the Italo-American mayor of New York held the position that was second in importance nationally to the Presidency of the United States. The election of La Guardia in 1933 signified the undoubted arrival of the New Immigrant in New York politics, and from that time on, political advancement in New York was opened to Polish-Americans, Greek-Americans, and others. And in this, as in other matters, other states came to follow the New York pattern. In New York, this new dispensation was fostered by La Guardia, who, in his own mind and in the mind of his non-Italo-American following, represented much more than the addition of one more ethnic group to political power.

"To put it sociologically," as Arthur Mann has written,

La Guardia was a marginal man who lived on the edge of many cultures, so that he was able to face in several directions at the same time. . . . Half Jewish and half Italian, born in Greenwich Village yet raised in Arizona, married first to a Catholic and then to a Lutheran but himself a Mason and an Episcopalian, Fiorello La Guardia was Mr. Brotherhood Week all by himself. . . . He was so many persons in one, so uniquely unparochial in that most parochial of cities, that New Yorkers of nearly every sort were able to identify themselves with him, although rarely for the same reasons. The hyphens of this many-hyphenated American were like magnets.

La Guardia, the undersized, roly-poly, shrill-voiced fireball, who campaigned vituperatively in six languages, was the exception to many rules, including the rule that Tammany could be beaten, if at all, only by a patrician reformer and then only for one term. That the time for a reform administration was at hand in 1933 was evident, following the fruitful investigation of Jimmy Walker's Tammany Hall by the patrician reformer Samuel Seabury. To the Good Government men, however, it was not evident that La Guardia should head the Fusion ticket. That decision was forced on the upper-class reform groups of the city by Seabury, who was, himself, descended from the Pilgrim Fathers, and who was the very pattern of a traditional New York reform mayor. As Mann has written, it was a victory made possible by the united efforts of the Mayflower and the Little Flower.

La Guardia went on to win a 40 percent plurality in a three-way race against the Tammany candidate and against the candidate of FDR's New York boss, Edward Flynn. In 1937 La Guardia returned, after four years of municipal reform unmatched in the city's history, and won reelection by an overwhelming mandate of the city, as he did again in 1941. His relations with Roosevelt's New Deal remained equivocal, but his influence upon the ideology of the New Deal was great. His was the most penetrating voice of the new Americanism of the emergent ethnocracy.

....

Prior to the New Immigration the American Jewish population had increased from 15,000 in 1840 to 250,000 in 1880, in the course of the German migration of that period, and had dispersed itself throughout the Midwest and in other areas of German settlement. These German Jews had chiefly engaged in trading, and consequently the Jewish peddler had become a stock American vaudeville character. This evidently was not looked upon by either Jews or non-Jews as a manifestation of anti-Semitism, which, down to the 1880's at least, was not much in evidence, except as a curiosity among genteel people to know who was Jewish and who was not and as a symbol in the minds of protesting farmers for the distant power of banking and finance.

Actually, Jews have not been prominently associated with many major banking enterprises in the United States—and these Jews were from the earlier German migration rather than from the much more numerous, but worse-advantaged New Immigration that began to arrive in the eighties. Indeed this is true of most large Jewish-American fortunes outside the entertainment industry. Members of this nineteenth-century German migration included in the business world, Solomon Loeb, Jacob Schiff, Otto Kahn, the Warburgs, the Guggenheims, and the founders of Gimbel's and Macy's. It also produced notable families of intellectuals, including the Brandeises, the Flexners, the Untermeyers, and the Frankfurters. In religion it was spoken for most influentially in the liberal Reform Judaism of Rabbi Isaac M. Wise and later, Stephen A. Wise.

Then, between 1880 and 1910 about 1.5 million Jewish refugees arrived on lower Manhattan Island. In religion as in language they were separate from the German-American Jews; but as anti-Semitism gained strength in America, Jewish organizations representing the separate groups increasingly worked toward unity of effort, the more so during World War I, when being German-American was much worse than being Jewish-American.

From the native American point of view, there did not seem much to distinguish the new Jewish immigrants from the rest of the New Immigrants, except for the beards and hats and cloaks. Unlike the other New Immigrants, who had been accustomed to isolated village life, however, the Jews were accustomed to city life and also the bicultural existence which faced them again in America. The Catholic New Immigrants from rural Europe had typically been imbued with the peasant's suspicion of learning and with the peasant's resigned acceptance of life as it was. The Jewish New Immigrants, by contrast, brought with them a veneration for learning and a faith in business enterprise. The Talmud enjoined them to "turn all thou hast into money and procure in marriage for thy son the daughter of a scholar, and for thy daughter a scholar." Jews pursued both wealth and education as religious duty.

The move from Minsk or Warsaw or Vienna to New York was a move from one ghetto to another, but it was also a move from the Old World of enforced segregation and pogroms to the New World of American opportunity. The immigrants, themselves, might wish only to remain Yiddish-speaking aliens in the New World, but they might still entertain other ideas of America as the land of opportunity for their children. There were American public schools for the children to attend, and there were colleges for the children who excelled in school. And, until the Great Depression, there were business opportunities for children who were not to be scholars. Many Jewish immigrants were not poor, at least by Russian standards, but extreme poverty was certainly very widespread among them. The first generation made their livings doing needlework in the garment district or engaging in other manual labor or in peddling or in shopkeeping; but they had faith that their children would do better.

Whereas patriarchal order was maintained in other New Immigrant ghettoes, the Jewish neighborhoods were fiercely filiarchal, in the parental sacrifices that were made to allow the children to advance above the parents in the alien world of America. The children were expected to learn American ways without becoming altogether Americanized; they were to "speak English and think Yiddish." Naturally the children often went too far, in the estimation of the parents; generations often divided on religious lines between Orthodox Judaism on the one hand and Reformed Judaism, or none at all, on the other. However, rebellion of Jewish youth against parental authority was, itself, often only an effort to find a new type of Jewish identity. Outright rebellion against parental authority can be clean-cut and final in a strictly patriarchal family; it is far less likely to occur so completely where authority has been shared in the family and where the child has been favored over the parents.

To a far greater extent than has been true in western European countries, American Jews have retained their self-awareness and communal identity, even in middle-class and upper middle-class circles. Prominent in stories of Jewish life in America are the possessive mamma, who is fiercely ambitious for her children, and the persistent fund raiser for Jewish community organizations and causes; these mothers and fund raisers have successfully held the Jewish family and the Jewish community together. According to a sample census taken in 1957, among married Jews in the United States, 96.5 percent had Jewish spouses.

This persistent Jewish-American cultural coherence was fostered by a growing American anti-Semitism which began to manifest itself at the outset of the New Immigration and to express itself, in part, in restrictive limitations against Jews in clubs, in residential areas, in colleges and medical schools, and in the higher reaches of industry and finance. In the 1930's the Nazis rose to power in Germany and advanced from intimidation of German Jews to the extermination of European Jewry. In America, German-American Bundists and other anti-Semitic groups organized and demonstrated. But the dominant and most lasting influence of Nazism was in the opposite direction, toward repudiating anti-Semitism in American life, and war against Nazi Germany drove this lesson home.

American Jews were always aware of Dachau and Belsen throughout the thirties, as non-Jews were not, and they were aware that America—particularly New York—was swiftly becoming the heartland of world Jewry. Albert Einstein, together with Chaim Weizmann and thousands of other European leaders and intellectuals escaped to America, to give this new development dramatic emphasis. One response was the tightening of Jewish ties; another was the association of Jewish aspirations with America more absolutely than before. Jewish intellectuals might be Marxian Socialists in theory and many might entertain romantic hopes for Russian communism—at least until the Russo-German pact of 1939—but in practice, their hopes for the world future of the Jews were now joined to their hopes for the future of America.

When it came to influencing the future of America, American Jews enjoyed an immense advantage in being concentrated in the national metropolis, where they still comprise about one-third of the nonblack, non-Puerto-Rican population. By comparison, old-stock white Americans make up only about one-twentieth of New York City's population. Jews were largely excluded from the New York worlds of Wall Street and Madison Avenue, and the publishing world remained predominantly Anglo-Saxon. Nevertheless, Jews had, for a generation, set the tone of New York cultural life in some respects. They had filled the concert halls and theaters of New York, and to that extent they had come to represent the national taste. They had influenced publishing by buying books in extraordinary quantities, where the publishing world favored their tastes. They had contributed largely to the world of Broadway entertainment; and to the world of popular music, they had contributed, among others, Irving Berlin, Jerome Kern, and George Gershwin. Even more influentially, they were a dominant force in the rise of the movie industry in Hollywood. And with the coming of the New Deal, the political consciousness of New York Jews came to be of national significance in the fields of New Deal reform, labor union reform, and literary-political Bohemian radicalism.

Together with the rise of Nazi Germany, the coming of the Great Depression and of the New Deal brought American Jews overwhelmingly into the party of President Franklin Roosevelt of New York. The Democratic governor of New York was Herbert Lehman, formerly lieutenant governor under Roosevelt, a leader in the financial community and a descendant of the old German-Jewish immigration. Jews continued to remain powerful in New Deal councils, from the wealthy and conservative Secretary of the Treasury Henry Morgenthau, Jr., to the militantly radical anti-Communist labor leaders, Sidney Hillman and David Dubinsky of the clothing trades. Many Jews who held the New Deal, as a whole, in contempt for its political and economic conservatism nevertheless venerated FDR as the founder of the new Americanism. This overwhelming Jewish loyalty to FDR and to FDR's Democratic party persisted in the postwar period and largely survived the rise to affluence and the move to the suburbs.

During the twenties and thirties the largest single Jewish community in the world may well have been Brownsville in Brooklyn, with a population of more than 200,000. It was an overcrowded and run-down area that had a poor reputation among New York Jews generally.

When one of our school teachers in an explosion of rage informed us that Brownsville was one huge cesspool of illiteracy and hoodlumism, a former Brownsville boy remembered, the students had all hastened to agree with her.

As was true elsewhere in New York, the small boys belonged to gangs, and outside the home and the school the standards they lived by were the standards of the juvenile gang.

On the other hand, according to another witness,

In Brownsville when I knew it, school was a major occupation, not of the children alone, but of the whole neighborhood. ... School to Brownsville represented a glorious future that would rescue it from want, deprivation and ugliness.

It had also been true, he added, that

among the Brownsville settlers there arose a group who prided themselves on being hard-headed and "American." They sneered at education

and their measure of a man was not how learned he was but how large
his bank balance: "How big a check can he write?" . . . But this same
group went into the market to buy professional men as husbands for
their daughters.

A Brownsville librarian later remembered that he was "constantly
beseeched for more books on sociology and for the best of Continental literature."

Your reading room is full of young men preparing themselves for civil
service and college-entrance examinations. Your reference desk is over-
taxed with demands or material for debate on every conceivable public
question . . . you have to be conservative and ever on your guard lest your
reading public increase three times as fast as the library's resources. . . .
Toward those books whose use some libraries restrict, the attitude of the
adults is very liberal. No explanation completely satisfies them and their
indignation rises high when they learn that libraries occasionally see fit to
withhold certain volumes of Tolstoy, of Zola, of Shaw.

Brownsville parents were ambitious to send their children to Harvard or Yale or Columbia or NYU, but City College of New York
was the most likely possibility. The enrollment of CCNY during the
twenties and thirties was about 80 percent Jewish, and close to half
of all American Jews with college degrees in 1940 had earned them
at CCNY, where admissions standards were driven sky high by the
competition.

Morris Freedman has drawn a composite image of the City College
student in the thirties as "an argumentative intellectual, a sometimes
brilliant, loquacious, rather truculent young man, who is partial to
radical politics, disrespectful of authority, and whose erudition is as
catholic and unselective as it is occasionally superficial." These students were anxious about economic security, about religion, about
their Jewishness and about politics; and the Communist party members on campus, though always relatively few in number, exercised a
continual terror. "If you didn't join, you might be branded loudly and
venomously as a fascist, a trotskyite (the party line was to use lower-
case letters for epithets) and, worst of all, as an ivory-tower aesthete
or wishy-washy liberal. There were no conservatives in those
days."

Whereas Bohemian radicalism for middle-class Anglo-Saxon

Americans had always represented a conscious rebellion against home and mother, the reverse was apt to be the case with Jewish radicals. Michael Gold, the leading spokesman for proletarian thought in the thirties, wrote in *Jews Without Money*,

Mother! Momma! I am still bound to you by the cords of birth. I cannot forget you. I must remain faithful to the poor because I cannot be faithless to you! I believe in the poor because I have known you. The world must be made gracious for the poor! Momma, you taught me that!

•••

Jewish and non-Jewish intellectuals alike were seeking, during the depression, to reformulate American ideals to make them relevant to depression society and to themselves. Among Jewish intellectuals, the results ranged from the corrosive cynicism of Nathanael West to the warmly affirmative Americanism of Alfred Kazin. Kazin had arrived at his understanding of the American character by studying American literature in Brownsville schools and the Brownsville public library. As a nineteen-year-old City College student, he started out his career as a literary critic by writing reviews for Malcolm Cowley on the *New Republic*. He attended Mark Van Doren's classes at Columbia, taught at the New School, and worked on V. S. Calverton's editorial enterprises, and at Calverton's place, became acquainted with Norman Thomas, Max Eastman, Sidney Hook, and other intellectual leaders of the anti-Communist left.

Encouraged by Carl Van Doren, the young Kazin wrote *On Native Grounds, A Study of American Prose Literature from 1890 to the Present,* which remains a classic historical exposition of what Kazin called "this new nationalism" in American literature, bent on "reclaiming the past for the strengthening of the present." For Kazin, the present was Greenwich Village in the era of Nazi Germany, the Spanish Civil War, the Great Depression, the New Deal, and the discordant Popular Front at home and abroad. To his way of thinking, Emerson, Thoreau, James, and Howells were all clearly relevant to this present.

For American intellectuals generally, America's literary heritage seemed more relevant to the depression era than did its political heritage, despite the political orientation of the decade, because its political heritage offered no constructive counsel on how to confront a depression which would not automatically revert to prosperity by following the natural moral law of supply and demand. For intellectuals of the New Immigration, there was the added objection to the American political heritage that it was no part of their own historic past. American literature, on the other hand, belonged, broadly speaking, to Judeo-Christian humanism, and, on that basis, the most recent immigrant to the United States could establish a valid kinship extending back to the New Zion of the first Puritans. This "shock of recognition," as Herman Melville had expressed it, was, if anything, more compelling to the new-stock Americans than to the old ones. Kazin's study remains, perhaps for this reason, a more compelling one than comparable studies by Van Wyck Brooks or Howard Mumford Jones or other old-stock Americans.

At the same time, the American heritage was particularly Anglo-Saxon and Protestant, as well as generally humanistic. It boasted a unique history, shaped by the frontier experience, and recent American stock had had no part in that experience. A positive approach, seeking rapport with the American character on universal grounds, was the one exemplified by Kazin. A negative approach, attacking that in American culture which was peculiarly American, was another possibility, and one which was taken during the 1930's in four short novels by Nathan Weinstein, writing under the pen name of Nathanael West.

West's *The Dream Life of Balso Snell* (1931) is a disorganized episodic scatology relating to art, love, and religion—one which has not been found by most critics to possess great literary merit. It is nevertheless a landmark in American literature, in the serious attempt it makes to be artistically obscene—a task which, according to accepted American literary standards, was impossible because it was self-contradictory. Influenced by James Branch Cabell's *Jurgen,* which had won its reputation by being banned in the twenties, and influenced by contemporary European literary arch-decadence, West, with *Balso Snell,* made an absolute break with the American past by avoiding any pretense whatever of conforming to any kind of moral standards.

West's *Miss Lonelyhearts* (1933) is a satiric look at some American varieties of abnormal psychology and a savage burlesque of American Christian sentimentalism. *A Cool Million* (1934) follows an ignorantly idealistic young Vermont bumpkin through a series of episodes which lampoon moralism, flag-waving patriotism, and rugged American individualism. Then, after an interval of five years spent by West in writing movie scripts in Hollywood, *The Day of the Locust* appeared in 1939, depicting the artificiality of civilization in Hollywood and Los Angeles and the American West generally.

The circle of West's admirers remained small in the thirties; he was not even mentioned in Kazin's book, although Kazin was acquainted with him personally. It has been chiefly since the mid-fifties, in the era of beatniks and black humor and New Left history, that West has come to be considered an important literary figure. He had invented the literary approach that demolished the American heritage by disfiguring it beyond belief, but that was more than most alienated radicals felt they could afford to do in the circumstances of the depression at home and fascism abroad.

West had by no means been alone in his literary use of obscenity to express hostility toward Yankee civilization; he had simply been the most advanced practitioner. Southern literary attitudes toward Yankee civilization shared some of West's points of view, and West seems to have borrowed from at least two contemporary southern writers. Some of his literary devices for his first novel appear to have been suggested by his reading of Cabell's *Jurgen,* and he seems also to have been influenced in the writing of his last novel by *Sanctuary,* written by his occasional hunting companion in Los Angeles, William Faulkner.

West and Kazin represented opposite poles of the literary world of the new Americanism. This world had been in process of creation since the early years of the century, beginning more or less with the literary criticism of Huneker and particularly with the literary controversy over Dreiser's *Sister Carrie* in 1900. During the first quarter of the century the German-Americans had been in the vanguard of this struggle, and during the 1920's H. L. Mencken was the doughtiest fighter against Anglophilism and moralism in literature. Mencken had actually won all of his points before the coming of the depression, anyway, but the depression demolished the comfortably bourgeois world he lived in, and then the Nazis discredited German-American humanism, itself, as an admissible American influence at all.

During the depression some old-stock Americans, including Van

Wyck Brooks, continued in the tradition of Emerson to foster American traits in literature. Others, notably Granville Hicks in *The Great Tradition,* accepted communism as the humanistic wave of the future and attempted to summon America's literary past in support of it. Edmund Wilson achieved for himself a unique position in the interwar period by his ability to remain relatively unencumbered, either by his American heritage or by his Marxist leanings, in his career as literary critic. Kazin wrote of Wilson that "he was the best example of the richness and exactitude that criticism in America had always missed in its modernist critics. In an age of fanaticism and special skills, he stood out as the quiet arbiter, the private reader of patience and wisdom whose very skills gave him public importance."

Brooks, Hicks, and Wilson, in their different ways, indicated that the Lost Generation never, as long as it lived, ceased to believe in its mission to instruct America and, more than that, to speak for it. But even more striking than this longevity of the Lost Generation during the depression and after, was the emergence in the field of literary criticism of two added schools: one representing the Lost Cause of southern American culture, and the other representing the Lost Tribes of New Immigration Jews.

The southern-oriented New Criticism, which expressed itself in scholarly journals such as *Kenyon Review* and *Southern Review,* was consciously agrarian and traditionalist; the New York-oriented new Americanism, which expressed itself in the *Partisan Review,* was consciously urban and radical in its politics. Nevertheless, when it came to viewing Yankee-Puritan civilization, the two schools of criticism shared much in common. Indeed, one American critic, the Southern-German-Jewish-American Ludwig Lewisohn had combined all of the main cultural elements of the new literary Americanism into one person, without, it is true, happily reconciling them in himself.

Negatively the two new schools of criticism could unite in opposition to the Yankee-Puritan idea that true art must always serve a moral purpose and that true morality in art was much the same thing as Victorian "good taste" or "edification." Positively they could unite in support of a conception of art as associated with civilization, in general, or at least Western civilization, and not simply the American civilization of the Yankee-Puritan heritage on the one hand or the American mass society of the twenties and thirties on the other. The

New Critic John Crowe Ransom wrote in *I'll Take My Stand,* "The South is unique on this continent for having founded and defended a culture which was according to the European principles of culture; and the European principles had better look to the South if they are to be perpetuated in this country." The children of immigrants could agree on European principles of culture without feeling the need to look to the South for them.

Both the neoconservatism of the *Southern Review* and the neo-Marxism of the *Partisan Review* were powerful influences on American thought. But culturally the future of America was with the urban New Immigration rather than with the agrarian Old South; and the neo-Marxism of the *Partisan Review* exerted the more profound influence upon the new Americanism, although not explicitly as neo-Marxism. The New Criticism, with its emphasis upon close textual analysis of poetry and prose, was ideally suited to classroom instruction; hence its most enduring influence has been an academic rather than a more broadly cultural one.

Partisan Review began its existence in 1934 as an organ of the John Reed Clubs, representing Communist party youth movements, but it went anti-Stalinist two years later in protest against the dictatorial policy of the party in literary matters. Although *Partisan Review* was never an organ of Jewish literary opinion—Dwight Macdonald, Mary McCarthy, Richard Chase, James Agee, and other non-Jewish intellectuals were among its inner circle—it nevertheless had the character, writes Norman Podhoretz, of a Jewish family group,

the term "Jewish" can be allowed to stand by clear majority rule and by various peculiarities of temper . . . and the term "family" by the fact that these were people who by virtue of their tastes, ideas, and general concerns found themselves stuck with one another against the rest of the world whether they liked it or not (and most did not). . . .

They formulated an avant-garde left-wing, anti-Stalinist literary position, and, Podhoretz writes,

out of that position developed an intellectual style which for a long while was almost unique to *Partisan Review* and which eventually came of its own force to be identified in the eyes of many with the quality of intellectuality itself.

It would be more precisely true to say that this style of thought came to be identified in the eyes of many with the term intellectual, rather than with the quality of intellectuality. Franklin and Jefferson and Emerson and Hawthorne had been associated with the quality of intellectuality, but they had not been "intellectuals," which was not a native American term. The original intellectuals, by name, were those European men and women of arts and letters, led by Emile Zola, who, in the 1890's successfully defended Captain Alfred Dreyfus against an anti-Semitic plot involving the French military caste and then the French government and the French Catholic Church as well.

Thereafter intellectuals, strictly speaking, were those Americans as well as Europeans who considered themselves to be the possessors of the quality of intellectuality and, in its name and in the tradition of Zola, the guardians of civilized values against the Philistines. The Sacco-Vanzetti case was viewed by intellectuals as an American re-enactment of the Dreyfus case thirty years later; indeed, without the Dreyfus case as a model, the Sacco-Vanzetti case might well never have come up in intellectual circles. Both the Dreyfus case and the Sacco-Vanzetti case were important in shaping the *Partisan Review* "intellectual" frame of mind, romantically uniting the intellectuals against the rest of the world whether they liked it or not (and, actually, whether the rest of the world might happen to be with them or against them).

Where *Partisan Review* represented the New York intellectuals, the *New Yorker* represented sophistication and wit and was an Anglo-Saxon family group in about the same measure that *Partisan Review* was a Jewish family group. The *New Yorker* advertised that it was not for "the little old lady from Dubuque," but it was aimed at the literate middle-class and upper-middle-class public as a whole. Intellectuals looked down upon the *New Yorker* somewhat but not altogether. Writers like Edmund Wilson and Mary McCarthy who were asked to write for both *Partisan Review* and the *New Yorker* were in a special class, even in the estimation of intellectuals.

Other New York-centered magazines which presented other claims to intellectual leadership included the Communist *New Masses,* the left-wing *New Republic* and *Nation,* and the moderately liberal *Harper's* and *Saturday Review of Literature. Time, Life* and *Fortune* did not appeal to intellectual audiences, but they were heavily staffed by intellectuals, who had succumbed, generally with some shamefacedness, to the offer of a good, steady salary. Working for the Luce publications at least allowed one the opportunity to engage in the radical and intellectual pursuits of the city on the side. The fate worse than Luce publications for New York intellectuals was Hollywood, a fate which befell many of them besides Nathanael West.

As an independent journal of radical opinion and as an advocate of thoroughgoing ethnocracy, V. S. Calverton's *Modern Monthly* was in a class by itself in the thirties. Calverton, whose real name was George Goetz, was a Johns Hopkins graduate from H. L. Mencken's German-American world of Baltimore. Like Mencken, Calverton was an avid and eclectic reader, but unlike Mencken, he was a Bohemian intellectual, dedicated to Marxism, free love, Freudianism, filiarchy, jazz and the New Negro. A "premature Marxist" in the twenties and a "premature anti-Stalinist" in the thirties, as Alfred Kazin has written, Calverton was always out of step with the main currents of thought in the interwar decades, and his death in 1940 at the age of 40 brought an end to his magazine as well as to his personal influence. Now, more than a quarter of a century after his death, in an age of filiarchy and of the black revolution, the times appear to have caught up with Calverton at last.

Kazin, who worked as Calverton's assistant on the *Modern Monthly*, found that

Calverton's house, like Calverton's magazine, was a natural gathering place for all sorts of radicals not in the Communist fold. . . . And among the European veterans and American Jews, who looked as if they had made their way to Calverton's house through a mine field, among all the sour, sedentary, guarded faces, were the characteristically lean, straight, bony Yankee individualists with ruddy faces and booming laughs, the old Harvard dissenters, leftover Abolitionists, Tolstoyans, single-taxers, Methodist ministers, Village rebels of 1912, everlasting Socialists and early psychoanalysts, who naturally turned up at George's house as friends of George's own heartiness, his great and open welcome to life.

To this cast of characters were added Negro reformers, novelists, historians, lawyers, sociologists, actors, artists, and jazz musicians. Perhaps no other white intellectual in the thirties was as well-informed as Calverton on what was happening in the intellectual world of black America. Calverton argued for a black culture in America which would determine its own cultural values within American society, but this was a form of ethnocratic radicalism that was far in advance of the times. Amid the desperate conditions of the depression, Negro intellectuals were unable to follow Calverton in his encouragement of black cultural nationalism within the white American culture, while few white intellectuals had any idea of what Calverton was thinking about.

....

Until the twentieth century the overwhelming majority of American Negroes had continued to live in the South; and to the extent that the Negro question was viewed as a southern question, it remained uncomplicated by the challenge of the new Americanism, which did not penetrate the Anglo-Saxon Protestant South. Southern whites could not avoid accepting the Negro as basic to southern society, and southern Negroes could not, practically speaking, avoid accepting the necessity of accommodating themselves to the subordinate position they had traditionally held in southern society.

At the turn of the century this necessary accommodation by southern Negroes meant submitting to Jim Crow segregation of black society from white. This was against the paternalistic southern tradition, which had accepted much racial intermingling. And since Jim Crow segregation constituted a radical reordering of southern society, it was inevitably carried out with great violence. The turn of the century marks the bloodiest period in the history of lynchings in America. Nor was the struggle entirely one of white against black, for there was bitter opposition among many southern whites to this repudiation of the traditional paternalistic southern code of behavior in race relations.

Racial segregation was the southern response to emancipation—a response that had been delayed for a generation by Reconstruction. The threat of federal intervention remained for a decade or more after Reconstruction, and no crises had occurred in the South during that time to disturb race relations unduly. Then, in the nineties Negroes challenged the authority of their paternalistic Bourbon protectors by joining the Populist movement; and with the defeat of

Populism, Bourbons and Populists alike joined in a comprehensive retribution against the Negro. The nineties was a period of rising racist sentiment nationally—a sentiment that expressed itself in the Anglo-Saxon imperialism of the Spanish-American War. Northern support for the rights of Negroes was tested during the nineties and found to be lacking. Segregation was by then being widely accepted in the South as the right way to keep the Negro in his place, when he no longer had a master to keep him in his place.

In one southern state after another Jim Crow legislation disfranchised the Negro and then segregated him to separate residential areas, schools, railroads cars, waiting rooms, parks, theaters, restaurants, and water fountains. Jim Crow became part of the southern way of life, as though it had always been the southern practice, and it was not effectively challenged until the Cold War era. It was during the first generation after the imposition of Jim Crow that the first mass migration of Negroes to northern cities took place.

Negroes did not escape Jim Crow by going north, for, during the Progressive era, Jim Crow segregation extended itself northward also. Racial discrimination was implicit in the exclusive sense of moral stewardship which characterized those Progressives who self-consciously set themselves apart from the "lesser breeds" and spoke of "the white man's burden" and of their "little brown brothers." When Theodore Roosevelt invited Booker T. Washington to luncheon at the White House, the criticism he received from Progressive supporters dissuaded him from making any further interracial gestures of the kind. During Roosevelt's, Taft's, and Wilson's administrations, Jim Crow regulations were introduced into federal government agencies.

This did not, it is true, reflect universal Progressive sentiment; for the National Association for the Advancement of Colored People was formed by white Progressives in 1909, and the National Urban League came into being a year later. These organizations represented only a small group of intellectuals, social workers, and lineal heirs of the original abolitionists, however. On the whole, Progressivism was lily-white and of the opinion that the disfranchisement and segregation of Negroes were in the interest of good government and sound morals.

Nor was Jim Crow as radical an innovation in the North as it was in the South. Even among the northern abolitionists themselves, there had never existed interracial fraternalism such as had persisted in the South, to some extent, down into the era of Jim Crow. The anti-slavery northerner Frederick Law Olmsted noted, in his classic account of antebellum southern society, that an amount of intermixing of the races went on in public such as northern abolitionists would have found hard to stomach. In fact, those abolitionists were frequently not far from putting Jim Crow into practice in the very abolitionist fight to which they were devoting their lives. The Negroes they were helping to freedom were the objects of their philanthropy, and, as such, were evidently expected to know their place. When a freed slave presumed to become a peer among the white abolitionists, as Frederick Douglass did, he was urged to return to the inferior role to which God had assigned him, and stick to repeating his personal story and the adventure of his escape from slavery to audiences that were arranged for him. When Douglass persisted in being an abolitionist leader in his own right, William Lloyd Garrison denounced him, in effect, for being an irresponsible, uppity Negro.

Negroes were frequently well enough received in the North—in communities where there were very few of them—but wherever they congregated in numbers, community pressures tended to force them into segregated and economically depressed ghettoes. Jim Crow in the form of actual legislation was a southern innovation, which was in some respects copied by the North; but Jim Crow as a customary practice, not requiring legislation, was already characteristic of northern society. Indeed, in the South, Jim Crow was part of the enterprising "New South" with its newly rising middle class, which was seeking to emulate the ways of the enterprising Yankee North.

The French demographic historian Philip Aries' history of the emergence of the institution of the modern family develops a social hypothesis that sheds light on the contrasting race attitudes of northerners and southerners in race matters. Antebellum southern society, by comparison to northern society, had been characterized by the quality of "sociability," to use Aries' term, of medieval society, before the emergence of the middle classes and of the modern family. It was reminiscent of that "rigid, polymorphous social body" of medieval times, where "people had lived on top of one another, masters and servants, children and adults, in houses open at all hours." Indeed, genteel southerners enthusiastically endorsed the medieval world of Sir Walter Scott's novels as the approved romantic model for their own society.

On the other hand, northern middle-class society exemplified the opposite quality of "domesticity," demanding family privacy against "the pressure of the multitude" and "the contact of the lower class." Northern middle-class democracy exemplified all the characteristics of that domesticity which, Aries wrote, "appear as manifestations of the same intolerance toward variety, the same insistence on uniformity" as marked the "concept of the family, the concept of class, and perhaps elsewhere the concept of race."

The antebellum north was characterized by anti-Negro opinion much more than it was by antislavery opinion. The Indiana constitution might declare "that all men are born equally free and independent, and have certain natural, inherent unalienable rights," whereas the Mississippi constitution was obliged to take the narrower view "that all freemen, when they form a social compact, are equal in rights." Nevertheless, Indiana, in a later constitution, added the provision that "no negro or mulatto shall come into, or settle in the State, after the adoption of this constitution." Northern opinion reacted against the Negro race as a threat to the family and the neighborhood, and when the "sociability" of the old slavocracy was destroyed, southern opinion came around to a similar point of view.

Whatever the differences have been between northern and southern attitudes toward the Negro race, it is a striking fact that Anglo-America as a whole has been characterized by far less race tolerance than Latin-American societies have shown. At the same time, Anglo-America has been far more successful in maintaining institutions of self-government than have Latin-American countries. The Spanish political philosopher Salvator de Madariaga observed that this Anglo-Saxon race-consciousness and this Anglo-Saxon aptitude for self-government were complementary qualities and not contradictory ones. Madariaga argued that, unlike the Englishman or the Anglo-American, the Spaniard or Spanish-American was individualistic in his point of view toward society, and that a society of Spaniards or Spanish-Americans was accordingly so atomistically individualistic as to require an authoritarian state and church to maintain social order. The Anglo-Saxon, on the other hand, habitually functioned as a member of a group, rather than as an individualist, and his voluntary associational activities in church, business, and civic organizations were the foundation stones of democracy in Anglo-Saxon communities.

The same contrasting ethnic characteristics of Spanish individualism on the one hand and Anglo-Saxon associationalism on the other, Madariaga argued, account for Spanish tolerance and Anglo-Saxon intolerance where race is concerned: "Hence in the Anglo-Saxon, a group-distance towards Blacks and Indians, which separates less a given man from a given man than a whole colour from a whole colour." Madariaga pointed out that, where opposition to racial barriers manifests itself in Anglo-Saxon communities, it tends to be a collective rather than an individual matter.

Anglo-American society had tended to keep its group-distance from others besides Negroes. It had done so with the Indians, the Irish, the Italians, the Jews, and most others of the New Immigration. The Anglo-American sense of domesticity reacted adversely to Irish-American sociability in the mid-nineteenth century much as it did to Afro-American sociability in the twentieth. However, the Irish had a society of their own and a religion of their own, and to the extent that they were not accepted by Anglo-America, they could adjust to the situation by strengthening their own social and religious ties. The Afro-Americans, on the contrary, had no such consciously held social model, independently of their native American culture. Racially they were more distinctively non-Anglo-American than any other major ethnic group, whereas culturally they were more thoroughly American than any other major ethnic group, lacking the recognizable hyphenated culture of another society to unify them in the alien northern cities of their native land.

Most old-stock northerners had little direct contact with Negroes, and their general attitude seems to have been one of comfortable condescension toward a race that was looked upon as mainly ignorant and shiftless but docile and not, on the whole, dangerous. The Negro was apt to be favorably represented, in the minds of the individual middle-class whites, by a particular cleaning woman who was an absolute jewel or a particular handyman who could always be relied on or the courteous doorman or the cheerful bootblack.

There was also a general recognition of "exceptional" Negroes, such as Booker T. Washington and George Washington Carver. Ne-

groes as a race, however, were considered morally and mentally subordinate to whites and therefore racially suited to subordinate roles in
society. Although anthropologists, led by Franz Boas, were methodically demolishing the current racial theories, these theories continued
to be taught in the nation's colleges and universities in the Progressive
period while to white Americans generally the proposition that white
was superior to black was self-evident.

That was not to say that white was thought superior to black in all
things. There was a willingness to credit Negroes with the virtues of
their supposed defects. An age that concerned itself with the dangers
of "overcivilization" could admire the Negro's primitive faith and
fortitude, and an age that placed an ever higher value upon youth was
one that could respond to what it recognized as childlike in Negro
culture. Many Americans who were emerging from the Mauve Decade
into a new century could discover elements to admire in the Negro's
"happy-go-lucky" freedom from puritanical restraint, especially as it
expressed itself in Negro music. It was preeminently through the
medium of music that the musically undistinguished descendants of
unmusical Puritans submitted to the influence of Negro America, all
the while maintaining that Anglo-Saxon group-distance from the
object of emulation. It was in this fashion, during the first quarter of
the twentieth century, that the Jim Crow era culminated in the Jazz
Age.

Thomas Jefferson wrote of Negroes in *Notes on Virginia* that "in
music they are more generally gifted than the whites, with accurate
ears for a tune and time, and they have been found capable of imag-
ining a small catch. . . . The instrument proper to them is the *banjar,*
which they brought hither from Africa." Negro slaves created work
songs for themselves in the fields. They were also willing converts to
Christianity and to hymn singing. The African-Americans were prohibited from doing their traditional African dances by their own
Negro ministers, who opposed these on moral grounds, but music
that encouraged work and religion was approved of by white owners
and Negro ministers alike.

Negro spirituals first became widely known outside the South in
1871, when the Fisk School in Nashville sent a group of students on a
singing tour in the hope of raising badly needed funds. The Fisk
Jubilee Singers performed in New York, New England, Washington,

D.C., London, Paris, and Moscow. They became known throughout the world and they introduced the world to "Roll, Jordan, Roll," "Steal Away to Jesus," "Go Down Moses," "Nobody Knows the Trouble I've Seen," and also to "Joshua Fit de Battle of Jericho," "Little David Play on Your Harp," and "All God's Chillun Got Shoes."

What Jefferson called the *banjar* was introduced by Negro slaves, together with the bones (polished small rib bones of sheep held between the fingers and played like castanets). Slave groups worked up routines accompanied by banjo and bones and other makeshift instruments. These became a form of entertainment patronized by plantation owners. Then, white performers in blackface copied the slave groups; and in the 1840's the minstrel show was developed, which remained the most popular form of professional entertainment in America down to the end of the century.

Musically the white minstrel show was at its best in the antebellum years, when the songs of Dan Emmett and Stephen Foster were written. The height of its popularity, however, was during the last quarter of the century, when it came to feature the ragtime music of "coon songs," which evoked the stereotyped Negro, with his love of watermelon-eating, chicken-stealing, woman-chasing, and razor-slashing.

The extraordinarily enduring popularity of the minstrel show is the best evidence there is of the nature of the meaningful role that the Negro played in Anglo-American culture. The minstrel show provided an equalitarian society with somebody to look down on and laugh at; it provided a moralistic society with an amoral spectacle which was acceptable, even though risqué, because it was about colored people; and it provided a prosaic culture with the universally appealing rhythms and music of Afro-America, as commercialized by the Christy Minstrels and their successors.

In addition to the white minstrel shows there were numerous all-Negro companies, which copied the routines that the white minstrels had copied from the slave groups. Negro minstrels wore the same burnt-cork makeup and mimicked the same broken English of the stereotype of the southern plantation Negro. Most successful of the Negro minstrels was James Bland, whose own compositions included "Oh, Dem Golden Slippers," "In the Evening by the Moonlight," and "Carry Me Back to Old Virginny." Bland was a college-educated northerner, for whom the subject matter of his songs and skits was almost as foreign as it had been for the Pennsylvanian Stephen Foster. Bland went to England in 1881 and remained there for twenty years, enjoying great success, first as The World's Greatest Minstrel Man and then, ridding himself of the burnt-cork makeup, as simply James Bland, one of the most popular musical performers in Europe.

Down to World War I only one Negro star was able to achieve in America the success that Bland achieved abroad. Bert Williams won fame in New York in the nineties with a song-and-dance routine that turned the old plantation and minstrel show dance, the cakewalk, into the popular dance of the day. Williams, with his partner George Walker, went on to star in the musical shows that were beginning to supplant minstrel shows in New York. In 1910 he became a star and the only Negro performer in the Ziegfeld Follies, continuing with the Follies for ten years. Performing in blackface, Williams sang such comedy songs as "Nobody," "Woodman Spare That Tree," and "You're on the Right Road But You're Going the Wrong Way."

It was Bert Williams who was the authority for the statement that, "it is no disgrace to be a Negro, but it is very inconvenient." Wealthy and universally acclaimed, Williams, shortly before his death, was moved to make the following reflection upon his career in a letter to a friend.

I was thinking about all the honors that are showered on me in the theater, how everyone wishes to shake my hand or get an autograph, a real hero you'd naturally think. However, when I reach my hotel, I am refused permission to ride on the passenger elevator, I cannot enter the dining room for my meals, and am Jim Crowed generally. But I am not complaining, particularly since I know this to be an *unbelievable* custom, I am just wondering. I would like to know when (my prediction) the ultimate changes come . . . if the new human beings will believe such persons as I am writing about actually lived?

••

The drift of Negroes to northern as well as southern cities had been going on since the Civil War, and by 1910 more than 90,000 Negroes lived in New York City, which rivaled Washington D.C. as the largest black community in the nation. Then war in Europe provided new jobs in war industries, while cutting off immigration from Europe, and the great migration to the northern cities was on. In the decade between 1910 and 1920 the Negro population outside the South increased by almost half a million. The cities that attracted the greatest numbers were Chicago, which offered industrial jobs and the civic boosting of the Negro *Defender,* and New York, which offered Harlem, fast developing into the black cultural capital of the world.

During the violent year that followed the Armistice, major race riots broke out in the cities across the nation, the worst of them in Chicago, lasting a week and leaving 38 dead—15 white and 23 black —and 537 wounded. Reactions to the riots included widespread white censure of the white teen-age gangs, which were the main aggressors, and widespread black pride for the resistance the Negroes had made against white terrorism. The Negro poet Claude McKay wrote a poem in 1919 beginning, "If we must die let it not be like hogs / Hunted and penned in an inglorious spot," which was widely circulated and widely committed to memory by Negroes.

The Chicago riot stimulated a postwar sense of black ethnic identity in urban America, which expressed itself most dramatically in Marcus Garvey's Back-to-Africa movement and then in the Harlem Renaissance and the idea of the New Negro. A full-blooded Negro from Jamaica, Garvey preached black racism and black Christianity. Organizing the Universal Negro Improvement Association, he called upon black America to "strike out to build industries, governments, and ultimately empires," arguing that "only then will we as a race prove to our Creator and to man in general that we are fit to survive and capable of shaping our own destiny." Denouncing American Negro leaders generally for supporting black integration in white America, Garvey won hundreds of thousands, perhaps millions, of Negroes to the cause of black nationalism. The power of the movement was broken when Garvey ran into financial difficulties and was finally, in 1925, convicted of fraud and imprisoned and later deported.

This first mass movement of American Negroes had been a frightening challenge to other American Negro leaders, and its failure was readily taken as proof of the falsely visionary nature of the concept of black nationalism in America. No other Negro leader in America touched so responsive a chord among the Negro masses, however, until the rise of Martin Luther King in the 1950's.

The Negro leader who, more than any other, was challenged by Garvey was W. E. B. Du Bois, the dominant figure in NAACP and, at the time of Garvey's rise, the most prominent figure in the American Negro world. Born in Massachusetts and educated at Fisk and at Harvard, where he received a Ph.D. in history in 1895, Du Bois had been the leading opponent of Booker T. Washington's program of Negro separatism and accommodation within the Jim Crow restrictions of white society. Du Bois had called upon Negroes to demand civic equality and the education of youth according to ability, without racial discrimination. Under his editorship, the NAACP *Crisis* rose to 100,000 in circulation by 1918, crusading for antilynching laws, honest implementation of the Fourteenth and Fifteenth Amendments, and an end to all forms of Jim Crow.

Du Bois shared with Garvey an interest in African civilization, and he favored a cultural pan-African movement. But his ambition for American Negroes was that they be, not Afro-Americans, but 100 percent Americans, accepting the white middle-class standards that Du Bois accepted. In common with most Negro intellectuals, Du Bois believed that African culture had not survived the middle passage and the centuries of American slavery in any meaningful way. The qualities that seemed to distinguish American Negro culture from American white culture, including even their unique contributions in the field of music, were explained by black as well as white scholars as largely the influence of the slave plantation environment upon European musical forms.

It was not until Melville Herskovitz's *The Myth of the Negro Past* in 1941 that serious scholarly consideration was given to the formative influences of African cultural survivals in black America—in music and dance forms, in languages and legends, and in family systems and religion. And it was not until the 1960's, in an era of resurgent black nationalism, that Herskovitz's general thesis came to receive any considerable measure of acceptance. In the meantime, those African cultural influences had been at work for centuries in the United States, as well as in South America and the West Indies; and in the United States those influences were shaping white as well as black culture in the Jazz Age.

Ragtime and jazz had originally emerged out of the relatively relaxed racial atmosphere as well as the relatively sophisticated musical influence of the Creole society of French Louisiana. Negroes in New Orleans and St. Louis heard classical and band music which was an integral part of the social life of the community, and they were permitted to participate in it and improvise on it. Ragtime was particularly associated with St. Louis, where it enjoyed its richest period of development during the nineties and the first decade of the new century. By the time Irving Berlin's "Alexander's Ragtime Band" was starting the dance craze for white America, the era of real ragtime, best remembered in Scott Joplin's "Maple Leaf Rag," was about over, making way for boogie-woogie and for jazz.

In New Orleans at the close of the nineteenth century, Buddy Bolden's band and others played jazz in the Storyville red-light district, where the dance-hall brothels provided Negro musicians with a lucrative source of income. Following the closing of the New Orleans red-light district in 1917, Negro jazz went north with the bands of King Oliver, Jelly Roll Morton, and Louis Armstrong. White musicians studied this jazz, and it was the white Original Dixieland Jazz Band from New Orleans which, with its records, started the rage for jazz in the North.

Fundamental to Negro jazz, as to Negro spirituals and work songs and blues songs, was what musicologists have called the "hot" treatment and what white moralists have denounced as savagery and downright beastliness. The moralists rightly felt that the hot treatment was African in origin and sensuous in an un-European and especially an un-Anglo-Saxon manner. This wailing, stomping, polyrhythmic, offbeat, off-note treatment created physical sensations that were novel to Western civilization. Lafcadio Hearn described this hot treatment in dancing as he observed it near the Cincinnati levee during the 1870's, before Jim Crow laws segregated American entertainment places.

The men, Hearn wrote, "patted juba"—clapped the rhythm of the plantation dance—and shouted:

the negro women danced with the most fantastic grace, their bodies describing almost incredible curves forward and backward; limbs intertwined rapidly in a wrestle with each other and with the music; the room presented a tide of swaying bodies and tossing arms, and flying hair. The white female dancers seemed heavy, cumbersome, ungainly by contrast with their dark companions; the spirit of the music was not upon them; they were abnormal to the life about them.

During the Jazz Age, however, the spirit of the music was upon the youth of middle-class white society to a marked degree, even though greatly watered down in Irving Berlin's pseudo ragtime, in the Tin Pan Alley imitation jazz, and in what Edmund Wilson called "the higher jazz" of Paul Whiteman and George Gershwin. "Race records" continued to give the full hot treatment to words as well as music, but the white jazz that was broadcast on radio and played in white dance halls was obliged to refine itself. White America, particularly the younger generation, came under the influence of the hot treatment, and white human nature's range of expression was accordingly increased.

The Jazz Age created a new Negro stereotype, which was almost officially represented by the dancer Bill "Bojangles" Robinson. This Negro was full of natural rhythm and vitality and always on the go, in contrast to the stereotype of the lazy, shiftless, "good-for-nothing" Negro. The Jazz Age Negro was glamorized as a primitive man in an era when primitivism was fashionable. He was admired as the natural extrovert, the naked id, in the midst of a putatively repressed and guilt-ridden white society, which continued to suffer from its Puritan heritage. He was a Freudian hero in a decade when young people who had any pretensions whatever to intellectualism were analyzing one another in a casual conversational way, noticing Freudian slips and being self-conscious about their inhibitions. Sad to say, he was a far cry from that other image of the New Negro which the genteel Bostonian liberal W. E. B. Du Bois had in mind.

During the Jazz Age a good deal was said and written about the New Negro and about the Black Renaissance, or Harlem Renaissance, which was the self-conscious cultural expression of the New Negro. The main leaders of the movement were Du Bois, James Weldon Johnson, and Alain Locke. Prominently figuring in the movement were the writers Langston Hughes, Claude McKay, Jessie Faunset, Jean Toomer, and Countee Cullen, while leading Negro actors and concert artists, notably Charles Gilpin, Paul Robeson, and

Roland Hayes, provided distinguished evidence of a flowering of Negro culture. In a considerably more equivocal manner the jazz musicians who were enjoying national acclaim—the Negro musicals on Broadway and the cabaret shows in Harlem—were also associated with the idea of a Harlem Renaissance.

The leaders of the movement were in agreement with Locke that "cultural recognition will come before political and economic equality because it is less dependent upon the condition of the masses," and that the "few at the top are the arbiters." Locke himself was a Rhodes Scholar and German-trained philosopher teaching at Howard University, and the other most active figures in the movement were college-educated: Johnson at Columbia, Hughes at Columbia and Lincoln College, Faunset at Cornell and the University of Pennsylvania, McKay at Kansas State and Tuskegee, and Walter White at Atlanta. The college, in Du Bois' opinion, was the key to the Negro's social salvation. Du Bois wrote in 1903 of southern Negro colleges that "the college trained in Greek and Latin and mathematics, 2,000 men; and these men trained full 50,000 others in morals and manners, and they in turn taught thrift and the alphabet to nine millions of men, who to-day hold $300,000,000 of property."

There was a cruel ambiguity in the thinking of these leaders which never satisfactorily resolved itself so far as the movement was concerned. They were divided between their pride in Negro accomplishments and Negro culture on the one hand and their acceptance of middle-class white standards of culture and their desire for white acceptance on the other. Du Bois and Locke were enthusiastic students of African culture and collectors of Africana, but they looked upon jazz as vulgar and thought it unfortunate that that was the aspect of Negro culture that was best known. Much of the literature of the Harlem Renaissance, such as Walter White's *Fire in the Flint* and Jessie Faunset's *There Is Confusion*, was self-consciously Victorian and un-Negroid. "The Negro critics and many of the intellectuals," wrote Langston Hughes, "were very sensitive about their race in books, (and still are). In anything that people were likely to read, they wanted to put their best foot forward, their politely polished and cultural foot—and only that foot."

Hughes and McKay counted themselves among the Bohemian Negro intellectuals. They were contemptuous of middle-class and upper-class Negroes who slavishly emulated a white middle-class society that would not admit them to its circle. Nor did they believe that the Harlem Renaissance would lead to a new age of tolerance for American Negroes. They enjoyed the culture of the Negroes in the ghettoes and the jazz joints, and they appreciated realism rather than Victorianism in Negro writing. As far as white America was concerned, they felt a bond of kinship with disillusioned and Bohemian whites and they believed that the Negro represented much of cultural value which the white world would do well to accept. Relations within the New Negro movement were consequently always somewhat difficult. The rather Victorian Johnson was impressed enough with McKay's realistically sexual *Home in Harlem* to urge McKay to return to the United States from France, but Du Bois wrote of it, "for the most part it nauseates me, and after the dirtier parts of the filth, I feel distinctly like taking a bath."

As a literary movement the Black Renaissance was remarkably productive of novelists, essayists, and poets and lively in its periodical literature: the NAACP's *Crisis,* the Urban League's *Opportunity,* and the more radical magazines, *Fire* and *Messenger.* Negro writers also were welcomed during the twenties in the pages of *Atlantic, Harper's, New Republic, Nation,* and *American Mercury.* From the point of view of white America, however, the activities of the Renaissance which chiefly attracted attention and had national influence were those that were happening on Broadway and on Lenox Avenue. On Broadway, Charles Gilpin received critical praise for his role in *Abraham Lincoln* in 1919 and went on to star in *Emperor Jones* the next year. His success in these roles broke the color barrier in the legitimate theater. In 1924 Paul Robeson played the lead in O'Neill's *All God's Children Got Wings* opposite a white actress, and the anticipated riots in connection with its opening failed to occur. In 1930 *Green Pastures* opened for its extraordinarily successful run. Even more of an influence on American culture than these, however, were the Negro musicals, beginning with *Shuffle Along* in 1921.

The musical revues and Harlem night clubs such as the Cotton Club with Duke Ellington's orchestra were jammed with white patrons. Club owners imposed Jim Crow rules excluding Negroes from the more successful Harlem clubs. Negroes resented this, but the whites were oblivious to their resentment and "came to Harlem night after night," as Langston Hughes wrote, "thinking the Negroes loved to have them there and firmly believed that all Harlemites left their houses at sundown to sing and dance in cabarets, because most of the whites saw nothing but the cabarets, not the homes." There they learned the Negro dances: the Lindy-Hop, the Charleston, and the Black Bottom, which swept the nation to become, with the jazz accompaniment, the most characteristic expression of the spirit of the twenties.

It was the jazzy New Negro of the Cotton Club and of the Savoy and of Carl Van Vechten's best-selling *Nigger Heaven* who captured the popular imagination and influenced popular culture. Then the crash came, and the public ceased to concern itself much with what went on in the cabarets. During the depression the Negro came to represent in the public mind the poverty which had always been one of his outstanding characteristics, even during the prosperous twenties. Negroes held the lowest-paying jobs and they were the first to lose them. During the New Deal the Negro stood as the representative of the underprivileged one-third of the nation. He was the lowest common denominator in the renewed struggle for social justice.

Northern Negroes responded to the New Deal by shifting from the Republican to the Democratic party. During the Reconstruction period, the Negro leader Frederick Douglass had preached that "the Republican Party is the ship, all else is the open sea. . . . I would as soon go to hell as vote Democratic." Following the World War I migration of Negroes to northern cities, however, Democratic machine politicians worked with some success for the Negro vote. In 1932 Walter White, secretary of the NAACP, denounced Hoover as "the man in the lily-white house," for seeking southern white votes, but a majority of northern Negroes voted for Hoover, anyway. By 1935 there were 3.5 million Negroes on relief and a growing number in government, some in positions of administrative responsibility.

The high proportion of Negroes on relief was a reflection of the high proportion of Negroes among the unemployed, rather than of partiality of the government; and the growing number of Negroes in government positions reflected the growth in the Negro professional class outside the government. It remained true that the New Deal took the Negroes seriously into account as no previous administration had done since Reconstruction, and in 1936 the Negroes overwhelmingly reciprocated at the polls.

The Great Depression brought the Negro to some extent into the mainstream of American life by reducing millions of white Americans to the Negroes' economic status. Nevertheless, the Negro continued to be fairly comprehensively Jim Crowed throughout the New Deal era to the extent of being denied many of the opportunities for advancement, of which new immigrants had traditionally availed themselves. Broadway was open to him, but Hollywood was not, except for a few stereotyped roles such as were played by Hattie McDaniels and Step'n Fetchit. In the world of sports Joe Louis was the heavyweight boxing champion of the world, and the track star Jesse Owens was the hero of the Olympic Games in Berlin. Both Louis and Owens were popular heroes representing American democracy against racist German Nazism; yet American Negroes continued to be Jim Crowed in most professional sports, including baseball and football. It was not until the 1950's that a new era opened in the Negro's struggle for his citizenship, when, in the course of the Cold War, Americans became increasingly conscious of, and even worried about, the minority position of whites in the world.

9.

Depression and Filiarchy

••

IN AMERICAN HISTORY, THE 1920's SEEM discon-
nected from the 1930's. Instead of a transition from the Dollar
Decade to the New Deal era, there was the separating cataclysm of
Wall Street. The old order collapsed, and the New Deal supplanted it;
and what resulted was a change that was even greater than the shift in
economic circumstances compounded by the shift in administrations.
There was a shift of American societies as well.

Whereas the main innovative tendencies of the twenties had been
old-stock, middle-class, and upper-middle-class tendencies—the technological and filiarchal conversion of the Protestant Republic—the
main innovative tendencies of the thirties were recent-immigrant,
working-class, even proletarian tendencies—the ideological and ethnocratic conquest of the Protestant Republic.

America is a middle-class nation that has always understood democracy to mean the rule of the middle classes. Democracy, by this definition, had appeared to be threatened during the plutocratic Gilded Age, and the middle-class Progressive movement was a response to this threat. During the 1930's democracy appeared to many to be threatened again; this time by the quasi-proletarian cosmopolitanism of the New Deal. It did not appear evident at the time that the long-range consequences would be to suburbanize much of the recent-immigrant and quasi-proletarian America into the middle classes, while attaching the loyalties of middle-class America to the practices, if not the principles, of the welfare state.

In the context of this New Deal ideological and ethnocratic conquest of the Protestant Republic, the decade of the thirties belongs to FDR and La Guardia and Huey Long and Francis E. Townsend and David Dubinsky and John L. Lewis and Studs Lonigan and Tom Joad. Since the New Deal did not rescind the technological society, however, it was also the age of Walt Disney and Shirley Temple and John Dillinger and Joe DiMaggio and Fred Allen and Benny Goodman and Sally Rand and "Wrong-Way" Corrigan.

The Angry Decade was also the Age of Swing; radio was in its prime, and movies were beginning to appear in living technicolor. The same technological procession of film stars and sports heroes and fads and fantastic events that had characterized the twenties continued on without letup throughout the depression. In many ways the age did better with circuses than it did with bread, and if the thirties are to be seen in a human perspective, the circuses should be remembered along with the bread shortages.

During the decade of prosperity, this technological procession had expressed the existential spirit of the technological filiarchy; during the decade of depression, it expressed the existential spirit of the technological society, but it was a society which was no longer authoritatively spoken for by the old order, and it was also a society which was no longer led by youth.

....

The automobile was as necessary for life and love in the thirties as it had been in the twenties, and it was almost as widely available, mostly in older models, of course. Used car lots and junk yards did a land-office business, and nearly everybody seemed to have a car of some kind from the Joads on up the economic scale. The automobile industry had pioneered in installment buying in the twenties, and it kept it up throughout the depression. The annual remodeling of new cars created just as much interest, if not as many sales, as during the twenties. When Ford went to the V-8 motor, it was an event in the thirties almost as exciting nationally as when Ford had gone to the Model-A in the previous decade.

The thirties was the great age of radio. Sports, news, and popular music remained staples during the daytime, along with the soap operas, such as "John's Other Wife" and "My Gal Sunday" to channel the daydreams of the American housewife. There were the serials for children in the late afternoon: "Orphan Annie" and "Jack Armstrong"; and evening serials for the men and boys: "Lone Ranger," "Green Hornet," and "Gang-Busters."

There were the comedy-variety shows, including those of Fred Allen, Bing Crosby, and Burns and Allen. The big bands, such as those of Benny Goodman and Tommy Dorsey and, slower and sweeter, Guy Lombardo and Horace Heidt, had their own weekly hour-long programs. "The Little Theater Off Times Square" was attended by the somewhat serious listener, as were the more pronouncedly cultural "Firestone Hour," "U.S. Steel Program" and the Metropolitan Opera, sponsored by the Texaco Company on Saturdays.

Movies continued to attract audiences through the depression at the rate of 85 million a week, the audiences being enticed in by cut-rate prices, ladies' nites, well-advertised "sneak previews," and bank nites with dishes and cars as prizes. The movie industry avoided controversial subjects, and almost no serious notice was given to the depression and its problems in commercial films.

Sex was more zealously guarded against than had been the case in the twenties. The ideal movie, from the point of view of producers, distributors, theater owners and, it was argued, the public weal, was the movie to which the whole family could go together. Mae West became one of the top box office attractions of the thirties, it is true, but she was far outdrawn by Shirley Temple. Walt Disney was perhaps the most successful innovator of the decade—from Mickey Mouse to *Three Little Pigs* to *Snow White* and to *Fantasia*.

The thirties was the heroic age of the newspaper comic strip, with

Buck Rogers, Flash Gordon, Tailspin Tommy, Captain Easy, and many others appealing to the spirit of adventure rather than to the sense of humor. Among them, none was more successful, with adults as well as children, than Dick Tracy, capitalizing on a national fascination with crime which the repeal of prohibition had done nothing to diminish.

The idea of labeling one criminal-at-large as public enemy number one and then concentrating national attention on his capture may or may not have been effective from the point of view of law enforcement. From the point of view of publicizing J. Edgar Hoover and the Federal Bureau of Investigation, its effect was immense, with the side result that the public enemies were unavoidably glorified also. Pretty Boy Floyd and Ma Parker received their share of attention; but until the FBI gunned him down under a movie theater marquee, John Dillinger reigned as the greatest bank robber the world had ever known, or at least the most publicized. He reigned during an era of many highly publicized bank robberies, which followed hard on the era of many highly publicized kidnappings.

The dance craze continued without letup throughout the depression. The Big Apple and the dance marathon were notable novelties of the day, but the main development was the arrival of the big band and swing and jitterbugging. The most popular bands included those of Count Basie, Duke Ellington, Benny Goodman, the Dorsey Brothers, Artie Shaw, Glenn Miller, and Harry James.

Everybody who managed to survive depression conditions at all shared more or less in these blessings of the technological society. The dust bowl farmers and the relief workers had their radios; and for most families, at least some of the time, the household budget could be cut to pay for the movies or for a round on one of the 30,000 or so miniature golf courses which appeared in vacant lots throughout the neighborhoods of the nation. If the budget could not be cut, there remained home life to be enjoyed. The game of Monopoly became more popular in the thirties than Mah-Jongg had been in the twenties, together with a craze for jigsaw puzzles. The Ouija Board enjoyed a vogue in the depression, and contract bridge became nationally popular, as did family poker.

Most Americans during the depression were conscious of being deprived of material wants, and the cliché that "nobody has starved" was repeatedly proved false; on the other hand, most Americans did not go from day to day worrying where their next meal was coming from. When depression statistics are looked at the other way around, four-fifths of the national labor force was employed before the recession of 1937. Even on relief, Americans had some reason to feel privileged. The London *Economist,* analyzing the New Deal sympathetically, was led to comment that the American relief program was only possible for a rich nation like the United States. Will Rogers remarked in the same vein that America had "the distinction of being the only nation that is goin' to the poorhouse in an automobile."

Perhaps no class in American society was more acutely conscious of being among the underprivileged than the really rich upper class was. Those fortunes of the rich which survived the stock market crash were but little disturbed by the exactions of the New Deal. The rich were not deprived of their money, but they were deprived of the position in society to which they considered their money entitled them. Henry Luce of *Time, Life,* and *Fortune* explained this situation of the rich in a talk that was not reprinted for the masses in *Life.*

"Without the aristocratic principle," Luce declared, "no society can endure," and America of the New Deal was without the aristocratic principle. Unlike others of his circle, however, Luce did not single out "that man in the White House" for sole responsibility. Rather he argued,

What slowly deadened our aristocratic sense was the expanding frontier, but more the expanding machine. . . . Money became more and more the only mark of success, but still we insisted that the rich man was no better than the poor man—and the rich man accepted the verdict. And so let me make it plain, the triumph of the mass mind is nowhere more apparent than in the frustration of the upper classes.

Throughout the depression the *Saturday Evening Post*, together with most of the nation's press, devoted itself to defending the right and duty of the rich to keep their money or spend it any way they wished to. The more money they spent, the more jobs there would be for the common man. Most people probably accepted this "trickle-down theory" as an economic fact; nevertheless, public opinion remained unsympathetic to the problems of the ultra-affluent. Richard Whitney of the New York Stock Exchange was the star performer in a cast of many millionaires who confessed to having helped themselves to large sums of other people's money, and they gave their whole class a bad public image.

The troubles of the nation's "poor little rich girls"—the Woolworth heiress, Barbara Hutton, and the tobacco heiress, Doris Duke —were regular Sunday supplement material throughout the decade, while the $11-per-week wage of Woolworth sales girls was one of the most widely circulated statistics of the depression era. Public sentiment was not aroused against the rich to the point of seriously calling for an expropriation of this wealth, except in the ambiguous terms of demagogues such as Huey Long and Father Coughlin, but public atmosphere was created which was unfavorable to the free exercise by the rich of their money. Coming-out parties for debutantes became less lavish or were dispensed with altogether, not because parents no longer could afford them, but because of the rudeness of the public reaction to them.

It was during the depression that the term "café society" became current to describe the swinging set among the wealthy of the nation. Café society was to an extent a self-conscious effort on the part of youth-oriented men and women of wealth to preserve the aristocratic principle in spite of the depression. Café society was seen by some, including Henry Luce, as a creative mixing of the aristocracy of wealth with the aristocracy of the performing arts, of the fine arts, and of the literary avant-garde. Soirees at private supper clubs in the era of repeal were more nearly abreast of the times than garden parties and cotillions.

Those who treasured aristocratic ambitions for café society were to be vindicated a generation later by the success of this concept in the jet set era. The depression was not the time for it, however, as the savage literary reaction against F. Scott Fitzgerald's writings early in the decade had demonstrated. Café society was a force for filiarchy, but it was an ineffective force. Otherwise, wealth tended to be characteristically reactionary, patriarchally revering the past and denouncing the present and disbelieving the future.

One might expect the forces of conservatism and reaction to be patriarchal in outlook, but this patriarchal outlook was at least equally typical of the forces of reform and of revolution. Within the Communist party, members were taught to revere Stalin and obey

Earl Browder and ask no questions. Socialists were led by the aging former Presbyterian minister, Norman Thomas. New Dealers were led by the squire from Hyde Park, who, with consummate artistry, created a father figure for the nation in his radio "fireside chats." Walter Reuther was an effective voice of youth in the labor movement, but organized labor spoke with its most eloquent militancy in the biblically patriarchal rumblings of John L. Lewis.

Student radicalism made its appearance on the college campuses, particularly during the Spanish Civil War and the Popular Front period that followed. Some young Americans enlisted in the Lincoln Brigade and fought in Spain, and a good many more joined the American Student Union to fight for left-wing causes. Such radicalism as this, however, was not really widespread among undergraduates. The student at Harvard who, in 1935, swallowed a live goldfish, aroused greater undergraduate excitement in the nation than any of the radical social causes could manage to muster.

....

In an effort to discover what the youth of America was thinking about during the depression, the sociologist Maxine Davis made a four-month tour of the country in her car, "talking with boys and girls every time I could." She found "that unemployment had afflicted them even more virulently than it has their seniors," and she noted that "the German situation is ever before us," as well as the Italian, where "youth is the strong right arm of Mussolini's Fascism." In America, however, "we never found revolt. We found nothing but a meek acceptance of the fate meted out to them, and a blind belief in a benign future based on nothing but wishful thinking."

While Maxine Davis feared the spread of fascism among American youth but could find no evidence of it, old-stock middle-class American parents more typically feared the spread of radical ideas or immoral ones among their children. Robert and Helen Lynd were told, on their return to Muncie, Indiana, in 1935, as they reported in *Middletown in Transition* (1937), that "parents are realizing the increasingly sharp divergence of their world and that of their children today as never before." In the face of this realization, the Lynds wrote, "the parents' world strikes back!"

According to the Lynds' previous survey in 1925, Middletown's emphasis in education had been on "the community values of group solidarity and patriotism." With continuing prosperity, this emphasis had somewhat relaxed by the end of the decade, but with the depression, there was renewed emphasis on control of the schools "in the public interest," amid a sense of "things being out of hand."

Middletown remained "heavily oriented towards the future and the next generation" in the thirties, just as it had been in the twenties; nevertheless its general outlook was decidedly less filiarchal amid depression conditions than it had been in prosperous times. Middletown parents had in many ways been distressed by the behavior of their children in the era of the flapper, but they had also, in some ways, accepted youthful ways as the ways of progress. From the parental point of view, youth in the depression was in some respects representative of the opposite of progress. Parental attitudes toward youth combined the guilty sense of failed responsibilities with a concern that the worsened conditions of life might deteriorate the character of the young people.

Sex education had been a daring cause in the twenties, and it was still taboo in most public schools during the thirties. The Lynds wrote that "the teacher knows and the community knows that the children ranged in their seats are wise in matters not in the curriculum, and that many of their children are rebelliously clamoring for the right to raise questions and to be outspoken in the face of the official and parental restraints." One teacher told them that "the things they say continually keep me on pins and needles for fear some of them will go home and tell their parents. I have an uneasy furtive sense about it all."

In spite of Parent-Teacher's Associations everywhere and the Hays Office in Hollywood, the trend in the thirties was away from the Comstockery that had persisted through the Jazz Age. Sally Rand gained renown at the Chicago World's Fair in 1933 for her nude fan dance, just as Little Egypt had with her hootchy-kootchy dance in the Chicago fair of 1893. More significantly, from the filiarchal point of view, James Joyce's *Ulysses* was upheld in court as literature and therefore not pornography; the censors had been discredited along with the prohibitionists, and theirs was to continue to be a losing fight.

Censorship, particularly of reading matter, had always been justified as a means of keeping the young in a state of innocence. Presumably the young could be excluded from shows such as Sally Rand's, which adult audiences were permitted to view. The *Ulysses* decision overrode the objection that complete censorship was necessary for the protection of children's minds.

Leading the fight against censorship during the thirties was *Esquire* which stood for the principle that sex was good clean fun and a fitting subject for sophisticated and even intellectual discourse. Except for the technological superiority of its glossy paper and bright colors and luscious skin tones, however, it was hardly more than a combination of *Smart Set* and *Police Gazette* of older times, much as *Playboy* is today. *Esquire* was a magazine for men, and as its image of "Mr. Esquire" as a jolly old roué indicated, it was the opposite of filiarchal in intent.

That America continued to idealize youth throughout the discouraging years of the depression is abundantly evident in the popularity of Shirley Temple and Charlie McCarthy and Walt Disney's productions and that technicolor classic, *The Wizard of Oz*. Filiarchy had decisively retreated, however, from the reality of Lindbergh's flight to Paris to the fantasy of Judy Garland rescuing the tin woodsman, the scarecrow, and the cowardly lion.

The first peacetime draft in American history went into effect in 1940, amid widespread concern as to whether it would be obediently accepted by American youth, many of whom had taken the Oxford Pledge never to fight in any future war. It turned out that there had been no cause for alarm. While the draft was assailed in Congress, the young men who got their draft notices reported as they were told to. Some of them were issued broomsticks instead of rifles at the beginning, and a good deal of scorn was heaped on that. They followed orders, and they were allowed to grumble about it, but their grumbling had to be good-natured. The best-selling *See Here, Private Hargrove* presented the nationally approved attitude for the draftees and the one which they characteristically took.

Taken together, they represented the Americans of the new era that had opened with the National Origins Act. Their education in Americanism had been in the direction of civics rather than history. American society in 1940 could not be inspirationally or even convincingly presented to most Americans as an evolution from the Pilgrims, no matter what the Daughters of the American Revolution wanted. Many good Americans traced their heritage back in a meaningful way only as far as 1933, when FDR had taken office. The unifying concept was the American Way, rather than any historic national tradition. In this sense America had less history in 1940 than it had had a century earlier in the days of Daniel Webster, John C. Calhoun, and Henry Clay.

It was as the world's great technological society that the American sense of national identity was most powerfully realized in 1940. There was a patriotic faith in American know-how, even at the fag end of the depression and even for the farm boy who had not known the benefits of rural electrification or for the second-generation immigrant from the cold-water flat. Lindbergh, who was an expert technologist and who had studied the German war machine, was convinced that American democracy could not match the Nazis, but in this he was putting himself in opposition to the dominant national faith. However ridiculous Private Hargrove's army might appear in the early stages of mobilization, the Americans who were drafted into it did not, by and large, suppose that when the time came for the big Blitzkrieg, anybody else was going to show America anything.

American patriotism in 1940, despite the depression, had confidence in the world of Detroit and Pittsburgh and also of Hollywood and Madison Avenue. Henry Luce's 1941 *Life* editorial "The American Century" told Americans what they believed: that American jazz, slang, movies, machines, and patented products were "in fact the only things that every community in the world, from Zanzibar to Hamburg, recognizes in common," and that the United States was "the powerhouse of the ideals of Freedom and Justice."

That was a machine-age brand of patriotism which any American could subscribe to, regardless of religion, ethnic origin, economic status, or family background; it was the standard brand of American patriotism in 1940 and a basic ingredient in G.I. morale thereafter.

....

This technological environment had been in poor working order during the thirties, but a generation later it was once again functioning brilliantly: televised, computerized, jet-sped, nuclear-powered, and nuclear-armed. The American technological environment of the fifties and sixties made society of the twenties appear antiquated, just as the steam-age America of 1900 had seemed antiquated from the retrospect of the 1920's: gas-driven, electrically operated, and "going like sixty." And American society in the 1950's and 1960's responded to its radically changing technological environment with correspondingly radical filiarchal tendencies.

Filiarchy, in the sense of the young as a ruling class, is a political phenomenon which the United States has not yet witnessed, although that certainly was an aspect of the presidential primary campaigns of Eugene McCarthy and Robert Kennedy in 1968. *Filiarchy, as it has manifested itself in twentieth-century American life, has been, to recapitulate, a cultural order arising out of the conditions of a continually developing technological environment; a society which relies on the young to acquire the new skills necessary to maintain and further re-create the environment; a society, furthermore, where social values are in a continual process of reinterpretation in relation to the changing environment and where the young, as the social product of the new environment, are superior to their elders in adaptability to the environment and in their understanding of it, and on that basis are qualified to act as authoritative exemplars of social change.*

Compared to the Old World, America has always thought of itself as a young nation, and youth in democratic America has always been accorded more freedom and more consideration than in aristocratic Europe. Nevertheless, filiarchy, has been distinctively a twentieth-century American phenomenon, and one which has represented, not simply an accentuation of former youth-oriented tendencies, but an actual reversal of authority from age and experience to youth and adaptability.

That democratic America of the Jacksonian era was far less patriarchally oriented than Regency England does not conflict with the fact that it was even further removed from the American filiarchal orientation of the 1920's or of the 1960's. Tocqueville devoted an extensive passage to the father-son relationship as he observed it in Jacksonian American society, which is worth quoting extensively:

It has been universally remarked that in our times the several members of a family stand upon an entirely new footing toward each other; that the distance which formerly separated a father from his sons has been lessened; and that paternal authority, if not destroyed, is at least impaired. Something analogous to this, but even more striking, may be observed in the United States. In America the family, in the Roman and aristocratic signification of the word, does not exist. All that remains of it are a few vestiges in the first years of childhood, when the father exercises, without opposition, that absolute domestic authority which the feebleness of his children renders necessary, and which their interest, as well as his own incontestable superiority, warrants. But as soon as the young American approaches manhood, the ties of filial obedience are relaxed day by day: master of his thoughts, he is soon master of his conduct. In America there is, strictly speaking, no adolescence: at the close of boyhood the man appears, and begins to trace out his own path. It would be an error to suppose that this is preceded by a domestic struggle, in which the son has obtained by a sort of moral violence the liberty that his father refused him. The same habits, the same principles which impel the one to assert his independence, predispose the other to consider the use of that independence as an incontestable right.

Implicit in this easy father-son relationship is the assumption that the son will learn from his father all that he is required to know in order to exercise his freedom to be his own man. He will be a chip off the old block. In 1830 that meant that he would probably take up farming, together with any business sidelines that might be profitable. By the time his own sons were growing up in the 1840's, it was quite possible that the business sidelines might be all they would need to know about.

By the turn of the twentieth century the odds were that the boy would not be raised on the farm, and if he was, the odds were that he, himself, would not go into farming. There might be a family business to go into; but, increasingly, the father would be apt to want his son to enjoy opportunities that he himself had not had: mainly to go to college and to work up from there. That son would belong to the best-educated generation of Americans in the nation's history up to that time, and every subsequent generation would literally be better educated than the previous one: a higher proportion of every subsequent generation would be college-educated than any previous one.

In this technological society of the twentieth century, children are expected to know more than their parents about the world they are living in; and they naturally do know more about it, and they naturally tend to know they do. They tend to know this, not because of being conscious of their superior education so much as because they recognize that their parents are behind the times.

Observing youth at the turn of the twentieth century, the psychologist G. Stanley Hall discovered that adolescence was the age when social attitudes were acquired which lasted a lifetime. (There would probably have been no way of discovering this in an earlier period, when social attitudes had not tended to vary perceptibly from generation to generation.) In twentieth-century America there have continued to be inner-directed persons, who have acquired their social values from their parents and from the social circumstances of their upbringings and who have retained these social values through life. There have also been comparatively other-directed persons, who have acquired their values chiefly from their childhood peers and thereafter have tended to adjust their social values to their changing social environment.

But, whether comparatively inner-directed or comparatively other-directed, twentieth-century Americans have been the products of a continually changing environment, and all remain influenced throughout their entire lives by the outmoded environment of their childhood, and particularly of their adolescence and postadolescence. The twentieth-century situation provokes conflict between generations, and in a democratic, youth-oriented society it must be a conflict in which the natural advantages weigh heavily on the side of youth.

Generation conflict is an ancient theme in history, about which both Plato and Aristotle had much to say. The phenomenon is therefore not one of the inventions of the technological society; indeed, sociologists have associated the phenomenon in the twentieth century particularly with underdeveloped regions, where the younger generations have rebelled against the old tribal ways of their elders.

Lewis Feuer's *The Conflict of Generations* concludes that generational conflict has been comparatively insignificant as an aspect of American life until the 1960's; that the normal condition in America has been that of "generational equilibrium," where youth has not found cause, as a generation, to unite against the older generation. Certain groups in American society have found cause to rebel against their parents—second-generation immigrant children, to take the most numerous category—but they have rebelled against a particular group of elders in society rather than against the older generation of society as a whole.

However, there nevertheless has been a history of generational conflict in America, which has been significant to American intellectual history, even though, until recent times, it has never enlisted a large following from any generation. The American Bohemianism, which first appeared in the 1850's, has remained a factor in American life down to the present generation of beatniks and hippies, and it has always taken the form of a revolt of youth against middle-class American culture.

Bohemianism persisted among youthful American intellectuals in the Gilded Age; and in the first two decades of the twentieth century, it formulated the ideology of radical filiarchy which remains substantially the ideology of student rebellion today. The Greenwich Village filiarchy attacked the moralism and hypocrisy of its elders; it flaunted free love; it converted itself to Marx and Freud in a freewheeling fashion, followed the latest in "pagan" dancing, upheld all radical causes, and self-consciously associated itself with the America of the non-Anglo-Saxons against the Anglo-American world of its parents. It was existential rather than programmatically ideological, and it saw the coming revolution, if at all, in terms of the coming to the fore of its own modern generation.

The Greenwich Village "liberation" was crushed during World War I; and the optimistic and eclectic radicalism of *Masses* became the more earnest and doctrinaire radicalism of *New Masses* in the era of the Jazz Age filiarchy and also of the Lost Generation. The 1930's marked the beginnings of organized student radicalism in America, as opposed to the postgraduate radicalism of Greenwich Village, but it was paternalistic rather than filiarchal in orientation. The radical college students of the depression era found no reason to suppose that they, as a generation, had anything new to offer society. Their elders had been arguing out the revolutionary issues, as between Stalinists and Trotskyites and Socialists and additional splinter groups, since the Bolshevik Revolution. As far as the depression generation was concerned, radicalism was received doctrine.

Then came World War II and the Cold War and the Korean War, extending the hiatus of American filiarchy from the opening of the depression era to the Eisenhower era of peacetime affluence. The

Eisenhower years witnessed filiarchal manifestations reminiscent of the 1920's, and the Kennedy and Johnson years, amid civil rights and Vietnam, witnessed "student involvement" and "paticipatory democracy," far in excess of the original Greenwich Village liberation but in a filiarchal pattern which is reminiscent of that earlier movement.

Evidently filiarchy is a natural condition of life in a democratic technological society; and paternalism, which has not ceased to be a condition of life despite an uncongenial environment for it, must continually make terms with filiarchy. It is futile to hope for a time when youth will once again accept its time-honored filial status in society, unless one is willing to make a devil's bargain for it either by abandoning democratic principles or by frankly counting on steady assistance against filiarchy from war or depression or other of the ancient horsemen of calamity.

Bibliographical
Acknowledgments

Bibliographical
Acknowledgments

··

It is not my intention to attempt to provide a general bibliography for
the subject of American civilization in the first machine age. Many
studies are omitted from these listings that would surely be included in
such a bibliography. The following are the particular writings from which
I have borrowed quotations and from which I am conscious of having
borrowed information and ideas in one way or another.

Part I
An Overview: Technology, Immigration,
and the American Character

THIS OVERVIEW IS BASED GENERALLY on sources that are
cited in the bibliographical listings for Chapters 1 through 9, and I will
repeat here only those which are specifically discussed or quoted or
otherwise drawn upon.

Michael McGiffert, ed., *The Character of Americans: A Book of Readings* (1964) is a collection of essays and selected passages, including the quoted statement by Lord Bryce and the essay by Seymour Martin Lipset, "A Changing American Character?" that is discussed and quoted in the overview. The Henry Adams quotation is from the famous introductory chapters to his *History of the United States*, 9 vols. (1889–91). Alton Ketchum, *Uncle Sam: The Man and the Legend* (1959) is a well-illustrated history. Kenneth S. Davis, *The Hero: Charles A. Lindbergh and the American Dream* (1959) is a brilliant biographical study.

The English translation of Philip Aries' study is *Centuries of Childhood: A Social History of Family Life* (1962). Bernard Bailyn, *Education in the Forming of American Society* (1960) is the source for the excerpts from the Massachusetts school laws as well as for the statement by Bailyn. Edmund Morgan is quoted from *The Puritan Family* (1944). The main authority for my discussion of the eighteenth-century American gentleman's view of progress is Stow Persons, "The Cyclical Theory of History in Eighteenth-Century America," *American Quarterly* (Summer 1954). The assertions of O'Sullivan, Paulding, and Wayland regarding progress are all from Russel B. Nye, *The Almost Chosen People* (1966).

Max Eastman's attitude toward Dewey is described in his autobiographical *Enjoyment of Living* (1945), and Hutchins Hapgood's attitude toward James appears in Hapgood's autobiographical *A Victorian in the Modern World* (1939). Lewis S. Feuer, *The Conflict of Generations* (1969) is an extensive and well-documented world history of the subject from the nineteenth century to the present. Floyd Dell is quoted from his autobiography, *Homecoming* (1933). The statement from *Fortune* magazine about college youth in the depression was quoted in Frederick Lewis Allen, *Since Yesterday* (1940). Ruth Miller Elson is quoted from *Guardians of Tradition: American Schoolbooks of the Nineteenth Century* (1964).

John Higham, *Strangers in the Land: Patterns of American Nativism* (rev. ed., 1963) is a political, social, and intellectual history of the subject down to the immigration restriction legislation of the 1920's. Nothing of a comparable scope and objectivity is available for the period from 1924 to the present, that I am aware of. Nathan Glazer and Daniel P. Moynihan, *Beyond the Melting Pot* (1963), a history of the main ethnic groups in New York City in modern times, exemplifies an approach to the history of American ethnocracy which is more productive of an understanding of the American character than have been the traditional approaches of immigration historians.

Theodore White, *The Making of a President, 1960* (1961) is the out-standing journalistic account of the election of 1960. Irwin Unger, "The 'New Left' and American History: Some Recent Trends in United States Historiography," *American Historical Review* (July 1967) is a thoughtful account of that development.

The Jefferson quotation is from his *Notes on Virginia* edited by William Peden (1954). The Frederick Jackson Turner quotations are from his essay "The Significance of the Frontier in American History." The Crèvecoeur statement on the "New American" is quoted from his *Letters from an American Farmer* (1782).

Chapter 1
The Protestant Republic

THE CARDINAL STATEMENTS on agrarian virtue are to be found in Hector St. John de Crèvecoeur, *Letters from an American Farmer* (1782); Thomas Jefferson, *Notes on Virginia,* ed. William Peden (1954); and William Jennings Bryan's "cross of gold" speech before the 1896 Democratic national convention. The Emerson statement is from his *Society and Solitude* (1870). Paul Glad, *The Trumpet Soundeth: William Jennings Bryan and His Democracy* (1960) analyzes the rural-evangelical orientation of Bryan's social thought. Henry Nash Smith, *Virgin Land* (1950) and Richard Hofstadter, *The Age of Reform* (1955) examine what they term the agrarian "myth," by which they mean the values Americans have historically attached to rural life and the frontier experience. Hofstadter's unsympathetic treatment of this subject in relation to the Populist movement was followed by a good deal of scholarly rebuttal. This controversy has been summarized in a bibliographical essay in Walter T. K. Nugent, *The Tolerant Populists: Kansas Populism and Nativism* (1963).

The University of Missouri catalog (1871) statement was pointed out to me a number of years ago by Katherine Gingrich, a student at Missouri. Paul H. Johnston, "Old Ideals Versus New Ideas in Farm Life," *U.S. Department of Agriculture Yearbook* (1940) demonstrates the relatively unimportant role played by farmers, as opposed to lawyers and businessmen, in rural political life. Booster and joiner attitudes in nineteenth-century American society are extensively discussed in Daniel Boorstin, *The Americans: The National Experience* (1965), as are the development of myths and symbols to explain the American Republic. Dixon Wecter, *Hero in America* (1941) discusses this myth-making process in relation to individual leading heroes. Stefan Lorant, *The Presi-*

dency: A Pictorial History of Presidential Elections from Washington to Truman (1951) illustrates the kinds of attempts made to present presidential candidates as images of American ideals. Alton Ketchum, *Uncle Sam: The Man and the Legend* (1959) is an illustrated history of the subject.

Lewis Atherton, *Main Street on the Middle Border* (1954) and Wilbert L. Anderson, *The Country Town: A Study of Rural Evolution* (1906) were the studies of small town society upon which I drew most heavily. Also useful were Ima Honaker Herron, *The Small Town in American Literature* (1939); James A. Williams, *An American Town* (1906); and Newell L. Sims, *A Hoosier Village* (1912). Informative personal reminiscences of childhood in small towns are included in Herbert Asbury, *Up from Methodism* (1926); Herbert Quick, *One Man's Life* (1925); O. J. Laylander, *The Chronicle of a Contented Man* (1928); and William Allen White, *Autobiography* (1946). Page Smith, *As a City Upon a Hill* (1967) contains a chapter titled "The Ideology of the Town."

Arthur W. Calhoun, *A Social History of the American Family,* 3 vols. (1919) contains much unevaluated information on the subject. Oscar Handlin, *Race and Nationality in American Life* (1948) discusses nineteenth-century sex attitudes; Barbara Welter, "The Cult of True Womanhood, 1820–1860," in *American Quarterly,* Vol. 43 (Summer, 1966) describes the image of woman as the divinely created custodian of virtue. The relevant quotations I have used are all from one or another of these two accounts. Andrew Sinclair, *The Better Half: The Emancipation of the American Woman* (1965) and Eric John Dingwall, *The American Woman: An Historical Study* (1956) are cocksure Freudian analyses by English writers which include a good deal of interesting information. August F. Fehlandt, *A Century of Drink Reform in the United States* (1904) contains perhaps as good an account as there is of the Woman's Crusade. Mary Earhart, *Frances Willard* (1944) is a scholarly biography and a good account of the early history of the WCTU. Eleanor Flexner, *Century of Struggle: The Woman's Rights Movement in the United States* (1959) is a scholarly history of the suffrage fight; and Alice Felt Tyler, *Freedom's Ferment: Phases of American Social History to 1860* (1944) is particularly good on reforms relating to the status of women. The quotation from the New York *Evening Post* and that by Josiah Strong are from Anderson, *Country Town.*

Lawrence A. Cremin, *The American Common School: An Historical Conception* (1951) traces the development of that conception to the mid-nineteenth century. David D. Van Tassel, *Recording America's Past: An Interpretation of the Development of Historical Studies in America, 1607–*

1884 (1960), and Richard D. Mosier, *Making the American Mind: Social and Moral Ideas in the McGuffey Readers* (1947) indicate the kind of indoctrination to which school children were exposed. Mark Sullivan, *Our Times, The United States, 1900–1925,* 9 vols (1926–35) contains an extensive discussion of the McGuffey Readers, as does Atherton, *Main Street,* from which I obtained the bit of verse concerning the little child who learns to pray.

Sidney E. Mead, *The Lively Experiment: The Shaping of Christianity in America* (1963) is a thoroughly convincing interpretive essay. Winthrop S. Hudson, *Religion in America* (1965) is an ample textbook on the subject; Hudson, *American Protestantism* (1961) is a brief historical survey with an informative bibliographical discussion. T. Scott Miyakawa, *Protestants and Pioneers: Individualism and Conformity on the American Frontier* (1964) does a good job of distinguishing the sects individually; and Timothy L. Smith, *Revivalism and Social Reform in Mid-nineteenth Century America* (1957) contains a clear discussion of the doctrinal differences of the leading denominations and a good brief bibliographical statement on related studies.

William G. McLoughlin, Jr., *Modern Revivalism, Charles Grandison Finney to Billy Graham* (1959) and J. C. Pollock, *Moody: A Biographical Portrait of the Pacesetter in Modern Mass Evangelism* (1963) analyze urban revivalism. Aaron I. Abell, *The Urban Impact on American Protestantism, 1865–1915* (1943); Henry F. May, *Protestant Churches and Industrial America* (1949); and Robert Cross, *The Emergence of Liberal Catholicism in America* (1958) examine church doctrines on social and economic matters. Charles H. Hopkins, *The Rise of the Social Gospel in American Protestantism, 1865–1915* (1940) is comprehensive and detailed. Barbara M. Cross, *Horace Bushnell* (1958) analyzes Bushnell's ideas and their influence. C. H. Cramer, *Royal Bob: The Life of Robert G. Ingersoll* (1952) and Paxton Hibben, *Henry Ward Beecher* (1927) are scholarly biographies.

Charles N. Glaab, ed., *The American City: A Documentary History* (1963) provides a survey of the history of American urbanization; Blake McKelvey, *The Urbanization of America, 1860–1915* (1963) is a substantial social study. American attitudes toward the city are examined in Anselm L. Strauss, *Images of the American City* (1962); Morton White and Lucia White, *The Intellectual Versus the City: From Thomas Jefferson to Frank Lloyd Wright* (1962); and Bessie L. Pierce, ed., *As Others See Chicago* (1933).

Scholarly studies of low life in late nineteenth-century America are lacking, but Herbert Asbury has compiled a great deal of information on the subject, without attempting to evaluate it in a scholarly way, in *The Barbary Coast* (1933), *The French Quarter* (1936), *The Gangs of New York* (1928), and *Gem of the Prairie: An Informal History of the Chicago Underworld* (1940). Informative contemporary accounts include Charles Loring Brace, *The Dangerous Classes of New York* (1872); Charles H. Parkhurst, *Our Fight with Tammany* (1895); and W. T. Stead, *If Christ Came to Chicago!* (1894). Willoughby C. Waterman, *Prostitution and Its Repression in New York City, 1900–1931* (1932) is a reliable study of a treacherously difficult subject. Allan Nevins, *The Emergence of Modern America, 1865–1878* (1927) and Arthur M. Schlesinger, *The Rise of the City, 1878–1893* (1933) contain informative chapters on urban social life. Jacob A. Riis, *How the Other Half Lives* (1890) is a brief lively repository of information. Robert C. Chapin, *The Standard of Living Among Workingmen's Families in New York City* (1909) and Frank H. Streightoff, *The Standard of Living Among the Industrial People of America* (1911) are graphic depictions of working-class life. John Koren, *Economic Aspects of the Liquor Problem* (1899) and Raymond Calkins, *Substitutes for the Saloon* (1919) are outstandingly good investigations of the saloon situation; Jack London, *John Barleycorn* (1913) is a vivid autobiographical portrayal of saloon society. The quotation from the Chicago *Tribune* and Masefield's statement are from Asbury's *Gem of the Prairie* and *Barbary Coast*.

Thomas Beer, *The Mauve Decade* (1926) is a witty evocation of polite society in the American nineties; Henry Seidel Canby, *The Age of Confidence* (1934) is an informative reminiscence of the period. Architecture and household furnishings are related to social change in Wayne Andrews, *Architecture, Ambition and Americans* (1955); Lewis Mumford, *The Brown Decades: A Study of the Arts in America, 1865–1895* (1931); John Kowenhoven, *Made in America: The Arts in Modern Civilization* (1948); and Siegfried Giedion, *Mechanization Takes Command* (1943). Among the studies of high society, Dixon Wecter, *The Saga of American Society, A Record of Social Aspiration, 1607–1937* (1937) is the most scholarly. E. L. Godkin, *Reflections and Comments, 1865–1895* (1895) contains comments on the current scene by an acknowledged arbiter on cultural matters. *The Woman's Book,* 3 vols. (1894) is a comprehensive and detailed account of upper-class canons of good taste. Arthur M. Schlesinger, *Learning How to Behave: A Historical Study of American Etiquette Books* (1947) is a brief survey. Mrs. Burton Harrison, *The Well-Bred Girl in Society* (1904) was considered a leading authority. The quotations from *Rag-Bag* and from Mrs. John Sherwood's etiquette books are in Dixon Wecter, *Saga of American Society* (1937). Frederick Lewis

Allen, *The Big Change* (1952) is a history of social change in America during the first half of the twentieth century, and it is the source for the statement by the New York gentleman. Andy Logan, *The Man Who Robbed the Robber Barons* (1965) is a biography of William D'Alton Mann and the source of the statement by Emily Post's son concerning *Town Topics*. The Ella Wheeler Wilcox quotations are from her *Poems of Passion* (1884); those by Eleanor Roosevelt from her *This I Remember* (1949).

Bernard W. Wishy, *The Child and the Republic* (1967) is a history of changing parental attitudes toward childhood from the postrevolutionary era to the early twentieth century. For colonial New England, Edmund Morgan, *The Puritan Family* (1944), together with Bernard Bailyn's *Education in the Forming of American Society* (1960), are significant studies; Philip Aries' *Childhood through the Centuries* (1962) is fundamental to an understanding of the subject, and Morgan's study indicates how thoroughly relevant Aries' thesis is to American circumstances.

Theodore Roosevelt's *Autobiography* (1913) is among those which tell a good deal about upper-class childhood in the late nineteenth century. Lawrence A. Cremin, *The Transformation of the School: Progressivism in American Education, 1876–1957* (1961) is a scholarly account that traces changes in upper-middle-class and intellectual attitudes toward childhood and child training. International Kindergarten Union, *Pioneers of the Kindergarten in America* (1924) summarizes the early history of the movement. Sally Gregory, a graduate student at Michigan State University, brought Emerson's statement concerning changing attitudes toward youth to my attention. R. E. Baber and E. A. Ross, *Changes in the Size of American Families* (1924) provides the statistics relating to the decline in the size of middle-class families.

Chapter 2
Paths of Righteousness

MY IDEAS CONCERNING AMERICAN attitudes toward political parties before the Civil War and my sources for these ideas appear in Ostrander, *The Rights of Man in America* (1960). Among the considerable number of studies relating to this subject which have appeared during the past decade, Shaw Livermore, *The Twilight of Federalism* (1962) is especially relevant to party attitudes of upper-middle-class Americans in the age of Jeffersonian Republicanism. Thomas H. O'Connor, *Lords of the Loom: The Cotton Whigs and the Coming of the Civil War* (1968) describes the attitudes of Boston businessmen to the rising

Republican party; Kenneth Stampp, *And the War Came* (1950) gives an idea of the complexity of northern business attitudes as a whole toward the South and secession.

David Donald, *Lincoln Reconsidered* (1959) is the source for the quotation of Lincoln on his own party regularity. John Sproat, *"The Best Men"; Liberal Reformers in the Gilded Age* (1969) gives a full account of the party attitudes of the Liberal Republicans. The main source for my discussion of political thought and practice in the Gilded Age has been Matthew Josephson, *The Politicos* (1938), from which the quotations of Wharton and Hearst are taken. I am aware of recent studies which have taken issue with Josephson's interpretation, but my own research for Ostrander, *Nevada, the Great Rotten Borough, 1859–1964* (1966) served to confirm for me Josephson's conclusions.

Irvin Wyllie, *The Self-Made Man in America* (1954) is the source for the quotations of Daniel Drew and of Theodore Roosevelt. Bishop Lawrence's statement occurs in his essay, "The Relation of Wealth to Morals," which appears in Gerald Grob and Robert Beck, eds., *American Ideas* (1963). The building of the Metropolitan Opera to outdo the exclusive Academy of Music is told in Dixon Wecter, *The Saga of American Society, A Record of Social Aspiration, 1607–1937* (1937).

Despite, or perhaps because of, the renewed interest in populism in American political thought, Solon J. Buck, *The Agrarian Crusade* (1920) and John D. Hicks, *The Populist Revolt* (1931) remain the most authoritative accounts. Norman Pollack, *The Populist Response to Industrial America* (1962) is a brief recent account which largely represents a return toward the older view. The main source for my discussion of Moody and late nineteenth-century evangelism is William McLoughlin, Jr., *Modern Revivalism* (1959), together with J. C. Pollock, *Moody* (1963). The Beecher statement regarding the great underclasses is taken from Sidney E. Mead, *The Lively Experiment: The Shaping of Christianity in America* (1963).

Robert Shaplen, *Free Love and Heavenly Sinners* (1954) is the account of the Beecher-Tilton affair which I have chiefly relied on; my discussion of Comstock is based on Heywood Broun and Margaret Leech, *Anthony Comstock: Roundsman of the Lord* (1927). James C. N. Paul and Murray L. Schwartz, *Federal Censorship, Obscenity in the Mail* (1961) and Morris L. Ernst and Alan U. Schwartz, *The Search for the Obscene* (1964) are clear factual accounts. Emanie Sachs, *The Terrible Siren: Victoria Woodhull, 1838–1927* (1928) is a biography based upon diligent interviewing of former neighbors and acquaintances as well as upon the available written evidence.

M. R. Werner, *It Happened in New York* (1957) is a detailed history of Parkhurst's antivice crusade, which, like Shaplan's history of the Beecher-Tilton episode and Andy Logan's *Man Who Robbed the Robber Barons* (1965) began as a series of articles in *The New Yorker*. Civic reform in Los Angeles is chronicled in George Baker Anderson, "What the Cranks Have Done," *Pacific Outlook*, May 18 and May 25, 1907, and in Dana Bartlett, *The Better City* (1907). A brief history of the Civic Federation of Chicago is given in Daniel Levine, *Varieties of Reform Thought* (1964).

J. C. Furnas, *The Life and Times of the Late Demon Rum* (1965); Andrew Sinclair, *Prohibition: The Era of Excess* (1962); and Herbert Asbury, *The Great Illusion: An Informal History of Prohibition* (1950) are conscientiously researched popular histories, of which Sinclair's is the most scholarly and Furnas' the most complete account. John Allen Krout, *The Origins of Prohibition* (1925) is authoritative for the pre-Civil War temperance movement, as is Peter H. Odegard, *Pressure Politics: The Story of the Anti-Saloon League* (1928) for that subject. I have drawn on my own study, *The Prohibition Movement in California: 1848–1933* (1957), and my main conclusions here are those which I arrived at in preparing that study. James H. Timberlake, *Prohibition and the Progressive Movement; 1900–1920* (1963) emphasizes the close relationship of the two movements. The statements by Russell were taken from Odegard, *Pressure Politics;* that by Gerrit Smith from Furnas' history; and those by A. C. Bane and the social-drinking Anti-Saloon League supporter (the editor Chester Rowell) from my study of California.

Robert H. Bremner, *From the Depths: The Discovery of Poverty in the United States* (1956), which I have relied on heavily, is a history of American philanthropy and, more than that, an intellectual history of changing national conceptions related to the subject. Amos Warner, *American Charities: A Study in Philanthropy and Economics* (1894) discusses the new tendencies of the time. The list of causes of poverty prepared by the New York Society for the Prevention of Pauperism is from John Bach McMaster, *History of the People of the United States from the Revolution to the Civil War*, 8 vols. (1883–1913). The quotations of Hartley, Du Bois and Dill, Weyl, and the Russell Sage Foundation monograph are from Bremner, *From the Depths*. For civic reform efforts of the time, I have consulted Frank M. Stewart, *A Half-century of Municipal Reform* (1950); Charles Zueblen, *American Municipal Progress* (1903); and Blake McKelvy, *The Urbanization of America, 1860–1915* (1963).

Harold U. Faulkner, *The Quest for Social Justice* (1931) remains the most complete available survey of Progressivism as a moral reform movement. George E. Mowry, *The Era of Theodore Roosevelt, 1900–1912* (1958) and Arthur S. Link, *Woodrow Wilson and the Progressive Era, 1910–1917* (1954) are primarily political histories that synthesize recent scholarship and then describe it in fairly detailed bibliographical discussions. Mark Sullivan, *Our Times, The United States, 1900–1925*, 6 vols. (1926–1935) is incomparable as a voluminous social and political record of the times from the contemporary point of view. It is a history of the American people in the manner of John Bach McMaster's history for the pre-Civil War period. It contains the best analysis of the significance of Theodore Roosevelt to American political life that I have read.

Among other writings on TR, I have made use of the somewhat denigrating Henry F. Pringle, *Theodore Roosevelt: A Biography* (1931) and the debunking essay by Richard Hofstadter in *The American Political Tradition and the Men Who Made It* (1949), as well as the warmly admiring William H. Harbaugh, *Power and Responsibility* (1958) and the laudatory John Morton Blum, *The Republican Roosevelt* (1962). John A. Garraty, *Henry Cabot Lodge: A Biography* (1953) is a sympathetic account. Margaret Leech, *In the Days of McKinley* (1959) re-creates the political climate at the close of the century and is successful to an extent in improving McKinley's reputation in history.

Biographical accounts of La Follette tend to be uncritically favorable; but Russel B. Nye, *Midwestern Progressive Politics* (1951) is a thorough, scholarly examination of the brand of Progressivism associated with La Follette. Walter Johnson, *William Allen White's America* (1947) and George E. Mowry, *The California Progressives* (1951) reveal the Progressive temper well and also indicate the character of the remarkable impact of Roosevelt's personality upon the atmosphere of local and state politics.

Paul Glad, *The Trumpet Soundeth: William Jennings Bryan and His Democracy* (1960) is a sympathetic analysis; and Paxton Hibben, *The Peerless Leader* (1929) is a sympathetic biography. The essay by Hofstadter in *The American Political Tradition*, from which I have taken the Bryan quotation, is hostile. George R. Poage, "The College Career of William Jennings Bryan," in *Mississippi Valley Historical Review*, Vol. 15 (September 1928), provides a basis for comparison with Wilson and his education. Ray Stannard Baker, *Woodrow Wilson, Life and Letters*, 8 vols. (1927–39) is authorized but intelligently critical. John Morton Blum, *Woodrow Wilson and the Politics of Morality* (1956) is a debunking study of Wilson which emphasizes Wilson's moralism without, however, placing it sufficiently in the moralistic context of the times. Particularly good accounts of this moralistic climate by those who had breathed it are William Allen White, *Autobiography* (1946); Brand Whitlock, *Forty Years of It* (1914); and Frederic C. Howe, *The Confessions of a Reformer* (1925). The Wilson quotation on Americans and morality is taken from Blum, *Woodrow Wilson*.

Chapter 3
The Evolutionary Outlook

GEORGE TEMPLETON STRONG'S COMMENT on Darwin's *Origins*, which appears in Strong's *Diary*, 4 vols. (1952), was pointed out to me by Douglas T. Miller. Bernard I. Cohen, "Science in America: The Nineteenth Century," in A. M. Schlesinger, Jr., and Morton White, eds., *Paths of American Thought* (1963), is an authoritative summary of the best writing on the subject. Bernard Jaffe, *Men of Science in America* (rev. ed., 1958) remains the best general history of American science. It is written for nonscientists and is biographically presented, and it has been my main source of reliance. A. Hunter Dupree, *Asa Gray* (1959) and Edward Lurie, *Louis Agassiz* (1960) examine the controversy over evolution among scientists. As a religious matter the controversy is discussed in Stow Persons, "Evolution and Theology in America" in Persons, ed., *Evolutionary Thought in America* (1950) and in Edward A. White, *Science and Religion in American Thought: The Impact of Naturalism* (1952). Milton Berman, *John Fiske: The Evolution of a Popularizer* (1961) demonstrates the influence of Herbert Spencer on American thought, as does the opening chapter of Richard Hofstadter, *Social Darwinism in American Thought* (1944). The quotations from Lowell and Silliman are from Jaffe, *Men of Science;* the Reid quotation is from Hofstadter, *Social Darwinism*. The Mather quotation is from his *The Christian Philosopher: A Collection of the Best Discoveries in Nature, with Religious Improvements* (1721).

Stow Persons presents a concise analysis of "Protestant Scholasticism" in America in his *American Minds: A History of Ideas* (1958), a subject that is examined in Herbert Schneider, *History of American Philosophy* (1946) and in other similar surveys. William F. Quillian, Jr., "Evolution and Moral Theory in America," in Persons, ed., *Evolutionary Thought* is a clear summary and the source of the relevant quotations of Darwin, Spencer, and Llano. Philip Wiener, *Evolution and Pragmatism* examines fully the Harvard origins of pragmatism and attaches major importance to the writings and discussions of Chauncy Wright and Charles S. Peirce. The quotations of Dewey and James are from Quillian, "Evolution and Moral Theory," in Persons, ed., *Evolutionary Thought*.

Among the many available histories of psychology, I have found particularly helpful J. C. Flugel and Donald J. West, *A Hundred Years of Psychology: 1833–1933* (1933) and Edna Heidbreder, *Seven Psychologies* (1933). Edwin G. Boring, "The Influence of Evolutionary Theory Upon American Psychological Thought" in Persons, ed., *Evolutionary Thought* is a valuable summary. D. E. Broadbent, *Behavior* (1961) examines the origins of behaviorism judiciously. C. P. Oberndorf, *A History of Psychoanalysis in America* (1953) is an informal medical history; Oscar Cargill, *Intellectual America* (1959) includes an extensive and imaginative discussion of the influence of Freudianism and variants of it on American culture, a subject also covered in Frederick J. Hoffman, *Freudianism and the Literary Mind* (1957). Sigmund Freud, *Autobiography* (1935) and Freud, *On the History of the Psycho-analytic Movement*, James Strachey, ed., (1966) contain Freud's comments on the Clark University ceremonies. The introduction to A. A. Brill, ed., *The Basic Writings of Sigmund Freud* (1938) gives an account of the introduction of Freudianism to America. The quotations from Freud on psychoanalysis are from his *Introductory Lectures on Psycho-analysis* (rev. ed., 1929). Lorine Pruette, *G. Stanley Hall: A Biography of the Mind* (1926) is a helpful supplement to Hall's autobiography. G. Stanley Hall, *Life and Confessions of a Psychologist* (1924) is a very substantial autobiography that is full of information on the introduction of Freudianism to America. This is true of a number of autobiographical writings of people who took up Freudianism, including Floyd Dell, *Homecoming* (1933) and Hutchins Hapgood, *A Victorian in the Modern World* (1939), which are quoted here on the subject.

John Higham, with Leonard Krieger and Felix Gilbert, *History: The Development of Historical Studies in the United States* (1965) is an outstanding intellectual history. Henry Adams is quoted from *The Education of Henry Adams* (1906). The Midwestern political and cultural temper at the close of the nineteenth century is described in Russel Nye, *Midwestern Progressive Politics* (1951) and, with emphasis upon Chicago and Illinois, by Ray Ginger, *Altgeld's America* (1958). The most recent roundup of literature dealing with the Turner thesis is contained in Ray Allen Billington, *The Frontier Thesis: Valid Interpretation of American History* (1966). A more extensive discussion is Gene M. Gressley, "The Turner Thesis—A Problem in Historiography," *Agricultural History*, Vol. 32 (1958). My view of the Turner thesis as a variant of the germ theory is presented in Ostrander, "Turner and the Germ Theory," *Agricultural History*, Vol. 32 (1958). For the discussion of Charles Beard, I have drawn particularly upon Cushing Strout, *The Pragmatic Revolt in History: Carl Becker and Charles Beard* (1958); Robert E. Brown, *Charles*

Beard and the Constitution (1956); and Eric F. Goldman, *Rendezvous with Destiny: A History of Modern American Reform* (1956). Stanley Elkins and Eric McKitrick, "The Founding Fathers: Young Men of the Revolution," Service Center for Teachers of History (1962), explains the appeal on non-Marxist grounds that Beard's argument had for Progressive reformers.

Frederick Rudolph, *The American College and University: A History* (1962) is a scholarly survey of higher education which treats the subject broadly in the context of the national culture, as does Laurence R. Veysey, *The Emergence of the American University* (1965) in his more detailed study of graduate education. R. Freeman Butts, *The College Charts Its Course* (1939) examines the controversies surrounding the curricular changes. Richard Hofstadter and Walter P. Metzger, *The Development of Academic Freedom in the United States* (1955) traces changes in national objectives for higher education; and Hofstadter and Wilson Smith, eds., *American Higher Education: A Documentary History*, 2 vols. (1961) is a full presentation of the arguments of the leading figures. Among the many histories of individual colleges, I have made particular use of Hugh Hawkins, *Pioneer: A History of the Johns Hopkins University, 1874–1889* (1960) and of Merle Curti and Vernon Carstensen, *The University of Wisconsin, 1848–1925*, 2 vols. (1949).

Luther Lee Bernard and J. Bernard, *Origins of American Sociology: The Social Science Movement in the United States* (1943) and Paul Buck, *Social Science at Harvard, 1860–1920* (1965) trace the development of disciplines; Howard W. Odum, ed., *American Masters of Social Science* (1927) discusses the development in terms of individual scholars. The impact of Franz Boas on American anthropology is emphasized in Melville Herskovitz, *Franz Boas: The Science of Man in the Making* (1953).

The main basis for my discussion of the origins of progressive education is Lawrence A. Cremin, *The Transformation of the School* (1961). Merle Curti's *Social Ideas of American Educators* (1935) is a series of biographical studies of leading educators, of whom John Dewey is by far Curti's favorite.

Aside from histories of individual women's colleges, I do not know of a good social and intellectual history of higher education for women. The subject is dealt with in Rudolph, *American College* and Ernest Earnest, *Academic Procession: An Informal History of the American College, 1636–1953* (1953) as well as in histories of women's rights, for instance, Eleanor Flexner, *Century of Struggle* (1959) and Aileen S. Kraditor, *The Ideas of the Woman Suffrage Movement, 1890–1920* (1965). Mark Sullivan, *Our Times, The United States, 1900–1925,* 9 vols. (1926–1935), is extremely good in describing the impact of college life on America in the pre-World War I period.

Chapter 4
American Bohemianism

ALBERT PARRY, *Garrets and Pretenders: A History of Bohemianism in America* (1933) is the pioneer history of this subject and the one upon which I have chiefly relied. Emily Hahn, *Romantic Rebels: An Informal History of Bohemianism in America* (1967) covers the same ground on the basis of Parry's book, as well as the considerable literature relating to the subject which appeared since Parry wrote his account. Allen Churchill, *The Improper Bohemians* (1959) concentrates on Greenwich Village. Henri Murger's *Scènes de la Vie de Bohème* was published in English as *The Latin Quarter* (1901).

William Bittner, *Poe: A Biography* (1962) is extremely good at unraveling the controversies surrounding Poe's reputation; Charles B. Willard, *Whitman's American Fame* (1950) gives a detailed history of the rise in Whitman's reputation. Perry Miller, *The Raven and the Whale* (1956) examines the journalistic-literary world of New York City in the times of Poe and Melville. Edmund Wilson, ed., *The Shock of Recognition: The Development of Literature in the United States Recorded by the Men Who Made It* (1943) includes the Whitman-Emerson correspondence and related writings about Poe by Lowell and others and also literary essays by Poe, including the famous one on Longfellow. Whitman's comments on Poe are also included in it.

The account of the Pfaffians is taken mainly from Parry's *Garrets and Pretenders,* but also from Van Wyck Brooks, *The Times of Melville and Whitman* (1947); Malcolm Easton, *Artists and Writers in Paris: The Bohemian Idea* (1964); Bernard Falk, *The Naked Lady* (1934), which is a biography of Adah Menken; and Vernon Loggins, *Where the Word Ends: The Life of Louis Moreau Gottschalk* (1958). Franklin Walker, *San Francisco's Literary Frontier* (1939) is an extensive history upon which I have chiefly relied. Ada Clare's letter to Gottschalk is from Loggins' biography, which has a good deal of information on her career. Ada Clare's definition of the Bohemian, together with the quotations of Howells, Winter, Burroughs, Sedman, Whitman on Clapp, and Lowell's letter to Aldrich—all were taken from Parry's book.

Thomas Beer, *The Mauve Decade* (1926) is an essay on American culture in the 1890's which discusses the Trilby craze. Hutchins Hapgood, *A Victorian in the Modern World* (1939) contains an informed account of the rise of the New Woman in that decade. Arnold T. Schwab, *James Gibbons Huneker* (1963) is an excellent biography and the best thing there is on Bohemianism in the nineties. It is the source for all of the quotations I have used by or about Huneker. Van Wyck Brooks, *The Confident Years,* 1885–1915 (1952) captures something of the stuffy respectability of the period, as do many of the writings of W. D. Howells, notably his *My Mark Twain* (1910). Andy Logan, *The Man Who Robbed the Robber Barons* (1965) is a biography of William D'Alton Mann.

Henry F. May, *The End of American Innocence: A Study of the First Years of Our Time, 1912–1917* (1959) is an intellectual history of the pre-World War I Greenwich Village movement, as is, for the most part, Christopher Lasch, *The New Radicalism in America* (1965), which approaches the problem biographically. Alson J. Smith, *Chicago's Left Bank* (1953) is a history of Chicago Bohemianism. Caroline Ware, *Greenwich Village, 1920–1930* (1931) is a sociological study which analyzes the cultures of all of the ethnic groups in the area, including the Anglo-Saxon Bohemians. Eleanor Flexner, *Century of Struggle: The Woman's Rights Movement in America* (1959) is a scholarly institutional study of the suffrage crusade. Richard Drinnon, *A Rebel in Paradise: A Biography of Emma Goldman* (1961) is a scholarly, sympathetic biography. Frederick Hoffman, with Charles Allen and Carolyn F. Ulrich, *The Little Magazine* (1947) catalogs these ventures from *Chap-Book* on.

Good autobiographies abound, relating to the prewar Greenwich Village era. Those which I have chiefly relied on are Max Eastman, *Enjoyment of Living* (1945); Floyd Dell, *Homecoming* (1933); Mabel Dodge Luhan, *Movers and Shakers* (1936); Margaret Anderson: *My Thirty Years' War* (1930); Isadora Duncan, *My Life* (1927); Lawrence Langner, *The Magic Curtain* (1951); and Hutchins Hapgood, *A Victorian in the Modern World* (1939). The quotation concerning *Chap-Book* is from Parry's book; Crystal Eastman is quoted in Max Eastman, *Enjoyment of Living;* Ina Coobrith is quoted in Walker, *San Francisco Literary Frontier;* and Ben Hecht's comments are from his autobiographical account, *A Child of the Century* (1954).

Chapter 5
The Mechanization of American Society

HUGO A. MEIER, "TECHNOLOGY AND DEMOCRACY, 1800–1860," *Mississippi Valley Historial Review,* Vol. 43 (1957) is a good historical summary. John W. Oliver, *History of American Technology* (1956) is a general survey; Roger Burlingame, *Engines of Democracy*

(1940) is an attempt to relate technology to democracy and to the creation of a unified national culture. Victor S. Clark, *History of Manufactures in the United States*, 3 vols. (1929) contains much information on technological changes. More significant than these studies as an analysis of the impact of technology on American culture is Siegfried Giedion, *Mechanization Takes Command* (1948), a detailed examination of the evolution of American parlors and kitchens and meat-packing plants and so on over the past century and more, accompanied by many illustrations and photographs. Giedion's book is the most important historical study I have seen of an important subject, technological determinism in America, with which American historians have not yet chosen to concern themselves. John A. Kouwenhoven has contributed a number of interesting essays on this subject in *Made in America: The Arts in Modern Civilization* (1948) and *The Beer Can by the Highway* (1961).

Leo Marx, *The Machine in the Garden* (1964) discusses the impact of the industrial revolution on American thought from Jefferson to Emerson, Whitman, Hawthorne, and Melville. My discussion, including the relevant quotations, is drawn primarily from Marx's book. Merrill Peterson, *The Jeffersonian Image in the American Mind* (1960) examines Jeffersonian agrarianism and its influence thoroughly. Russel B. Nye, *The Almost Chosen People* (1966) and Arthur Ekirch, *The Idea of Progress in America, 1815–1860* (1951) are studies which demonstrate America's utter confidence in progress and its unquestioning acceptance of machinery as a means to progress.

For the early period of the industrial revolution in America, I have found useful Dirk J. Struik, *Yankee Science in the Making* (1948); Constance McL. Green, *Eli Whitney and the Birth of American Technology* (1956); and, particularly, George Rogers Taylor, *The Transportation Revolution, 1815–1860* (1951). Merle Curti, "America at the World Fairs, 1815–1893," in Curti, *Probing Our Past* (1955), is the basis for my account of that subject, together with Friedrich Klemm, *A History of Western Technology* (1959) and H. J. Habakkuk, *American and British Technology in the Nineteenth Century: The Search for Labour Saving Inventions* (1962). The European comments on American technology were taken from Klemm's study. Jefferson's opinion of Evans' invention is quoted in Giedion *Mechanization Takes Command.*

Norman Ware, *The Industrial Worker, 1840–1860* (1924) is a highly significant history of the workingman's reorientation in the industrial revolution. It is the source for the statements from the pre-Civil War labor spokesmen regarding capital and labor. Edward C. Kirkland, *Industry Comes of Age: Business, Labor, and Public Policy, 1860–1897* (1961) emphasizes the positive contributions of technology for industrial workers as well as for others, and of the role of engineers in late nineteenth-century American society. Giedion, *Mechanization Takes Command* is excellent on the history of scientific management; Samuel Haber, *Efficiency and Uplift: Scientific Management in the Progressive Era* (1964) examines the expansion of influence of the concept of labor, management in political circles. Frank B. Gilbreth, *Primer of Scientific Management* (1914) is a kind of catechism on the subject. TR's comment on scientific management is from Gilbreth's *Primer* and Wilson's is from Haber, *Efficiency and Uplift*. Irving Bernstein, *The Lean Years: A History of the Worker, 1920–1933* (1960) is a study, not of labor unions, but of workers generally.

Elizabeth Faulkner Baker, *Technology and Woman's Work* (1946), a detailed scholarly study, is the main basis for my account of women in the American industrial revolution and the source of the quotation from *Fortune*. There are two good histories of the typewriter: Richard N. Current, *The Typewriter and the Men Who Made It* (1954), which concentrates on technological developments, and Bruce Bliven, Jr., *The Wonderful Writing Machine* (1954), which devotes more attention to the social impact of the machine. Hardly any attention has been paid by historians to the serving classes in American society, but Lucy M. Salmon, *Domestic Service* (1901) contains much information on the subject for the turn of the century. I have relied without restraint, here and in the next chapter, on Robert S. Lynd and Helen M. Lynd, *Middletown* (1929), a superlative study of Muncie, Indiana, society in the mid-twenties. The comment of the woman on canning all summer is from *Middletown*. I have relied similarly on Frederick Lewis Allen, *Only Yesterday* (1931), which remains a remarkably true as well as lively depiction of American society in the 1920's. Allen's *The Big Change* (1950) includes an excellent description of middle-class life in America in 1900 and one which I have made full use of. William Leuchtenberg, *The Perils of Prosperity* (1958) presents a good brief statistical visualization of technological change in the 1910's and 1920's.

Norbert Wiener's comment on Edison is from his *The Human Use of Human Beings* (1954). Henry Ford's *Edison as I Knew Him* (1930) was written with the assistance of Samuel Crowther, as were his other writings. Matthew Josephson, *Edison* (1959) describes Edison's image as well as his accomplishments. Particularly valuable among the considerable literature on Henry Ford are the brief biography by Roger Burlingame, *Henry Ford* (1955) and the more substantial, judiciously debunking, *The Legend of Henry Ford* (1948) by Keith Sward. John B. Rae, *The Ameri-*

can Automobile (1965) is a brief scholarly survey. Godfrey M. Lebhar, *Chain Stores in America, 1859–1959* (1959) is an informative survey. Edward L. Throm, ed., *Fifty Years of Popular Mechanics, 1902–1952* (1952) provides a visual impression of how inventions appealed to the national imagination. Ford's announcement of the Model T is quoted in Burlingame; Ford's comments on the social results of overproduction are from his *My Life and Work*.

Alfred D. Chandler, ed., *Giant Enterprise* (1964) is a documentary study of the organizational history of the automobile industry, which I have relied on, in conjunction with William H. Whyte, *The Organization Man* (1956) and Alfred P. Sloan, Jr., assisted by Boyden Sparkes, *Adventures of a White-Collar Man* (1941), for the businessman's conception of free enterprise in the 1920's. Henry Ford, with Samuel Crowther, *My Life and Work* (1922) and Edward A. Filene, *Successful Living in the Machine Age* (1932) are revealing statements of American businessmen's idea of progress. C. Wright Mills, *White Collar: The American Middle Classes* (1951) is an interesting, statistically informative attempt to define what the middle class is and the direction in which it is going. James Playsted Wood, *The Story of Advertising* (1958) and Joseph J. Seldin, *The Golden Fleece* (1963) are informative popular surveys of the history of American advertising.

Fred J. Ringel, ed., *America as Americans See It* (1932) is, taken as a whole, an extremely good collection of short essays by many people on many facets of American life of the time. The particular essays I have made use of are: Clifton Fadiman, "What Does America Read?"; Faith Baldwin, "Love and Romance"; Clare Boothe Brokaw, "American Society and Near-Society"; Walter B. Pitkin, "The American: How He Lives"; John Held, Jr., "College Life"; Clarence Cook Little, "Higher Education"; Doris E. Fleischman, "Women: Types and Movements"; John R. Tunis, "The Business of American Sports"; and Bruce Bliven, "Worshipping the American Hero." Foster Rhea Dulles, *America Learns to Play, A History of Popular Recreation, 1607–1940* (1940) is an informative account that is particularly good for the period of the last quarter of the nineteenth century and the first quarter of the twentieth. I have also used Jesse Frederick Steiner, *Americans at Play: Recent Trends in Recreation and Leisure Time Activities* (1933) and Allison Danzig and Peter Brandwein, ed., *Sport's Golden Age: A Close-up of the Fabulous Twenties* (1948), which is the source for the Grantland Rice comment.

Silas Bent, *Ballyhoo, The Voice of the Press* (1927) is the main source for my discussion of that subject and the source for the editorial statement in the Chicago *Tribune*. Gordon W. Allport, *The Psychology of*

Radio (1935) is the source for the information concerning the impact of radio on children. Marshall McLuhan, *Understanding Media* (1964) argues the thesis that "societies have been shaped more by the nature of the media by which men communicate than by the content of the communication," and discusses the psychological impacts of newspapers, telephones, radios, movies, and other media. William C. de Mille is quoted from his *Hollywood Saga* (1939).

Chapter 6
The Technological Filiarchy

WINTHROP'S COMMENTS ARE FROM HIS FAMOUS remarks on liberty to the Massachusetts General Court in 1645, recorded in his *Journals*, J. J. Hosmer, ed., 2 vols. (1908). Hezakiah Niles on saucy girls is quoted in George Rogers Taylor, *Transportation Revolution, 1815–1860* (1951). Early seventeenth-century English society and social thought, as they relate to American settlement, are authoritatively described in Wallace Notestein, *The English People on the Eve of Colonization* (1954). E. M. W. Tillyard, *The Elizabethan World Picture* (1943) describes the patriarchal idea of the great chain of being as Englishmen understood it.

Pearl Binder, *Muffs and Morals* (1954) is an informative popular history of changing styles and the moral attitudes that accompanied the changes. Carrie A. Hall, *From Hoopskirts to Nudity* (1938) is a brief historical survey of women's fashions in America, with illustrations. James Laver, *Women's Dress in the Jazz Age* (1964), mainly pictures, is an English account. Paul Nystrom, *The Economics of Fashion* (1928) is a substantial and scholarly account which examines the subject from anthropological and sociological as well as economic points of view. Mary Ellen Roach and Joanne Bubolz Eicher, eds., *Dress, Adornment and the Social Order* (1965) is a compilation of sociological, psychological, anthropological, and fashion expertise relating to the subject. An excellent 59-page annotated bibliography is appended. The Sears, Roebuck catalog is on microfilm from 1894.

The studies on childhood listed in Chapter 3 are all relevant to this discussion. In addition Monica M. Kiefer, *American Children Through Their Books, 1700–1835* (1948) is a significant study. Lewis Atherton, *Main Street on the Middle Border* (1954) is informative for children in small-town America at the turn of the century, and Foster Rhea Dulles, *America Learns to Play, a History of Popular Recreation, 1607–1940* (1940) includes much that is related to the subject. Histories of education mainly have remarkably little to say about children. Two opposing views of childhood in America in the latter half of the nineteenth century are to be found in Catharine E. Beecher and Harriet Beecher Stowe, *The American Woman's Home* (1869) and a two-volume compilation of articles, *The Woman's Home* (1894), which is the source for the statement concerning the influence of *Little Lord Fauntleroy* on children's dress.

The social ideas of Dorothy Dix are from her *Dorothy Dix, Her Book: Every-Day Help for Every-Day People* (1926). Faith Baldwin's comment on Mrs. Dix is in Fred J. Ringel, ed., *America as Americans See It* (1932). Lawrence A. Cremin, *Transformation of the Schools; Progressivism in American Education, 1876–1957* (1961) is the main basis for the discussion of the change in orientation of Progressive education. The account of Muncie, Indiana, is, of course, from Robert S. Lynd and Helen M. Lynd, *Middletown* (1929). George Mowry, ed., *The Twenties: Fords, Flappers & Fanatics* (1963) is a good selection of contemporary newspaper and magazine articles, two of which I have quoted from here: "Flapping Not Repented Of" from *The New York Times,* July 16, 1922, and Eleanor Rowland Wembridge, "Petting and the Campus," from *Survey*, July 1, 1925. Woodrow Wilson's comment on automobiles and socialism is from Dulles, *America Learns to Play.* F. Scott Fitzgerald's comment is from his article, "Echoes of the Jazz Age," in *Scribner's Magazine,* November 1931. The statement from the *Journal of Commerce* and those by the presidents of the Christian Endeavor Society and the University of Florida are from Frederick Lewis Allen, *Only Yesterday* (1931). The discussion of the dance craze is drawn primarily from Mark Sullivan, *Our Times, The United States, 1900–1925,* 9 vols. (1926–35); and also from Dulles, *America Learns to Play;* David Ewen, *Panorama of American Popular Music* (1957); and Isaac Goldberg, *Tin Pan Alley* (1930). Mencken on the flapper is quoted in Henry F. May, *The End of American Innocence: A Study of the First Years of Our Time, 1912–1917* (1959).

Most of the studies related to college education which are cited in the bibliography for Chapter 3 are relevant here, especially Frederick Rudolph, *The American College and University: A History* (1962), which includes a detailed account of the rise of college football. Ernest Earnest, *Academic Procession: An Informal History of the American College, 1936–1953* (1953) is especially good on changes in college social life. Edgar O. Reynolds, *The Social and Economic Status of College Students* (1927) is an authoritative and significant nationwide statistical study. The comments of John Held, Jr., and former University of Michigan president Clarence Cook Little are in Ringel, ed., *America as*

Americans See It. John O. Lyons, *The College Novel in America* (1962) summarizes the plots of novels dealing with college life. The account by Christian Gauss is from his *Life in College* (1930). James Wechsler, *Revolt on the Campus* (1935) is concerned with the revolt of political radicals and, from that standpoint, is good on the ideas of college intellectuals in the Jazz Age and the depression. *Fortune* magazine (June, 1936) made a survey of campus mores, particularly in the Ivy League. Allen in *Only Yesterday* considered the subject in an influential chapter, "The Revolution in Manners and Morals," which he followed up for the period of the thirties in *Since Yesterday* (1940). Alfred C. Kinsey et al., *Sexual Behavior in the Human Male* (1948) and *Sexual Behavior in the Human Female* (1953) is a conclusively exhaustive and careful study so far as the sex habits of college-educated Americans are concerned. *Sex and the College Student* (1966), by the Group for the Advancement of Psychiatry, includes an annotated bibliography on the subject.

Adam Winthrop's letter to Margaret Tyndall is from Joseph Hopkins Twitchell, ed., *Some Old Puritan Love-Letters: John and Margaret Winthrop, 1618–1636* (1894). I have altered spelling and punctuation. The verse about short skirts is from Hall, *Hoopskirts to Nudity;* the Fitzgerald statement from his "Echoes of the Jazz Age." The opinion concerning the typical American's religious views are those of H. Paul Douglass from the article "Protestant Faiths," in Harold E. Stearns, ed., *America Now* (1938). Abraham Holtzman, *The Townsend Movement* (1936), a significant scholarly monograph, is the basis for my discussion of that subject.

Kenneth S. Davis, *The Hero: Charles A. Lindbergh and the American Dream* (1959) is a brilliant, full biographical study of Lindbergh's life and times. It is the basis for my discussion and the source for the relevant quotations. Jeremiah Milbank, Jr., *The First Century of Flight in America* (1943) is a good survey of the history of balloons and airplanes in America and also of the impact of the flight on American thought, a subject also considered in Frank Donovan, *The Early Eagles* (1962).

Chapter 7
Americanization and Counter-Americanization

MALDWYN ALLEN JONES, *American Immigration* (1960) is a brief scholarly survey with an informative bibliographical discussion. Carl Wittke, *We Who Built America* (1939) presents a substantial history of the New Immigration; Oscar Handlin, *The Uprooted* (1951) portrays the subject from the point of view of the immigrants. So far as I know, the intellectual history of the American ideal which is symbolized by the Statue of Liberty has not yet been written. The antidemocratic influence of immigration on American society is discussed briefly in Frederick Lewis Allen, *The Big Change* (1952); George Rogers Taylor, *The Transportation Revolution, 1815–1860* (1951); and Gilman Ostrander, *The Rights of Man in America, 1606–1861* (1960); and in greater detail for New York State in Douglas T. Miller, *Jacksonian Aristocracy* (1967). Immigration historians have tended to ignore that significant aspect of their subject. John Higham, *Strangers in the Land: Patterns of American Nativism* (rev. ed., 1963) examines the circumstances surrounding passage of the National Origins Act; Barbara M. Solomon, *Ancestors and Immigrants* (1956) discusses the intellectual background of the restrictionist movement. Robert A. Divine, *American Immigration Policy, 1924–1952* (1957) is a chronological record of developments from the National Origins Act to McCarran's immigration law. William S. Bernard, ed., *American Immigration Policy, 1924–1952* (1957) attempts to evaluate the consequences of the quota system as well as its causes. The quotation of Hezakiah Niles is from Taylor, *Transportation Revolution*. The quotation of Ruth Miller Elson is from her *Guardians of Tradition, American Schoolbooks of the Nineteenth Century* (1964).

Ray Allen Billington, *The Protestant Crusade, 1800–1860* (1938) and Higham, *Strangers in the Land* are thorough, scholarly accounts, and I have relied on the latter study particularly. Carl Wittke, *German-Americans and the World War* (1936) is perhaps the best study of the subject, which has yet to be treated as an important event in American cultural history. Edward N. Saveth, *American Historians and European Immigrants, 1875–1925* (1948) examines the differing racial theories of individual leading historians, noting the relevance of the ethnic background of the individual historian to his brand of racial theory. Edward G. Hartmann, *The Movement to Americanize the Immigrant* (1948) deals chiefly with the wartime period. The Roosevelt statement on speaking United States is from Hartmann's account; *The New York Times* editorial is from Higham, *Strangers in the Land*.

David A. Shannon, *The Socialist Party of America: A History* (1955), Paul F. Brissenden, *The I.W.W.: A Study of American Syndicalism* (1955), and John S. Gambs, *The Decline of the I.W.W.* (1932) are scholarly accounts. William Preston, Jr., *Aliens and Dissenters: Federal Suppression of Radicals, 1903–1933* (1963) is a detailed history based upon government documents and other manuscript collections, notably those of the American Civil Liberties Union. Robert K. Murray, *Red Scare: A Study in National Hysteria* (1955) is a history of events in terms of their public impact and is the main basis for my discussion of the subject. Willard Waller, *The Veteran Comes Back* (1944) and Dixon Wecter, *When Johnny Comes Marching Home* (1944) are both scholarly studies of the veteran in American society.

David M. Chalmers, *Hooded Americanism* (1965) and W. Pierce Randel, *The Ku Klux Klan* (1965), both study the Klans in detail on a state-to-state basis. The statement by Evans is from his "The Klan's Fight for Americanism," *North American Review* (March 1925), reprinted in George Mowry, ed., *The Twenties: Fords, Flappers & Fanatics* (1963). My discussion of fundamentalism is based primarily on Stewart G. Cole, *The History of Fundamentalism* (1963). Ray Ginger, *Six Days or Forever?* (1958) is a brief, absorbing account of the Scopes trial and the basis for my discussion, including all related quotations. An interesting compilation relating to the case, which includes Mencken's articles for the *Sun* and later statements by Scopes and Roger Baldwin, is Jerry R. Tompkins, ed., *D-Days at Dayton: Reflections on the Scopes Trial* (1965).

John Tracy Ellis, *American Catholicism* (1955) is a brief scholarly survey with a useful bibliographical discussion. William V. Shannon, *The American Irish* (1963) is a substantial scholarly history. Nathan Glazer and Daniel P. Moynihan, *Beyond the Melting Pot* (1963) is a brilliant study, which breaks with the dominant filiopietistic tradition of immigration history and analyzes the impact of varied ethnic groups upon the recent history and culture of New York City. I have relied heavily here on Moynihan's account of the New York Irish and, in Chapter 8, on Glazer's account of the New York Jews and Italians. Elmer Ellis, *Mr. Dooley's America: A Life of Finley Peter Dunn* (1941) is the basis for my account of Dunn. Frank L. Christ and Gerard E. Sherry, eds., *American Catholicism and the Intellectual Ideal* (1961) is a collection of articles, many of them written in the twenties, by Catholic intellectuals, commenting, generally critically, on the role of the Catholic Church in American intellectual life. Edmund A. Moore, *A Catholic Runs for President: The Campaign of 1928* (1956) is the basis for my account of the election. The Methodist temperance committee statement is from Ostrander, *Prohibition Movement in California.*

For biographical information on Mencken, I have chiefly relied on William Manchester, *Disturber of the Peace: H. L. Mencken* (1951), which is the source for the Mencken quotations and those about him. My discussion of Lewis is based on Mark Schorer, *Sinclair Lewis* (1961). Lewis' "The American Fear of Literature" is reprinted in Erik Karlfeldt, *Why Sinclair Lewis Got the Nobel Prize* (1931).

Malcolm Cowley, *Exile's Return: A Literary Odyssey of the 1920's* (1934) reflects the point of view of a member of the younger Lost

Generation which grew up during the war, as opposed to the writers for Harold E. Sterns, ed., *Civilization in the United States* (1922) who were of the prewar generation. Alfred Kazin, *On Native Grounds: An Interpretation of Modern American Prose* (1942) is a balanced and evocative history of American literature from the late nineteenth century. The statement about the importance of Van Wyck Brooks' old-stock New England status is made by Bernard Smith in his article on Brooks in Malcolm Cowley, ed., *After the Genteel Tradition: American Writers Since 1910* (1959). Louis G. Joughin and Edmund M. Morgan, *The Legacy of Sacco and Vanzetti* (1948) is an extensive history of the case, which is particularly valuable for Morgan's examination of the case in its purely legal aspects. David Felix, *Protest: Sacco-Vanzetti and the Intellectuals* (1965) is an extremely well-presented, rather brief analysis of the case as a celebrated cause among intellectuals. This is an important study, and it is a serious reflection against the American community of intellectuals that it lacked the power of self-analysis to produce a study such as this until more than a generation after the fact. Daniel Aaron, *Writers on the Left* (1961) is a scholarly and sympathetic history of a painful subject.

Albert U. Romasco, *The Poverty of Abundance: Hoover, the Nation, the Depression* (1965) is a straightforward account of the miseries of the depression and the moralistic and miserly conduct of the Hoover administration, and it is the basis for my discussion of that policy, including Hoover's statements and the social worker's testimony before the congressional committee. David A. Shannon, ed., *The Great Depression* (1960) is a collection of articles from *The New York Times* and other sources dealing with depression conditions. It is the source of the statements about relief in St. Paul and Scranton and the problem of people sleeping in parks. Robert and Helen Lynd's sequel to *Middletown* is *Middletown in Transition* (1937). William E. Leuchtenburg, *Franklin D. Roosevelt and the New Deal* (1963) is a balanced, clearly written survey with a full bibliographical discussion of the subject. Arthur Meier Schlesinger, Jr., *The Coming of the New Deal* (1959) and *The Politics of Upheaval* (1960) are large-scale studies of the shifting political circumstances, ideas, and alignments within the administration and outside it.

Chapter 8
A New Nationalism

FOR FDR'S CAREER as governor of New York and his election as President, I have relied mainly on A. M. Schlesinger, Jr., *The Crisis of the Old Order* (1958) and *The Coming of the New Deal*

(1959); Frank Freidel, *Franklin D. Roosevelt,* 3 vols. (1952–56); and Alfred B. Rollins, *Roosevelt and Howe* (1962). Joseph J. Huthmacher, *Senator Robert F. Wagner and the Rise of Urban Liberalism* (1968) argues the thesis that I have substantially accepted here concerning the Tammany origins of New Deal liberalism. Francis Perkins is quoted from her *The Roosevelt I Knew* (1946). My account of La Guardia's election is from Arthur Mann, *La Guardia Comes to Power, 1933* (1965); the quotation from Mann on La Guardia is from his *La Guardia, A Fighter Against His Times* (1959).

R. A. Schermerhorn, *These Our People: Minorities in American Culture* (1949) is a substantial survey of each of the major ethnic groups which is informative and balanced in its treatment. Caroline Ware, *Greenwich Village, 1920–1930* (1931) discusses the Italian section as does Herbert J. Gans, *The Urban Villagers: Group and Class in the Life of Italian-Americans* (1962) for Boston a generation later. Among the individual ethnic histories, I have found most useful Lawrence F. Pisani, *The Italian in America* (1957) and Oscar Handlin, *Adventures in Freedom: Three Hundred Years of Jewish Life in America* (1954). For New York City the chapters by Glazer on the Italians, Jews, and Negroes in Nathan Glazer and Daniel P. Moynihan, *Beyond the Melting Pot* (1963); Moses Richin, *The Promised City, New York's Jews 1870–1914* (1962); and Gilbert Osofsky, *Harlem: The Making of a Ghetto* (1966) are scholarly and absorbing studies. Judith R. Kramer and Seymour Leventman, *Children of the Gilded Ghetto: Conflict Resolutions of Three Generations of American Jews* (1961) and Irvin L. Child, *Italian or American? The Second Generation in Conflict* (1943) are both carefully researched, factual studies.

The discussion of Jewish society in Brownsville is based primarily on Elliot E. Cohen, ed., *Commentary on the American Scene* (1953), a collection of articles from *Commentary* magazine, from which all of the quotations relating to Brownsville were taken. Alfred Kazin's brilliant autobiographical essays, *Starting Out in the Thirties* (1965), also deal with Brownsville as well as with radical intellectual life in New York City during the depression. Kazin is quoted on the new nationalism in literature and later on Edmund Wilson from his *On Native Grounds.*

Granville Hicks, *Part of the Truth* (1965) is a clear account of how Hicks's set of intellectuals moved in and then out of the Communist party. Norman Podhoretz is quoted on *Partisan Review* from his autobiographical *Making It* (1967). Kazin's quotation on V. S. Calverton's parties is from his *Starting Out in the Thirties.* Calverton's *The New Generation* (1930) is an argument for filiarchy published at a very inopportune time for the subject. Very remarkably, no history of the intellectual in American society has as yet been written. There are American intellectual histories in print, but they are concerned with the American character rather than with the American intellectual.

For the history of the American Negro, I have, in general, relied on John Hope Franklin, *From Slavery to Freedom: A History of American Negroes* (rev. ed. 1956); August Meier and Elliott Rudwick, *From Plantation to Ghetto* (1966); and Leslie Fishel, Jr., and Benjamin Quarles, eds., *The Negro American: A Documentary History* (1967).

C. Vann Woodward, *The Strange Career of Jim Crow* (1955) is the source for my account of that subject; for the conflicting programs of Washington and Du Bois I have relied particularly on August Meier, *Negro Thought in America, 1880–1915* (1963). Francis L. Broderick and August Meier, eds., *Negro Protest Thought in the Twentieth Century* (1965) is a source book. Meier and Rudwick, "The Rise of Segregation in the Federal Bureaucracy, 1900–1930," *Phylon* (Summer 1967) traces segregation back to TR's administration.

Salvator de Madariaga is quoted from his *The Fall of the Spanish American Empire* (1948). David Brion Davis, *The Problem of Slavery in Western Culture* (1966) is critical of the idea that Latin-American and Anglo-American slave systems were distinctively different, and on this score he opposes himself to standard authorities, notably Frank Tannenbaum, *Slave and Citizen: The Negro in the Americas* (1946) and Stanley Elkins, *Slavery: A Problem in American Institutional and Intellectual Life* (1959). However, Davis does not present evidence to modify the accepted view that sharply contrasting racial attitudes existed in the two cultures, and he accepts as authoritative C. R. Boxer's *Race Relations in the Portuguese Colonial Empire, 1415–1825* (1963), which opposes the accepted view only to the extent of asserting "that race relations in the old Portuguese colonial empire did not invariably present ... a picture of harmonious integration." William Byrd's *Secret Diary* and Jefferson's *Notes on Virginia* are sources for the quotations by those two men. The discussion of the impact of slavery on state constitutions is from Ostrander, *Rights of Man in America*. The discussion of the Fisk singers, Bland and Andrews, is drawn from Langston Hughes, *Famous Negro Music Makers* (1955).

My discussion of the New Negro and the Black Renaissance is mainly based on Alain Locke, ed., *The New Negro, An Interpretation* (1925); James Weldon Johnson, *Black Manhattan* (1940); Langston Hughes' autobiography, *The Big Sea* (1940); and V. F. Calverton, "The Negro," in Harold E. Stearns, ed., *America Now* (1938). Samuel Lubell, *White and Black* (1966) is the source for the quotation of Douglass on the Republican party and of Walter White on Hoover.

Among the histories of jazz, Rudi Blesh, *Shining Trumpets* (rev. ed. 1958) is probably the most painstakingly researched account, but it is excessively dogmatic in insisting upon an extremely arbitrary thesis. An excellent account of the origins of jazz in New Orleans, which emphasizes the European rather than the African influences, is Henry A. Kmen, *Music in New Orleans: The Formative Years, 1791–1841* (1966). The quotation by Lafcadio Hearn is from Gilbert Chase, *America's Music, From the Pilgrims to the Present* (rev. 2nd ed., 1966), which includes the most balanced and musically knowledgeable history of jazz that I have read. The quotation of Alain Locke is from his *The New Negro* (1925). Du Bois' praise of the liberal arts education is from his *Souls of Black Folk* (1903). The statements by Langston Hughes are from *The Big Sea* (1940).

Chapter 9
Depression and Filiarchy

FREDERICK LEWIS ALLEN followed *Only Yesterday* with *Since Yesterday* (1940) about the events and everyday happenings of the depression decade. The depression did not lend itself to Allen's spritely style and upper-middle-class viewpoint, however, and other historians concentrated their attention on the political developments and the grim realities of the decade, ignoring the lighter realities of the era almost altogether. During the past two or three years, a variety of accounts of the 1930's have appeared, indicating a growing interest in the general social history of the era.

Robert and Helen Lynd followed up *Middletown* with *Middletown in Transition* (1937), which emphasizes the persistence of traditional attitudes in the face of alien circumstances. Maxine Davis's report was published as *The Lost Generation* (1936). Luce's "The American Century" editorial appeared in *Life* magazine on February 17, 1941. Luce's statement on the decline of aristocracy in America is quoted in Woolcott Gibbs's profile of Luce in *The New Yorker*, November 23, 1936.

Index

72 73 74   12 11 10 9 8 7 6 5 4 3 2 1

Revised January, 1970

harper ⚡ torchbooks

American Studies: General

HENRY ADAMS Degradation of the Democratic Dogma. ‡ *Introduction by Charles Hirschfeld.* TB/1450
LOUIS D. BRANDEIS: Other People's Money, *and How the Bankers Use It. Ed. with Intro. by Richard M. Abrams* TB/3081
HENRY STEELE COMMAGER, Ed.: The Struggle for Racial Equality TB/1300
CARL N. DEGLER: Out of Our Past: *The Forces that Shaped Modern America* CN/2
CARL N. DEGLER, Ed.: Pivotal Interpretations of American History
Vol. I TB/1240; Vol. II TB/1241
A. S. EISENSTADT, Ed.: The Craft of American History: *Selected Essays*
Vol. I TB/1255; Vol. II TB/1256
LAWRENCE H. FUCHS, Ed.: American Ethnic Politics TB/1368
MARCUS LEE HANSEN: The Atlantic Migration: 1607-1860. *Edited by Arthur M. Schlesinger. Introduction by Oscar Handlin* TB/1052
MARCUS LEE HANSEN: The Immigrant in American History. *Edited with a Foreword by Arthur M. Schlesinger* TB/1120
ROBERT L. HEILBRONER: The Limits of American Capitalism TB/1305
JOHN HIGHAM, Ed.: The Reconstruction of American History TB/1068
ROBERT H. JACKSON: The Supreme Court in the American System of Government TB/1106
JOHN F. KENNEDY: A Nation of Immigrants. *Illus. Revised and Enlarged. Introduction by Robert F. Kennedy* TB/1118
LEONARD W. LEVY, Ed.: American Constitutional Law: *Historical Essays* TB/1285
LEONARD W. LEVY, Ed.: Judicial Review and the Supreme Court TB/1296
LEONARD W. LEVY: The Law of the Commonwealth and Chief Justice Shaw: *The Evolution of American Law, 1830-1860* TB/1309
GORDON K. LEWIS: Puerto Rico: *Freedom and Power in the Caribbean. Abridged edition* TB/1371
RICHARD B. MORRIS: Fair Trial: *Fourteen Who Stood Accused, from Anne Hutchinson to Alger Hiss* TB/1335
GUNNAR MYRDAL: An American Dilemma: *The Negro Problem and Modern Democracy. Introduction by the Author.*
Vol. I TB/1443; Vol. II TB/1444

GILBERT OSOFSKY, Ed.: The Burden of Race: *A Documentary History of Negro-White Relations in America* TB/1405
CONYERS READ, Ed.: The Constitution Reconsidered. *Revised Edition. Preface by Richrd B. Morris* TB/1384
ARNOLD ROSE: The Negro in America: *The Condensed Version of Gunnar Myrdal's* An American Dilemma. *Second Edition* TB/3048
JOHN E. SMITH: Themes in American Philosophy: *Purpose, Experience and Community* TB/1466
WILLIAM R. TAYLOR: Cavalier and Yankee: *The Old South and American National Character* TB/1474

American Studies: Colonial

BERNARD BAILYN: The New England Merchants in the Seventeenth Century TB/1149
ROBERT E. BROWN: Middle-Class Democracy and Revolution in Massachusetts, 1691-1780. *New Introduction by Author* TB/1413
JOSEPH CHARLES: The Origins of the American Party System TB/1049
HENRY STEELE COMMAGER & ELMO GIORDANETTI, Eds.: Was America a Mistake? *An Eighteenth Century Controversy* TB/1329
WESLEY FRANK CRAVEN: The Colonies in Transition: 1660-1712† TB/3084
CHARLES GIBSON: Spain in America † TB/3077
CHARLES GIBSON, Ed.: The Spanish Tradition in America + HR/1351
LAWRENCE HENRY GIPSON: The Coming of the Revolution: 1763-1775. † *Illus.* TB/3007
JACK P. GREENE, Ed.: Great Britain and the American Colonies: 1606-1763. + *Introduction by the Author* HR/1477
AUBREY C. LAND, Ed.: Bases of the Plantation Society + HR/1429
JOHN LANKFORD, Ed.: Captain John Smith's America: *Selections* from his Writings ‡ TB/3078
LEONARD W. LEVY: Freedom of Speech and Press in Early American History: *Legacy of Suppression* TB/1109
PERRY MILLER: Errand Into the Wilderness TB/1139
PERRY MILLER   T. H. JOHNSON, Eds.: The Puritans: *A Sourcebook of Their Writings*
Vol. I TB/1093; Vol. II TB/1094

---

† The New American Nation Series, edited by Henry Steele Commager and Richard B. Morris.
‡ American Perspectives series, edited by Bernard Wishy and William E. Leuchtenburg.
a History of Europe series, edited by J. H. Plumb.
§ The Library of Religion and Culture, edited by Benjamin Nelson.
‖ Researches in the Social, Cultural, and Behavioral Sciences, edited by Benjamin Nelson.
Σ Harper Modern Science Series, edited by James A. Newman.
° Not for sale in Canada.
+ Documentary History of the United States series, edited by Richard B. Morris.
# Documentary History of Western Civilization series, edited by Eugene C. Black and Leonard W. Levy.
Λ The Economic History of the United States series, edited by Henry David et al.
¶ European Perspectives series, edited by Eugene C. Black.
** Contemporary Essays series, edited by Leonard W. Levy.
* The Stratum Series, edited by John Hale.

EDMUND S. MORGAN: The Puritan Family: *Religion and Domestic Relations in Seventeenth Century New England*   TB/1227

RICHARD B. MORRIS: Government and Labor in Early America   TB/1244

WALLACE NOTESTEIN: The English People on the Eve of Colonization: 1603-1630. † *Illus.*   TB/3006

FRANCIS PARKMAN: The Seven Years War: *A Narrative Taken from* Montcalm and Wolfe, The Conspiracy of Pontiac, *and* A Half-Century of Conflict. *Edited by John H. McCallum*   TB/3083

LOUIS B. WRIGHT: The Cultural Life of the American Colonies: 1607-1763. † *Illus.*   TB/3005

YVES F. ZOLTVANY, Ed.: The French Tradition in America +   HR/1425

American Studies: The Revolution to 1860

JOHN R. ALDEN: The American Revolution: 1775-1783. † *Illus.*   TB/3011

MAX BELOFF, Ed.: The Debate on the American Revolution, 1761-1783: *A Sourcebook*   TB/1225

RAY A. BILLINGTON: The Far Western Frontier: 1830-1860. † *Illus.*   TB/3012

STUART BRUCHEY: The Roots of American Economic Growth, 1607-1861: *An Essay in Social Causation. New Introduction by the Author.*   TB/1350

WHITNEY R. CROSS: The Burned-Over District: *The Social and Intellectual History of Enthusiastic Religion in Western New York, 1800-1850*   TB/1242

NOBLE E. CUNNINGHAM, JR., Ed.: The Early Republic, 1789-1828 +   HR/1394

GEORGE DANGERFIELD: The Awakening of American Nationalism, 1815-1828. † *Illus.*   TB/3061

CLEMENT EATON: The Freedom-of-Thought Struggle in the Old South. *Revised and Enlarged. Illus.*   TB/1150

CLEMENT EATON: The Growth of Southern Civilization, 1790-1860. † *Illus.*   TB/3040

ROBERT H. FERRELL, Ed.: Foundations of American Diplomacy, 1775-1872   HR/1393

LOUIS FILLER: The Crusade against Slavery: 1830-1860. † *Illus.*   TB/3029

DAVID H. FISCHER: The Revolution of American Conservatism: *The Federalist Party in the Era of Jeffersonian Democracy*   TB/1449

WILLIAM W. FREEHLING, Ed.: The Nullification Era: *A Documentary Record* ‡   TB/3079

WILLIM W. FREEHLING: Prelude to Civil War: *The Nullification Controversy in South Carolina, 1816-1836*   TB/1359

PAUL W. GATES: The Farmer's Age: *Agriculture, 1815-1860* Δ   TB/1398

FELIX GILBERT: The Beginnings of American Foreign Policy: *To the Farewell Address*   TB/1200

ALEXANDER HAMILTON: The Reports of Alexander Hamilton. ‡ *Edited by Jacob E. Cooke*   TB/3060

THOMAS JEFFERSON: Notes on the State of Virginia. ‡ *Edited by Thomas P. Abernethy*   TB/3052

FORREST MCDONALD, Ed.: Confederation and Constitution, 1781-1789 +   HR/1396

BERNARD MAYO: Myths and Men: *Patrick Henry, George Washington, Thomas Jefferson*   TB/1108

JOHN C. MILLER: Alexander Hamilton and the Growth of the New Nation   TB/3057

JOHN C. MILLER: The Federalist Era: 1789-1801. † *Illus.*   TB/3027

RICHARD B. MORRIS, Ed.: Alexander Hamilton and the Founding of the Nation. *New Introduction by the Editor*   TB/1448

RICHARD B. MORRIS: The American Revolution Reconsidered   TB/1363

CURTIS P. NETTELS: The Emergence of a National Economy, 1775-1815 Δ   TB/1438

DOUGLASS C. NORTH & ROBERT PAUL THOMAS, Eds.: *The Growth of the American Economy to 1860* +   HR/1352

R. B. NYE: The Cultural Life of the New Nation: 1776-1830. † *Illus.*   TB/3026

GILBERT OSOFSKY, Ed.: Puttin' On Ole Massa: *The Slave Narratives of Henry Bibb, William Wells Brown, and Solomon Northup* ‡   TB/1432

JAMES PARTON: The Presidency of Andrew Jackson. *From Volume III of the* Life of Andrew Jackson. *Ed. with Intro. by Robert V. Remini*   TB/3080

FRANCIS S. PHILBRICK: The Rise of the West, 1754-1830. † *Illus.*   TB/3067

MARSHALL SMELSER: The Democratic Republic, 1801-1815 †   TB/1406

TIMOTHY L. SMITH: Revivalism and Social Reform: *American Protestantism on the Eve of the Civil War*   TB/1229

JACK M. SOSIN, Ed.: The Opening of the West +   HR/1424

GEORGE ROGERS TAYLOR: The Transportation Revolution, 1815-1860 Δ   TB/1347

A. F. TYLER: Freedom's Ferment: *Phases of American Social History from the Revolution to the Outbreak of the Civil War. Illus.*   TB/1074

GLYNDON G. VAN DEUSEN: The Jacksonian Era: 1828-1848. † *Illus.*   TB/3028

LOUIS B. WRIGHT: Culture on the Moving Frontier   TB/1053

American Studies: The Civil War to 1900

W. R. BROCK: An American Crisis: *Congress and Reconstruction, 1865-67* °   TB/1283

T. C. COCHRAN & WILLIAM MILLER: The Age of Enterprise: *A Social History of Industrial America*   TB/1054

W. A. DUNNING: Reconstruction, Political and Economic: 1865-1877   TB/1073

HAROLD U. FAULKNER: Politics, Reform and Expansion: 1890-1900. † *Illus.*   TB/3020

GEORGE M. FREDRICKSON: The Inner Civil War: *Northern Intellectuals and the Crisis of the Union*   TB/1358

JOHN A. GARRATY: The New Commonwealth, 1877-1890 +   TB/1410

JOHN A. GARRATY, Ed.: The Transformation of American Society, 1870-1890 +   HR/1395

HELEN HUNT JACKSON: A Century of Dishonor: *The Early Crusade for Indian Reform.* † *Edited by Andrew F. Rolle*   TB/3063

ALBERT D. KIRWAN: Revolt of the Rednecks: *Mississippi Politics, 1876-1925*   TB/1199

ARTHUR MANN: Yankee Reforms in the Urban Age: *Social Reform in Boston, 1800-1900*   TB/1247

ARNOLD M. PAUL: Conservative Crisis and the Rule of Law: *Attitudes of Bar and Bench, 1887-1895. New Introduction by Author*   TB/1415

JAMES S. PIKE: The Prostrate State: *South Carolina under Negro Government.* ‡ *Intro. by Robert F. Durden*   TB/3085

WHITELAW REID: After the War: *A Tour of the Southern States, 1865-1866.* ‡ *Edited by C. Vann Woodward*   TB/3066

FRED A. SHANNON: The Farmer's Last Frontier: *Agriculture, 1860-1897*   TB/1348

VERNON LANE WHARTON: The Negro in Mississippi, 1865-1890   TB/1178

American Studies: The Twentieth Century

RICHARD M. ABRAMS, Ed.: The Issues of the Populist and Progressive Eras, 1892-1912 +
HR/1428
RAY STANNARD BAKER: Following the Color Line: American Negro Citizenship in Progressive Era. ‡ Edited by Dewey W. Grantham, Jr. Illus.   TB/3053
RANDOLPH S. BOURNE: War and the Intellectuals: Collected Essays, 1915-1919. ‡ Edited by Carl Resek   TB/3043
A. RUSSELL BUCHANAN: The United States and World War II. † Illus.
Vol. I TB/3044; Vol. II TB/3045
THOMAS C. COCHRAN: The American Business System: A Historical Perspective, 1900-1955
TB/1080
FOSTER RHEA DULLES: America's Rise to World Power: 1898-1954. † Illus.   TB/3021
JEAN-BAPTISTE DUROSELLE: From Wilson to Roosevelt: Foreign Policy of the United States, 1913-1945. Trans. by Nancy Lyman Roelker   TB/1370
HAROLD U. FAULKNER: The Decline of Laissez Faire, 1897-1917   TB/1397
JOHN D. HICKS: Republican Ascendancy: 1921-1933. † Illus.   TB/3041
ROBERT HUNTER: Poverty: Social Conscience in the Progressive Era. ‡ Edited by Peter d'A. Jones   TB/3065
WILLIAM E. LEUCHTENBURG: Franklin D. Roosevelt and the New Deal: 1932-1940. † Illus.
TB/3025
WILLIAM E. LEUCHTENBURG, Ed.: The New Deal: A Documentary History +   HR/1354
ARTHUR S. LINK: Woodrow Wilson and the Progressive Era: 1910-1917. † Illus. TB/3023
BROADUS MITCHELL: Depression Decade: From New Era through New Deal, 1929-1941 ∆
TB/1439
GEORGE E. MOWRY: The Era of Theodore Roosevelt and the Birth of Modern America: 1900-1912. † Illus.   TB/3022
WILLIAM PRESTON, JR.: Aliens and Dissenters: Federal Suppression of Radicals, 1903-1933
TB/1287
WALTER RAUSCHENBUSCH: Christianity and the Social Crisis. ‡ Edited by Robert D. Cross
TB/3059
GEORGE SOULE: Prosperity Decade: From War to Depression, 1917-1929 ∆   TB/1349
GEORGE B. TINDALL, Ed.: A Populist Reader: Selections from the Works of American Populist Leaders   TB/3069
TWELVE SOUTHERNERS: I'll Take My Stand: The South and the Agrarian Tradition. Intro. by Louis D. Rubin, Jr.; Biographical Essays by Virginia Rock   TB/1072

Art, Art History, Aesthetics

CREIGHTON GILBERT, Ed.: Renaissance Art **
Illus.   TB/1465
EMILE MALE: The Gothic Image: Religious Art in France of the Thirteenth Century. § 190 illus.   TB/344
MILLARD MEISS: Painting in Florence and Siena After the Black Death: The Arts, Religion and Society in the Mid-Fourteenth Century. 169 illus.   TB/1148
ERWIN PANOFSKY: Renaissance and Renascences in Western Art. Illus.   TB/1447
ERWIN PANOFSKY: Studies in Iconology: Humanistic Themes in the Art of the Renaissance. 180 illus.   TB/1077

JEAN SEZNEC: The Survival of the Pagan Gods: The Mythological Tradition and Its Place in Renaissance Humanism and Art. 108 illus.
TB/2004
OTTO VON SIMSON: The Gothic Cathedral: Origins of Gothic Architecture and the Medieval Concept of Order. 58 illus.   TB/2018
HEINRICH ZIMMER: Myths and Symbols in Indian Art and Civilization. 70 illus. TB/2005

Asian Studies

WOLFGANG FRANKE: China and the West: The Cultural Encounter, 13th to 20th Centuries. Trans. by R. A. Wilson   TB/1326
L. CARRINGTON GOODRICH: A Short History of the Chinese People. Illus.   TB/3015
DAN N. JACOBS, Ed.: The New Communist Manifesto and Related Documents. 3rd revised edn.   TB/1078
DAN N. JACOBS & HANS H. BAERWALD, Eds.: Chinese Communism: Selected Documents
TB/3031
BENJAMIN I. SCHWARTZ: Chinese Communism and the Rise of Mao   TB/1308
BENJAMIN I. SCHWARTZ: In Search of Wealth and Power: Yen Fu and the West   TB/1422

Economics & Economic History

C. E. BLACK: The Dynamics of Modernization: A Study in Comparative History   TB/1321
STUART BRUCHEY: The Roots of American Economic Growth, 1607-1861: An Essay in Social Causation. New Introduction by the Author.
TB/1350
GILBERT BURCK & EDITORS OF Fortune: The Computer Age: And its Potential for Management   TB/1179
JOHN ELLIOTT CAIRNES: The Slave Power. ‡ Edited with Introduction by Harold D. Woodman   TB/1433
SHEPARD B. CLOUGH, THOMAS MOODIE & CAROL MOODIE, Eds.: Economic History of Europe: Twentieth Century #   HR/1388
THOMAS C. COCHRAN: The American Business System: A Historical Perspective, 1900-1955
TB/1180
ROBERT A. DAHL & CHARLES E. LINDBLOM: Politics, Economics, and Welfare: Planning and Politico-Economic Systems Resolved into Basic Social Processes   TB/3037
PETER F. DRUCKER: The New Society: The Anatomy of Industrial Order   TB/1082
HAROLD U. FAULKNER: The Decline of Laissez Faire, 1897-1917 ∆   TB/1397
PAUL W. GATES: The Farmer's Age: Agriculture, 1815-1860 ∆   TB/1398
WILLIAM GREENLEAF, Ed.: American Economic Development Since 1860 +   HR/1353
J. L. & BARBARA HAMMOND: The Rise of Modern Industry. || Introduction by R. M. Hartwell
TB/1417
ROBERT L. HEILBRONER: The Future as History: The Historic Currents of Our Time and the Direction in Which They Are Taking America
TB/1386
ROBERT L. HEILBRONER: The Great Ascent: The Struggle for Economic Development in Our Time   TB/3030
FRANK H. KNIGHT: The Economic Organization
TB/1214
DAVID S. LANDES: Bankers and Pashas: International Finance and Economic Imperialism in Egypt. New Preface by the Author TB/1412
ROBERT LATOUCHE: The Birth of Western Economy: Economic Aspects of the Dark Ages
TB/1290

W. ARTHUR LEWIS: Economic Survey, 1919-1939
TB/1446
W. ARTHUR LEWIS: The Principles of Economic Planning. *New Introduction by the Author°*
TB/1436
ROBERT GREEN MC CLOSKEY: American Conservatism in the Age of Enterprise   TB/1137
PAUL MANTOUX: The Industrial Revolution in the Eighteenth Century: *An Outline of the Beginnings of the Modern Factory System in England°*   TB/1079
WILLIAM MILLER, Ed.: Men in Business: *Essays on the Historical Role of the Entrepreneur*
TB/1081
GUNNAR MYRDAL: An International Economy. *New Introduction by the Author*   TB/1445
RICHARD S. WECKSTEIN, Ed.: Expansion of World Trade and the Growth of National Economies **   TB/1373

Historiography and History of Ideas

HERSCHEL BAKER: The Image of Man: *A Study of the Idea of Human Dignity in Classical Antiquity, the Middle Ages, and the Renaissance*   TB/1047
J. BRONOWSKI & BRUCE MAZLISH: The Western Intellectual Tradition: *From Leonardo to Hegel*   TB/3001
EDMUND BURKE: On Revolution. Ed. by Robert A. Smith   TB/1401
WILHELM DILTHEY: Pattern and Meaning in History: *Thoughts on History and Society.° Edited with an Intro. by H. P. Rickman*
TB/1075
ALEXANDER GRAY: The Socialist Tradition: *Moses to Lenin °*   TB/1375
J. H. HEXTER: More's Utopia: *The Biography of an Idea. Epilogue by the Author*   TB/1195
H. STUART HUGHES: History as Art and as Science: *Twin Vistas on the Past*   TB/1207
ARTHUR O. LOVEJOY: The Great Chain of Being: *A Study of the History of an Idea*   TB/1009
JOSE ORTEGA Y GASSET: The Modern Theme. *Introduction by Jose Ferrater Mora*   TB/1038
RICHARD H. POPKIN: The History of Scenticism from Erasmus to Descartes. *Revised Edition*
TB/1391
G. J. RENIER: History: *Its Purpose and Method*
TB/1209
MASSIMO SALVADORI, Ed.: Modern Socialism #
HR/1374
BRUNO SNELL: The Discovery of the Mind: *The Greek Origins of European Thought*   TB/1018
W. WARREN WAGER, ed.: European Intellectual History Since Darwin and Marx   TB/1297
W. H. WALSH: Philosophy of History: In Introduction   TB/1020

History: General

HANS KOHN: The Age of Nationalism: *The First Era of Global History*   TB/1380
BERNARD LEWIS: The Arabs in History TB/1029
BERNARD LEWIS: The Middle East and the West °   TB/1274

History: Ancient

A. ANDREWS: The Greek Tyrants   TB/1103
ERNST LUDWIG EHRLICH: A Concise History of Israel: *From the Earliest Times to the Destruction of the Temple in A.D. 70°* TB/128

THEODOR H. GASTER: Thespis: *Ritual Myth and Drama in the Ancient Near East*   TB/1281
MICHAEL GRANT: Ancient History °   TB/1190
A. H. M. JONES, Ed.: A History of Rome through the Fifgth Century # *Vol. I: The Republic*   HR/1364
Vol. II The Empire: HR/1460
SAMUEL NOAH KRAMER: Sumerian Mythology
TB/1055
NAPHTALI LEWIS & MEYER REINHOLD, Eds.: Roman Civilization *Vol. I: The Republic*
TB/1231
Vol. II: The Empire   TB/1232

History: Medieval

MARSHALL W. BALDWIN, Ed.: Christianity Through the 13th Century #   HR/1468
MARC BLOCH: Land and Work in Medieval Europe. *Translated by J. E. Anderson*
TB/1452
HELEN CAM: England Before Elizabeth TB/1026
NORMAN COHN: The Pursuit of the Millennium: *Revolutionary Messianism in Medieval and Reformation Europe*   TB/1037
G. G. COULTON: Medieval Village, Manor, and Monastery   HR/1022
HEINRICH FICHTENAU: The Carolingian Empire: *The Age of Charlemagne. Translated with an Introduction by Peter Munz*   TB/1142
GALBERT OF BRUGES: The Murder of Charles the Good: *A Contemporary Record of Revolutionary Change in 12th Century Flanders. Translated with an Introduction by James Bruce Ross*   TB/1311
F. L. GANSHOF: Feudalism   TB/1058
F. L. GANSHOF: The Middle Ages: *A History of International Relations. Translated by Rémy Hall*   TB/1411
DENYS HAY: The Medieval Centuries ° TB/1192
DAVID HERLIHY, Ed.: Medieval Culture and Society #   HR/1340
J. M. HUSSEY: The Byzantine World   TB/1057
ROBERT LATOUCHE: The Birth of Western Economy: *Economic Aspects of the Dark Ages °*
TB/1290
HENRY CHARLES LEA: The Inquisition of the Middle Ages. || *Introduction by Walter Ullmann*   TB/1456
FERDINARD LOT: The End of the Ancient World and the Beginnings of the Middle Ages. *Introduction by Glanville Downey*   TB/1044
H. R. LOYN: The Norman Conquest   TB/1457
GUIBERT DE NOGENT: Self and Society in Medieval France: *The Memoirs of Guilbert de Nogent.* || Edited by John F. Benton TB/1471
MARSILIUS OF PADUA: The Defender of Peace. *The Defensor Pacis. Translated with an Introduction by Alan Gewirth*   TB/1310
CHARLES PETET-DUTAILLIS: The Feudal Monarchy in France and England: *From the Tenth to the Thirteenth Century °*   TB/1165
STEVEN RUNCIMAN: A History of the Crusades *Vol. I: The First Crusade and the Foundation of the Kingdom of Jerusalem. Illus.*
TB/1143
Vol. II: The Kingdom of Jerusalem and the Frankish East 1100-1187. Illus.   TB/1243
Vol. III: The Kingdom of Acre and the Later Crusades. Illus.   TB/1298
J. M. WALLACE-HADRILL: The Barbarian West: *The Early Middle Ages, A.D. 400-1000*
TB/1061

JACOB BURCKHARDT: The Civilization of the Renaissance in Italy. *Introduction by Benjamin Nelson and Charles Trinkaus. Illus.* Vol. I TB/40; Vol. II TB/41

JOHN CALVIN & JACOPO SADOLETO: A Reformation Debate. *Edited by John C. Olin* TB/1239

FEDERICO CHABOD: Machiavelli and the Renaissance TB/1193

THOMAS CROMWELL: Thomas Cromwell. *Selected Letters on Church and Commonwealth, 1523-1540.* ¶ *Ed. with an Intro. by Arthur J. Slavin* TB/1462

R. TREVOR DAVIES: The Golden Century of Spain, 1501-1621 ° TB/1194

J. H. ELLIOTT: Europe Divided, 1559-1598 *a* ° TB/1414

G. R. ELTON: Reformation Europe, 1517-1559 ° *a* TB/1270

DESIDERIUS ERASMUS: Christian Humanism and the Reformation: *Selected Writings. Edited and Translated by John C. Olin* TB/1166

DESIDERIUS ERASMUS: Erasmus and His Age: *Selected Letters. Edited with an Introduction by Hans J. Hillerbrand. Translated by Marcus A. Haworth* TB/1461

WALLACE K. FERGUSON et al.: Facets of the Renaissance TB/1098

WALLACE K. FERGUSON et al.: The Renaissance: *Six Essays. Illus.* TB/1084

FRANCESCO GUICCIARDINI: History of Florence. *Translated with an Introduction and Notes by Mario Domandi* TB/1470

WERNER L. GUNDERSHEIMER, Ed.: French Humanism, 1470-1600. * *Illus.* TB/1473

MARIE BOAS HALL, Ed.: Nature and Nature's Laws: *Documents of the Scientific Revolution* # HR/1420

HANS J. HILLERBRAND, Ed., The Protestant Reformation HR/1342

JOHAN HUIZINGA: Erasmus and the Age of Reformation. *Illus.* TB/19

JOEL HURSTFIELD: The Elizabethan Nation TB/1312

JOEL HURSTFIELD, Ed.: The Reformation Crisis TB/1267

PAUL OSKAR KRISTELLER: Renaissance Thought: *The Classic, Scholastic, and Humanist Strains* TB/1048

PAUL OSKAR KRISTELLER: Renaissance Thought II: *Papers on Humanism and the Arts* TB/1163

PAUL O. KRISTELLER & PHILIP P. WIENER, Eds.: Renaissance Essays TB/1392

DAVID LITTLE: Religion, Order and Law: *A Study in Pre-Revolutionary England.* § *Preface by R. Bellah* TB/1418

NICCOLO MACHIAVELLI: History of Florence and of the Affairs of Italy: *From the Earliest Times to the Death of Lorenzo the Magnificent. Introduction by Felix Gilbert* TB/1027

ALFRED VON MARTIN: Sociology of the Renaissance. ° *Introduction by W. K. Ferguson* TB/1099

GARRETT MATTINGLY et al.: Renaissance Profiles. *Edited by J. H. Plumb* TB/1162

J. E. NEALE: The Age of Catherine de Medici ° TB/1085

J. H. PARRY: The Establishment of the European Hegemony: 1415-1715: *Trade and Exploration in the Age of the Renaissance* TB/1045

J. H. PARRY, Ed.: The European Reconnaissance: *Selected Documents* # HR/1345

BUONACCORSO PITTI & GREGORIO DATI: Two Memoirs of Renaissance Florence: *The Diaries of Buonaccorso Pitti and Gregorio Dati. Edited with Intro. by Gene Brucker. Trans. by Julia Martines* TB/1333

J. H. PLUMB: The Italian Renaissance: *A Concise Survey of Its History and Culture* TB/1161

A. F. POLLARD: Henry VIII. *Introduction by A. G. Dickens.* ° TB/1249

RICHARD H. POPKIN: The History of Scepticism from Erasmus to Descartes TB/1391

PAOLO ROSSI: Philosophy, Technology, and the Arts, in the Early Modern Era 1400-1700. || *Edited by Benjamin Nelson. Translated by Salvator Attanasio* TB/1458

FERDINAND SCHEVILL: The Medici. *Illus.* TB/1010

FERDINAND SCHEVILL: Medieval and Renaissance Florence. *Illus. Vol. I: Medieval Florence* TB/1090

Vol. II: The Coming of Humanism and the Age of the Medici TB/1091

R. H. TAWNEY: The Agrarian Problem in the Sixteenth Century. *Intro. by Lawrence Stone* TB/1315

H. R. TREVOR-ROPER: The European Witch-craze of the Sixteenth and Seventeenth Centuries and Other Essays ° TB/1416

VESPASIANO: Rennaissance Princes, Popes, and XVth Century: *The Vespasiano Memoirs. Introduction by Myron P. Gilmore. Illus.* TB/1111

History: Modern European

RENE ALBRECHT-CARRIE, Ed.: The Concert of Europe # HR/1341

MAX BELOFF: The Age of Absolutism, 1660-1815 TB/1062

OTTO VON BISMARCK: Reflections and Reminiscences. *Ed. with Intro. by Theodore S. Hamerow* ¶ TB/1357

EUGENE C. BLACK, Ed.: British Politics in the Nineteenth Century # HR/1427

EUGENE C. BLACK, Ed.: European Political History, 1815-1870: *Aspects of Liberalism* ¶ TB/1331

ASA BRIGGS: The Making of Modern England, 1783-1867: *The Age of Improvement* ° TB/1203

ALAN BULLOCK: Hitler, A Study in Tyranny. ° *Revised Edition. Illus.* TB/1123

EDMUND BURKE: On Revolution. *Ed. by Robert A. Smith* TB/1401

E. R. CARR: International Relations Between the Two World Wars. 1919-1939 ° TB/1279

E. H. CARR: The Twenty Years' Crisis, 1919-1939: *An Introduction to the Study of International Relations* ° TB/1122

GORDON A. CRAIG: From Bismarck to Adenauer: *Aspects of German Statecraft. Revised Edition* TB/1171

LESTER G. CROCKER, Ed.: The Age of Enlightenment # HR/1423

DENIS DIDEROT: The Encyclopedia: *Selections. Edited and Translated with Introduction by Stephen Gendzier* TB/1299

JACQUES DROZ: Europe between Revolutions, 1815-1848. ° *a Trans. by Robert Baldick* TB/1346

JOHANN GOTTLIEB FICHTE: Addresses to the German Nation. *Ed. with Intro. by George A. Kelly* ¶ TB/1366

ROBERT & ELBORG FORSTER, Eds.: European Society in the Eighteenth Century # HR/1404

C. C. GILLISPIE: Genesis and Geology: *The Decades before Darwin* § TB/51

Literature & Literary Criticism

Philosophy

ERNST CASSIRER: Rousseau, Kant and Goethe. *Intro.* by Peter Gay   TB/1092
FREDERICK COPLESTON, S. J.: Medieval Philosophy   TB/376
F. M. CORNFORD: From Religion to Philosophy: *A Study in the Origins of Western Speculation* §   TB/20
WILFRID DESAN: The Tragic Finale: *An Essay on the Philosophy of Jean-Paul Sartre*   TB/1030
MARVIN FARBER: The Aims of Phenomenology: *The Motives, Methods, and Impact of Husserl's Thought*   TB/1291
MARVIN FARBER: Basic Issues of Philosophy: *Experience, Reality, and Human Values*
                                                       TB/1344
MARVIN FARBERS: Phenomenology and Existence: *Towards a Philosophy within Nature* TB/1295
PAUL FRIEDLANDER: `Plato: *An Introduction*
                                                       TB/2017
MICHAEL GELVEN: A Commentary on Heidegger's "Being and Time"   TB/1464
J. GLENN GRAY: Hegel and Greek Thought
                                                       TB/1409
W. K. C. GUTHRIE: The Greek Philosophers: *From Thales to Aristotle* °   TB/1008
G. W. F. HEGEL: On Art, Religion Philosophy: *Introductory Lectures to the Realm of Absolute Spirit.* || *Edited with an Introduction by J. Glenn Gray*   TB/1463
G. W. F. HEGEL: Phenomenology of Mind. ° || *Introduction by George Lichtheim*   TB/1303
MARTIN HEIDEGGER: Discourse on Thinking. *Translated with a Preface by John M. Anderson and E. Hans Freund. Introduction by John M. Anderson*   TB/1459
F. H. HEINEMANN: Existentialism and the Modern Predicament   TB/28
WERER HEISENBERG: Physics and Philosophy: *The Revolution in Modern Science. Intro. by F. S. C. Northrop*   TB/549
EDMUND HUSSERL: Phenomenology and the Crisis of Philosophy. § *Translated with an Introduction by Quentin Lauer*   TB/1170
IMMANUEL KANT: Groundwork of the Metaphysic of Morals. *Translated and Analyzed by H. J. Paton*   TB/1159
IMMANUEL KANT: Lectures on Ethics. § *Introduction by Lewis White Beck*   TB/105
WALTER KAUFMANN, Ed.: Religion From Tolstoy to Camus: *Basic Writings on Religious Truth and Morals*   TB/123
QUENTIN LAUER: Phenomenology: *Its Genesis and Prospect. Preface by Aron Gurwitsch*
                                                       TB/1169
MAURICE MANDELBAUM: The Problem of Historical Knowledge: *An Answer to Relativism*
                                                       TB/1198
H. J. PATON: The Categorical Imperative: *A Study in Kant's Moral Philosophy*   TB/1325
MICHAEL POLANYI: Personal Knowledge: *Towards a Post-Critical Philosophy*   TB/1158
KARL R. POPPER: Conjectures and Refutations: *The Growth of Scientific Knowledge* TB/1376
WILLARD VAN ORMAN QUINE: Elementary Logic *Revised Edition*   TB/577
WILLARD VAN ORMAN QUINE: From a Logical Point of View: *Logico-Philosophical Essays*
                                                       TB/566
JOHN E. SMITH: Themes in American Philosophy: *Purpose, Experience and Community*
                                                       TB/1466
MORTON WHITE: Foundations of Historical Knowledge   TB/1440
WILHELM WINDELBAND: A History of Philosophy *Vol. I: Greek, Roman, Medieval*   TB/38
Vol. II: Renaissance, Enlightenment, Modern
                                                       TB/39

LUDWIG WITTGENSTEIN: The Blue and Brown Books °   TB/1211
LUDWIG WITTGENSTEIN: Notebooks, 1914-1916
                                                       TB/1441

Political Science & Government

C. E. BLACK: The Dynamics of Modernization: *A Study in Comparative History*   TB/1321
DENIS W. BROGAN: Politics in America. *New Introduction by the Author*   TB/1469
CRANE BRINTON: English Political Thought in the Nineteenth Century   TB/1071
ROBERT CONQUEST: Power and Policy in the USSR: *The Study of Soviet Dynastics* °
                                                       TB/1307
ROBERT A. DAHL & CHARLES E. LINDBLOM: Politics, Economics, and Welfare: *Planning and Politico-Economic Systems Resolved into Basic Social Processes*   TB/1277
HANS KOHN: Political Ideologies of the 20th Century   TB/1277
ROY C. MACRIDIS, Ed.: Political Parties: *Contemporary Trends and Ideas* **   TB/1322
ROBERT GREEN MC CLOSKEY: American Conservatism in the Age of Enterprise, 1865-1910
                                                       TB/1137
MARSILIUS OF PADUA: The Defender of Peace. *The Defensor Pacis. Translated with an Introduction by Alan Gewirth*   TB/1310
KINGSLEY MARTIN: French Liberal Thought in the Eighteenth Century: *A Study of Political Ideas from Bayle to Condorcet*   TB/1114
BARRINGTON MOORE, JR.: Political Power and Social Theory: *Seven Studies* || TB/1221
BARRINGTON MOORE, JR.: Soviet Politics—The Dilemma of Power: *The Role of Ideas in Social Change* || TB/1222
BARRINGTON MOORE, JR.: Terror and Progress—USSR: *Some Sources of Change and Stability*
JOHN B. MORRALL: Political Thought in Medieval Times   TB/1076
KARL R. POPPER: The Open Society and Its Enemies *Vol. I: The Spell of Plato* TB/1101
Vol. II: The High Tide of Prophecy: Hegel, Marx, and the Aftermath   TB/1102
CONYERS READ, Ed.: The Constitution Reconsidered. *Revised Edition, Preface by Richard B. Morris*   TB/1384
JOHN P. ROCHE, Ed.: Origins of American Political Thought: *Selected Readings* TB/1301
JOHN P. ROCHE, Ed.: American Political Thought: *From Jefferson to Progressivism*
                                                       TB/1332
HENRI DE SAINT-SIMON: Social Organization, The Science of Man, and Other Writings. || *Edited and Translated with an Introduction by Felix Markham*   TB/1152
CHARLES SCHOTTLAND, Ed.: The Welfare State **
                                                       TB/1323
JOSEPH A. SCHUMPETER: Capitalism, Socialism and Democracy   TB/3008

Psychology

ALFRED ADLER: The Individual Psychology of Alfred Adler: *A Systematic Presentation in Selections from His Writings. Edited by Heinz L. & Rowena R. Ansbacher* TB/1154
LUDWIG BINSWANGER: Being-in-the-World: *Selected Papers. || Trans. with Intro. by Jacob Needleman*   TB/1365
HADLEY CANTRIL: The Invasion from Mars: *A Study in the Psychology of Panic* || TB/1282
MIRCEA ELIADE: Cosmos and History: *The Myth of the Eternal Return* §   TB/2050
MIRCEA ELIADE: Myth and Reality   TB/1369

7

edited by Robert W. Funk and Gerhard Ebeling TB/253

SOREN KIERKEGAARD: On Authority and Revelation: *The Book on Adler, or a Cycle of Ethico-Religious Essays.* Introduction by F. Sontag TB/139

SOREN KIERKEGAARD: Crisis in the Life of an Actress, *and Other Essays on Drama.* Translated with an Introduction by Stephen Crites TB/145

SOREN KIERKEGAARD: Edifying Discourses. *Edited with an Intro.* by Paul Holmer TB/32

SOREN KIERKEGAARD: The Journals of Kierkegaard. ° *Edited with an Intro.* by Alexander Dru TB/52

SOREN KIERKEGAARD: The Point of View for My Work as an Author: *A Report to History.* § Preface by Benjamin Nelson TB/88

SOREN KIERKEGAARD: The Present Age. § *Translated and edited by Alexander Dru.* Introduction by Walter Kaufmann TB/94

SOREN KIERKEGAARD: Purity of Heart. *Trans.* by Douglas Steere TB/4

SOREN KIERKEGAARD: Repetition: *An Essay in Experimental Psychology* § TB/117

SOREN KIERKEGAARD: Works of Love: *Some Christian Reflections in the Form of Discourses* TB/122

WILLIAM G. MCLOUGHLIN, Ed.: The American Evangelicals: 1800-1900: *An Anthology* TB/1382

WOLFHART PANNENBERG, et al.: History and Hermeneutic. *Volume 4 of* Journal for Theology and the Church, *edited by Robert W. Funk and Gerhard Ebeling* TB/254

JAMES M. ROBINSON, et al.: The Bultmann School of Biblical Interpretation: New Directions? *Volume 1 of* Journal for Theology and the Church, *edited by Robert W. Funk and Gerhard Ebeling* TB/251

F. SCHLEIERMACHER: The Christian Faith. *Introduction by Richard R. Niebuhr.*
Vol. I TB/108; Vol. II TB/109

F. SCHLEIERMACHER: On Religion: *Speeches to Its Cultured Despisers.* Intro. by Rudolf Otto TB/36

TIMOTHY L. SMITH: Revivalism and Social Reform: *American Protestantism on the Eve of the Civil War* TB/1229

PAUL TILLICH: Dynamics of Faith TB/42

PAUL TILLICH: Morality and Beyond TB/142

EVELYN UNDERHILL: Worship TB/10

Religion: The Roman & Eastern Christian Traditions

A. ROBERT CAPONIGRI, Ed.: Modern Catholic Thinkers II: *The Church and the Political Order* TB/307

G. P. FEDOTOV: The Russian Religious Mind: *Kievan Christianity, the tenth to the thirteenth Centuries* TB/370

GABRIEL MARCEL: Being and Having: *An Existential Diary.* Introduction by James Collins TB/310

GABRIEL MARCEL: Homo Viator: *Introduction to a Metaphysic of Hope* TB/397

Religion: Oriental Religions

TOR ANDRAE: Mohammed: *The Man and His Faith* § TB/62

EDWARD CONZE: Buddhism: *Its Essence and Development.* ° *Foreword by Arthur Waley* TB/58

EDWARD CONZE: Buddhist Meditation TB/1442

EDWARD CONZE et al, Editors: Buddhist Texts through the Ages TB/113

ANANDA COOMARASWAMY: Buddha and the Gospel of Buddhism TB/119

H. G. CREEL: Confucius and the Chinese Way TB/63

FRANKLIN EDGERTON, Trans. & Ed.: The Bhagavad Gita TB/115

SWAMI NIKHILANANDA, Trans. & Ed.: The Upanishads TB/114

D. T. SUZUKI: On Indian Mahayana Buddhism. ° *Ed. with Intro. by Edward Conze.* TB/1403

Religion: Philosophy, Culture, and Society

NICOLAS BERDYAEV: The Destiny of Man TB/61

RUDOLF BULTMANN: History and Eschatology: *The Presence of Eternity* ° TB/91

RUDOLF BULTMANN AND FIVE CRITICS: Kerygma and Myth: *A Theological Debate* TB/80

RUDOLF BULTMANN and KARL KUNDSIN: Form Criticism: *Two Essays on New Testament Research.* Trans. by F. C. Grant TB/96

WILLIAM A. CLEBSCH & CHARLES R. JAEKLE: Pastoral Care in Historical Perspective: *An Essay with Exhibits* TB/148

FREDERICK FERRE: Language, Logic and God. *New Preface by the Author* TB/1407

LUDWIG FEUERBACH: The Essence of Christianity. § *Introduction by Karl Barth.* Foreword by H. Richard Niebuhr TB/11

ADOLF HARNACK: What Is Christianity? § *Introduction by Rudolf Bultmann* TB/17

KYLE HASELDEN: The Racial Problem in Christian Perspective TB/116

MARTIN HEIDEGGER: Discourse on Thinking. *Translated with a Preface by John M. Anderson and E. Hans Freund.* Introduction by John M. Anderson TB/1459

IMMANUEL KANT: Religion Within the Limits of Reason Alone. § *Introduction by Theodore M. Greene and John Silber* TB/FG

WALTER KAUFMANN, Ed.: Religion from Tolstoy to Camus: *Basic Writings on Religious Truth and Morals.* Enlarged Edition TB/123

H. RICHARD NIEBUHR: Christ and Culture TB/3

H. RICHARD NIEBUHR: The Kingdom of God in America TB/49

ANDERS NYGREN: Agape and Eros. *Translated by Philip S. Watson* ° TB/1430

JOHN H. RANDALL, JR.: The Meaning of Religion for Man. *Revised with New Intro. by the Author* TB/1379

WALTER RAUSCHENBUSCHS Christianity and the Social Crisis. ‡ *Edited by Robert D. Cross* TB/3059

Science and Mathematics

JOHN TYLER BONNER: The Ideas of Biology. Σ *Illus.* TB/570

W. E. LE GROS CLARK: The Antecedents of Man: *An Introduction to the Evolution of the Primates.* ° *Illus.* TB/559

ROBERT E. COKER: Streams, Lakes, Ponds. *Illus.* TB/586

ROBERT E. COKER: This Great and Wide Sea: *An Introduction to Oceanography and Marine Biology. Illus.* TB/551

W. H. DOWDESWELL: Animal Ecology. *61 illus.* TB/543

C. V. DURELL: Readable Relativity. *Foreword by Freeman J. Dyson* TB/530

GEORGE GAMOW: Biography of Physics. Σ *Illus.* TB/567

F. K. HARE: The Restless Atmosphere TB/560

J. R. PIERCE: Symbols, Signals and Noise: *The Nature and Process of Communication* Σ TB/574

WILLARD VAN ORMAN QUINE: Mathematical Logic TB/558

Science: History

MARIE BOAS: The Scientific Renaissance, 1450-1630 ° TB/583

STEPHEN TOULMIN & JUNE GOODFIELD: The Architecture of Matter: *The Physics, Chemistry and Physiology of Matter, Both Animate and Inanimate, as it has Evolved since the Beginnings of Science* TB/584

STEPHEN TOULMIN & JUNE GOODFIELD: The Discovery TB/576

STEPHEN TOULMIN & JUNE GOODFIELD: The Fabric of the Heavens: *The Development of Astronomy and Dynamics* TB/579

Science: Philosophy

J. M. BOCHENSKI: The Methods of Contemporary Thought. *Tr. by Peter Caws* TB/1377

J. BRONOWSKI: Science and Human Values. *Revised and Enlarged. Illus.* TB/505

WERNER HEISENBERG: Physics and Philosophy: *The Revolution in Modern Science. Introduction by F. S. C. Northrop* TB/549

KARL R. POPPER: Conjectures and Refutations: *The Growth of Scientific Knowledge* TB/1376

KARL R. POPPER: The Logic of Scientific Discovery TB/1376

STEPHEN TOULMIN: Foresight and Understanding: *An Enquiry into the Aims of Science. Foreword by Jacques Barzun* TB/564

STEPHEN TOULMIN: The Philosophy of Science: *An Introduction* TB/513

Sociology and Anthropology

REINHARD BENDIX: Work and Authority in Industry: *Ideologies of Management in the Course of Industrialization* TB/3035

BERNARD BERELSON, Ed.: The Behavioral Sciences Today TB/1127

JOSEPH B. CASAGRANDE, Ed.: In the Company of Man: *Twenty Portraits of Anthropological Informants. Illus.* TB/3047

KENNETH B. CLARK: Dark Ghetto: *Dilemmas of Social Power. Foreword by Gunnar Myrdal* TB/1317

KENNETH CLARK & JEANNETTE HOPKINS: A Relevant War Against Poverty: *A Study of Community Action Programs and Observable Social Change* TB/1480

LEWIS COSER, Ed.: Political Sociology TB/1293

ROSE L. COSER, Ed.: Life Cycle and Achievement in America ** TB/1434

ALLISON DAVIS & JOHN DOLLARD: Children of Bondage: *The Personality Development of Negro Youth in the Urban South* || TB/3049

PETER F. DRUCKER: The New Society: *The Anatomy of Industrial Order* TB/1082

CORA DU BOIS: The People of Alor. *With a Preface by the Author*
Vol. I *Illus.* TB/1042; Vol. II TB/1043

EMILE DURKHEIM et al.: Essays on Sociology and Philosophy: *with Appraisals of Durkheim's Life and Thought.* || *Edited by Kurt H. Wolff* TB/1151

LEON FESTINGER, HENRY W. RIECKEN, STANLEY SCHACHTER: When Prophecy Fails: *A Social and Psychological Study of a Modern Group that Predicted the Destruction of the World* || TB/1132

CHARLES Y. GLOCK & RODNEY STARK: Christian Beliefs and Anti-Semitism. *Introduction by the Authors* TB/1454

ALVIN W. GOULDNER: The Hellenic World TB/1479

ALVIN W. GOULDNER: Wildcat Strike: *A Study in Worker-Management Relationships* TB/1176

CESAR GRANA: Modernity and Its Discontents: *French Society and the French Man of Letters in the Nineteenth Century* TB/1318

L. S. B. LEAKEY: Adam's Ancestors: *The Evolution of Man and His Culture. Illus.* TB/1019

KURT LEWIN: Field Theory in Social Science: *Selected Theoretical Papers.* || *Edited by Dorwin Cartwright* TB/1135

RITCHIE P. LOWRY: Who's Running This Town? *Community Leadership and Social Change* TB/1383

R. M. MACIVER: Social Causation TB/1153

GARY T. MARX: Protest and Prejudice: *A Study of Belief in the Black Community* TB/1435

ROBERT K. MERTON, LEONARD BROOM, LEONARD S. COTTRELL, JR., Editors: Sociology Today: *Problems and Prospects* ||
Vol. I TB/1173; Vol. II TB/1174

GILBERT OSOFSKY, Ed.: The Burden of Race: A Documentary History of Negro-White Relations in America TB/1405

GILBERT OSOFSKY: Harlem: The Making of a Ghetto: *Negro New York 1890-1930* TB/1381

TALCOTT PARSONS & EDWARD A. SHILS, Editors: Toward a General Theory of Action: *Theoretical Foundations for the Social Sciences* TB/1083

PHILIP RIEFF: The Triumph of the Therapeutic: *Uses of Faith After Freud* TB/1360

JOHN H. ROHRER & MUNRO S. EDMONSON, Eds.: The Eighth Generation Grows Up: *Cultures and Personalities of New Orleans Negroes* || TB/3050

ARNOLD ROSE: The Negro in America: *The Condensed Version of Gunnar Myrdal's An American Dilemma. Second Edition* TB/3048

GEORGE ROSEN: Madness in Society: *Chapters in the Historical Sociology of Mental Illness.* || *Preface by Benjamin Nelson* TB/1337

PHILIP SELZNICK: TVA and the Grass Roots: *A Study in the Sociology of Formal Organization* TB/1230

PITIRIM A. SOROKIN: Contemporary Sociological Theories: *Through the First Quarter of the Twentieth Century* TB/3046

MAURICE R. STEIN: The Eclipse of Community: *An Interpretation of American Studies* TB/1128

EDWARD A. TIRYAKIAN, Ed.: Sociological Theory, Values and Sociocultural Change: *Essays in Honor of Pitirim A. Sorokin* ° TB/1316

FERDINAND TONNIES: Community and Society: *Gemeinschaft und Gesellschaft. Translated and Edited by Charles P. Loomis* TB/1116

SAMUEL E. WALLACE: Skid Row as a Way of Life TB/1367

W. LLOYD WARNER: Social Class in America: *The Evaluation of Status* TB/1013

FLORIAN ZNANIECKI: The Social Role of the Man of Knowledge. *Introduction by Lewis A. Coser* TB/1372

10